The Science of Optimism and Hope

LAWS OF LIFE SYMPOSIA SERIES

VOLUME 1, DIMENSIONS OF FORGIVENESS:
PSYCHOLOGICAL RESEARCH & THEOLOGICAL PERSPECTIVES
Edited by Everett L. Worthington, Jr.

VOLUME 2, THE SCIENCE OF OPTIMISM AND HOPE:
RESEARCH ESSAYS IN HONOR OF MARTIN E.P. SELIGMAN
Edited by Jane E. Gillham

VOLUME 3, UNDERSTANDING WISDOM:
SOURCES, SCIENCE, AND SOCIETY
Edited by Warren S. Brown

The Science of Optimism and Hope

✦

Research Essays in Honor of Martin E. P. Seligman

Edited by
Jane E. Gillham

TEMPLETON FOUNDATION PRESS
PHILADELPHIA & LONDON

Templeton Foundation Press
Five Radnor Corporate Center, Suite 120
100 Matsonford Road
Radnor, Pennsylvania 19087

Library of Congress Cataloging-in-Publication Data
The science of optimism & hope : research essays in honor of Martin E. P. Seligman / edited by Jane E. Gillham
p. cm. — (Laws of life symposia series ; v. 2)
Based on the Optimism and Hope Symposium, held Feb. 10, 1998 in Philadelphia, Pa.
Includes bibliographical references and index.
ISBN 1-890151-24-6 (alk. paper) —
ISBN 1-890151-26-2 (pbk. : alk. paper)
1. Optimism—Congresses. 2. Hope—Congresses. I. Title: Science of optimism and hope. II. Seligman, Martin E.P. III. Gillham, Jane. IV. Optimism and Hope Symposium (1998 : Philadelphia, PA.) V. Series

BF698.35.O57 S43 2000
149'.5—dc21 00-055220

Designed and typeset by Gopa Design
Cover design by Gopa and the Bear; Image © Photodisc
Printed in the United States of America

00 01 02 03 04 05 06 10 9 8 7 6 5 4 3 2 1

Contents

Part III. Optimism in Families and Cultures

✦ Preface ✦

THIS BOOK is the second in the Laws of Life Symposia Series, a series resulting from symposia dedicated to research on the scientific foundations of effective living. The series explores the personal qualities and virtues that enhance well-being and increase meaning in the lives of individuals and societies. The first volume, published in 1998, was devoted to psychological research and theological perspectives on forgiveness. Forthcoming volumes in the series will focus on wisdom, creativity, and spirituality, among other topics.

The present volume is devoted to research on optimism and hope. The book's chapters are based on presentations given at the symposium *The Science of Optimism and Hope*, sponsored by the John Templeton Foundation and held on February 10, 1998, in Philadelphia. Thirty eminent and developing scholars from around the world were invited to present their work at the symposium. A major goal of the symposium (and the Laws of Life Symposia Series) was to encourage a new generation of scholars to pursue work on positive human qualities. To that end, funding was provided for each scholar to bring his or her top students to the symposium.

The Optimism and Hope Symposium, and this volume, were created in honor of Martin E. P. Seligman. Over the past thirty-five years, Seligman has conducted groundbreaking research on the qualities that allow people to rise to life's challenges, overcome adversity, resist illness and depression, and lead happier, more successful lives. This research has inspired much of the work in this volume. Indeed, Seligman has served as dissertation advisor and mentor for many of the contributors, including me.

At the time of the symposium, Seligman had just begun his term as president of the American Psychological Association. As president,

Seligman's accomplishments were numerous. I believe his greatest accomplishment was reminding psychologists that psychology's focus had strayed, that many of us were ignoring the most important aspects of life—those experiences and human strengths that make life most worth living. Marty's mission—to revive and launch positive psychology as a field—is consonant with Sir John Templeton's vision of a science that explores the virtues that enhance life.

The symposium and this volume reflect just two steps toward a positive psychology or science of human virtue. In the two years since the symposium, several events have moved us further toward this goal. First, on the day of the symposium, the Templeton Foundation announced that it would sponsor an award, in Seligman's honor, for outstanding dissertation research on the science of optimism and hope. Second, the Templeton Foundation now sponsors four annual awards for outstanding research in the field of positive psychology. The first prize is currently the largest cash award in the field of psychology. These prizes are helping to jump-start the field of positive psychology by rewarding young and established scholars for pursuing work in this area. Third, the millennial issue (January 2000) of the *American Psychologist*, the flagship journal of the APA, was devoted to positive psychology and the January 2001 issue will contain a supplement on positive psychology. Fourth, a positive psychology newsgroup (positive psychology@lists.apa.org) has been created to facilitate discussion among researchers interested in this field. Finally, with Seligman's assistance, a network of scholars interested in pursuing positive psychology is being formed and has begun to meet regularly. The goal of this network is to organize a critical mass of leading and rising scholars who will catalyze a change in the focus of psychology. The network will hold conferences, encourage collaborations, and generate ideas for future research. Clearly, a movement is underway.

It is my hope that, by highlighting current theory, research, and questions, this volume will increase readers' understanding and interest in the scientific study of optimism and hope, and provide scholars with a starting point for future work.

Part I

History

✦ Introduction ✦

Jane E. Gillham

In his book, *Worldwide Laws of Life,* Sir John Templeton describes virtues that have been emphasized by philosophers, religious leaders, politicians, inventors, entrepreneurs, scientists, and poets over the centuries. Included among these are the virtues of optimism and hope. Like many before him, Templeton argues that we find what we look for in life: "good or evil, problems or solutions," that a "measure of mental health is the disposition to find good everywhere," and that we can improve our lives by changing our mindset. Templeton proposes that social sciences can teach us about the merits of these virtues and how to live more satisfying, productive, and fulfilling lives.

These sentiments will sound familiar to scholars aware of Martin Seligman's career. In his early work (during the late 1960s and early 1970s), Seligman observed that exposure to uncontrollable negative events leads to helplessness. In a series of famous experiments, Seligman and his colleagues demonstrated that animals exposed to uncontrollable shock become passive, develop symptoms that resemble depression and are more prone to physical ailments. This passivity of "helplessness" persists even when shock later becomes controllable. Additional studies demonstrated that the phenomenon of learned helplessness applies to people as well. For example, college students who are initially given unsolvable anagrams show less persistence than their peers do on solvable problems. To explain these findings, Seligman proposed that individuals develop expectancies about the occurrence of adversity in their lives. These expectancies are powerful predictors of behavior. The expectation that adversity will continue and that one will be powerless in its wake leads to helplessness, passivity, withdrawal, anxiety, depression, and even physical illness. Expectations of control lead to persistence, coping, and resilience from depression and physical health problems.

Thus, our beliefs can determine what happens to us in life.

In the mid to late 1970s, Seligman began to focus more on humans and the phenomenon of clinical depression. He observed that there are individual differences in reactions to adversity. While many people develop helpless expectancies following uncontrollable negative events, others do not. Seligman became interested in the origins of helpless expectations; he and his colleagues proposed that expectations generate in large part from the habitual ways in which people explain the good and bad events in their lives (attributional or explanatory styles). Individuals with pessimistic explanatory styles attribute adversity to stable, global, and internal factors (e.g., "I'm stupid," "I'm unlovable"). They attribute positive events to temporary, specific, and external factors (e.g., "it was just luck"). Individuals with optimistic styles display the opposite pattern of attributions. They attribute negative events to causes that are temporary, specific, and external (e.g., "I didn't make the deadline because it was unreasonable") and positive events to causes that are stable, global, and internal (e.g., "I'm good with people"). Seligman and colleagues proposed that a pessimistic style, particularly for negative events, leads to helpless expectancies.

Over the past twenty years, hundreds of studies (many by Seligman) have explored the correlates and consequences of pessimistic and optimistic explanatory styles. Individuals with pessimistic explanatory styles are more likely to experience depression, academic failure, and physical health problems. In contrast, individuals with optimistic styles demonstrate greater academic success, job performance, and resilience to depression and illness. Scheier, Carver, and their colleagues (e.g., Scheier & Carver, 1992, 1993) have found that optimistic and pessimistic outlooks (expectancies) are linked to many of the same outcomes as explanatory style. Thus, the disposition to find the good is linked to mental as well as physical health.

Recently, Seligman has demonstrated that pessimists can be taught the skills of optimism. Adults and children who acquire these skills are less vulnerable to depression. Although this work is still in its early stages, it suggests that we may be able to improve our lives by changing the way we think.

Like most clinical and research psychologists, Seligman has focused largely on the things that can go wrong in life—on depression, failure, and disease (or their absence)—and the psychological variables that may put us at risk. However, Seligman has recently argued that psychology's negative focus has blinded us to the qualities that make life most worthwhile. Living optimally is much more than the absence of pathology. Seligman's current work focuses on identifying and fostering the human virtues, strengths, and experiences that promote success, meaning, satisfaction, and joy.

Research on optimism and hope is not new. Seligman's career has already spanned more than three decades and several other research groups have explored the costs of pessimism and the benefits of optimism. However, the past few years have produced many exciting findings and raised extremely important questions for the field. This volume describes current research and scholarship on optimism and hope. It is dedicated to Martin Seligman and he inspired much of the work within. Seligman has served as a mentor for many of the contributors and most of the contributors can trace the origins of their work to Seligman's own work on helplessness, explanatory style, and the skills of optimism.

In this volume, contributors focus on several different (but overlapping) concepts related to optimism and hope, including expectancies, explanatory style, goal setting, future mindedness, control, and choice. Several of the chapters address issues related to Seligman's recent push for a positive psychology.

The book is divided into four parts. In the second and third parts of the book, chapters describing research are followed by commentaries. Commentaries discuss the previous chapter and often describe additional related research. This structure reflects the structure of the symposium on which the book is based, although the order of topics has been changed slightly in the written volume. In addition, a few of the symposium discussants were unable to write commentaries for the volume.

Part 1 of this volume focuses on the history of Seligman's career to date. It includes a chapter written by three of his colleagues and oldest friends, Steven Maier, Christopher Peterson, and Barry Schwartz. It is easy to look back in time and see the logical progression of Seligman's career. Many of his research questions and findings seem obvious given the perspective of hindsight, but Maier, Peterson, and Schwartz remind us that Seligman's contribution to psychology is even larger than we might imagine. By placing his early work in the context of the accepted theories and paradigms of its time, these authors reveal that Seligman asked radical questions and often produced unexpected and revolutionary findings. The chapter provides a good introduction to questions and methods used in a wide variety of studies described throughout the volume.

Part 2 focuses on the link between optimism and well-being in individuals. The first section explores the neurobiological underpinnings of helplessness, resilience, and coping. Steven Maier, Linda Watkins, and Robert Drugan describe their recent research on the neurobiological events that may lead to helplessness or resilience in animals.

The second section in Part 2 explores the link between optimism and psychological well-being in humans. Hundreds of studies have linked explanatory style to depressive symptoms and depression. However, few studies have adequately evaluated whether a pessimistic explanatory style is a risk factor for depression (or whether an optimistic style is a protective factor). Existing studies yield conflicting findings and are often plagued by methodological problems. Many are cross sectional and yield only correlational findings. Even so, recent research by Lyn Abramson, Lauren Alloy, and their colleagues provides strong evidence that an optimistic explanatory style protects young adults against future episodes of clinical depression. Thomas Joiner comments on the methodology employed by Abramson and colleagues and outlines the methods required for establishing psychological variables as risk or protective factors. Susan Nolen-Hoeksema and Rick Snyder discuss hope, optimism, and resilience following the loss of a loved one. Their work reminds us that human beings have a remarkable capacity to adapt, find meaning, and grow even when facing the worst traumas imaginable. Sadly, this capacity has largely been ignored and unexplained by psychologists.

The third section of Part 2 explores the relationship between optimism and health. Christopher Peterson reviews research linking a pessimistic explanatory style to physical health problems, and describes the possible mechanisms involved. Lisa Aspinwall and Susanne Brunhart explore the relationship between optimism and the avoidance or denial of physical health concerns. Optimism and hope have often been condemned by philosophers and writers who argue that these outlooks are irrational, lead to extreme risk taking and, ultimately, to catastrophe. Thus, Voltaire's Candide defines optimism as "a mania for maintaining that all is well when things are going badly." Havelock Ellis cautioned, "The place where optimism most flourishes is in the lunatic asylum." Yet, Albert Einstein countered, "I would rather be an optimist and a fool, than a pessimist and right." Are optimists out of touch with reality? Is optimism harmful? These are two of the questions that Aspinwall and Brunhart address in their research. Lauren Alloy, Lyn Abramson, and Alexandra Chiara then offer a commentary and present some contradictory findings.

The fourth section explores intervention programs designed to promote optimism and hope. Andrew Shatté, Jane Gillham, and Karen Reivich discuss the Penn Optimism Program, a school-based intervention designed to promote optimism and thereby prevent depressive symptoms in children and adolescents. Kevin Stark and Janay Boswell critique this program and give suggestions for broadening it and enhancing its effects on children, their families, and their schools.

Stanley Rachman and Robert DeRubeis provide general commentaries on the material covered in Part 2. Both authors critique the research presented and describe questions and directions for future investigations. Rachman describes his own work, which, like Seligman's, has shifted focus from weakness and negative experience (e.g., fear, depression) to strength and positive experience (e.g., courage, optimism). DeRubeis discusses the possible origins of explanatory styles, calls for a distinction between passive versus active optimism, and suggests that a focus on negative experience may have an important role in a positive psychology.

Most of the research on optimism and hope has focused on the well-being of individuals, without attending to the larger systems of which they are a part. Part 3 explores optimism and hope in a broader context. Specifically, the role of these qualities in families, religions, societies, and cultures is explored. Although most of the work focuses on optimism and hope, there is discussion of other positive experiences, including happiness and flow.

In the first section in Part 3, Frank Fincham discusses the relationship between explanatory style and the quality of family relationships. Judy Garber offers a commentary in which she explores the parenting practices that may promote or stifle optimism in children. Fincham and Garber raise important questions about the ways in which optimism and pessimism have been defined and operationalized in research. Investigators have typically assumed, for example, that optimism and pessimism are two poles of a single continuum—with lower pessimism equal to greater optimism. While optimism and pessimism overlap, they may not be perfectly or even strongly correlated. The factors that reduce one do not necessarily promote the other.

Everett Worthington also offers a commentary on Fincham's work. He raises deep questions about the methodology employed in most longitudinal research and our ability to detect profound changes in the quality of relationships.

The second section of Part 3 explores the relationship of hope and well-being to social factors. David Myers explores the question of "Who is happier and why?" He reviews research on the link between happiness and a variety of demographic and interpersonal variables including wealth, religious faith, optimism, and relationships with others. Commentaries by Lisa Miller and Rabbi Yechiel Eckstein discuss the link between religion, faith, hope, and well-being.

In the third section, the link between optimism, culture, and history is explored. Jason Satterfield examines the role of optimism in shaping historical and cultural events, including military aggression by political leaders. Satterfield proposes that optimism is most adaptive when combined with integrative complexity (the ability or tendency to think deeply about problems and consider situations from multiple perspectives). His chapter reminds us of the potential dangers of optimism that is out of touch with reality. In their commentary, Christopher Peterson and Michael Bishop describe the origins of the CAVE technique, the technique used by Satterfield and others to code explanatory style in famous individuals from the explanations given in their speeches, letters, and other historical documents. Peterson and Bishop describe some intriguing studies that challenge our assumption that the dimensions of explanatory style apply to all individuals.

In the fourth section, Mihaly Csikszentmihalyi describes his research on flow, the experience people have when they are engaged in an activity they truly enjoy. Flow is often characterized by intense focus, complete immersion in the activity, forgetting oneself, and losing track of time. Csikszentmihalyi describes the qualities of people who experience flow and the factors that make flow more likely. Many of these qualities coincide with those identified by Templeton in the *Worldwide Laws of Life*.

Part 3 ends with a commentary by Barry Schwartz, who warns against the possible dangers of a psychology that focuses primarily on building optimism, hope, and happiness. Schwartz reminds us of an important paradox. Although opportunities for individual choice and control have increased in the past 100 years, rates of clinical depression have also risen dramatically. Schwartz discusses the relationship between choice and well-being, the tension that often exists between truth and happiness, and the possibility that changing our mindset may prevent us from making important changes in the world.

In Part 4, Martin Seligman summarizes the honorary address he gave at the conclusion of the symposium. This address also summarizes his main mission as president of the American Psychological Association. The chapter discusses the origins and consequences of psychology's negative focus—on the causes, treatment, and prevention of damage. Seligman argues that the time has come for researchers to apply their methods to understanding and promoting the highest human qualities.

Seligman's plea echoes Templeton's vision that "the secret of a productive life can be sought and found." In the past two years, a systematic, organized movement of positive psychology has begun. It is exciting to think about the road ahead. Although the scholarship described in this volume points to many questions and directions for future exploration, it has already begun to teach us an enormous amount about optimism, hope, and the qualities that make life most worthwhile.

REFERENCES

Scheier, M.F., & Carver, C.S. (1992). Effects of optimism on psychological and physical well-being: Theoretical overview and empirical update. *Cognitive Therapy and Research, 16,* 201–228.

Scheier, M.F., & Carver, C.S. (1993). On the power of positive thinking: The benefits of being optimistic. *Current Directions in Psychological Science, 2,* 26–30.

Templeton, J.M. (1997). *Worldwide Laws of Life.* Philadelphia, PA: Templeton Foundation Press.

CHAPTER 1

From Helplessness to Hope: The Seminal Career of Martin Seligman

Steven F. Maier, Christopher Peterson, and Barry Schwartz

THIS BOOK explores a specific field of psychological research, but it also celebrates the profound contributions to this field of Martin E. P. Seligman. Therefore, the book blends the history of this research enterprise and Seligman's own intellectual history. This chapter reviews the modest origins of the phenomenon of "learned helplessness" in the animal laboratory, its extensions to human beings (especially those displaying dramatic failures of adaptation), and its eventual emergence as "learned optimism." The remainder of the book documents two major themes. First, the insights arising out of research on learned helplessness have been extended to almost every domain of modern psychology. And second, Seligman has played a significant role in almost all of these extensions. In fact, this book makes a fitting tribute to the man whose fingerprints appear on every chapter.

Although the research discussed in this book focuses on optimism and hope, the research story does not begin there. Rather, it begins with the opposite end of the pole—helplessness. As will become apparent, Seligman is now a strong proponent of the development of a positive psychology, but the historic, intellectual seeds of the view that underlies this new emphasis are very much in negative psychology. The critical first step in thinking that made this development possible was an appreciation of the negative consequences of the inability to control important environmental events. It is this inability that produces the learned helplessness phenomenon.

The history of research on learned helplessness and learned optimism as well as Seligman's own involvement in these areas reflects a large element of chance. Furthermore, the development of research in this area also illustrates two other important lessons in how science actually proceeds. First, it is often difficult to predict at the outset where research will lead. Work on learned helplessness began in the animal laboratory and for several years was directed at deep theoretical issues in the psychology of learning and not at depression, academic achievement, and other significant human phenomena. And second, the history of learned helplessness research demonstrates the continuity between basic and applied research in the way that it has moved effortlessly between fundamental issues in learning, cognition, and motivation on the one hand, and attempts to deal with problems of human adaptation and obstacles to the achievement of human potential on the other.

LEARNED HELPLESSNESS IN ANIMALS

Early Experiments

Learned helplessness research, and Seligman's own work, began in the mid-1960s in the animal learning laboratory of Richard L. Solomon at the University of Pennsylvania. At that time, the focus in the Solomon laboratory was on the rigorous testing of a new theory designed to explain the occurrence of avoidance learning. In avoidance learning, some warning signal (e.g., a light) precedes the onset of an aversive stimulus (e.g., a shock) by a short period of time (e.g., ten seconds). A response by the animal (e.g., jumping a hurdle) after the aversive event has started enables it to escape the aversive stimulus. And a response during the warning signal enables it to *avoid* the aversive event.

Animals readily learn to make avoidance responses in such experiments, and this fact created a significant theoretical puzzle. According to the dominant theories of the day, for a response to be learned, some event had to occur that reinforced it. The reinforcer for escape responses was obvious—termination of shock. But what was the reinforcer for avoidance responses? This also seems obvious—the absence of shock. But not so fast. If the absence of shock is a reinforcer, then why doesn't it reinforce everything an animal does? After all, before the experiment, the animal went through its life seeking food, grooming, sleeping, exploring, and each of these behaviors was accompanied by the absence of shock. While this sort of account is clearly absurd, it demonstrates why calling the absence of shock a reinforcer is problematic. If the absence of shock constitutes a reinforcer in the avoidance experiment, it must be because the shock is otherwise *expected*. This account makes obvious sense. The animal expects something (shock) to happen if it doesn't respond. So it responds, thereby preventing the "expected" event. It is thus the absence of this expected aversive event that is the reinforcer of avoidance.

For researchers and theorists of the day, dominated as they were by the principles of behaviorism, the problem with this account was that a major aim of their enterprise was to explain behavior without having to appeal to mental entities like "expectations." Solomon and his students typified this enterprise and developed a theory—*two-process theory*—to do that job for avoidance learning. The theory argued that fear becomes classically conditioned (Process 1) to the warning signal on the early trials before the animal has learned to jump the hurdle. The warning signal and the shock are paired together in Pavlovian fashion on those trials. Avoidance responses do not occur until later trials, and when they do, they *escape* the fear-provoking warning signal (Process 2) and are followed by a rapid reduction in conditioned fear. The theory thus maintained that the animal does not really learn to "avoid" the aversive event. Rather, the so-called "avoidance" response is really an escape response; the animal, motivated by conditioned fear produced by the warning signal, escapes this fear.

Solomon and his students attempted to test this explanation of avoidance learning with what was called a "transfer of control" experiment, in which the intention was to conduct straightforward classical conditioning of fear by pairing a neutral stimulus (e.g., a light) with an aversive stimulus. Then, in a different environment, avoidance learning would be conducted using some other stimulus (e.g., a tone) as the warning signal. After the avoidance response was well established and the animal was responding reliably to the tone, the crucial third phase of the experiment would be conducted. The light would be turned on during the avoidance procedure, and the question was whether the animal would now perform the avoidance response, even though the light had never been used as a warning signal in the avoidance apparatus.

This was a key prediction made by two-process theory: If "avoidance" responding was really "escape" from a fear-provoking warning signal, then any time you presented such a signal, it ought to trigger the already learned avoidance response. However, when Leaf and Overmier, graduate students in the Solomon laboratory, set out to test the prediction, they had difficulty in conducting the experiment. The problem was that when, after classical conditioning of fear had been established, the animals were exposed to an avoidance procedure, they often failed to learn to avoid shock. Indeed, they often failed even to learn to escape shock (Overmier, 1968; Overmier and Leaf, 1965). This was quite surprising given that such tasks are typically learned rapidly.

Because having learned to avoid shock was a precondition for testing this key prediction, the prediction could not be tested. The solution to the problem, as it turned out, was to reverse phases 1 and 2 and conduct the avoidance training first and the classical conditioning second. This was indeed done, and the testing of two-process theory proceeded successfully. It seemed that somehow the prior occurrence of classical conditioning interfered with the learning of the instrumental escape and avoidance responses.

For researchers committed to rigorous testing of two-process theory, this peculiar, accidentally discovered order effect was largely a methodological nuisance. However, another graduate student in the Solomon laboratory (Seligman), and a graduate student in Henry Gleitman's laboratory, which was right next door (Maier), thought that the "nuisance" deserved study in its own right and might even be more interesting than the theory that was being tested. The question was what was it about the shock animals received during classical conditioning that interfered with subsequent learning?

It is the very defining feature of classical conditioning that the behavior of the subject has no impact on the occurrence of the unconditioned stimulus (the UCS) or its properties. Could this have been important? This question led to what is arguably the single most important experiment in the entire literature concerning helplessness and optimism. Overmier and Seligman (1967) first gave animals a series of either escapable shocks—shocks that could be terminated by a response—or exactly matched but inescapable shocks, as in classical conditioning. The animals were later tested for escape and avoidance learning in a different apparatus. It turned out that the animals that had initially received escapable shock learned normally, while those that had initially received physically identical inescapable shocks failed to learn. This demonstration was quickly followed by experiments in which it was found that an experience of escapable shock "immunized" animals so that a later exposure to inescapable shock was without effect on later learning (Seligman and Maier, 1967), and ideas about control, helplessness, and optimism were born.

Learned Helplessness Theory

Why should inescapable shock interfere with later learning? The process of attempting to answer this question became a crossroads for Seligman and Maier. Explanatory concepts existed within the behaviorist theories that dominated the 1960s that could provide an "explanation" (e.g., Bracewell and Black, 1974). However, the explanation seemed contorted and inelegant, and seemed to trivialize the phenomenon. If one added to this a growing disenchantment with the pinched behaviorist theories of the time, as well as two personalities who wanted to "push the envelope," it was over-determined that a new theory would be developed.

Seligman and Maier reasoned that it must be something about what the animal *learned* about inescapable shock that was critical, rather than the shock per se, because inescapable and escapable shocks were physically identical, yet had drastically different effects. What could the animals be learning? Seligman and Maier together pondered this seemingly easy-to-answer question for months, consulted scholars in various disciplines, and could not come up with a meaningful answer within the context of learning theory. Presumably, the key was that the shock was inescapable. But what did that really mean? How can that fact about shock be learned? This question obviously does not seem difficult now, and probably would not have seemed all that difficult back then, to someone not fortunate enough to have been immersed in the learning theories of the day. However, Seligman and Maier *were* immersed in those theories. And those theories emphasized what might be called "magic moments" of temporal conjunction of conditioned stimulus and unconditioned stimulus, response and reinforcer. The language of "control" and "lack of control" that seems so natural today was completely absent in the 1960s and early 1970s. An organism could never learn about lack of control if it were locked into processing the world as a series of these magic moments.

Influenced by some revolutionary experiments and ideas coming from another lab mate (e.g., Rescorla, 1967), Seligman and Maier ultimately reasoned that the animal must be learning that responding and shock termination are *independent.* This required that organisms be sensitive to the probability of an outcome (e.g., shock termination) given that they had made some response, to the probability of the outcome given that they had not made that response, and to the relation between these two probabilities. Act and outcome were independent when these two probabilities were equal, and Seligman and Maier argued that this is what the animal learns about inescapable shock—that shock termination is independent of voluntary responses.

It was not long before Seligman and Maier realized that the comparison of these two probabilities defined a dimension that could be called "behavioral control over environmental events." Learning about this dimension—the "computing" of probabilities—is quite far removed from the "magic moments" of earlier theories. However, this still did not explain why animals exposed to inescapable shock later fail to learn to escape. Seligman and Maier argued that the learning that shock termination is independent of behavior has two major consequences. First, this learning interferes with the subsequent formation of associations between the escape response and shock termination. Second, this learning undermines the motivation to attempt to escape. This entire set of conjectures was first published in a chapter by Maier, Seligman, and Solomon (1969) and was collectively called the *learned helplessness hypothesis.*

Research from 1970–1985

Animal research on learned helplessness in the next 10–15 years went in two different directions. The first one focused on the behavioral phenomenon itself and revolved around its generality and limits. Was the interference with escape learning produced by inescapable shock restricted to escaping shock, or would the organism also fail to escape other aversive events? Would an inescapable event other than electric shock produce the same phenomenon? Did uncontrollable aversive events affect aspects of behavior other than escape learning? Did uncontrollable positive events produce analogous outcomes? How long did the effects persist? What was the range of species that showed helplessness phenomena? Could helplessness be demonstrated in humans? Questions such as these were addressed by a growing number of investigators, and answers to these questions indicated that the phenomenon was quite robust and general (see Maier and Seligman, 1976).

The second direction concentrated on theory testing. The learned helplessness theory initially not only met with great resistance but also generated quite a controversy. This should be no surprise since the assumptions about the nature of the learning process made by the theory were opposed to the ideas that were then dominant. In addition to criticizing the ideas involved in the theory of learned helplessness, opponents suggested alternative explanations of the basic interference with escape learning produced by inescapable shock. There were two categories of alternative theories. One category was behavioral. As a class, these theories argued that exposure to inescapable shock taught organisms some response that interfered with the one they were later required to learn. The second category was neurochemical, derived from some pioneering work by Weiss (Weiss, 1968; Weiss, Stone, & Harrell, 1970). These theories argued that inescapable shock depleted a neurotransmitter, typically norepinephrine, that was necessary for the mediation of movement. Therefore, helplessness was not the result of an interference with learning per se, but rather it was the result of neurochemically based movement impairment. What the behavioral and neurochemical accounts have in common is an appeal to peripheral (movement based) rather than central (learning based) mechanisms to explain interference.

The idea that the learned helplessness phenomenon could be explained by the learning of interfering motor responses was relatively easy to disprove (Maier, 1970). However, the neurochemical depletion and movement deficit ideas were more challenging. It became clear that animals that had been exposed to uncontrollable aversive events *did* later move less in the presence of aversive events than did other animals. However, this could be explained readily by both theories. Reduced motivation to escape consequent to learning uncontrollability, as well as depletion of transmitters required for movement, would predict reduced movement.

The difference between the views thus came to be focused on whether or not there was a true interference with associative processes, *as well as* a reduction in movement, following exposure to uncontrollable aversive events. The difficulty was that the learning tasks used in learned helplessness experiments confounded poor learning with reduced movement. That is, all the tasks that had been used required active motor output (e.g., jumping over the hurdle) as the index of learning. A series of experiments attempted to resolve this issue by assessing learning in tasks in which there was either no correlation (Jackson, Alexander, & Maier, 1980), or even a negative correlation between learning and movement (Minor, Jackson, & Maier, 1984). In the latter category of study, the behavior needed to escape was the *withholding* of an active motor response, and animals previously exposed to uncontrollable stressors continued to emit this active motor response, thereby failing to learn to escape. Here, failure to learn was reflected in *greater* movement rather than reduced movement.

Synthesis

Despite this research, there still were numerous difficulties for learned helplessness theory. First, even at the level of psychological theory, learned helplessness was vague concerning the mechanism by which uncontrollable stressors produce later associative interference. Exactly what was interfered with? Second, despite the existence of a true associative interference, movement per se was nevertheless often still reduced. Third, learned helplessness theory had no satisfactory explanation for many of the behavioral effects of uncontrollable stressors that occurred in addition to interference with escape learning. Why should uncontrollable stressors reduce aggressiveness, interfere with maternal behavior, exaggerate fear conditioning, reduce food and water intake, and increase responsiveness to opiate drugs such as morphine? The list of consequences of uncontrollable stressors is long, and reduced incentive to escape and associative interference can not explain all, or even most of them.

Purely behavioral research continues to make progress on the nature of the alterations in associative processes that are produced by exposure to uncontrollable stressors. The bulk of the evidence suggests that exposure to uncontrollable stressors produces an attentional shift away from "internal," response-produced cues and toward external cues (Lee & Maier, 1988). This might suggest that uncontrollable stressors produce a change in learning style, not a deficit per se. Indeed, it might be expected that uncontrollably stressed organisms would learn better than normals in tasks requiring detailed attention to external cues, and this is actually the case (Lee & Maier, 1988).

However, purely behavioral research has not been able to provide much insight into how uncontrollable stressors alter other types of behavior. Here, neuroscience and neurochemistry have been able to provide great advances. A number of investigators have elucidated the neural and neurochemical consequences of uncontrollability in fine detail (e.g., Anisman, Zalcman, Shanks, & Kacharko, 1991; Maswood, Barter, Watkins, & Maier, 1998; Petty, Kramer, & Moeller, 1994; Simson & Weiss, 1988). The tremendous explosion of knowledge concerning how the brain works and how it regulates behavior has made it possible to tie the neurochemical consequences of uncontrollability to the behavioral consequences that occur. It is now possible, for example, to state *why* uncontrollable stressors reduce aggressiveness rather than increase it, *why* they increase fear, and so on. Indeed, a knowledge of the underlying neurocircuitry has allowed a priori prediction of new, unexplored consequences of uncontrollability. For example, from what is known about neurocircuitry, one can make the counter-intuitive prediction that uncontrollably stressed animals will find opiate drugs, but not stimulants, more rewarding and addictive than normal animals (Will,

Watkins, and Maier, 1998). Such a prediction would be unlikely based on purely behavioral knowledge.

Future Directions

The powerful techniques now available to researchers in the neurosciences, added to rapidly accumulating detailed knowledge, suggest that animal research in the foreseeable future will be focused at the neurobiological level. This neurobiological emphasis is also related to the medical need to develop animal models of pathology. Effective biomedical research requires animal models, and the neurobiological work on learned helplessness indicates that it may be an especially useful model of a number of psychopathologies (e.g., Basoglu & Mineka, 1992). The fact that learned helplessness in animals has been proposed as a model of a number of different disorders should not be disturbing. Disorders such as depression, post-traumatic stress disorder, and the like are syndromal nosological categories, not biological entities. A given biological phenomenon, like learned helplessness, could be common to a number of disorders. Furthermore, it could reveal the common core cause of a diversity of pathologies. It is a real testimony to the power and importance of basic research and theory to realize that these broad and exciting new directions, full of potential significance for application, have flowed from the accidental discovery that dogs with a certain history were unable to learn what for other dogs was a trivial task. But it should also be clear that for progress to be made, "accidents" like this have to happen to the right people, and Seligman is such a person.

LEARNED HELPLESSNESS IN HUMANS

Mapping the behavioral scope of learned helplessness in animals, articulating the theory, and defending it against the many challenges that arose would have been more than enough to keep even the most energetic scientist busy for years—but not Seligman. For as the developments just described were unfolding, Seligman was also taking the helplessness phenomenon in an entirely different direction, by asking about its scope and character in human beings.

The earliest studies of human helplessness were strictly analogous to those done with animals, exposing human research participants to aversive events—typically bursts of white noise—that could neither be escaped nor avoided. Participants were then tested on tasks that *could* be mastered, for example, unscrambling anagrams. And just as with animals, the reliable finding was that relative to individuals who either had no previous experimental experience, or experience with controllable events, those who had experienced uncontrollability often showed deficits, including negative affect, slower problem-solving, more failures to master tasks, and perseveration with unproductive strategies.

One of the most widely cited papers from this early era of human helplessness research was by Seligman and Hiroto (Hiroto & Seligman, 1975), which reported four parallel studies testing the transfer of helplessness deficits from one sort of pretreatment to a second sort of test task. Two pretreatment tasks were used, an "instrumental" pretreatment, in which participants had to press buttons to terminate a noise, and a "cognitive" pretreatment, in which participants had to solve concept-identification problems. Two test tasks were used, one "instrumental" (moving a lever to escape or avoid a noise) and the other "cognitive" (unscrambling anagrams). The four studies were made up of all possible combinations of the pretreatments and test tasks.

It was hardly surprising that deficits were evident when the test tasks were similar to the pretreatments; these results would be predicted by almost any theory. More interesting were the findings that deficits were *also* evident when the test tasks and the pretreatments were dissimilar. Using jargon popular at the time, Hiroto and Seligman concluded that "cross-modal helplessness" had been produced and that this was strong support for the theory that helplessness involved learning that one did not have control over events.

In retrospect, the distinction between "instrumental" and "cognitive" pretreatments and test tasks may seem artificial, but it provides a useful reminder that Hiroto and Seligman did their experiments at a time when there was still broad skepticism in the field about the necessity or utility of mentalistic accounts of behavior that relied on things like "expectations." The cognitive revolution was still being fought, and behaviorism had yet to surrender. The investigation of learned helplessness, among humans as well as animals, was one of the important battlegrounds.

Perhaps because helplessness theory was fighting a rear-guard action against behaviorism, the early research in helplessness paid scant attention to the *detailed* development of helplessness theory as an alternative. The original helplessness story was a very simple, straightforward account of how experience with uncontrollable events produces subsequent deficits. Helplessness theory argued that uncontrollable events produce an expectation of response-outcome independence, which in turn produces a variety of deficits, and left it at that. Introducing the construct of "expectation" was a sufficient departure from prevailing theory that researchers did not scrutinize this construct until some time later. Indeed, very few early studies even tried to measure expectations, despite the central role they were accorded in helplessness theory. Animals, of course, cannot directly report on what they expect. But people can. Yet, perhaps because helplessness theory was firmly grounded in the animal learning tradition, the earliest investigators of human helplessness did not turn immediately to such contemporary theoretical frames as Rotter's social learning theory (1954). Rotter (1966, 1975) wrote extensively about generalized expectancies (such as locus of control and interpersonal trust) and provided means with which to investigate them.

Cronbach (1957) distinguished between two traditions of scientific psychology—an experimental tradition, emphasizing external objective events and their effects on behavior, and a correlational tradition, emphasizing internal subjective events and their effects. Cronbach called for the unification of these traditions, acknowledging that it would be difficult to do so. Researchers in each tradition not only ask different questions about behavior, but also use different research and analytical strategies. Seligman led other helplessness researchers to bridge the gap described by Cronbach when he asked whether the helplessness phenomenon, as produced in animal and human laboratories, was similar to certain failures of human adaptation.

The best-known of these applications was Seligman's proposal that learned helplessness played a causal role in depression (1974, 1975).

Though animal models of psychopathology had been around at least since the time of Pavlov, Seligman significantly advanced such efforts by specifying explicitly a set of rigorous ground rules for establishing the goodness of a laboratory model (e.g., Miller, Rosellini, & Seligman, 1977). According to Seligman, it was critical that researchers move back and forth between the model and the clinical phenomenon, evaluating the parallels vis-à-vis symptoms, causes, treatments, and preventions. Even today, some researchers touting animal models of various maladies, psychological and physical, do not sufficiently validate their models against the actual clinical phenomena they purport to clarify. A wry comment by Judah Folkman, the laboratory researcher whose studies of a possible new type of cancer treatment received massive publicity in the spring of 1998, exemplifies this well: "We know a great deal about how to cure cancer in mice." In contrast, Seligman knows a great deal about helplessness and its consequences in dogs, rats, and human beings.

Helplessness and Attributional Style

A major turning point in the development of research and theory on human helplessness came in 1978, when Seligman, in collaboration with Abramson and Teasdale, published a revised theory of helplessness and depression (Abramson, Seligman, & Teasdale, 1978). The new theory incorporated ideas from attribution theory, which for years had been the private domain of social psychology. From this point forward, simple claims about the relation among experience, expectations, and behavior were replaced by efforts designed to detail the processes by which expectations were formed. The revised theory started with an attempt to make sense of some anomalous data. As researchers investigated parallels between learned helplessness on the one hand and failures of adaptation like depression on the other, it became clear that problems like depression were more complex than the helplessness theory allowed. Sometimes human helplessness following uncontrollability was chronic; other times, it was transient. Sometimes human helplessness was pervasive; other times, it was circumscribed. And sometimes human helplessness was marked by a striking loss of self-esteem; other times, it was not. The original helplessness theory was silent regarding these variations.

Abramson, Seligman, and Teasdale (1978) revised the learned helplessness theory as it applied to people, and especially to depression, by proposing that when individuals encounter an uncontrollable aversive event, they ask themselves why. The answer people give to this question—the causal attribution they entertain—sets the parameters for the helplessness that ensues. Three dimensions of causal attribution were claimed to be important. If the attributed cause were *stable* ("it's going to last forever") rather than unstable, then helplessness would be long-lasting. If it were *global* ("it's going to undermine everything") rather than specific, then helplessness would be general. And if the causal attribution were *internal* ("it's me") rather than external, then helplessness would be accompanied by a loss of self-esteem. The pattern of causal attributions for a particular instance of uncontrollability would affect a person's expectations for the future. And these expectations would in turn affect the person's behavior.

Reality or social consensus may sometimes dictate the causal explanation that a person embraces; but in more ambiguous circumstances, the individual relies on habitual tendencies to explain bad events in a given way, a personality characteristic described by Seligman as explanatory (or attributional) style (Peterson & Seligman, 1984). Those people who tend to offer stable and global explanations for bad events are not only at risk for helplessness, but also for the failures of adaptation in which helplessness figures in the wake of uncontrollability. Those people who tend to offer internal explanations for bad events are at risk for self-esteem loss in the wake of uncontrollability.

This revised account of learned helplessness—the attributional reformulation—is an explanation of human problems that presupposes that people are rational, acting "logically" in accordance with their interpretation of the causes of events. The rationality inherent in the processes proposed by the attributional reformulation of helplessness theory may be what allows it to be used in the service of a positive psychology. For this rationality can explain resilience as readily as helplessness, hope as well as despair, and good cheer as well as depression. It tells us how to intervene to undo passivity as well as how to prevent passivity in the first place. In all cases, how a person *thinks* about the things he or she experiences is taken seriously. At the same time, it is important to stress that one of the potent determinants of explanatory style is reality, so that interventions cannot be so simple as just urging people to "think positive" when the world in which they live is relentlessly negative.

The attribution reformulation of helplessness theory is a diathesis-stress theory, proposing that the conjunction of objective bad events (the stress) and a pessimistic explanatory style (the diathesis) is necessary for negative behavioral outcomes to ensue. This position builds from the roots of the helplessness approach in the experimental psychology of animal learning, where bad events—the stress (e.g., uncontrollable electric shocks)—are presented to research participants. When guiding research with people, the attributional reformulation has usually focused on the cognitive diathesis, which proves a consistent correlate of expected outcomes.

When one of us (Peterson) originally went to the University of Pennsylvania in 1979 to work with Seligman, Seligman supervised both a thriving animal laboratory and a thriving human laboratory. The attributional reformulation of helplessness theory had just been proposed, an Attributional Style Questionnaire (ASQ) to measure attributional style had been created, and the initial investigation of explanatory style had just been published (Seligman, Abramson, Semmel, & von Baeyer, 1979). Over the years, explanatory style research has become increasingly popular, and many ways to measure this individual difference variable are now available. The original Attributional Style Questionnaire (Peterson, Semmel, von Baeyer, Abramson, Metalsky, & Seligman, 1982) was expanded, to boost reliability (Peterson & Villanova, 1988), and then simplified (Dykema, Bergbower, Doctora, & Peterson, 1996), to facilitate use with general population samples. A Children's ASQ with a forced choice format was developed by Kaslow and Tanenbaum (Seligman, Peterson, Kaslow, Tanenbaum, Alloy, & Abramson, 1984) and then refined (Thompson, Kaslow, Weiss, & Nolen-Hoeksema, 1998). Forced-choice measures suitable for use with adults are in the process of being created (Reivich, 1995). A content analysis strategy dubbed the CAVE technique (Content Analysis of Verbatim Explanations) was created that allowed pre-existing written or spoken material to be scored for explanatory style (Peterson, Schulman, Castellon, & Seligman, 1992). Still other strategies have been reported, including ways to score Minnesota

Multiphasic Personality Inventory (MMPI) responses (Colligan, Offord, Malinchoc, Schulman, & Seligman, 1994) and Thematic Apperception Test (TAT) protocols (Peterson & Ulrey, 1994) for explanatory style.

In their monograph *Learned Helplessness: A Theory for the Age of Personal Control*, Peterson, Maier, and Seligman (1993) took a step back from the details of current helplessness research and tried to account for its popularity. One of the reasons they cited was the availability of relatively simple and straightforward methods for conducting helplessness research. The family of explanatory style measures just described exemplifies this point. Countless researchers have used one or another of these approaches to investigate the correlates of pessimistic versus optimistic explanatory style. Some of this work has been theory-driven, for example, the several hundred investigations of explanatory style and depression (Sweeney, Anderson, & Bailey, 1986). But other studies have been exploratory and opportunistic, such as Peterson's investigations of explanatory style as a risk factor for traumatic injuries (see Chapter 8). In any case, explanatory style has emerged from its connection to helplessness as a personality characteristic in its own right, one that is broadly associated with coping, adaptation, and well-being (Buchanan & Seligman, 1995).

Important questions about explanatory style remain, of course (Peterson, 1991). For example, what are the origins of explanatory style, especially its pessimistic manifestation? One can readily explain why a pessimistic style maintains itself, because of the vicious cycles it can set into motion, but why would anyone start out with this view of the causes of events? Here research has only begun to scratch the surface, but there are hints that the explanatory styles of parents and children converge (Seligman et al., 1984). Also, failure and trauma early in life seem to foreshadow pessimism later in life (Peterson, Maier, & Seligman, 1993). Finally, in a study of twins, Schulman, Keith, and Seligman (1993) reported that explanatory style was moderately heritable. We should probably not interpret this to mean that there is a specific causal attribution gene waiting to be discovered. However, some of the factors that lead to success or failure in life—intelligence, attractiveness, health, physical prowess, and the like—are indisputably heritable, and the experiences that they enable or block may well shape the individual's explanatory style.

Perhaps more important, especially for a future positive psychology of optimism and hope, is the question of how an optimistic explanatory style can be encouraged. Intervention studies by Seligman's research group demonstrate that children can be taught with cognitive-behavioral exercises to look at events in a more optimistic fashion, and that this instruction seems to have long-term benefits (see Chapter 11). And Beck's cognitive therapy for depression has the effect of making pessimistic individuals more optimistic; changes in explanatory style seem to go in lock-step with symptom relief and may confer protection against the recurrence of depression (Seligman, Castellon, Cacciola, Schulman, Luborsky, Ollove, & Downing, 1988).

As the multiple available measures of explanatory style facilitate rapid progress, the downside of these measures could be premature preoccupation with the particular constellation of attributional dimensions hypothesized by Abramson, Seligman, and Teasdale in their reformulation of helplessness theory. To be sure, the internality, stability, and globality of causal attributions are important, but they are hardly the only attributional dimensions of potential interest (Weiner, 1986). There is no doubt that whether events are inside the skin or outside (internality), whether they persist across time or not (stability), and whether they generalize across situations or not (globality) are key dimensions of the psychological universe. But the universe must have more key dimensions than this. What are they?

For example, what about the controllability of events? One might think that perceived controllability should have been included as an additional dimension measured by the ASQ and its descendants, but the reformulation of helplessness theory—inspired as it was by data from controlled laboratory experiments—took it for granted that the controllability or uncontrollability of events was objectively known, and not a part of experience open to interpretation and sensitive to individual differences. As the revised theory is increasingly applied outside the laboratory, this neglect of controllability as a possible dimension of explanatory style becomes more and more unfortunate. For example, studies suggest that ostensible "pessimism" (internal, stable, and global causal explanations) concerning bad events seen as controllable may have desirable consequences (Sellers & Peterson, 1993), perhaps because they constitute an assertion that things can be different.

Similarly, what about the importance (e.g., magnitude or severity) of the events about which attributions are made? Again, the reformulation did not consider this parameter because in laboratory experiments the aversive events to which research participants were exposed were held constant. The earliest version of the ASQ *did* ask respondents to rate the importance of the hypothetical events that were presented, but these ratings rarely proved interesting, perhaps because they did not span a broad enough range of possible importance.

This neglect of the importance of events in helplessness theory has recently been rectified. In their hopelessness theory of depression, Abramson, Metalsky, and Alloy (1989) made the importance of events a cornerstone in what has become the next major reformulation of helplessness theory. Stoplights and pollen counts are uncontrollable and aversive, but it is doubtful that depression is ever precipitated by these events, no matter how they are interpreted. They are simply not important enough.

Along similar lines, the original ASQ deliberately included achievement-related and interpersonal types of events, under the assumption that explanatory style might show some domain specificity. Again, this distinction rarely proved interesting, largely because respondents treated these different sorts of events as very similar. But perhaps young adult college students in the United States, the typical participants in the earliest studies of explanatory style, are likely to conflate achievement and interpersonal outcomes. Good grades and high salaries can boost one's social status, turning achievement into something social. And interpersonal success can be reflected by how many "best" friends one has, turning social circumstances into opportunities for achievement. As the attributional reformulation of helplessness is extended into other settings—other age groups, other socioeconomic classes, and other cultures—it would be wise to revisit the possibility that there are domain-specific explanatory styles. It is already clear, for example, that the internal versus external distinction can prove problematic when assessed in collectivist cultures, where the distinction between self (internal) and others (external) is not given the same significance that it has in the contemporary United States (cf. Miller, 1984).

One of the interesting extensions of the attributional reformulation targets these other populations. The ASQ has been translated into a variety of languages, and investigators have begun to explore explanatory style in other cultures. To date, results are largely consistent with the findings from the United States. A pessimistic explanatory style has undesirable correlates, whereas an optimistic explanatory style has desirable ones. But this research has been oriented toward confirmation, and the possibility that the ASQ (and of course the accompanying attributional reformulation of helplessness) needs to be made more culturally appropriate has yet to be considered seriously. We anticipate that an exciting chapter in the learned helplessness tradition will be written when such cross-cultural investigations are begun in earnest.

What about the role of objective events? As psychologists in the learned helplessness tradition poise themselves to help develop a positive social science (Seligman, 1998), it is crucial that the role of reality be remembered. From the uncontrollable events that predispose people to helplessness to the actual causal texture of the world that (sometimes) dictates a particular type of causal attribution, the outcomes of interest to "positive" social scientists are as much influenced by what the situation does or does not afford as they are by attitudes of hope and optimism. One would not want to stroll into Lebanon, Northern Ireland, the former Yugoslavia, or West Philadelphia and advise their residents simply to be more optimistic in their outlooks. A positive social science needs to encourage appropriate changes in social conditions so that optimism can exist as a viable worldview.

CONCLUSION

This chapter tried to accomplish two things: provide a brief history, as background for the compelling contributions to this book, and establish a sense of the magnitude of Martin Seligman's contributions to date. It is true that much about helplessness and optimism still needs to be explored. Helplessness and its consequences are not as simple as people once thought, and many details need to be worked out. Many big questions remain to be answered, and some big questions have yet to be asked. Nevertheless, what is already notable about the research spawned by learned helplessness, especially Seligman's contributions to that research, is that they constitute a rare example of what Cronbach envisioned forty years ago.

We suggest an informative exercise: Access PsycINFO or PsycLIT, and enter "au=Seligman, Martin E. P." Your first thought may be "Oh, the E. P. stands for "ever publishing," but the sheer number of articles that Seligman has had a hand in is not the point. Rather, look at the range of journals in which Seligman and his colleagues have published studies of learned helplessness, from *Journal of Comparative and Physiological Psychology* to *Journal of Consulting and Clinical Psychology*, from *Journal of Experimental Psychology* to *Journal of Personality and Social Psychology*, from *Behaviour Research and Therapy* to *Cognitive Therapy and Research*, from *American Psychologist* to *Journal of Abnormal Psychology*, from *Psychology Today* to *Science*. With Seligman taking the lead, the phenomenon of learned helplessness has produced research as broad in scope as is psychology itself.

To locate Seligman further in the broad history of psychology, we must also note that he is among the rare psychologists who has heeded the plea George Miller (1969) made in his American Psychological Association Presidential speech to "give psychology away." Many serious researchers are reluctant to take their ideas to the general public, but Seligman, the president of APA in 1998, has never been shy about doing so. His popular books are as laudable as his monographs and journal articles. They make difficult and important ideas accessible to untrained readers without oversimplifying or pandering to current fashion. The point is that Seligman has always had something worth giving away. His basic research has legitimized his popular presentations. At the same time, his writing for the general public has stimulated interest in basic research among several generations of academic psychologists, and it continues to do so.

Finally, as evidenced by this book and by Seligman's other recent contributions (e.g., Seligman, 1998), Seligman is leading his many students and collaborators in the next major new direction—taking the insights gained from research on learned helplessness and putting them to use in creating a psychology that emphasizes the nurture of what is good rather than just the repair of what is broken. Seligman's most recent endeavor is a call for psychology to be as focused on strength as weakness, as interested in building the best things in life as repairing the worst, and as concerned with making the lives of normal people fulfilling as healing pathology. He dubs this "positive psychology," and although his interest in this topic stems from decades of studying what can go wrong with the human condition, positive psychology represents a radical reframing of Seligman's research program.

To be sure, everything learned about helplessness and its relation to depression, failure, and illness informs our knowledge of the absence of these conditions (Peterson, Maier, & Seligman, 1993). But there is more to positive psychology than the study of what does not go wrong. The "neutral" points of the typical outcome measures in the learned helplessness research tradition signify not being depressed, not failing, and not being ill. To extend past findings beyond these neutral points and offer conclusions about emotional fulfillment, achievement, and wellness, positive psychologists must study not just *independent* variables that pertain to strength but also appropriate *dependent* variables. And different questions must be posed by positive psychologists than have been asked by researchers who work within a disease or deficiency framework. Possible topics of interest to positive psychology include hope, creativity, optimism, happiness, flow, courage, emotional intelligence, giftedness, genius, future-mindedness, interpersonal skills, and honesty.

In approaching these topics, positive psychologists should heed certain lessons from past attempts to understand human strengths and skills. From the fate of humanistic psychology of the 1960s and 1970s, positive psychologists should learn the importance of relying on empirical research. Humanists were skeptical about the scientific method and what it could yield yet were unable to offer an alternative other than the unsupported assertion that people were good. In contrast, positive psychologists must see both strength and weakness as authentic and as amenable to scientific understanding.

From the fate of past studies of creativity, positive psychologists should learn to keep an open mind about appropriate operational definitions of the topics of interest to them. Although self-report questionnaire measures are often useful and valid, not everything of interest to positive psychologists can be so assessed. Already we are seeing researchers searching for questionnaire measures of emotional intelligence (Schutte et al., 1998), but there is good reason to suspect that these measures will need to be supplemented if not altogether replaced by more complex measures that rely on the observation of actual behavior (Davies, Stankov, & Roberts, 1998).

From the fate of intelligence testing throughout the twentieth century, positive psychologists should learn several lessons as well. Desirable psychological states should not be reified; they should not be studied out of context; and they should not be used to rank order all people along a single continuum. Most importantly, positive psychologists should not regard what is "right" about people as unalterable, the result of fortuitous genetic or environmental circumstances. Indeed, the central goal of positive psychology is to cultivate and encourage the good psychological life for all people. That would be a legacy worthy of Martin Seligman.

REFERENCES

Abramson, L.Y., Metalsky, G.I., & Alloy, L.B. (1989). Hopelessness depression: A theory-based subtype of depression. *Psychological Review, 96,* 358–372.

Abramson, L.Y., Seligman, M.E.P., & Teasdale, J.D. (1978). Learned helplessness in humans: Critique and reformulation. *Journal of Abnormal Psychology, 87,* 49–74.

Anisman, H., Zalcman, S., Shanks, N., & Kacharko, R.M. (1991). *Multisystem regulation of performance deficits induced by stressors: An animal model of depression.* Clifton, NJ: Humana Press.

Basoglu, M., & Mineka, S. (1992). *The role of uncontrollable and unpredictable stress in post-traumatic stress response in torture survivors.* Cambridge: Cambridge University Press.

Bracewell, R.J., & Black, A.H. (1974). The effects of restraint and noncontingent pre-shock on subsequent escape learning in the rat. *Learning and Motivation, 5,* 53–69.

Buchanan, G.M., & Seligman, M.E.P. (Eds.) (1995). *Explanatory style.* Hillsdale, NJ: Erlbaum.

Colligan, R.C., Offord, K.P., Malinchoc, M., Schulman, P., & Seligman, M.E.P. (1994). CAVEing the MMPI for an optimism-pessimism scale: Seligman's attributional model and the assessment of explanatory style. *Journal of Clinical Psychology, 50,* 71–95.

Cronbach, L.J. (1957). The two disciplines of scientific psychology. *American Psychologist, 12,* 671–684.

Davies, M., Stankov, L., & Roberts, R.D. (1998). Emotional intelligence: In search of an elusive construct. *Journal of Personality and Social Psychology, 75,* 989–1015.

Dykema, K., Bergbower, K., Doctora, J.D., & Peterson, C. (1996). An Attributional Style Questionnaire for general use. *Journal of Psychoeducational Assessment, 14,* 100–108.

Hiroto, D.S., & Seligman, M.E.P. (1975). Generality of learned helplessness in man. *Journal of Personality and Social Psychology, 31,* 311–327.

Jackson, R.L., Alexander, J.H., & Maier, S.F. (1980). Learned helplessness, inactivity, and associative deficits: Effects of inescapable shock on response choice escape learning. *Journal of Experimental Psychology: Animal Behavior Processes, 6,* 1–20.

Lee, R.K.K., & Maier, S.F. (1988). Inescapable shock and attention to internal versus external cues in a water escape discrimination task. *Journal of Experimental Psychology: Animal Behavior Processes, 14,* 302–311.

Maier, S.F. (1970). Failure to escape traumatic shock: Incompatible skeletal motor response or learned helplessness. *Learning and Motivation, 1,* 157–170.

Maier, S.F., & Seligman, M.E.P. (1976). Learned helplessness: Theory and evidence. *Journal of Experimental Psychology: General, 105,* 3–46.

Maier, S.F., Seligman, M.E.P., & Solomon, R. (1969). *Pavlovian fear conditioning and learned helplessness.* New York: Appleton-Century-Crofts.

Maswood, S., Barter, J.E., Watkins, L.R., & Maier, S.F. (1998). Exposure to inescapable but not to escapable stress increases extracellular levels of 5-HT in the dorsal raphe nucleus of the rat. *Brain Research, 783,* 115–120.

Miller, G.A. (1969). Psychology as a means of promoting human welfare. *American Psychologist, 24,* 1063–1075.

Miller, J.G. (1984). Culture and the development of everyday social explanation. *Journal of Personality and Social Psychology, 46,* 961–978.

Miller, W.R., Rosellini, R.A., & Seligman, M.E.P. (1977). Learned helplessness and depression. In J.D. Maser & M.E.P. Seligman (Eds.), *Psychopathology: Experimental models* (pp. 104–130). San Francisco: Freeman.

Minor, T.R., Jackson, R.L., & Maier, S.F. (1984). Effects of task irrelevant cues and reinforcement delay on choice escape learning following inescapable shock: Evidence for a deficit in selective attention. *Journal of Experimental Psychology: Animal Behavior Processes, 10,* 543–556.

Overmier, J.B. (1968). Interference with avoidance behavior: Failure to avoid traumatic shock. *Journal of Experimental Psychology, 78,* 340–343.

Overmier, J.B., & Leaf, R.C. (1965). Effects of discriminative Pavlovian fear conditioning upon previously or subsequently acquired avoidance responding. *Journal of Comparative and Physiological Psychology, 60,* 213–217.

Overmier, J.B., & Seligman, M.E.P. (1967). Effects of inescapable shock on subsequent escape and avoidance behavior. *Journal of Comparative Physiology and Psychology, 63,* 23–33.

Peterson, C. (1991). Meaning and measurement of explanatory style. *Psychological Inquiry, 2,* 1–10.

Peterson, C., Maier, S.F., & Seligman, M.E.P. (1993). *Learned helplessness: A theory for the age of personal control.* New York: Oxford University Press.

Peterson, C., Schulman, P., Castellon, C., & Seligman, M.E.P. (1992). CAVE: Content analysis of verbatim explanations. In C. P. Smith (Ed.), *Motivation and personality: Handbook of thematic content analysis* (pp. 383–392). New York: Cambridge University Press.

Peterson, C., & Seligman, M.E.P. (1984). Causal explanations as a risk factor for depression: Theory and evidence. *Psychological Review, 91,* 347–374.

Peterson, C., Semmel, A., von Baeyer, C., Abramson, L.Y., Metalsky, G.I., & Seligman, M.E.P. (1982). The Attributional Style Questionnaire. *Cognitive Therapy and Research, 6,* 287–299.

Peterson, C., & Ulrey, L.M. (1994). Can explanatory style be scored from TAT protocols? *Personality and Social Psychology Bulletin, 20,* 102–106.

Peterson, C., & Villanova, P. (1988). An expanded Attributional Style Questionnaire. *Journal of Abnormal Psychology, 97,* 87–89.

Petty, F., Kramer, G., & Moeller, M. (1994). Does learned helplessness induction by Haloperidol involve serotonin mediation? *Pharmacology, Biochemistry, & Behavior, 48,* 671–676.

Reivich, K. (1995). The measurement of explanatory style. In G.M. Buchanan & M.E.P. Seligman (Eds.), *Explanatory style* (pp. 21–47). Hillsdale, NJ: Erlbaum.

Rescorla, R.A. (1967). Pavlovian conditioning and its proper control procedures. *Psychological Review, 74,* 71–80.

Rotter, J.B. (1954). *Social learning and clinical psychology*. Englewood Cliffs, NJ: Prentice-Hall.

Rotter, J.B. (1966). Generalized expectancies for internal versus external control of reinforcement. *Psychological Monographs, 81*(1, Whole No. 609).

Rotter, J.B. (1975). Some problems and misconceptions related to the construct of internal versus external reinforcement. *Journal of Consulting and Clinical Psychology, 43,* 56–67.

Schulman, O., Keith, D., & Seligman, M.E.P. (1993). Is optimism heritable? A study of twins. *Behaviour Research and Therapy, 31,* 569–574.

Schutte, N.S., Malouff, J.M., Hall, L.E., Haggerty, D.J., Cooper, J.T., Golden, C.J., & Dornheim, L. (1998). Development and validation of a measure of emotional intelligence. *Personality and Individual Differences, 25,* 167–177.

Seligman, M.E.P. (1974). Depression and learned helplessness. In R.J. Friedman & M.M. Katz (Eds.), *The psychology of depression: Contemporary theory and research* (pp. 83–113). Washington, DC: Winston.

Seligman, M.E.P. (1975). *Helplessness: On depression, development, and death.* San Francisco: Freeman.

Seligman, M.E.P. (1998). Positive social science. *APA Monitor, 29(4),* 2, 5.

Seligman, M.E.P., Abramson, L.Y., Semmel, A., & von Baeyer, C. (1979). Depressive attributional style. *Journal of Abnormal Psychology, 88,* 242–247.

Seligman, M.E.P., Castellon, C., Cacciola, J., Schulman, P., Luborsky, L., Ollove, M., & Downing, R. (1988). Explanatory style change during cognitive therapy for unipolar depression. *Journal of Abnormal Psychology, 97,* 13–18.

Seligman, M.E.P., & Maier, S.F. (1967). Failure to escape traumatic shock. *Journal of Experimental Psychology, 74,* 1–9.

Seligman, M.E.P., Peterson, C., Kaslow, N.J., Tanenbaum, R.L., Alloy, L.B., & Abramson, L.Y. (1984). Attributional style and depressive symptoms among children. *Journal of Abnormal Psychology, 93,* 235–238.

Sellers, R.M., & Peterson, C. (1993). Explanatory style and coping with controllable events by student-athletes. *Cognition and Emotion, 7,* 431–441.

Simson, P.E., & Weiss, J.M. (1988). Altered activity of the locus coeruleus in an animal model of depression. *Neuropharmacology, 1,* 287–295.

Sweeney, P.D., Anderson, K., & Bailey, S. (1986). Attributional style in depression: A meta-analytic review. *Journal of Personality and Social Psychology, 50,* 974–991.

Thompson, M., Kaslow, N.J., Weiss, B., & Nolen-Hoeksema, S. (1998). Children's Attributional Style Questionnaire-Revised (CASQ-R): Psychometric examination. Unpublished manuscript, Emory University.

Weiner, B. (1986). *An attributional theory of motivation and emotion.* New York: Springer-Verlag.

Weiss, J.M. (1968). Effects of coping responses on stress. *Journal of Comparative and Physiological Psychology, 65,* 251–260.

Weiss, J.M., Stone, E.A., & Harrell, N. (1970). Coping behavior and brain norepinephrine in rats. *Journal of Comparative and Physiological Psychology, 72,* 153–160.

Will, M.J., Watkins, L.R., & Maier, S.F. (1998). Uncontrollable stress potentiates morphine's rewarding properties. *Pharmacology, Biochemistry, & Behavior, 60,* 655–664.

Part II

✦

Optimism and Well-Being in Individuals

Section A. The Neurobiology of Optimism

CHAPTER 2

The Neurobiology of Stressor Controllability

Steven F. Maier and Linda R. Watkins

THIS CHAPTER discusses the neurobiology of helplessness and its converse, perseverance and resilience. Because research on helplessness and optimism began in the animal laboratory where Leaf, Overmier, Seligman, and Maier conducted experiments, this chapter contains an important historical perspective as well. It is neither possible to review all the neurobiology of these phenomena in the few pages in this single chapter, nor would this be useful for the likely reader. Instead, this chapter develops two objectives. The first briefly explains the existence of the phenomena—in non-human animals—that are the subject of this volume. This becomes necessary because the invasive techniques that are needed to study neural functioning at a mechanistic level of detail can only be used in non-humans. Thus, if phenomena of helplessness/optimism cannot be studied in animals, then a deep understanding of neural mechanisms will be difficult to attain. The second objective is to offer the reader some appreciation of the modern neuroscientific techniques used to study the neural mechanisms that mediate helplessness, optimism, and resilience. The intent is to convey some sense of the power of these techniques. It should be stated at the outset that although a considerable body of knowledge concerning the neurobiology of learned helplessness and related phenomena exists, there is almost nothing known about the neurobiology of optimism and hope. However, these may be opposite sides of the same coin or opposite poles of the same continuum. Thus the techniques that have been used to study one can be used to explore the other.

HELPLESSNESS/OPTIMISM IN ANIMALS

Although earlier studies (e.g., Mowrer & Viek, 1948) suggested the importance of the degree of control that an organism has over stressors, sustained research on stressor controllability actually began with the discovery that animals exposed to aversive events over which they have no control later fail to learn control in different situations where control is possible. In contrast, the experience of controllable aversive events has no such consequence (Overmier & Seligman, 1967; Seligman & Maier, 1967). Even though the initial focus was on the animal that lacked control, it became clear from the outset that the experience of control was not merely a neutral condition that failed to have an impact. Indeed, some early experiments demonstrated that the animal, which first experiences control, later persists in attempting to escape (more than do animals that have not experienced the aversive event), even under conditions in which escape or control is not possible (Volpicelli, Ulm, Altenor, & Seligman, 1983). An experience of control made the animals into behavioral optimists. Furthermore, an original experience with control had protective effects and immunized animals against the later effects of uncontrollable stressors (Seligman & Maier, 1967). A variety of effects of exposure to uncontrollable stressors were abrogated if the organism were first exposed to controllable stressors (Williams & Maier, 1977), particularly if the experience with control came early in life (Seligman, Rosellini, & Kozak, 1975).

Further work uncovered a broad array of outcomes that follow uncontrollable, but not controllable stressors. Animals do not merely fail to escape; they also become less active in the presence of aversive events, less aggressive, less dominant, and less interested in eating and drinking. In addition, they lose interest in sex, do not engage in appropriate maternal behavior (e.g., retrieving pups from the nest), become neophobic, display anxious behavior, and show exaggerated fear conditioning (see Maier, 1993, for a review). Consequently, a very elaborate slice of an animal's behavior is sensitive to the dimension of control over events to which it is exposed.

Some insight into the existence of these phenomena in a rat, for example, can be gleaned from the fact that this sort of sensitivity to control (helplessness after lack of control, and persistence and resilience to the effects of stress after control) has been demonstrated in a wide range of species and seems to have been conserved throughout much of evolution (Eisenstein & Carlson, 1997). This suggests that both persistence and optimism, together with helplessness, are adaptive. Typically, helplessness is not thought of as adaptive, but perhaps the most adaptive strategy that can be adopted when events are truly uncontrollable—as they sometimes are in nature—is to cease attempts at control or escape, thereby conserving energy resources (Minor & Saade, 1997). Conversely, when control is possible persistence is adaptive. Because environmental circumstances in nature often do not change rapidly, helplessness for a period of time after encountering uncontrollability and persistence for a period of time after encountering control would both be adaptive. This indicates that these states should be somewhat prolonged, although temporary. Failure to learn to escape, anxious behavior, and reduced activity persist for two to three days after exposure to a bout of uncontrollable stress and then dissipate (Maier, Coon, McDaniel, & Jackson, 1979). If more than a few days elapse between exposure to uncontrollable stress and behavioral testing, the usual effects of the uncontrollable stressor are not present. Of course, repeated experience with uncontrollability can make these effects much more permanent and this would also be adaptive.

It would thus appear that the precursors of the phenomena under discussion in this volume may be adaptive and promote survival. If this is so, the mechanisms that produce them may have been made part of the genome and therefore may indeed be present in non-human animals and so may be studied at that level. Of course, this does not mean that the phenomena are identical to those in the human, which surely have been elaborated and embellished. Research suggests that the expectation of future controllability or uncontrollability produce the symptoms of learned helplessness and its converse. In non-humans, the expectation follows fairly directly from the experience, but in humans, a variety of cognitive factors—attributions, beliefs, personality—may determine what expectations will result from a particular experience. Thus, the animal studies, arguably, allow the study of the mechanisms specifically involved in the link between experience and expectation that do not involve attributions and the like, as well as the link between expectation and determination of the behavioral sequelae of the expectations.

NEUROBIOLOGICAL MECHANISMS

Behavior and the Amygdala

When we began our research into learned helplessness thirty years ago, searching for neural mechanisms that mediated complex phenomena resembled a search for the proverbial "needle in a haystack." Even the possibility of isolating a discrete neural circuit and the set of mechanisms that might be responsible seemed unlikely. However, the explosive development that has occurred in neuroscience has changed everything. Sufficient knowledge now exists about the brain that it is possible to form *a priori* hypotheses, which can then be tested.

For example, recall that exposure to uncontrollable stressors produces a wide spectrum of behavioral changes. One way to summarize this alteration is that the experience of uncontrollability interferes with defensive behavior and exaggerates fear-related behavior. Or alternatively, it may be that control blunts the effects of stress on defensive and fear-related behavior. If this represents an accurate summary, it is then possible to inquire into what is now known about how the brain organizes defensive behavior and fear.

Fear responses are known to be organized in the amygdala (Davis, 1992). Signals for danger activate pathways that converge on discrete nuclei in the basal and lateral regions of the amygdala, and the association between danger and cues for danger are actually formed here. Thus, in the amygdala the association between the conditioned stimulus (CS) (e.g., a tone) and the unconditioned stimulus (UCS) (e.g., a foot shock) is formed during fear conditioning. The message then is transmitted to the central nucleus of the amygdala, where commands from the central nucleus journey to discrete regions of the brain that produce the behavioral, endocrine, and autonomic aspects of fear. So, for example, projections travel to ventral regions of the periaqueductal gray, where activation produces the freezing behavior that occurs during fear, and to nuclei in the hypothalamus that regulate blood pressure.

The final common path in producing defensive responses—escape, fighting, and the like—are nuclei within the dorsal part of the periaqueductal gray of the brain (Fanselow, 1991). Stimulation in this region induces defensive behavior, and lesions in this area prevent defensive responses to threatening stimuli. If subjects exposed to uncontrollability show inhibited defensive behavior and facilitated fear-related behavior, then current knowledge of the brain would suggest that perhaps they possess augmented amygdala function and depressed dorsal periaqueductal gray function.

The Dorsal Raphe Nucleus

Continuing on this path, the search would then be for a region that simultaneously activates the amygdala and inhibits the dorsal periaqueductal gray when activated. The dorsal raphe nucleus is one such possible region. It projects to both the amygdala and the dorsal periaqueductal gray, and can activate the amygdala and inhibit the dorsal periaqueductal gray (e.g., Kiser, Brown, Sanghera, & German, 1980). The dorsal raphe nucleus presents many interesting features. Virtually all of the serotonin neurons in the brain have their cell bodies in the raphe nuclei, and axons from the raphe nuclei provide serotonin to much of the forebrain. Of course, serotonin is of special interest since most of the currently popular anti-depressant and the newer anti-anxiety drugs work by altering serotonin levels. The projections from the dorsal raphe to the amygdala and periaqueductal gray are indeed serotonergic—serotonin is released in the amygdala and dorsal periaqueductal gray when the dorsal raphe nucleus is active and serotonin does activate the output of the amygdala and inhibit dorsal periaqueductal gray output. It has these opposing effects because there are different types of serotonin receptors in these structures, as well as different microcircuitries.

The pattern of behavior, observed after exposure to uncontrollable stressors, would follow if uncontrollability activated serotonergic neurons in the dorsal raphe nucleus. This would lead to excessive amounts of serotonin being released in the projection regions of the dorsal raphe nucleus, such as the amygdala and the dorsal periaqueductal gray. Of course, a possible alternative implies that stressors activate the dorsal raphe nucleus, but that control blunts this effect. Without the neuroscientific knowledge that now exists, no actual reason to focus on the dorsal raphe nucleus would have arisen; moreover, it is unlikely that a theoretically unguided, random search through the brain would have uncovered its role in learned helplessness.

Persistent questions remain: Does stress activate serotonergic neurons in the dorsal raphe nucleus? Are these neurons sensitive to controllability? How could one determine these answers? Simply placing electrodes into the dorsal raphe nucleus and measuring electrical activity by itself is not sufficient, because only about one-third of the cells in the dorsal raphe nucleus contain serotonin. While it is possible to determine whether a cell, from which a recording is being made, is serotonergic, this procedure is quite difficult, especially in an awake animal that is experiencing uncontrollable and controllable stressors. Thankfully, new techniques that are now available allow fresh approaches, and otherwise difficult questions yield answers.

When a neuron becomes active, it utilizes many proteins and enzymes in the process of generating an action potential and releasing neurotransmitters from axon terminals. These enzymes and proteins must be replenished by the neuron, and the neuron also must engage in a variety of other "housekeeping" operations during and after activation. To manufacture these proteins, the neuron must first transcribe the appropriate DNA sequences into RNA, and the RNA will then be translated into the relevant protein. This gene transcription first requires the production of numerous "transcription factors," which directly bind to DNA to induce gene transcription. Thus, the genes for these transcription factors are induced before the other genes, and are therefore called immediate-early genes. In effect, it is possible to inquire whether a neuron has been activated by determining either gene activation for these transcription factors or production of the transcription protein product. These transcription factors are a consequence of neural activity; if the neuron has been active they should be present. To summarize, if the messenger RNA for the transcription factor or the protein itself is detected in a neuron, then it can be inferred that the neuron has been activated.

An obvious experiment would involve administering a controllable stressor, a yoked uncontrollable stressor, or a control treatment to rats, and then determining the presence or absence of transcription factors in dorsal raphe neurons to assess their activation status. Grahn has successfully conducted this exact experiment in our laboratory, one that ten years ago would have been impossible to perform (Grahn, Maswood, McQueen, Watkins, & Maier, in press.). The transcription factor examined was one called *c-fos*. Figure 2.1 illustrates how this is done using a technique called immunohistochemistry.[1] The results of one such experiment are shown in figure 2.2.

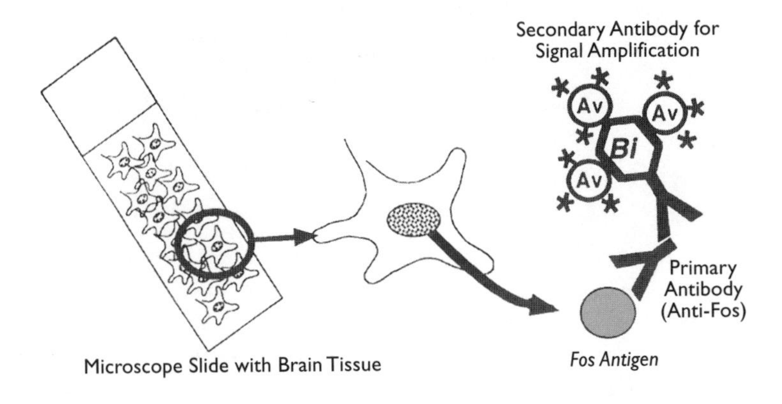

Figure 2.1. Immunohistochemical method for visualizing c-fos *protein in neurons.*

No *fos* labeling occurs at all in animals that receive no stress, so control data is not included in the figure. Clearly, uncontrollable stressors, relative to controllable stressors, do activate serotonergic neurons in middle and caudal regions of the dorsal raphe nucleus. Furthermore, these cells do respond to the controllability dimension. Other techniques can be used to measure the messenger RNA for the fos protein, but description would be more complex.

Is serotonin indeed released in the amygdala and dorsal periaqueductal gray? Advances in neurochemistry now permit the actual measurement of neurotransmitters released in discrete brain nuclei—in real time—in awake, behaving animals. Figure 2.3 illustrates the technique of *in vivo* micro dialysis.

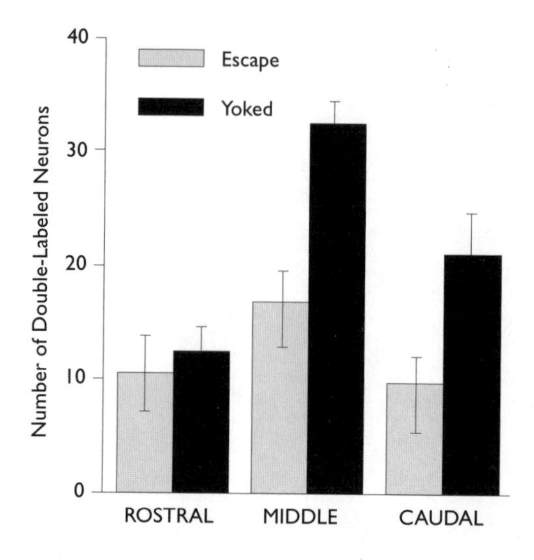

Figure 2.2. Number of neurons in the dorsal raphe nucleus double-labeled for serotonin and c-fos after exposure to escapable or yoked inescapable shock.

Very small probes, cartooned in cross-section in the figure, are implanted in the brain region of interest, for example the amygdala. The probe consists of a thin tube with an open end at the bottom; the top of the tube is fixed outside the subject's head. A physiologically neutral solution, such as cerebrospinal fluid, is continuously infused through the probe at a constant rate, which collects in small tubes that are changed every few minutes. A dialysis membrane is attached to the end of the probe. Obviously, no serotonin or other neurotransmitter exists inside the probe because none is added to the infused cerebrospinal fluid. Therefore, if the neurons in the region of the probe tip release serotonin from their axon terminals into the extracellular synaptic space, then serotonin molecules will diffuse through the membrane due to a concentration gradient. The serotonin, released by the neurons, will then simply collect in the tubes. The final step remains to measure the amount of serotonin in the tubes, which constitute quite small amounts of serotonin. These amounts result from the small number of neurons in the region of the probe tip—in real time—that will have released serotonin. Modern analytical chemistry, fortunately, allows the

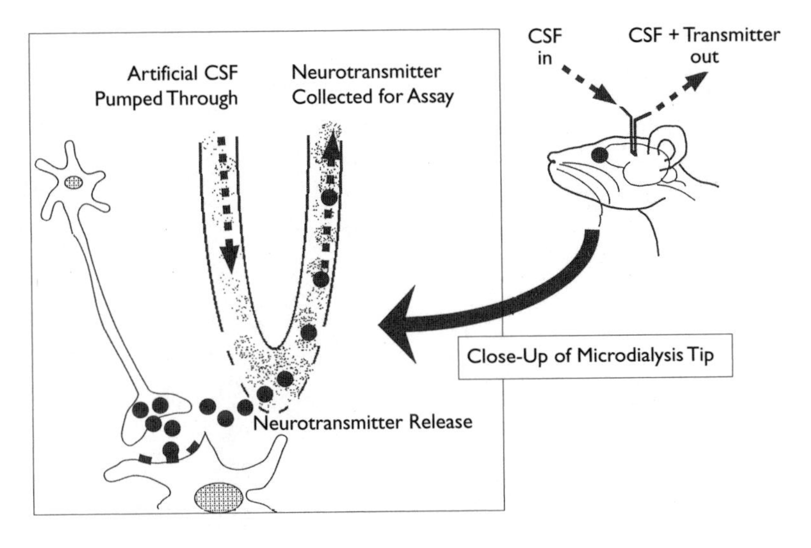

Figure 2.3. In vivo *micro dialysis method for measurement of serotonin release in brain.*

measurement of small amounts. In our laboratory we use high performance liquid chromatography with electrochemical detection, and can detect roughly two femptagrams of serotonin—that is, 2×10^{-12} grams.

Figure 2.4 details the resulting data and shows the amount of serotonin released in the basolateral amygdala as a percentage of the basal levels of serotonin. Dialysis began while the animals were in a safe and familiar environment in order to determine baseline levels of serotonin release; it continued while the animals were moved to the experimental room and placed in the apparatus. As can be seen, movement and placement in the apparatus produced a release of serotonin in the amygdala. Separate groups were then exposed to either controllable (escapable) tailshock, uncontrollable (inescapable) tailshock, or merely remained in the apparatus. As is also evident, controllable shock did not produce any further release of serotonin. However, the uncontrollable shock, even though physically identical to the controllable shock, produced a large and sustained release of serotonin, with levels remaining high for a long period of time after the termination of the stress session and return to the home cage environment.

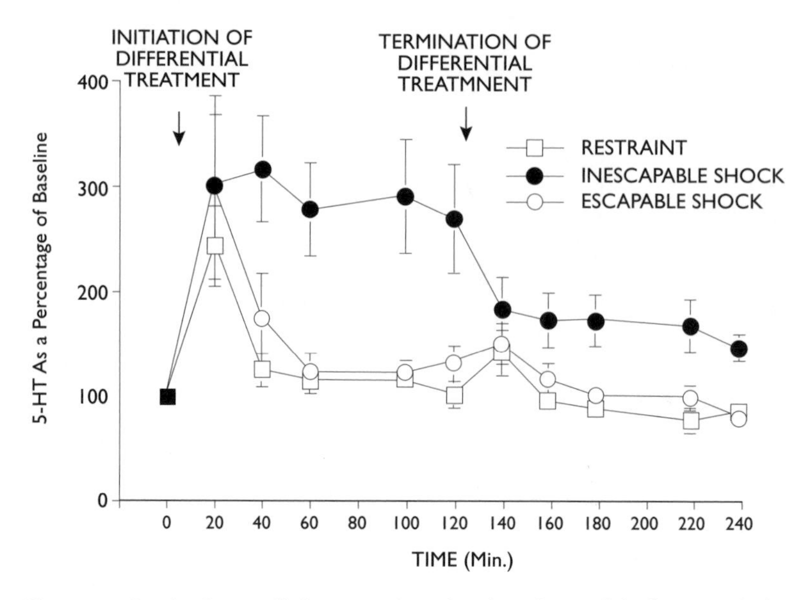

Figure 2.4. Levels of extracellular serotonin in basolateral amygdala during and after escapable shock, yoked inescapable shock, or restraint in the apparatus.

In sum, serotonergic cells in the dorsal raphe nucleus are sensitive to control, and differential release of serotonin in regions such as the amygdala does occur. However, remember that learned helplessness effects persist for about three days. Why should the animal fail to escape or show enhanced fear a number of days later? One answer is that these serotonergic neurons are sensitized by uncontrollable stressors so that they respond in an exaggerated fashion for about three days. How does this happen? The internal organization of the dorsal raphe nucleus is somewhat unusual. The soma and dendrites of serotonergic neurons in the dorsal raphe express receptors of the 5-HT_{1A} type. These receptors inhibit activation of the neurons on which they are located when serotonin binds to them, and they thus function as inhibitory autoreceptors (Radja, Laporte, Daval, Vergé, Goslan, & Hamon, 1991). Serotonergic neurons in the dorsal raphe nucleus release serotonin within the raphe itself when they are activated, not just in the terminal projection regions. This means that these neurons are normally under "self-inhibition." Anything that interferes with or reduces this self-inhibition should exaggerate the activity of these cells, since normal restraint on their activity has been reduced. It is known that the presence of a large amount of serotonin within the dorsal raphe will reduce the number of these receptors that are present on the surface of the neurons (Short, 1997), a process that requires several hours. Importantly, uncontrollable stressors release large amounts of serotonin within the dorsal raphe nucleus itself, as measured with the *in vivo* microdialysis procedure described above (Maswood, Barter, Watkins, & Maier, 1998). This large amount of serotonin then down regulates the 5-HT_{1A} receptors as measured by receptor binding techniques (Short, 1997), yielding hyper-reactive dorsal raphe neurons for a number of days. They are hyper-reactive because the normal self-inhibitory restraint that regulates their function has been reduced. Thus, any input that would normally activate these cells will produce an exaggerated release of serotonin in projection regions such as the amygdala. Indeed, the test tasks that are used to assess learned helplessness, such as escape training, do activate these neurons. Therefore, the proximate cause of behavioral learned helplessness effects may be exaggerated release of serotonin in regions that control the behaviors in question, such as the amygdala.

The data presented thus far do not indicate that these serotonergic changes are either necessary or sufficient to produce helplessness and its converse. Fortunately, these questions can now be answered. To determine if activation of serotonergic neurons in the dorsal raphe nucleus is necessary, the strategy would be to prevent the neurons from becoming activated during exposure to uncontrollable stressors. This can be accomplished through microinjecting into the dorsal raphe—during exposure to uncontrollable stressors—very small amounts of substances that specifically inhibit serotonergic neuronal activation, but no other neural activation. This should block learned helplessness. Similarly, it can be determined whether activating these cells is sufficient to produce learned helplessness. In effect, the strategy would be to microinject substances into the dorsal raphe that activate serotonergic neurons and determine whether this, by itself, with no exposure to a stressor, produces learned helplessness. Research using these techniques cannot be reviewed here, but many such experiments have now been conducted (Maier, Busch, Maswood, Grahn, & Watkins, 1995a; Maier, Grahn,

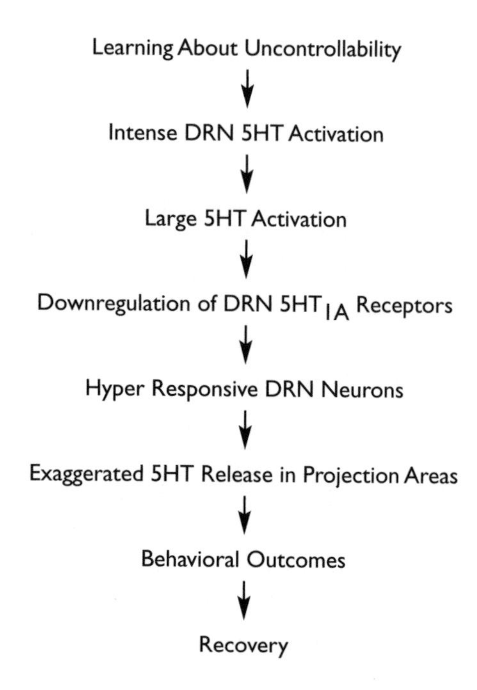

Figure 2.5. Proposed neural scheme for the induction of learned helplessness.

Maswood, & Watkins, 1995b; Maier, Grahn, & Watkins, 1995c).

To summarize, the scheme, shown in figure 2.5, is that uncontrollable stressors produce an intense activation of serotonergic cells in the dorsal raphe nucleus; large amounts of serotonin are released within the raphe, as well as in projection regions; this down regulates 5-HT$_{1A}$ inhibitory auto-receptors in the dorsal raphe nucleus (DRN); hyper-reactive neurons result for a period of time; input to the raphe during this period produces an exaggerated release of serotonin in projection regions; and finally, this serotonin produces the behavioral outcomes. We seem to have isolated a critical neural circuit that mediates learned helplessness, and perhaps its converse—resilience. The next step must determine the mechanisms by which controllable and uncontrollable events have differential effects on these cells in the dorsal raphe. Such studies are not only well underway, but also a number of inputs to the raphe, following exposure to uncontrollable stressors, are already clear (Grahn et al., 1998). Whether or not the mechanisms described here prove to be critical, the important points for this chapter highlight these available tools, which permit a new level of analysis for researchers, as well as the formation of *a priori* hypotheses about the brain for guiding researchers.

CONCLUSIONS

Research has provided a large body of knowledge about neural mechanisms by which uncontrollable events produce helplessness; however, little knowledge exists about how control exerts its blunting power and makes subjects resilient. Interestingly, Drugan has discovered a molecule that seems to be released by cells in the brain only under conditions of control (Drugan, Basile, Ha, & Ferland, 1994). This molecule has characteristics expected to inhibit serotonergic cells in the dorsal raphe nucleus. Whether this inhibition actually takes place or not is a topic to be explored. However, if this inhibition does occur it would provide a mechanism for resilience, which leads to intriguing questions with regard to individual differences. Only about half of the subjects that receive uncontrollable stressors actually show helplessness effects. What distinguishes the resistant subjects? Although we don't know, the tools for discovery are in place.

Seligman and Maier started together, literally running experiments side by side. We think it is fair to say that both have come a long way, albeit in very different directions. As Seligman has commented, he has "reached outward" while Maier has "reached inward," attempting to understand the same set of phenomena. It would be useful for these divergent directions to come together. Seligman is striving for a psychology of optimism and human potential, and we believe it is now possible to discover something of the neurobiology of these processes. We would argue that true understanding emerges only when a set of phenomena are apprehended at multiple levels of analysis, and the possibility, seems to us, more than a pipe dream.

NOTES

1 In Grahn's experiment, at various times after the behavioral treatments, brains are removed and very thin sections made of the dorsal raphe nucleus. These sections are placed on slides, and are then incubated with antibodies raised in goats against the rat *c-fos* protein. These antibodies will, of course, bind to any *c-fos* protein that is expressed in the neurons on the slide. After a period of time, the slides are washed extensively, and so the only antibody that remains on the slides will be that bound to the *c-fos* proteins. The slides are then incubated with a second antibody that will recognize and bind to any goat antibody. This second antibody will, therefore, bind to the antibody that is bound to the *c-fos* protein. However, this second antibody is first treated in such a way that biotin molecules have become attached to the end of the antibody that does not recognize and attach itself to the goat antibody. Thus, wherever there has been *fos* protein on the slide there will now be free biotin (at the end of the second antibody).

This procedure unfolds in this manner because avidin cross-links strongly to biotin, and molecules such as horseradish peroxidase, which form a colored product that can be seen, can be linked to avidin. Thus the next step involves incubation with an avidin-horseradish peroxidase complex. Now horseradish peroxidase appears wherever there was *fos* protein, and this reacts to form a dark product, specifically, a black dot emerges wherever there is *fos* protein. Because *c-fos* protein is restricted to the nucleus of the neurons, activated neurons have a visible black dot in the nucleus. When the slides are then viewed under a microscope and the neurons in the dorsal raphe whose nucleus contains *fos* protein—visualized as a black dot—appear, they can be successfully counted. Indeed, these images are so clear that they can be digitized and counted by a computer program.

This *c-fos* immunohistochemistry can indicate how many neurons were activated, but as mentioned above, not all neurons in the dorsal raphe nucleus are serotonergic. How do we know that these activated neurons are serotonergic neurons? We use a further antibody that recognizes serotonin, but here with a red tag added for visualization rather than a black tag as for the *fos*. Since serotonin is not restricted to the nucleus, the whole neuron stains red if it is serotonergic. Again, one simply counts the number of red neurons with a black dot in their nucleus, and this indicates the number of activated serotonin neurons.

REFERENCES

Davis, M. (1992). The role of the amygdala in conditioned fear. In J.P. Aggleton (Ed.), *The amygdala* (pp. 255–307). New York: Wiley-Liss.

Drugan, R.C., Basile, A.S., Ha, J.H., & Ferland, R.J. (1994). The protective effects of stress control may be mediated by increased brain levels of benzodiazepine receptor agonists. *Brain Research, 661,* 127–136.

Eisenstein, E.M., & Carlson, A.D. (1997). A comparative approach to the behavior called "learned helplessness." *Behavioral Brain Research, 68,* 149–160.

Fanselow, M.S. (1991). The midbrain periaqueductal gray as a coordinator of action in response to fear and anxiety. In A. Depaulis & R. Bandler (Eds.), *The midbrain periaqueductal gray matter* (pp. 151–173). New York: Plenum Press.

Grahn, R.E., Maswood, S., McQueen, M.B., Watkins, L.R., & Maier, S.F. (1999). Opioid-dependent effects of inescapable shock on escape behavior and conditioned fear responding are mediated by the dorsal raphe nucleus. *Behavioural Brain Research, 99,* 153–167.

Kiser, R.S., Brown, C.A., Sanghera, M.K., & German, D.C. (1980). Dorsal raphe nucleus stimulation reduces centrally-elicited fearlike behavior. *Brain Research, 191,* 265–272.

Maier, S.F., Busch, C., Maswood, C., Grahn, R.E., & Watkins, L.R. (1995a). The dorsal raphe nucleus is a site of action mediating the behavioral effects of the benzodiazepine receptor inverse agonist DMCM. *Behavioral Neuroscience, 106,* 759–766.

Maier, S.F., Coon, D.J., McDaniel, M.A., & Jackson, R.L. (1979). The time course of learned helplessness, inactivity, and nociceptive deficits in rats. *Learning and Motivation, 10,* 467–488.

Maier, S.F., Grahn, R.E., Maswood, S., & Watkins, L.R. (1995b). The benzodiazepine receptor antagonists flumazenil and CGS8216 block the enhancement of fear conditioning and interference with escape behavior produced by inescapable shock. *Psychopharmacology, 121,* 250–258.

Maier, S.F., Grahn, R.E., & Watkins, L.R. (1995c). 8-OH-DPAT micro injected in the region of the dorsal raphe nucleus blocks and reverses the enhancement of fear conditioning and the interference with escape produced by exposure to inescapable shock. *Behavioral Neuroscience, 109,* 404–413.

Maswood, S., Barter, J.E., Watkins, L.R., & Maier, S.F. (1998). Exposure to inescapable but not to escapable stress increases extra cellular levels of 5-HT in the dorsal raphe nucleus of the rat. *Brain Research, 783,* 115–120.

Minor, T.R., & Saade, S. (1997). Poststress glucose mitigates behavioral impairment in rats in the "learned helplessness" model of psychopathology. *Biological Psychiatry, 1997(42),* 324–334.

Mowrer, O.H., & Viek, P. (1948). An experimental analogue of fear from a sense of helplessness. *Journal of Abnormal and Social Psychology, 43,* 193–200.

Overmier, J.B., & Seligman, M.E.P. (1967). Effects of inescapable shock upon subsequent escape and avoidance learning. *Journal of Comparative and Physiological Psychology, 63,* 28–33.

Radja, F., Laporte, A.M., Daval, G., Vergé, D., Gozlan, H., & Hamon, M. (1991). Auto-radiography of serotonin receptor subtypes in the central nervous system. *Neurochemistry International, 18,* 1–15.

Seligman, M.E.P., & Maier, S.F. (1967). Failure to escape traumatic shock. *Journal of Experimental Psychology, 74,* 1–9.

Seligman, M.E.P., Rosellini, R.A., & Kozak, M. (1975). Learned helplessness in the rat: Reversibility, time course, and immunization. *Journal of Comparative and Physiological Psychology, 88,* 542–547.

Short, K.R. (1997). Inescapable stress, a benzodiazepine receptor inverse agonist or serotonin in the dorsal raphe nucleus increases anxiety and decreases 5-HT_{1A} receptor binding in rat dorsal raphe. *Society for Neuroscience Abstracts, 27,* 1078.

Volpicelli, J.R., Ulm, R.R., Altenor, A., & Seligman, M.E.P. (1983). Learned mastery in the rat. *Learning and Motivation, 14,* 204–222.

Williams, J.L., & Maier, S.F. (1977). Transituational immunization and therapy of learned helplessness in the rat. *Journal of Experimental Psychology: Animal Behavior Processes, 3,* 240–253.

✦ CHAPTER 3 ✦

The Neurochemistry of Stress Resilience and Coping: A Quest for Nature's Own Antidote to Illness

Robert C. Drugan

IT IS AN HONOR to discuss the research of my mentor, Steve Maier. Even though his pioneering work illustrates only a piece of the neurobiology of stress and coping picture that his laboratory and others have constructed over the past several decades, nevertheless, his research demonstrates the remarkable reach of the tentacles of stress controllability. This reach includes modifying such essential, fundamental biological processes as pain perception (Maier, Drugan, and Grau, 1982; Drugan, Ader, & Maier, 1985) and immunocompetence (Laudenslager, Ryan, Drugan, Hyson, & Maier, 1983). This work underscores the exquisite regulation of bodily processes that psychological dynamics of stress can achieve. These findings, therefore, have raised our level of appreciation for the reciprocal neural highway connecting brain, behavior, and body.

As a college sophomore, I chose the citation classic "Learned Helplessness: Theory and Evidence" by Maier and Seligman (1976) as an article in a research methods class. This paper inspired a three-year honors thesis project in Jim Misanin's lab, where possible stress controllability-induced changes in pain sensitivity, as contributing to learned helplessness effects, were studied. My research continued on the psychopharmacology of stress and coping as a graduate student in Maier's lab, and I continue to investigate the neurochemical consequences of stress resilience and coping to this day.

The neural circuits orchestrating fear and defensive behaviors, activated by uncontrollable but not controllable stress exposure (e.g., dorsal raphe nucleus, amygdala, and periaqueductal gray matter) (Maier et al., 1995; Maier, Grahn, Maswood, & Watkins, 1995; Maier, Grahn, & Watkins, 1995; Sutton, Grahn, Wiertelak, Watkins, & Maier, 1997) provide a framework for the development of novel pharmacotherapies for stress-related disorders in humans. The advent of modern neurobiological tools, coupled with the innovative animal model work of Maier and others in the field of stress and coping has, to embellish Maier's analogy further, equipped researchers with a metal detector for finding that "needle in the haystack." The "on-line" analysis of neurochemical and cellular processes by early gene expression and microdialysis allows neuroscientists to make great strides in localizing, quantifying, and comparing the neurochemical status of behaviorally divergent groups of subjects during or following a stress experience. This fine-tuned analysis will provide answers to questions concerning the etiology of individual differences in response to stress.

Maier has recently focused his investigations on the serotonergic (5-HT) system, particularly the dorsal raphe. This site is a critical relay center for both ascending and descending information, which modifies not only emotionality, but also pain reactivity and defensive behavior as well. The 5-HT system is the one of choice for the new generation non-benzodiazepine anxiolytics (e.g., buspirone, Buspar) as well as serotonin specific reuptake inhibitors (SSRI) used as antidepressants (e.g., fluoxetine, Prozac). Although these compounds have a much improved therapeutic window, improvements regarding toleration, side effects, and withdrawal symptoms remain an active area of research. Maier's work alerts pharmaceutical bench science to target specific receptor subtypes for serotonin, located in these areas, and hasten the arrival of a "magic bullet" for stress-related disorders in humans. The implementation of molecular biology in drug development affords the pharmaceutical industry to take this information and "fast-forward" the time line from drug discovery at the bench to its arrival at the clinical bedside.

The elegance of using early gene expression (e.g., c-*fos*) or microdialysis becomes apparent when illustrating neurochemical changes in the living, awake organism and demonstrating cellular activity sensitive to stress controllability. As a psychologist, I am particularly excited about Maier's discoveries that unequivocally reveal that early gene expression and neurotransmitter activity can be modified by an organism's capability to cope (or not to cope) with stress.

I would like to revisit Maier's concepts raised about coping and fear and add complementary empirical finding about two concepts regarding individual differences in stress reactivity (resilient versus vulnerable organisms). Ever since my original work with the learned helplessness paradigm in 1976, I noted a markedly different behavioral profile of coping (escapable stress) and non-coping (yoked-inescapable stress) subjects during the initial stress exposure. I continued to examine the role of fear/anxiety as a mediator of these stress controllability effects as a graduate student in Maier's lab. I was fascinated as to why the coping (escape) subjects remained resilient, even though they were exposed to the identical physical stress as their yoked counterparts. I took the road less traveled to study resilience.

STRESS RESILIENCE

In addition to the anatomical sites mediating fear as Maier described, there are specific neurochemical receptors or drug recognition sites in the brain that specifically bind minor tranquilizers, such as valium. These benzodiazepine receptors are associated with the major inhibitory neurotransmitter in the brain, gamma aminobutyric acid (GABA). These receptors are found in high density in emotional centers of the brain including the amygdala, as well as in midbrain areas such as the raphe nucleus and periaqueductal gray matter (Mohler & Okada, 1977; Squires & Braestrup, 1977). The GABAergic system influences and is influenced by many neurotransmitters, including serotonin (Iverson, 1983). Environmental stress also rapidly alters benzodiazepine receptors (Braestrup, Nielsen, Nielsen, & Lyon, 1979; Drugan et al., 1989; Trullas, Havoundjian, Zamir, Paul, & Skolnick, 1987).

My original hypothesis was that coping afforded stress resilience by reducing fear or anxiety during the stress experience. GABA antagonist-induced seizures (via bicuculline injection) in rats provide a behavioral "window into the brain," which indicate GABAergic "tone" or levels in brain. Bicuculline-induced seizures are remarkably sensitive to prior stress controllability experience. Those rats, given the opportunity to actively cope with stress, are protected from seizures, while uncontrollably-stressed subjects exhibit a hyper-reactivity to seizures (Drugan, McIntryre, Alpern, & Maier, 1985). Thus, behavioral pharmacology data, from intact rats, indicated that coping with stress was associated with the release of an anti-convulsant compound in brain.

Neurochemical techniques allow researchers to both survey and quantify drug recognition sites in brain. In vitro radioligand binding analysis involves taking behaviorally treated (e.g., controllable versus uncontrollable stress) rats and dissecting, homogenizing, and preparing brain tissue areas (e.g., cortex, hippocampus, amygdala) so that they can be incubated with radioactively-tagged drugs, such as valium. The labeling of the drug allows the neuroscientist the capability of quantifying the attraction between the drug and the receptor (i.e., affinity), as well as the number of available receptors (i.e., density). We conducted these analyses on rats previously exposed to either escapable stress, inescapable stress, or no stress. Interestingly, the escapable stress or coping subjects showed an increased GABA binding (as measured with [3H] muscimol), as well as a decreased convulsant site binding (as measured with [35S] TBPS [Drugan, Basile, Ha, & Ferland, 1994]). These benzodiazepine/GABA receptor complex (BGRC) changes are identical to the effects one would observe if an untreated rat were given valium.

Because some subjects exposed to uncontrollable stress do not develop behavioral, physiological, or immunological pathology, perhaps resilience is achieved through a similar neurochemical pathway as active behavioral coping—by way of the BGRC. In order to test this possibility, we exposed rats to either no stress or inescapable shock stress. Twenty-four hours later, all subjects were tested for their performance in a shuttle escape task, the behavioral "litmus test" for learned helplessness. Those subjects that do not learn are considered stress vulnerable, while those subjects that learn in a fashion similar to unstressed controls are deemed stress resilient. Using our particular stress paradigm, we find a somewhat bimodal distribution with 50% showing resilience, and 50% exhibiting vulnerability. In vitro radioligand binding analyses of these groups revealed that the resilient group showed an identical pattern of binding changes as the active behavioral coping rats mentioned above. More specifically, the stress resilient rats exhibited increased GABA binding and decreased binding to the convulsant site in cortex and hippocampus (Drugan et al., 1989; Drugan, Paul, & Crawley, 1993). This suggested that coping and stress resilience-induced effects may be due to the activation of a neurochemical final common pathway in the brain. In sum, both of these stress resilient groups showed BGRC changes reminiscent of giving the subject an injection of valium.

COPING AND THE RELEASE OF AN ANTI-ANXIETY COMPOUND IN THE BRAIN

While similar receptor alterations in coping and stress resilient subjects interest researchers, the isolation and characterization of the brain substance responsible for producing these BGRC changes constitutes essential data. Recent techniques in neurochemistry, such as brain extraction and subsequent receptor competition analyses, offer researchers an indication as to the specific sites in the brain where brain-derived compounds may have their actions. Procedures for isolating benzodiazepines in mammalian brain tissue arose for analysis in pharmacokinetics (drug biodistribution), as well as for the quantification of brain-released substances in certain psychiatric or pathologic states (Ha, Pannell, Drugan, Ferland, & Basile, 1996). Using a procedure that is a modification of a technique developed by Osselton (1978) and Foerster, Mason, and Mason (1974), and Foerster, Hatchett, and Garriott (1978), Basile and colleagues at the National Institute of Diabetes, Digestive and Kidney Disorders Institute (NIDDK), at the National Institutes of Health, developed a technique that allows extraction of benzodiazepine receptor ligands from mammalian brain tissue (Basile et al., 1991; Ha et al., 1996; Yurdaydin et al., 1993). In collaboration with Basile, we examined the brains of rats exposed to escapable stress, yoked-inescapable stress, or no stress (naïve). Two hours following the escapable stress exposure, we observed a two- to three-fold increase in whole brain levels of a substance that competes with valium for the BGRC (see figure 3.1). Thus, active behavioral coping or stress control is associated with the enhanced release of a valium-like substance in the brain in comparison to both yoked inescapable stress and nonstressed controls (Drugan et al., 1994). This substance may be a mechanism whereby coping with stress protects against subsequent stress pathology.

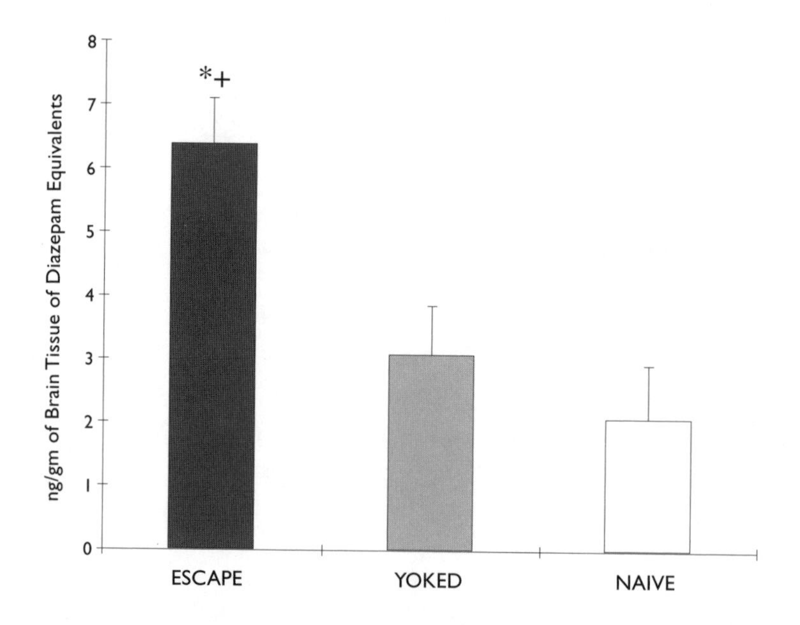

Figure 3.1. Mean brain levels of benzodiazepine receptor agonists in naïve (no stress), inescapably-shocked, and escapably-shocked rats analyzed two hours following treatment. Vertical bars represent mean + Standard Error of the Mean (n = *10 rats/group). The asterisk (*) indicates significant difference in comparison to naive controls* ($p < .01$)*; the plus sign (+) indicates significant difference in comparison to yoked-inescapable shock group* ($p < .05$) *by Newman-Keuls post hoc comparisons after Analysis of Variance (ANOVA) (Drugan et al., 1994).*

If coping with stress or stress resilience is associated with the release of a GABA-enhancing, anxiolytic (valium-like substance), memory interference might be expected, since many of these anti-anxiety compounds have amnestic properties (Izquierdo & Medina, 1991; Lister, 1985; Lucki et al., 1987; Thiebot, 1985; Venault et al., 1986). The protection afforded to stress resilient subjects on subsequent behavior and physiology may be, in part, mediated by an impairment of the memory of the prior stress experience. This memory deficit might be beneficial for the organism in reducing the proactive interference of the initial stress exposure on subsequent behavior and physiology.

We evaluated the above coping-memory hypothesis by training rats immediately after the stress session on a spatial learning and memory task, the Morris water maze (Morris, 1981). A place-learning task was used, due to its sensitivity to the integrity of the hippocampus, a brain area known to have changes in GABAergic function in response to stress (Foy, Stanton, Levine, & Thompson, 1987; Petty & Sherman, 1981), as well as BGRC changes in coping and stress resilient rats (Drugan et al., 1994; Drugan, Paul, & Crawley, 1993). If stress control or resilience causes the release of a valium-like compound in the brain, then coping subjects should show poorer retention of the location of a submerged platform in comparison to yoked-inescapable stress and nonstress controls. Stress controllability did not alter the acquisition of this navigational learning task, but markedly influenced the memory of the event. Coping subjects showed poorer retention for the platform location twenty-four hours later in comparison to the other groups, which did not differ from one another (Healy & Drugan, 1996).

We were intrigued as to the identity of the coping-induced substance in the brain that possesses anxiolytic, anti-convulsant, and amnestic properties. Neuroactive steroids are those steroids released from sites in the peripheral nervous system (e.g., deoxycorticosterone, from adrenal gland) and have actions in brain tissue. Neurosteroids are synthesized, released, and subsequently have their effects in the brain (Baulieu, 1981). Traditional endocrinology ascribes genomic actions of steroid hormones at sites in the nucleus of cells that, in turn, modifies gene expression (McEwen, 1991). However, recent work illustrates another action of steroids termed non-genomic, that is, having its effects on cell surface receptors and modifying ion-gated channels (e.g., NMDA-glutamate and GABA) in a fashion reminiscent of classic neurotransmitters

(McEwen, 1991). Metabolites of the parent hormones progesterone and deoxycorticosterone, such as allopregnanolone (AP) and tetrahydrodeoxycorticosterone (THDOC), are positive modulators of the BGRC (Majewska et al., 1986). More specifically, these GABA-positive steroid metabolites have valium-like actions. Perhaps coping with stress causes the accumulation of these metabolites in the brain several hours poststress. Conversely, other neurosteroids such as dehydroepiandrosterone sulfate (DHEAS) and pregnenolone sulfate (PS) are negative modulators of the BGRC and interfere with GABAergic transmission (Majewska and Schwartz, 1987; Majewska, Demirgören, Spivak, and London, 1990).

Stress-induced increases in BGRC positive neurosteroids have been demonstrated by several laboratories (Barbaccia et al., 1996; Purdy, Morrow, Moore, & Paul, 1991). The increase in these compounds is sufficient to modulate the BGRC function. Since these compounds act in a fashion similar to valium, they might be expected to have a similar anxiolytic, anticonvulsant, and amnestic profile. Recent research verifies that these steroid metabolites reduce anxiety (Crawley, Glowa, Majewska, & Paul, 1986), are anti-convulsant in nature (Belelli, Lan, & Gee, 1990) and have memory-impairing effects (Mayo et al., 1993).

We tested the involvement of these neurosteroids in coping animals by administering a drug prior to stress that inhibits the synthesis of these BGRC positive neurosteroids. N, N-diethyl-4-methyl-3-oxo-4-aza-5 alpha androstane-17 beta-carboxamide (4-MA) is a potent inhibitor of the 5-alpha reductase enzyme, responsible for catalyzing the reduction of the parent steroid hormones into the bioactive BGRC positive modulators, allopregnanolone and THDOC (Toomey, Goode, Petrow, & Neubauer, 1991). If the coping-induced memory deficit twenty-four hours post-training is the result of an endogenous BGRC active neurosteroid compound, then one would expect to see a reversal of this effect following the administration of the steroid synthesis inhibitor, 4-MA. 4-MA reversed the escapable stress-induced deficit in memory of the previous platform location twenty-four hours later (Healy & Drugan, 1996). Thus, memory alterations due to active coping behavior appear to result from the release of neurosteroids in the brain. Figure 3.2 presents a schematic diagram that incorporates the above findings into a model, which illustrates the anxiolytic and mnemonic actions that may impart stress resiliency in coping subjects by brain derived GABA positive steroids acting at the BGRC. Conversely, in the non-coping group is the putative release of GABA-negative steroids that result in anxiety, seizure susceptibility, and enhanced memory of the stress event by interfering with GABAergic transmission in the brain.

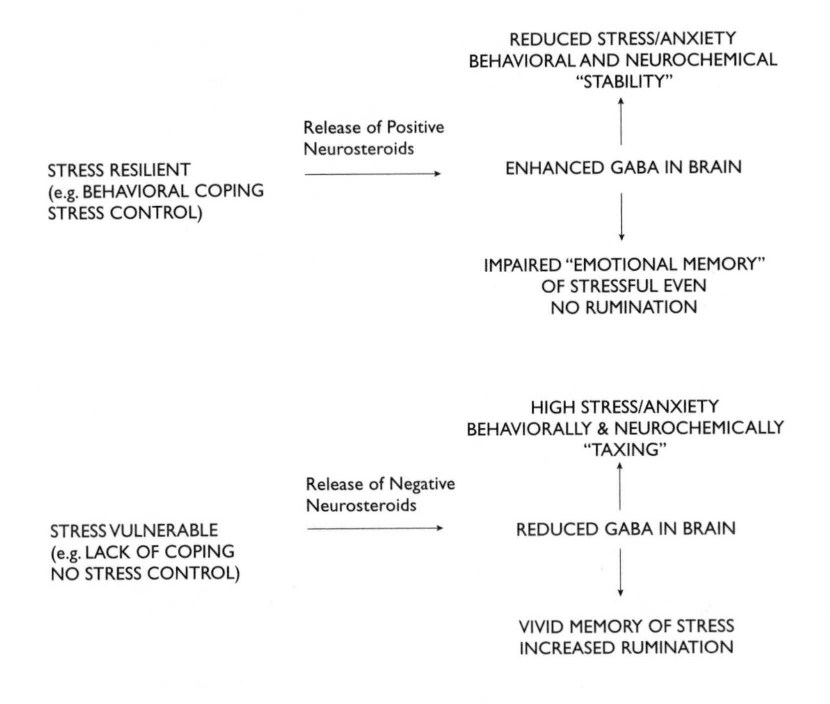

Figure 3.2. A model indicates the release of neurosteroids in both coping and non-coping subjects, and how these substances may impart either stress resilience or vulnerability by altering anxiety as well as memory.

The data that I have presented, focusing on the BGRC receptor as a critical mediator in affording stress resilience in animals, is not mutually exclusive of the work presented by Maier on the serotonergic (5-HT) system. Due to the ubiquitous nature of GABA in the brain, this neurotransmitter has important connections with the 5-HT system as presented by Maier and colleagues in a recent paper (Sutton et al., 1997).

Maier and colleagues have provided unequivocal evidence for a BGRC/5-HT-stress interaction in the dorsal raphe nucleus (Sutton et al., 1997), which verifies and extends earlier electrophysiological work using micro injection and single unit recording in the raphe nucleus (Gallagher, 1978). Furthermore, the pervasiveness of GABA in the brain is exemplified in electrophysiological estimates that 20% to 40% of neurons in the brain contain this neurotransmitter (Bloom & Iverson, 1971). The GABAergic system, therefore, not only influences the cell body domain of 5-HT, but also has influences in the terminal projection fields including periaqueductal gray matter (PAG), amygdala, as well as cortex. Thus, the GABAergic changes presented herein are likely acting in concert with the 5-HT system, described by Maier to influence both stress vulnerability and resilience.

In summary, our appreciation of a multiple, yet synergistic transmitter etiology for both stress vulnerability and resilience will allow researchers to develop a more sophisticated battery of treatments. This multifaceted approach will guide titration of therapy in light of the marked individual differences in the expression of psychopathology in humans. Maier's breakthroughs in the neurobiology of stress and coping, coupled with Seligman's clinical discoveries, have made a monumental contribution to the field of biological psychiatry. Furthermore, Seligman's vision of ushering in an era of "positive" psychology will not only immediately benefit society, but will also refocus the traditional biomedical model from one of "anatomy of an illness" to a future mission of searching for "nature's own antidote to illness." The outcome of such an innovative about-face may hasten the discovery of novel behavioral and pharmacological therapies that will allow people to live happier and more productive lives. Generally speaking, this may be conceptualized as the reallocation of resources toward preserving and maximizing health, rather than exclusively irradicating illness.

REFERENCES

Barbaccia, M.L., Roscetti, G., Bolacchi, F., Concas, A., Mostallino, M.C., Purdy, R.H., & Biggio, G. (1996). Stress-induced increase in brain neuroactive steroids: Antagonism by abecarnil. *Pharmacology, Biochemistry and Behavior, 54,* 205–210.

Basile, A.S., Hughes, R.D., Harrison, P.M., Murata, Y., Pannell, L., Jones, E.A., Williams, R., & Skolnick, P. (1991). Elevated brain concentrations of 1,4 benzodiazepines in fulminant hepatic failure. *New England Journal of Medicine, 325,* 473–478.

Baulieu, E.E. (1981). Steroid hormones in the brain: Several mechanisms? In K. Fuxe, J.A. Gustafsson, and L. Wetterberg (Eds.), *Steroid hormone regulation of the brain* (pp. 3–17). New York: Pergamon Press, Oxford University Press, 3–17.

Belelli, D., Lan, N.C., & Gee, K.W. (1990). Anti-convulsant steroids and the GABA/benzodiazepine receptor-chloride ionophore complex. *Neuroscience and Biobehavioral Reviews, 14,* 315–325.

Bloom, F.E., & Iverson, L. (1971). Localizing [3H] GABA in nerve terminals of rat cerebral cortex by electron microscopic autoradiography. *Nature, 229,* 628–630.

Braestrup, C., Nielsen, M., Nielsen, E.B., & Lyon, M. (1979). Benzodiazepine receptors in the brain as affected by different experimental stresses: The changes are small and not unidirectional. *Psychopharmacology, 65,* 273–277.

Crawley, J.N., Glowa, J.R., Majewska, M.D. , & Paul, S.M. (1986). Anxiolytic activity of an endogenous adrenal steroid. *Brain Research, 398,* 382–385.

Drugan, R.C., Ader, D.N., & Maier, S.F. (1985). Shock controllability and the nature of stress-induced analgesia. *Behavioral Neuroscience, 99,* 791–801.

Drugan, R.C., Basile, A.S., Ha, J.H., & Ferland, R.J. (1994). The protective effects of stress control may be mediated by increased brain levels of benzodiazepine receptor agonists. *Brain Research, 661,* 127–136.

Drugan, R.C., Deutsch, S.I., Weizman, R., Weizman, A., Vocci, F.J., Crawley, J.N., Skolnick, P., & Paul, S.M. (1989). Molecular mechanisms of stress and anxiety: Alterations in the Benzodiazepine/GABA receptor complex. In

H. Weiner, I. Florin, R. Murison, and D. Hellhammer (Eds.), *Frontiers of stress research, control of bodily function: Basic and clinical aspects* (pp. 148–159). *Vol. 3*. Toronto: Hans Huber Publishers.

Drugan, R.C., McIntryre, T.D., Alpern, H.P., & Maier, S.F. (1985). Coping and seizure susceptibility: Control over shock protects against bicuculline-induced seizures. *Brain Research, 342,* 9–17.

Drugan, R.C., Morrow, A.L., Weizman, R., Weizman, A., Deutsch, S.I., Crawley, J.N., & Paul, S.M. (1989). Stress-induced behavioral depression is associated with a decrease in GABA receptor-mediated chloride ion flux and brain benzodiazepine receptor occupancy. *Brain Research, 487,* 45–51.

Drugan, R.C., Paul, S.M., & Crawley, J.N. (1993). Decreased forebrain [35S]TBPS binding and increased [3H]muscimol binding in rats that do not develop stress-induced behavioral depression. *Brain Research, 631,* 270–276.

Drugan, R.C., Skolnick, P., Paul, S.M., & Crawley, J.N. (1989). A pretest procedure reliably predicts performance in two animal models of inescapable stress. *Pharmacology, Biochemistry and Behavior, 33,* 649–654.

Foerster, E.H., Hatchett, D., & Garriott, J.C. (1978). A rapid, comprehensive screening procedure for basic drugs in blood or tissues by gas chromatography. *Journal of Analytical Toxicology, 2,* 50–55.

Foerster, E.H., Mason, M.S., & Mason, M.F. (1974). Preliminary studies on the use of n-butyl chloride as an extractant in a drug screening procedure. *Journal of Forensic Science, 19,* 155–160.

Foy, M.R., Stanton, M.E., Levine, S., & Thompson, R.F. (1987). Behavioral stress impairs long-term potentiation in rodent hippocampus. *Behavioral and Neural Biology, 48,* 138–149.

Gallagher, D.W. (1978). Benzodiazepines: Potentiation of a GABA inhibitor response in the dorsal raphe nucleus. *European Journal of Pharmacology, 49,* 133–143.

Ha, J.H., Pannell, L., Drugan, R.C., Ferland, R.J., & Basile, A.S. (1996). Extraction of benzodiazepine receptor ligands from mammalian tissues. *Neuroscience Protocols, 2,* 1–12.

Healy, D.J., & Drugan, R.C. (1996). Escapable stress modulates retention of spatial learning in rats: Preliminary evidence for involvement of neurosteroids. *Psychobiology, 24,* 110–117.

Iverson, S. (1983). Where in the brain do the benzodiazepines act? In M.R. Trimble (Ed.), *Benzodiazepines divided: A multidisciplinary review* (pp. 167–185). New York: John Wiley and Sons.

Izquierdo, I., & Medina, J.H. (1991). GABAa receptor modulation of memory: The role of endogenous benzodiazepines. *Trends in Pharmaceutical Science, 12,* 260–265.

Laudenslager, M.L., Ryan, S.M., Drugan, R.C., Hyson, R.L., & Maier, S.F. (1983). Coping and immunosuppression: Inescapable but not escapable shock suppresses lymphocyte proliferation. *Science, 221,* 568–571.

Lister, R.G. (1985). The amnestic action of benzodiazepines in man. *Neuroscience and Biobehavioral Reviews, 9,* 87–94.

Lucki, I., Rickels, K., Giesecke, A., & Geller, A. (1987). Differential effects of anxiolytic drugs, diazepam and buspirone, on memory function. *British Journal of Clinical Pharmacology, 23,* 207–211.

Maier, S.F., Busch, C., Maswood, S., Grahn, R.E., & Watkins, L.R. (1995). The dorsal raphe nucleus is a site of action mediating the behavioral effects of the benzodiazepine receptor inverse agonist DMCM. *Behavioral Neuroscience, 109,* 759–766.

Maier, S.F., Drugan, R.C., & Grau, J.W. (1982). Controllability, coping behavior and stress-induced analgesia in the rat. *Pain, 12,* 47–56.

Maier, S.F., Grahn, R.E., Maswood, S., & Watkins, L.R. (1995). The benzodiazepine receptor antagonist flumazenil and CGS 8216 block the enhancement of fear conditioning and interference with escape behavior produced by inescapable shock. *Psychopharmacology, 121,* 250–259.

Maier, S.F., Grahn, R.E., & Watkins, L.R. (1995). 8-OH-DPAT microinjected in the region of the dorsal raphe nucleus blocks and reverses the enhanced fear conditioning and the interference with escape produced by exposure to inescapable shock. *Behavioral Neuroscience, 109,* 404–412.

Maier, S.F., & Seligman, M.E.P. (1976). Learned helplessness: Theory and evidence. *Journal of Experimental Psychology: General, 105,* 3–46.

Maier, S.F., & Warren, D.A. Controllability and safety signals exert dissimilar proactive effects on nociception and escape performance. *Journal of Experimental Psychology: Animal Behavior Processes, 14,* 18–25.

Majewska, M.D., Demirgören, S. Spivak, C.E., & London, E.D. (1990). The neurosteroid dehydroepiandrosterone sulfate is an allosteric antagonist of the $GABA_A$ receptor. *Brain Research, 526,* 143–146.

Majewska, M.D., Harrison, N.L., Schwartz, R.D., Barker, J.L., & Paul, S.M. (1986). Steroid hormone metabolites are barbiturate-like modulators of the GABAa receptor. *Science, 232,* 1004–1007.

Majewska, M.D. and Schwartz, R.D. (1987). Pregnenolone-sulfate: An endogenous antagonist of the gamma-aminobytyric acid receptor complex in brain? *Brain Research, 404,* 355–360.

Mayo, W., Dellu, F., Robel, P., Cherkaoui, J., LeMoal, M., Baulieu, E.E., & Simon, H. (1993). Infusion of neurosteroids into the nucleus basalis magnocellularis affects cognitive processes in the rat. *Brain Research, 607,* 324–330.

McEwen, B.S. (1991). Steroid hormones are multifunctional messengers in the brain. *Trends in Pharmacological Sciences, 12,* 141–150.

Mohler, H., & Okada, T. (1977). The benzodiazepine receptor: Demonstration in the central nervous system. *Science, 198,* 849–851.

Morris, R.G.M. (1981). Spatial localization does not require the presence of local cues. *Learning and Motivation, 12,* 239–260.

Osselton, M.D. (1978). The release of basic drugs by the enzymatic digestion of tissues in cases of poisoning. *Journal of the Forensic Scientific Society, 17,* 189–194.

Petty, F., & Sherman, A.D. (1981). GABAergic modulation of learned helplessness. *Pharmacology, Biochemistry and Behavior, 15,* 453–457.

Purdy, R.H., Morrow, A.L., Moore, P.H., & Paul, S.M. (1991). Stress-induced elevations of gamma-aminobutyric acid type A receptor-active steroids in the rat brain. *Proceedings of the National Academy of Sciences, 88,* 4553–4557.

Seligman, M.E.P. (1996). Science as an ally of practice. *American Psychologist, 51,* 1072–1079.

Squires, R., & Braestrup, C. (1977) Benzodiazepine receptors in rat brain. *Nature, 266,* 732–734.

Sutton, L.C., Grahn, R.E., Wiertelak, E.P., Watkins, L.R., & Maier, S.F. (1997). Inescapable shock-induced potentiation of morphine analgesia in rats: Involvement of opioid, GABAergic and serotonergic mechanisms in the dorsal raphe nucleus. *Behavioral Neuroscience, 111,* 816–824.

Thiebot, M. (1985). Some evidence for amnestic-like effects of benzodiazepines in animals. *Neuroscience and Biobehavioral Reviews, 9,* 95–100.

Toomey, R.E., Goode, R.L., Petrow, V., & Neubauer, B.L. (1991). In vivo essay for conversion of testosterone to dihydrotestosterone by rat prostatic steroid 5a-reductase and comparison of two inhibitors. *The Prostate, 19,* 63–72.

Trullas, R., Havoundjian, H., Zamir, H., Paul, S.M., & Skolnick, P. (1987). Environmentally-induced modification of the benzodiazepine/GABA receptor coupled chloride ionophore. *Psychopharmacology, 97,* 384–390.

Venault, P., Chapouthier, G., Prado De Carvalho, L., Simiand, J., Morre, M., Dodd, R.H., & Rossier, J. (1986). Benzodiazepine impairs and B-carboline enhances performance in learning and memory tasks. *Nature, 321,* 864–866.

Yurdaydin, C., Gu, Z.Q., Fromm, C., Holt, G., & Basile, A.S. (1993). Benzodiazepine receptor ligands in an animal model of hepatic encephalopathy: Correlation between concentration, severity of encephalopathy and benzodiazepine receptor antagonist efficacy. *Journal of Pharmacology and Experimental Therapeutics, 265,* 565–571.

Section B. Psychological Resilience

✦

✦ CHAPTER 4 ✦

Optimistic Cognitive Styles and Invulnerability to Depression

Lyn Y. Abramson, Lauren B. Alloy, Benjamin L. Hankin, Caroline M. Clements, Lin Zhu, Michael E. Hogan, and Wayne G. Whitehouse

COGNITIVE INVULNERABILITY HYPOTHESIS OF PROTECTION FROM DEPRESSION

WHY ARE SOME PEOPLE invulnerable to depression even in the face of adversity? According to the cognitive perspective, the way people typically interpret or explain events in their lives—their cognitive styles—importantly affects their vulnerability to depression. For example, according to the hopelessness theory (Abramson, Metalsky, & Alloy, 1989), some people exhibit pessimistic cognitive styles and characteristically attribute negative life events to stable and global causes, infer that further negative consequences will follow from a current negative life event, and believe that the occurrence of a negative event in their lives means that there is something fundamentally wrong with themselves. In contrast, people with more optimistic cognitive styles typically attribute negative events to unstable and specific causes, infer that negative consequences will not follow from a current negative event, and believe that the occurrence of a negative event in their lives does not mean that they are flawed in any way. According to the hopelessness theory, people with optimistic cognitive styles are more likely to remain hopeful and thus less likely to develop episodes of depression when they confront negative life events than people with pessimistic cognitive styles.

For example, imagine a woman whose fiancé breaks off their engagement. If the woman pessimistically infers that the cause of the breakup is her flawed personality (a stable and global cause), she is likely to expect further negative events in a wide variety of life domains (e.g., with friends, at work, etc.), to become hopeless and, in turn, depressed. Similarly, if she infers that a consequence of the breakup is that she will never marry and have children as she desires, she will be more likely to become hopeless. Finally, her inference that she must be worthless given that her fiancé broke up with her also will contribute to hopelessness. In contrast, if the woman makes more benign optimistic inferences, she is more likely to remain hopeful, and, in turn, nondepressed. For example, attributing the breakup to this man's temporary commitment phobia, inferring that the breakup has saved her from an unhappy marriage to a difficult man, and believing that the breakup doesn't reflect on her will enable the woman to remain hopeful and, thus, protect her from depression.

Beck (1967; 1987) similarly underscores the importance of optimistic cognitive styles in protecting people from depression. According to the cognitive perspective, then, people with optimistic cognitive styles are at lower risk for depression than people with pessimistic cognitive styles.

MIDDLE TO LATE ADOLESCENCE AND THE SURGE OF DEPRESSION

An important first step toward understanding factors associated with risk for and protection against depression is to delineate a developmental timeline for the emergence of depression. To construct such a developmental timeline for depression from preadolescence to young adulthood, Hankin, Abramson, Moffitt, Silva, and McGee (1998) used a prospective, longitudinal approach with structured diagnostic interviews administered 5 times over the course of 10 years, from age 11 to age 21, among the same members of a complete birth cohort in New

Zealand. Results showed that the rates of clinical depression stayed relatively level (about 2%) from age 11 to age 15, then increased dramatically to 17% at age 18, and remained at a high level of 18% at age 21. The greatest increase in new cases of depression occurred between ages 15 and 18. Given the dramatic upsurge in depression during middle to late adolescence (age 15 to 18) and maintenance of this high level of depression in young adulthood (age 21), this developmental period is ideal for testing the cognitive invulnerability hypothesis. Does an optimistic cognitive style protect adolescents and young adults from this surge of depression? Below we answer this question with a series of studies with middle to older adolescents and young adults.

TESTING THE COGNITIVE INVULNERABILITY HYPOTHESIS: THE BEHAVIORAL HIGH-RISK DESIGN

A powerful strategy for testing the cognitive invulnerability hypothesis is the "behavioral high-risk design" (e.g., Depue et al., 1981). Similar to the genetic high-risk paradigm, the behavioral high-risk design involves studying participants who do not currently have the disorder of interest but who are hypothesized to be at high or low risk for developing it. In contrast to the genetic high-risk paradigm, in the behavioral high-risk study individuals are selected on the basis of hypothesized psychological, rather than genetic, vulnerability or invulnerability to the disorder. Thus, to test the cognitive invulnerability hypothesis of depression, one would want to select nondepressed people who were at low versus high risk for depression based on exhibiting optimistic versus pessimistic cognitive styles, respectively. One would then compare these optimists and pessimists on their likelihood of exhibiting depression both in the past, in a retrospective version of the design, and in the future, in a prospective version of the design. The prospective version of the design is superior to the retrospective version because the cognitive "vulnerability" that is assessed in the latter might actually be a scar of a prior depressive episode (Rohde, Lewinsohn, & Seeley, 1990) rather than a *causal* factor in that prior episode (Gotlib & Abramson, 1999).

The results of studies that have used methods less optimal than the behavioral high-risk design to test the cognitive invulnerability hypothesis of depression have been equivocal (see Barnett & Gotlib, 1988 for a review). In contrast, recent studies using or approximating a behavioral high-risk design have obtained considerable support for the cognitive invulnerability hypothesis of depression. For example, using a retrospective behavioral high-risk design, Alloy, Lipman, and Abramson (1992) tested the attributional invulnerability hypothesis of the hopelessness theory for clinically significant depression. In this study, rates of past major depressive disorder and hopelessness depression (HD) over a two-year period were examined for two groups of college students: those who exhibited the attributional vulnerability for depression with low self-esteem (pessimists) and those who did not (optimists). Consistent with the cognitive invulnerability hypothesis, optimistic students were less likely to have exhibited major depressive disorder and the syndrome of HD over the previous two years and experienced fewer episodes of these disorders than pessimistic students. Moreover, recent studies that have used variants of the prospective behavioral high-risk design consistently have found that people who exhibit optimistic cognitive styles are less likely to develop depressive moods and/or depressive symptoms when they experience negative life events than are individuals with pessimistic styles (Alloy & Clements, 1998; Alloy, Just, & Panzarella, 1997b; Metalsky, Halberstadt, & Abramson, 1987; Metalsky & Joiner, 1992; Metalsky, Joiner, Hardin, & Abramson, 1993; Nolen-Hoeksema, Girgus, & Seligman, 1992).

THE TEMPLE-WISCONSIN COGNITIVE VULNERABILITY TO DEPRESSION (CVD) PROJECT

The ongoing Temple-Wisconsin Cognitive Vulnerability to Depression (CVD) Project is a collaborative, 2-site study that uses a prospective behavioral high-risk design to test the cognitive invulnerability and other etiological hypotheses of hopelessness and Beck's theories of depression. In the CVD Project, optimistic and pessimistic first-year college students who were nondepressed and had no other current Axis

I psychopathology at the outset of the study were followed for approximately five years.

Because the optimists were required to score in the lowest quartile on measures of the cognitive vulnerabilities featured in both the hopelessness theory (Cognitive Style Questionnaire [CSQ]; Abramson, Metalsky, & Alloy, 1998) and Beck's theory (expanded Dysfunctional Attitude Scale [DAS]; Weissman & Beck, 1978), and the pessimists were required to score in the highest quartile on both of these measures, the CVD Project provides a broad test of a "generic" cognitive invulnerability hypothesis. A strength of this study is that the two sites permit a built-in assessment of replicability of results. Whereas the University of Wisconsin sample has a high representation of Caucasian individuals from rural, farming, small town, and suburban backgrounds, the Temple University sample is more urban, with a high representation of minority (largely African Americans) and lower socioeconomic participants. Importantly, all of the results reported below replicated across the two sites.

COGNITIVE INVULNERABILITY AND THE PREDICTION OF DEPRESSION AND SUICIDALITY

The CVD Project behavioral high-risk design allows for retrospective and prospective tests of the cognitive invulnerability hypothesis. We now review findings on the predictive validity of optimistic and pessimistic cognitive styles for depressive disorders and suicidality.

Retrospective Lifetime History of Depression

Based on the cognitive invulnerability hypothesis and evidence that attributional styles exhibit some stability over the life span (Burns & Seligman, 1989), Alloy, Abramson, Hogan, and colleagues (in press) examined the lifetime prevalence rates of DSM-III-R (Diagnostic and Statistical Manual of Mental Disorders, Third Edition, Revised) and RDC (Research Diagnostic Criteria) depressive disorders, the syndrome of HD, and other Axis I disorders in optimists versus pessimists. Consistent with the cognitive invulnerability hypothesis, the optimists showed lower lifetime prevalence than the pessimists of major depressive disorder (DSM and RDC; 17% versus 39%), RDC minor depressive disorder (12% versus 22%), HD (12% versus 40%), and depressive spectrum disorders (RDC labile personality [1% versus 8%] and subaffective dysthymia [0% versus 4%]). Indeed, the optimists showed half the rate of lifetime major depression of the pessimists, and only one-third the rate of HD. Moreover, these group differences were specific to depressive disorders. The groups did not differ on lifetime prevalence rates of anxiety disorders, alcohol and drug abuse, or other Axis I disorders. These findings suggest that optimistic cognitive styles may indeed confer protection from full-blown, clinically significant depressive disorders and from HD, and that the protection may be specific to depression.

One possible confound in interpreting these lifetime history findings is that the risk group differences may be due to differential residual depressive symptoms associated with pessimism (even though no one with current episodes of psychopathology was allowed in the final sample). To rule out this possibility, Alloy, Abramson, Hogan, and colleagues (in press) examined the Beck Depression Inventory (BDI; Beck, Rush, Shaw, & Emery, 1979) scores at the time of the cognitive invulnerability assessment as a covariate. Although differences in RDC minor depression and the depressive spectrum disorders were no longer statistically significant, the group differences on lifetime history of major depression and HD were maintained. Note that the use of the BDI as a covariate in these analyses provides a very conservative test of the cognitive invulnerability hypothesis.

Alloy, Abramson, Hogan, and colleagues (in press) also examined several other hypothesized cognitive vulnerability factors for depression, including self-consciousness (Ingram, 1990), sociotropy and autonomy (Beck, 1987), and inferential style for positive events (Alloy, Reilly-Harrington, Fresco, Whitehouse, & Zechmeister, 1999). These other variables did not predict lifetime history of depressive disorders (major, minor, and HD) and moreover, the differences between optimists and pessimists in lifetime prevalence of major, minor, and HD remained when these other hypothesized vulnerability factors were used as covariates. (The only exception to this pattern was that when sociotropy was used as a covariate, the optimists and pessimists did not differ in lifetime prevalence of minor depression.) Thus, these results support the importance of the cognitive and schematic invulnerabilities featured in hopelessness and Beck's theories.

These findings provide the first demonstration that, as predicted, optimistic cognitive styles may confer protection against full-blown, clinically significant depressive disorders and against the hypothesized subtype of HD. This is noteworthy because a criticism of the cognitive theories of depression is that they may apply only to mild depression (Coyne & Gotlib, 1983). The results of the study by Alloy, Abramson, Hogan, and colleagues (in press) suggest that this criticism is inappropriate and that these theories are relevant to explain more severe, clinically significant forms of depression. Second, the results also provide support for the hypothesis that the specific subtype of HD exists in nature and conforms to theoretical description. Of course, the major conceptual limitation of the retrospective findings of Alloy, Abramson, Hogan, and colleagues (in press) is that the causal direction of the association between cognitive vulnerability and increased lifetime rates of depressive disorders is unclear. Did the pessimistic cognitive styles temporally precede and contribute to the onset of the past episodes of depression, or did these styles develop as a result of the past depression? To more clearly test whether optimistic cognitive styles actually decrease risk for depression, a prospective test of the cognitive invulnerability hypothesis is needed.

Prospective Incidence of First Onsets and Recurrences of Depression

Alloy, Abramson, Whitehouse, and colleagues (1998) examined CVD Project findings on the prospective incidence of first onsets and recurrences of depressive and anxiety disorders for the first two and one-half years of follow-up at both sites. More than half of the CVD Project sample entered college with no prior history of clinically significant depression. These participants potentially could experience their very first episode of clinical depression during the prospective follow-up period. Did an optimistic cognitive style actually decrease the likelihood that these participants would develop a first episode of depression during their college years?

Consistent with the cognitive invulnerability hypothesis, Alloy, Abramson, Whitehouse, and colleagues (1998) reported that optimists were less likely than pessimists to develop a first onset of DSM or RDC major depressive disorder (1% versus 17%), RDC minor depressive disorder (6% versus 39%), and the subtype of HD (5% versus 41%). In contrast, there were no risk group differences in the development of anxiety disorders during the prospective follow-up period among this sample (3% versus 7%). Even with initial BDI scores controlled, the impressive risk group differences in rates of first onsets of depressive episodes were maintained. These findings provide especially important support for the cognitive invulnerability hypothesis because they are based on a truly prospective test, uncontaminated by prior history of depression. Moreover, they suggest that optimistic cognitive styles confer protection against first onsets of depression, and in particular, the subtype of HD, but not for anxiety disorders.

Recall that with our selection strategy, we excluded any potential participant who exhibited any current Axis I diagnosis. However, as demonstrated by the results from our retrospective analyses, we did include participants with a past history of clinical depression as long as they were not experiencing a current episode of depression at the outset of the study. What about these participants who, though nondepressed at the outset of the CVD Project, did have a prior history of clinically significant depression? This subsample allows a test of whether the cognitive invulnerability hypothesis holds for protection against recurrences of depression, which is particularly important given that depression often is a recurrent disorder (Belsher & Costello, 1988; Judd, 1997).

Of the 161 students with a past history of depression, 63 were classified as optimists and 98 were classified as pessimists. Alloy, Abramson, Whitehouse, and colleagues (1998) reported that optimists with a past history of depression were less likely than pessimists with prior depression to develop recurrences of DSM and RDC major depression (6% versus 27%), RDC minor depression (26.5% versus 50%), and HD

(22% versus 52%), and these differences were maintained even when initial BDI scores were controlled. Optimists with a prior history of depression also were less likely than previously depressed pessimists to experience onsets of anxiety disorder (2% versus 11%). Thus, the cognitive invulnerability hypothesis was upheld for both recurrences and first onsets, suggesting that similar processes may, at least in part, underlie initial as well as subsequent episodes of depression. The prospective CVD Project results are exciting because they provide the first demonstration that optimistic cognitive styles (or for that matter, any hypothesized psychological invulnerability factor) confer protection against clinically significant depressive episodes.

Of interest, Steinberg, Alloy, and Abramson (1998) reported that pessimism did not worsen following episodes of depression. That is, participants' inferences for stressful events did not increase in negativity from before to after each recurrence of major or minor depression, supporting the stability of pessimistic cognitive styles.

Prospective Incidence of Suicidality

The cognitive theories of depression also may be especially useful for understanding the processes giving rise to suicidality. Drawing on prior research demonstrating a powerful link between hopelessness and suicide (e.g., Beck, Brown, Berchick, Stewart, & Steer, 1990; Minkoff, Bergman, Beck, & Beck, 1973), Abramson and colleagues (1989) speculated that suicidality, on a continuum from suicidal ideation to completed suicide, may be a core symptom of HD. Indeed, according to both hopelessness and Beck's theories, individuals exhibiting pessimistic cognitive styles should be at risk for suicidality mediated by hopelessness whereas optimists should not. In support of this hypothesis, Joiner and Rudd (1995) found that college students with a pessimistic attributional style for negative interpersonal events showed increases in suicidality when they experienced interpersonal stressors.

Using CVD Project data from the first two and one-half years of prospective follow-up, Abramson, Alloy, Hogan, and colleagues (1998a) also tested the cognitive invulnerability hypothesis of suicidality. They found that optimists were less likely than the pessimists to exhibit suicidality as assessed by structured diagnostic interview (12.6% versus 28%). In addition, the optimists exhibited lower levels of suicidality than the pessimists as assessed by questionnaire self-report. Further, optimists were less likely than pessimists to exhibit other hypothesized risk factors for suicidality not explicitly specified in hopelessness or Beck's theories, including prior history of suicidality (e.g., Beck, Steer, & Brown, 1993), personal history of depressive disorders (e.g., Hawton, 1987; Lewinsohn, Rohde, & Seeley, 1993), borderline personality dysfunction (Isometsa et al., 1996), and parental history of depression (e.g., Wagner, 1997). Given that cognitive vulnerability was related to these other hypothesized risk factors for suicidality, Abramson, Alloy, Hogan, and colleagues (1998a) controlled statistically for these other risk factors and found that cognitive risk status continued to predict prospective suicidality. Finally, Abramson, Alloy, Hogan, and colleagues (1998a) found that hopelessness across the two and one-half year follow-up completely mediated the relationship between cognitive vulnerability and prospective suicidality as measured by both interview and questionnaire, even when controlling for prior history of suicidality. It should be noted that controlling for prior history of suicidality in tests of the cognitive vulnerability hypothesis may be overly conservative because prior history of suicidality may, at least in part, be a result of cognitive vulnerability.

COGNITIVE INVULNERABILITY AND PROTECTION AGAINST DEPRESSION IN THE FACE OF ADVERSITY AMONG HIGH-SCHOOL STUDENTS

Recall that the dramatic surge in depression among middle to late adolescents starts at about age 15 (Hankin et al., 1998). Does the cognitive invulnerability hypothesis hold for middle to late adolescents from ages 15 to 18? Hankin, Abramson, and Siler (in press) used a prospective design to test the cognitive invulnerability hypothesis among high school students. High school students completed measures of attributional style for negative life events, the occurrence of negative life events, hopelessness, and depressive symptoms at two times separated by five weeks. High school students with an optimistic attributional style were less likely than those with a pessimistic style to become hopeless and, in turn, experience depressive symptoms when they experienced many negative life events. In sum, this study showed that an optimistic attributional style in the face of adversity protected against depression during middle to late adolescence, a developmental period marked by rapidly increasing rates of depression.

ILLUSORY OPTIMISM AND INVULNERABILITY TO DEPRESSION

Above, we summarized studies showing that optimism provides invulnerability to depression. But what if the optimism is illusory? One type of illusory optimism is an "illusion of control." People exhibit an illusion of control when they believe they have control over objectively uncontrollable events. Does an illusion of control protect people from depression? Is depression associated with the absence of an illusion of control?

To answer these questions, we gave the participants at the Temple site of the CVD Project a judgment of control task at both the first and the second yearly assessments during the prospective follow-up phase. To determine whether participants showed an illusion of control on a laboratory task, they were presented with objectively uncontrollable outcomes on a computer monitor and each time the outcome of interest (a white square) occurred, the participant won a quarter. All participants won five dollars noncontingently even though they had no control over the occurrence of the outcome. Zhu and Alloy (1998) found that individuals who had developed a DSM-III-R and/or RDC diagnosis of major or minor depressive disorder during the first two years of the CVD project gave relatively realistic estimates of control for the laboratory task at the end of the second-year follow-up. On the other hand, participants who were invulnerable to depression during the same two years of follow-up were overly optimistic and showed an illusion of control on the laboratory task. Thus, clinically significant depression appears to be associated with a lack of illusory optimism.

If depressed individuals tend to show more realistic estimates of control than nondepressed individuals, then would an illusion of control provide protection from depression? To answer this question, in a separate study Alloy and Clements (1992) measured college students' illusions of control for a laboratory task. Those participants who believed they had control over an objectively uncontrollable event (whether or not a white square appeared on a computer screen) were dubbed "optimists" whereas those who accurately noted that they had no control over the event were called "realists." The investigators then evaluated whether the optimists were protected from developing depressed mood following failure on a laboratory task (unsolvable puzzles) as well as from developing depressive symptoms over the next month when confronted with naturally occurring negative events outside of the laboratory. Consistent with the cognitive invulnerability hypothesis, optimists were less likely than realists to report depressed mood after laboratory failure. The optimists also were protected from developing depressive symptoms in their natural environments when confronted with negative life events whereas the realists were not. Moreover, the optimists became less hopeless than the realists after experiencing naturalistic stressors. Finally, the optimists' reduced discouragement in the face of negative life events partially mediated the association between the illusion of control and protection from depressive affect. This reduced hopelessness following negative events provides one mechanism through which an illusion of control may decrease risk for depression. Thus, even when optimism is illusory, it provides protection from depression.

SELF-REFERENT INFORMATION PROCESSING: A MECHANISM UNDERLYING COGNITIVE VULNERABILITY?

According to the cognitive theories of depression, people with pessimistic cognitive styles are vulnerable to depression, in part, because they tend to engage in negatively toned information processing about themselves when they encounter negative life events. Thus, Alloy, Abramson, Murray, Whitehouse, and Hogan (1997a) examined whether nondepressed individuals with pessimistic cognitive styles do, in fact, process information about themselves more negatively than do those with optimistic styles, based on a Self-Referent Information Processing (SRIP) Task Battery administered to the pessimistic and optimistic participants in the CVD Project at the outset of the study. This battery consisted of four tasks that yielded five measures of information processing about the self. Each task utilized four types of trait adjectives, matched for word length and frequency: positive and negative adjectives that were either relevant or irrelevant to a depressive self-concept (e.g., "incompetent" is a negative, depression-relevant adjective; "effective" is a positive, depression-relevant adjective; "polite" and "rude" are examples of positive and negative depression-irrelevant adjectives, respectively). In Task 1, participants were presented with the adjectives on a computer monitor and asked to judge whether each one was self-descriptive or not. Response times for making these judgments also were recorded without the awareness of the participants. In Task 2, participants received a booklet containing three adjectives of each of the four types. For each adjective that they judged to be self-descriptive, they were asked to provide specific evidence from their own past behaviors that indicated why the adjective described them. For example, if a participant believed that he or she was incompetent, he or she had to provide specific examples of past incompetent behaviors in his or her life. On this task, the measure of self-referent information processing was the number of behavioral examples provided for each of the four types of adjectives. In Task 3, participants read twenty-four statements describing hypothetical behaviors from each of the four adjective domains (e.g., negative depression-relevant, etc.). They were asked to judge the probability (0%–100%) that they would behave or react in the way described if they were in that situation in the future. Task 4 was an incidental free recall test for the adjectives participants had judged as self-descriptive or not in Task 1. The total time between Task 1 and the beginning of Task 4 was two hours.

Consistent with prediction, Alloy and colleagues (1997a) found that relative to optimists, pessimists showed preferential processing of self-referent negative depression-relevant information. When faced with negative self-referent information (e.g., worthless), pessimists showed greater endorsement, faster response times, more elaboration (i.e., more past behavioral examples and higher future probability judgments), and enhanced recall of the threatening information than did optimists. Even more consistent across the SRIP measures, pessimists also were less likely to process positive depression-relevant stimuli (e.g., competent) than were optimists. Pessimists showed less endorsement, slower response times, less elaboration (i.e., fewer past behavioral examples and lower future probability judgments), and less recall of the positive information than did optimists. These differences between pessimists and optimists in self-referent information processing remained even when current levels of depressive symptoms were controlled, suggesting that the self-referent information processing differences associated with cognitive vulnerability status are not due to any residual differences in the depressive symptoms of the two groups.

These findings of differences in self-referent information processing between pessimists and optimists are important for two reasons. First, they indicate that negatively toned self-referent information processing previously demonstrated to be characteristic of depressed individuals (e.g., Segal, 1988) also occurs among nondepressed individuals who are vulnerable to depression by virtue of exhibiting pessimistic cognitive styles. Second, from a methodological perspective, the findings provide converging evidence for information processing effects of cognitive styles on laboratory tasks adapted from cognitive science paradigms and, thereby, further support the construct validity of the cognitive style questionnaire measures.

DEVELOPMENTAL ORIGINS OF COGNITIVE VULNERABILITY AND INVULNERABILITY TO DEPRESSION

If pessimistic cognitive styles do confer vulnerability for depression and suicidality, as indicated by the CVD Project findings, then it is important to understand the antecedents of these cognitive styles. What are the developmental origins of cognitive vulnerability to depression? In the CVD Project, we directly studied the parents of the pessimists and optimists with respect to parents' cognitive styles, parenting behaviors, psychopathology, and personality as well as the pessimists' and optimists' early childhood life events and neglect and maltreatment experiences. Below, we briefly review preliminary findings from the CVD Project and several related studies on possible developmental precursors of pessimism and optimism. We emphasize that the CVD Project findings presented in this section indeed are preliminary because analyses still are in progress. Moreover, many of our initial explorations of potential precursors of cognitive styles have relied on retrospective designs and, thus, should be construed as generating hypotheses for more definitive testing with future prospective designs.

Parental Psychopathology and Children's Cognitive Vulnerability to Depression

Prior research has demonstrated that children of depressed parents are at increased risk for depression themselves (e.g., Downey & Coyne, 1990). Parental depression may contribute to the development of pessimistic cognitive styles and, thus, cognitive vulnerability to depression in offspring through a variety of mechanisms including genetic transmission, modeling, and negative parenting practices, among others. To explore the possible familial origins of pessimistic cognitive styles, Abramson, Alloy, Tashman, Whitehouse, and Hogan (1998b) examined the association between CVD Project participants' cognitive risk status and their parents' depression based on the participants' reports of their parents' psychiatric history using the family history RDC method (Andreasen, Endicott, Spitzer, & Winokur, 1977) as well as direct interview of the parents themselves with the SADS-L (Endicott & Spitzer, 1978). Child and parent reports of parental psychopathology showed significant, but modest, agreement, with phi coefficients ranging from .18 to .43 for various disorders.

Based on the child (CVD participants) reports of parental psychopathology, Abramson and colleagues (1998b) found that pessimists' mothers were significantly more likely to have a history of depressive disorder than were optimists' mothers (35% versus 18%). There was a trend for the fathers of pessimists to be more likely than the fathers of optimists to have a history of depressive disorder (18% versus 12%). There were no differences in rates of other disorders between the pessimists' and optimists' parents. With the direct interview of parents, Abramson and colleagues (1998b) found that mothers of pessimists had greater lifetime histories of depression than mothers of optimists whereas fathers of pessimists and optimists didn't differ. In sum, both child and parent reports about parents' depression were consistent in showing greater lifetime depression in the mothers of pessimists than optimists. These findings are consistent with the hypothesis that mothers' depression may contribute to the development of cognitive vulnerability to depression in their offspring.

Modeling, Parental Inferential Feedback, and Cognitive Vulnerability to Depression.

Children may learn their cognitive styles in part from significant others, in particular their parents. If modeling of parents' styles is a contributor to the development of cognitive vulnerability versus invulnerability to depression, then children's cognitive styles should correlate with those of their mothers or fathers. In addition to modeling, the feedback parents provide to their children about causes and consequences of negative events in the child's life may contribute to the child's cognitive risk for depression. Children may be taught, implicitly or explicitly, to make the same inferences about events in their lives as those made by their parents for the children's events. If parental feedback contributes to children's cognitive risk, then parents' typical inferential communications to their children should be correlated with the children's cognitive styles.

Alloy, Abramson, Tashman, and colleagues (in press) examined the modeling and feedback hypotheses with data from the CVD Project. To test the modeling hypothesis, the same cognitive style measures (CSQ and DAS) were administered to the parents of the pessimistic and optimistic participants as to the participants themselves. To test the feedback hypothesis, parent and child report versions of the Parent Attributions for Children's Events Scale (PACE; Steinberg, Tashman, Alloy, & Abramson, 1998), a questionnaire that assessed parents' typical feedback to their child regarding the causes and consequences of negative events in the child's life, were administered. Consistent with the modeling hypothesis, parents of pessimists had more dysfunctional attitudes than parents of optimists. However, the inferential styles of these two groups of parents did not differ. Supporting the feedback hypothesis, according to the child reports of parental behavior, both mothers and fathers of pessimists provided more depressogenic feedback about causes and consequences of negative life events that happened to their child than did mothers and fathers of optimists. Thus, not only may children model the cognitive styles of their parents, but they also may be directly taught habitual ways of interpreting events by the inferential feedback they receive from their parents.

Developmental Maltreatment and Cognitive Vulnerability to Depression

Rose and Abramson (1998) hypothesized that a developmental history of maltreatment and neglect may contribute to the origins of cognitive vulnerability to depression. Noting that research on "depressive realism" suggests that depressives may not be as irrational as originally portrayed in Beck's cognitive distortion theory of depression (e.g., Alloy, Albright, Abramson, & Dykman, 1990), Rose and Abramson suggested that the pessimistic cognitive styles exhibited by depressives might be the internal representations of maltreatment or adverse environments they actually experienced rather than cognitive distortions.

Consistent with their formulation, Rose and Abramson (1998) found that adults who exhibited marked cognitive vulnerability for depression were more likely than others to report growing up in environments characterized by emotional, sexual, and physical maltreatment as well as neglect. According to Rose and Abramson, emotional maltreatment may be a particularly virulent contributor to cognitive vulnerability to depression because, unlike physical or sexual maltreatment, the abuser, by definition, supplies negative cognitions to the victim. For example, the individual may be told why negative events happen (e.g., "Of course you didn't get invited to the prom. You're ugly.") and internalize these attributions. Anecdotally, Rose and Abramson noted that participants spontaneously provided support for this position while they were being interviewed about their early maltreatment. Participants who had experienced multiple forms of abuse made comments such as, "Bruises heal. Unless you end up needing reconstructive surgery, getting beaten isn't the worst thing. But I could not forget those terrible things my mother said to me. I can't get the names she called me out of my head." Of course, the correlational data obtained by Rose and Abramson (1998) cannot establish that the association between early maltreatment and cognitive risk for depression is causal; however, they are consistent with the hypothesis that developmental maltreatment predisposes cognitive vulnerability to depression and underscore the importance of future prospective tests of this hypothesis.

CONCLUSION

We have reviewed promising evidence from the CVD Project and related studies indicating that the cognitive styles featured in hopelessness and Beck's theories of depression indeed confer vulnerability and invulnerability for full-blown clinically significant depressive disorders, depressive symptoms and mood, and suicidality. Pessimism increases vulnerability for suicidality, first onsets and subsequent recurrences of depressive episodes, and symptoms of depression. In contrast, optimism, even when illusory, protects against depression.

In concluding, we note that researchers in the field of depression have focused, understandably, on what makes people depressed. This is a very important question. However, we have tried to show that it also is important to ask what protects people from depression. In this regard, a passage from Solzhenitsyn's (1973) writings on the destructive labor camps in the Gulag Archipelago is provocative. In discussing corruption of prisoners in the camps, Solzhenitsyn says he is not going to explain the cases of corruption. Why, he says, should we worry about explaining the house that in subzero weather loses its warmth? What needs to be explained, he goes on to say, is that there are houses that retain their warmth even in subzero weather. Analogously, we suggest that perhaps what is to be explained by the depression researcher is not why certain people succumb to depression when confronted with the insults nature and our fellow humans deal to all of us, but rather why many people maintain a nondepressed state in what sometimes is the psychological equivalent of subzero temperatures. We suggest that an optimistic cognitive style provides protection from depression even in the face of adversity.

REFERENCES

Abramson, L.Y., Alloy, L.B., Hogan, M.E., Whitehouse, W.G., Cornette, M., Akhavan, S., & Chiara, A. (1998a). Suicidality and cognitive vulnerability to depression among college students: A prospective study. *Journal of Adolescence, 21,* 157–171.

Abramson, L.Y., Alloy, L.B., Tashman, N., Whitehouse, W.G., & Hogan, M.E. (1998b). The Temple-Wisconsin Cognitive Vulnerability to Depression (CVD) Project: Axis I and II psychopathology in the parents of individuals at high and low cognitive risk for depression. Manuscript in preparation, University of Wisconsin.

Abramson, L.Y., Metalsky, G.I., & Alloy, L.B. (1989). Hopelessness depression: A theory-based subtype of depression. *Psychological Review, 96,* 358–372.

Abramson, L.Y., Metalsky, G.I., & Alloy, L.B. (1998). The Cognitive Style Questionnaire: A measure of the vulnerability featured in the hopelessness theory of depression. Manuscript in preparation, University of Wisconsin-Madison.

Alloy, L.B., Abramson, L.Y., Hogan, M.E., Whitehouse, W.G., Rose, D.T., Robinson, M.S., Kim, R., & Lapkin, J.B. (in press). The Temple-Wisconsin Cognitive Vulnerability to Depression (CVD) Project: Lifetime history of Axis I psychopathology in individuals at high and low cognitive risk for depression. *Journal of Abnormal Psychology.*

Alloy, L.B., Abramson, L.Y., Murray, L.A., Whitehouse, W.G., & Hogan, M.E. (1997a). Self-referent information-processing in individuals at high and low cognitive risk for depression. *Cognition and Emotion, 11,* 539–568.

Alloy, L.B., Abramson, L.Y., Tashman, N., Steinberg, D.L., Whitehouse, W.G., & Hogan, M.E. (in press). The Temple-Wisconsin Cognitive Vulnerability to Depression (CVD) Project: Cognitive and inferential feedback styles of the parents of individuals at high and low cognitive risk for depression. *Cognitive Therapy and Research.*

Alloy, L.B., Abramson, L.Y., Whitehouse, W.G., Hogan, M.E., Panzarella, C., Robinson, M.S., Lapkin, J.B., & Rose, D.T. (1998). The Temple-Wisconsin Cognitive Vulnerability to Depression (CVD) Project: Prospective incidence of first onsets and recurrences of Axis I disorders in individuals at high and low cognitive risk for depression. Manuscript in preparation, Temple University.

Alloy, L.B., Albright, J.S., Abramson, L.Y., & Dykman, B.M. (1990). Depressive realism and nondepressive optimistic illusions: The role of the self. In R.E. Ingram (Ed.), *Contemporary psychological approaches to depression: treatment, research, and theory* (pp. 71–86). New York: Plenum Press.

Alloy, L.B., & Clements, C.M. (1992). Illusion of control: Invulnerability to negative affect and depressive symptoms after laboratory and natural stressors. *Journal of Abnormal Psychology, 101,* 234–245.

Alloy, L.B., & Clements, C.M. (1998). Hopelessness theory of depression: Tests of the symptom component. *Cognitive Therapy and Research, 22,* 303–335.

Alloy, L.B., Just, N., & Panzarella, C. (1997b). Attributional style, daily life events, and hopelessness depression: Subtype validation by prospective variability and specificity of symptoms. *Cognitive Therapy and Research, 21,* 321–344.

Alloy, L.B., Lipman, A., & Abramson, L.Y. (1992). Attributional style as a vulnerability factor for depression: Validation by past history of mood disorders. *Cognitive Therapy and Research, 16,* 391–407.

Alloy, L.B., Reilly-Harrington, N., Fresco, D., Whitehouse, W.G., & Zechmeister, J.S. (1999). Cognitive styles and life events in subsyndromal unipolar and bipolar disorders: Stability and prospective prediction of depressive and hypomanic mood swings. *Journal of Cognitive Psychotherapy: An International Quarterly, 13,* 21–40.

Andreasen, N., Endicott, J., Spitzer, R.L., & Winokur, G. (1977). The family history method using diagnostic criteria: Reliability and validity. *Archives of General Psychiatry, 34,* 1229–1235.

Barnett, P.A., & Gotlib, I.H. (1988). Psychosocial functioning and depression: Distinguishing among antecedents, concomitants, and consequences. *Psychological Bulletin, 104,* 97–126.

Beck, A.T. (1967). *Depression: Clinical, experimental, and theoretical aspects.* New York: Harper & Row.

Beck, A.T. (1987). Cognitive models of depression. *Journal of Cognitive Psychotherapy: An International Quarterly, 1,* 5–37.

Beck, A.T., Brown, G., Berchick, R.J., Stewart, B.L., & Steer, R.A. (1990). Relationship between hopelessness and ultimate suicide: A replication with psychiatric patients. *American Journal of Psychiatry, 147,* 190–195.

Beck, A.T., Rush, A.J., Shaw, B.F., & Emery, G. (1979). *Cognitive therapy of depression.* New York: Guilford.

Beck, A.T., Steer, R.A., & Brown, G. (1993). Dysfunctional attitudes and suicidal ideation in psychiatric outpatients. *Suicide and Life-Threatening Behavior, 23,* 11–20.

Belsher, G., & Costello, C.G. (1988). Relapse after recovery from unipolar depression: A critical review. *Psychological Bulletin, 104,* 84–96.

Burns, M.O., & Seligman, M.E.P. (1989). Explanatory style across the life span: Evidence for stability over 52 years. *Journal of Personality and Social Psychology, 56,* 471–477.

Coyne, J.C., & Gotlib, I.H. (1983). The role of cognition in depression: A critical appraisal. *Psychological Bulletin, 94,* 472–505.

Depue, R.A., Slater, J., Wolfstetter-Kausch, H., Klein, D., Goplerud, E., & Farr, D. (1981). A behavioral paradigm for identifying persons at risk for bipolar depressive disorder: A conceptual framework and five validation studies (Monograph). *Journal of Abnormal Psychology, 90,* 381–437.

Downey, G., & Coyne, J.C. (1990). Children of depressed parents: An integrative review. *Psychological Bulletin, 108,* 50–76.

Endicott, J., & Spitzer, R.A. (1978). A diagnostic interview: The schedule for affective disorders and schizophrenia. *Archives of General Psychiatry, 35,* 837–844.

Gotlib, I.H., & Abramson, L.Y. (1999). Attributional theories of emotion. In T. Dalgleish & M. Power (Eds.), *Handbook of cognition and emotion* (pp. 613–636). New York: Wiley.

Hankin, B.L., Abramson, L.Y., Moffitt, T.E., Silva, P.A., & McGee, R. (1998). Development of depression from preadolescence to young adulthood: Emerging gender differences in a 10-year longitudinal study. *Journal of Abnormal Psychology, 107,* 128–140.

Hankin, B.L., Abramson, L.Y., & Siler, M. (in press). A prospective test of the hopelessness theory of depression in adolescence. *Cognitive Therapy and Research.*

Hawton, K. (1987). Assessment of suicide risk. *British Journal of Psychiatry, 150,* 145–153.

Ingram, R.E. (1990). Self-focused attention in clinical disorders: Review and a conceptual model. *Psychological Bulletin, 107,* 156–176.

Isometsa, E.T., Henriiksson, M.M., Heikkinen, M.E., Aro, H.M., Martunnen, M.J., Kuoppasalmi, K.II., & Lonnqvist, J.K. (1996). Suicide among subjects with personality disorders. *American Journal of Psychiatry, 153,* 667–673.

Joiner, T.E., & Rudd, M.D. (1995). Negative attributional style for interpersonal events and the occurrence of severe interpersonal disruptions as predictors of self-reported suicidal ideation. *Suicide and Life-Threatening Behavior, 25,* 297–304.

Judd, L.L. (1997). The clinical course of unipolar major depressive disorders. *Archives of General Psychiatry, 54,* 989–991.

Lewinsohn, P.M., Rohde, P., & Seeley, J.R. (1993). Psychosocial characteristics of adolescents with a history of suicide attempt. *Journal of the American Academy for Child and Adolescent Psychiatry, 32,* 60–68.

Metalsky, G.I., Halberstadt, L.J., & Abramson, L.Y. (1987). Vulnerability to depressive mood reactions: Toward a more powerful test of the diathesis-stress and causal mediation components of the reformulated theory of depression. *Journal of Personality and Social Psychology, 52,* 386–393.

Metalsky, G.I., & Joiner, T.E. (1992). Vulnerability to depressive symptomatology: A prospective test of the diathesis-stress and causal mediation components of the hopelessness theory of depression. *Journal of Personality and Social Psychology, 63,* 667–675.

Metalsky, G.I., Joiner, T.E., Hardin, T.S., & Abramson, L.Y. (1993). Depressive reactions to failure in a naturalistic setting: A test of the hopelessness and self-esteem theories of depression. *Journal of Abnormal Psychology, 102,* 101–109.

Minkoff, K., Bergman, E., Beck, A.T., & Beck, R. (1973). Hopelessness, depression, and attempted suicide. *American Journal of Psychiatry, 130,* 455–459.

Nolen-Hoeksema, S., Girgus, J.S., & Seligman, M.E.P. (1992). Predictors and consequences of childhood depressive symptoms: A 5-year longitudinal study. *Journal of Abnormal Psychology, 101,* 405–422.

Rohde, P., Lewinsohn, P.M., & Seeley, J.R. (1990). Are people changed by the experience of having an episode of depression? A further test of the scar hypothesis. *Journal of Abnormal Psychology, 99,* 264–271.

Rose, D.T., & Abramson, L.Y. (1998). Developmental maltreatment and cognitive vulnerability to depression. Manuscript in preparation, University of Wisconsin.

Segal, Z.V. (1988). Appraisal of the self-schema construct in cognitive models of depression. *Psychological Bulletin, 103,* 147–162.

Solzhenitsyn, A.I. (1973). *The Gulag Archipelago, 1918–1956.* New York: Harper & Row.

Steinberg, D.L., Alloy, L.B., & Abramson, L.Y. (1998). Predictors of relapse and recurrence of depression: The scar hypothesis and the impact of depressive episodes. Manuscript in preparation, New York State Psychiatric Institute.

Steinberg, D.L., Tashman, N., Alloy, L.B., & Abramson, L.Y. (1998). The Parent Attributions for Children's Events Scale (PACE). Manuscript in preparation, Temple University.

Wagner, B.M. (1997). Family risk factors for child and adolescent suicidal behavior. *Psychological Bulletin, 121,* 246–298.

Weissman, A., & Beck, A.T. (1978). Development and validation of the

Dysfunctional Attitude Scale: A preliminary investigation. Paper presented at the meeting of the American Educational Research Association, Toronto, Canada.

Zhu, L., & Alloy, L.B. (1998). Predictors of judged control: Depression and private self-consciousness. Paper presented at the APA Meeting, San Francisco, CA.

ACKNOWLEDGMENTS

The research reviewed in this chapter was supported by National Institute of Mental Health Grants MH 43866 to Lyn Y. Abramson and MH 48216 to Lauren B. Alloy. We would like to thank the following CVD Project staff for their contributions to this chapter: Sogoli Akhavan, Sue Amundson, Michelle Armstrong, Monica Calkins, Mark Cenite, Alexandra Chiara, Judith Cronholm, Rayna Dombro, Patricia Donovan, Ilene Dyller, Kimberly Eberbach, Erika Francis, Teresa Gannon, Stephanie Johnson, Nancy Just, Rita Kekstas, Ray Kim, Christine Klitz, Joanna Lapkin, Alan Lipman, Susan Luebke, Gary Marshall, Laura Murray, Catherine Panzarella, David Raniere, Noreen Reilly-Harrington, Matthew Robinson, Donna Rose, Pamela Shapiro, Janet Shriberg, Deborah Small, Laurie Teraspulsky, Sandra Tierney, Aaron Torrance, and Ann Whitehouse.

The first two authors contributed equally to this chapter.

✦ CHAPTER 5 ✦

Commentary on the Temple-Wisconsin Cognitive Vulnerability to Depression Project: Causality in Non-Experimental Mental Health Research

Thomas E. Joiner, Jr.

IN THE CONTEXT of non-experimental research on resilience, vulnerability, and mental health, how does one demonstrate that a proposed resilience or vulnerability factor is causal? In true experimental research designs, the goal is to control and manipulate one variable, holding constant all others, to assess the specific effect on a second variable. In achieving control of one variable and constancy of others, considerable ingenuity is often required. But of course, regarding human psychopathology and resilience research, the variables in question—things like attitudes, personality, stress levels, and the like—make up people's lives, and "control and manipulation" of such is impossible, ingenuity notwithstanding.

Far from abandoning causal theories, resilience and psychopathology researchers have provided detailed descriptions of factors and processes that protect against, and those that produce, psychopathology. And far from abandoning rigorous empirical scrutiny of their theories, these researchers have developed alternative, non-experimental means to assess the causal status of proposed vulnerability and buffering factors ("non-experimental" is used in the sense that full experimental control and manipulation are not available, not in the sense of "non-scientific"). Here, too, ingenuity is required, not in achieving full experimental control, but in developing criteria to assess causality, and in designing non-experimental studies to test these criteria.

CRITERIA FOR VULNERABILITY AND PROTECTIVE FACTORS IN MENTAL HEALTH RESEARCH

Garber and Hollon (1991) summarized three criteria for demonstrating, insofar as possible, whether a variable serves as a vulnerability factor in non-experimental research (the same logic applies to protective factors). First, a vulnerability factor and an outcome should *covary*, at least to the extent predicted by theory. That is, the more one experiences a vulnerability factor, the more one should experience symptoms. Second, a vulnerability should *temporally precede* an outcome. That is, the vulnerability factor should exist before the onset of symptoms and should be associated with future increases in symptoms. And third, the relationship between a vulnerability and an outcome should be *non-spurious* (e.g., should not be better accounted for by a third variable). The main purpose of this commentary is to apply the criteria of covariation, temporal precedence, and non-spuriousness to the findings described by Abramson, Alloy, and colleagues (see Chapter 4). Does an optimistic cognitive style meet these criteria and therefore deserve consideration as a true protective factor?

THE THEORY

The reader is referred to Chapter 4 by Abramson, Alloy, and colleagues for a full description of their theory. By way of brief overview, in earlier work, they have postulated that the tendency to attribute negative events to stable and global causes (as well as other negative inferential styles) represents a diathesis, which, in the presence but not the absence of negative life stress, increases vulnerability to depression specifically, not to psychopathology generally (Abramson, Metalsky, & Alloy, 1989). As applied to optimistic styles and resilience, similar logic holds. That is, those with an optimistic style are thought to be buffered against the depression-inducing effects of negative life events. In the Temple-Wisconsin Vulnerability study, participants were classified as having an optimistic cognitive style if they displayed a positive attributional style emphasized in the theory of Abramson and her colleagues and they were relatively free of the dysfunctional attitudes emphasized in Beck's (e.g., 1983) theoretical work. The procedures of the project involved originally symptom-free participants being regularly assessed over the course of approximately 2.5 years.

THE EVIDENCE

Covariation

Does an optimistic cognitive style covary with depression-free functioning, at least to the extent predicted by the theory? The clear answer is yes. In study after study with both adults and children, the correlation between cognitive style and depressive symptoms is in the predicted direction, statistically significant, and of moderate magnitude (for reviews see Joiner & Wagner, 1995 and Peterson & Seligman, 1984).

Interestingly, Abramson, Alloy, and colleagues' chapter (see Chapter 4) does not emphasize the concurrent correlation between cognitive style and depression, for at least two probable reasons. First, as described in the next section, their focus is rightly on prospective results, which speak to the criterion of temporal antecedence. Second, and this point is sometimes overlooked, their theory predicts a relation between cognitive style and depression *only* in the presence of negative life events. Theirs is a resilience-to-stress theory, in which the presence of both the protective factor (cognitive style) and the stress (negative life events) is required to reliably predict the outcome (being depression-free). It turns out that cognitive style, even considered alone, *does* covary with depression; the important point, however, is that even if cognitive style had *not* covaried with depression (and an occasional study finds this), such would be irrelevant to the theory, which predicts a resilience-to-stress configuration of the relations between cognitive style, negative life events, and depression. This is an example of how the criteria put forth by Garber and Hollon (1991), as useful as they are, cannot be applied by rote; they are heuristics, which, only when combined with the particulars of a theory, produce testable conditions for causality.

Temporal Antecedence

Past research on whether cognitive style meets the temporal antecedence criterion has been mixed, which is one reason that the very clear findings from the Temple-Wisconsin project are important. In this study, cognitive style, measured at one point in time when *all* participants were nondepressed, predicted the *maintenance* of depression-free functioning measured at later points in time. This was true regarding self-reported depressive symptoms, as well as the onset of interviewer-determined clinical depression. Whereas several studies had previously supported the prospective relationship of negative cognitive style to self-reported depressive symptoms (e.g., Metalsky, Joiner, Hardin, & Abramson, 1993), the Temple-Wisconsin study is the first to my knowledge to rigorously demonstrate the prospective relation of optimistic cognitive style to protection from clinical depression. It is interesting to note that the relation between clinical depression and self-reported depressive symptoms is controversial, with some arguing for continuity (e.g., Vredenburg, Flett, & Krames, 1993), and others arguing that they are completely different things (e.g., Coyne, 1994). This controversy is moot with regard to the Temple-Wisconsin project, in that optimistic cognitive style protected against *both*.

The possibility remains, however, that the prospective relation between cognitive style and future symptoms is spurious, attributable to some third variable. An important feature of the Temple-Wisconsin project is the attempt to rule out as many such variables as possible.

Non-Spuriousness

A key form of non-spuriousness, and one that is implicit in the criterion of temporal antecedence, is that the relation of a proposed vulnerability or resilience factor to *later* symptoms is not merely due to the relation of the proposed vulnerability/resilience factor to *current* symptoms. Accordingly, a standard in longitudinal psychopathology research is to statistically or otherwise control for baseline symptoms when assessing the predictive effect of a putative risk factor on later symptoms. In their Temple-Wisconsin project, Abramson, Alloy, and colleagues take a satisfying approach to this issue, in that they ensure that *all* participants are symptom-free at baseline. Thus, the detected predictive relation of optimistic cognitive style to future depression-free functioning necessarily applies to the *maintenance* of *future* mental health.

Abramson, Alloy, and colleagues use two other controls against non-spuriousness, which deserve comment. First, because depression is clearly a chronic and often episodic disorder, it is possible that even those who are symptom-free at baseline nonetheless have a past history of depression. Moreover, it may be that optimistic cognitive style appears to protect against later depression merely because both cognitive style and later depression are each related to a third variable—namely, past depression. Here, again, Abramson, Alloy, and colleagues address this possibility, in that the same pattern of results held when people with a past history of depression were excluded from analyses.

Second, as pointed out by Hollon, Kendall, and Lumry (1986), any variable hypothesized to have causal status regarding a psychopathological syndrome should be relatively specific to that syndrome, and should not covary with other clinical phenomena believed to be distinct from the syndrome of interest (in the current case, depression). This criterion for non-spuriousness is quite stringent, because it is possible that depressive symptoms may covary with the proposed vulnerability/resilience factor, even in the absence of a depressive *diagnosis*. Nonetheless, here again, the results provided by Abramson, Alloy, and colleagues meet this criterion. For example, as a general rule, optimistic cognitive style was more protective against depressive diagnoses than against anxiety disorders, even despite the high overlap of these two classes of disorders.

The Temple-Wisconsin project was thus designed to eliminate at least three important sources of non-spuriousness: 1) the relation of baseline to future symptoms; 2) the effects of past history of a syndrome; and 3) diagnostic specificity. The fact that supportive results emerged even given these stringent controls provides compelling support for the thesis of Abramson, Alloy, and colleagues that an optimistic cognitive style is protective against episodes of depression

CONCLUSION

Non-experimental designs are forced upon researchers investigating human resilience, vulnerability, and mental health. Even so, careful research designs can provide probative information about the possible causal relation of a factor to mental health. Three criteria—covariation, temporal antecedence, and non-spuriousness—represent useful heuristics for designing maximally probative non-experimental studies. The Temple-Wisconsin Project represents a successful application of these criteria, with implications for the causal status of an optimistic cognitive style in relation to good mental health.

REFERENCES

Abramson, L.Y., Metalsky, G.I., & Alloy, L.B. (1989). Hopelessness depression: A theory-based subtype of depression. *Psychological Review, 96,* 358–372.

Beck, A.T. (1983). Cognitive therapy of depression: New perspectives. In P. Clayton & J. E. Barret (Eds.), *Treatment of depression: Old controversies and new approaches* (pp. 265–290). New York: Raven.

Coyne, J. C. (1994). Self-reported distress: Analog or ersatz depression? *Psychological Bulletin, 116,* 29–45.

Garber, J., & Hollon, S.D. (1991). What can specificity designs say about causality in psychopathology research? *Psychological Bulletin, 110,* 129–136.

Hollon, S.D., Kendall, P.C., & Lumry, A. (1986). Specificity of depressotypic cognitions in clinical depression. *Journal of Abnormal Psychology, 95,* 52–59.

Joiner, Jr., T.E., & Wagner, K.D. (1995). Attributional style and depression in children and adolescents: A meta-analytic review. *Clinical Psychology Review, 8,* 777–798.

Metalsky, G. I., Joiner, Jr., T. E., Hardin, T.S., & Abramson, L.Y. (1993). Depressive reactions to failure in a naturalistic setting: A test of the hopelessness and self-esteem theories of depression. *Journal of Abnormal Psychology, 102,* 101–109.

Peterson, C.R., & Seligman, M.E.P. (1984). Causal explanations as a risk factor for depression: Theory and evidence. *Psychological Review, 91,* 347–374.

Vredenburg, K., Flett, G.L., & Krames, L. (1993). Analogue versus clinical depression: A critical appraisal. *Psychological Bulletin, 113,* 327–344.

✦ CHAPTER 6 ✦

Growth and Resilience Among Bereaved People

Susan Nolen-Hoeksema

PSYCHOLOGISTS HAVE LONG been interested in the negative effects of traumatic experiences, such as the loss of a loved one or being diagnosed with a life-threatening disease. Hundreds of studies detailing various kinds of trauma have shown that people often experience significant symptoms of distress following such traumas, and for some people, this distress lingers for years after the trauma (see Janoff-Bulman, 1992 for a review).

Traumatic experiences, however, do not always create long-term distress in people. Indeed, some people experience traumatic events as opportunities to grow and learn more about themselves and the world (Frankl, 1984; Miles & Crandall, 1983; Tedeschi & Calhoun, 1996). Studies of bereaved people, cancer patients, myocardial infarction patients, bone marrow transplant patients, stroke victims and their caregivers, and men testing positive for HIV find that, as a consequence of their experience, they now valued relationships more, gained important self-knowledge, reorganized their priorities, and developed new attitudes toward life (Collins, Taylor, & Skokan, 1990; Curbow, Somerfield, Baker, Wingard, & Legro, 1993; Laerum, Johnsen, Smith, & Larsen, 1987; Lehman et al., 1993; Michela, 1987; Park & Cohen, 1993; Taylor, Kemeny, Reed, & Aspinwall, 1991; Tedeschi & Calhoun, 1996). For example, below are some comments from those who lost a close loved one in recent months (from Nolen-Hoeksema & Larson, 1999):

> Thinking back on it, if I had not done this, look at all I would have missed—all this growth, all this understanding. (Vera, 65, who lost a 90-year-old father to leukemia)

> I tend to look at it generally as if all the things that happen in my life are a gift, for whatever reason, or however they happen. It doesn't necessarily have to be only pleasant gifts, but everything that happens . . . there's a meaning. I've had a lot of suffering in my life . . . and through that I've learned a great deal. While I wouldn't want to go back and relive that, I'm grateful for that because it makes me who I am. There's a lot of joys and sorrows, but they all enrich life. (Alicia, 50, whose 70-year-old father died of cancer)

> I like who I am now because I find at 44 that I really like myself. If I didn't go through a lot of the hardships that I had, I wouldn't be who I am. So in a lot of ways, it's been an OK journey. And if I hadn't had people like that in my life, I wouldn't have a good sense of humor, which is one of the things that helps you get through, right? I feel extremely fortunate lately. (Norma, 44, whose 60-year-old father died of cancer)

In this chapter, I explore the idea that traumatic experiences such as the death of a close loved one can be watershed experiences, leading to positive change and growth in many people. The data I report in this chapter come from a longitudinal study of bereavement conducted in the San Francisco Bay Area (see Davis, Nolen-Hoeksema, & Larson, 1999; Nolen-Hoeksema & Larson, 1999). In this study, several hundred adults, ranging in age from 18 to 84, were interviewed within one month of the death of a close loved one, usually due to cancer. They were then reinterviewed six, thirteen, and eighteen months after the loss. I will focus on data from 240 participants who provided full data at all interviews.

At the end of each interview, we asked this question of the participants: "Sometimes people who lose a loved one find some positive aspect in the experience. For example, some people feel they learn something about themselves or others. Have you found anything positive in this experience?"

Although some respondents reacted negatively to this question (one man said, "No. Make that hell no!"), the overwhelming response to the question was affirmative. Sixty-five percent of the respondents said "yes" to this question at the six, thirteen, and eighteen month interviews.

First, I will describe some of the ways people in our study said they had grown or found something positive in the loss of their loved one, and use the participants' own words to illustrate these themes. Next, I will examine the relationship between perceiving something positive in a loss and psychological adjustment. Finally, I will investigate who finds it possible to grow following a loss, and who does not.

REPRIORITIZING ONE'S LIFE AND GOALS

One of the most common responses people gave when asked what they had found positive in the experience of their loss was that it had caused them to reprioritize their lives and to make major changes in the ways they ran their lives. The loss was often experienced as a "wake-up call" triggering the realization that they were not living their lives as they truly wished. Often, people decided to focus more on the here and now, rather than always concentrating on future goals or past failures. The loss of their loved ones had made them acutely aware of the shortness of time and the fragility of life. Some people decided to reduce the time spent on jobs and careers to spend more time with family. Others decided to pursue a new career or education, which they had always been putting off for the future.

> One thing I learned is to take each day to deal with whatever you're doing, day by day. For sure, I make it a point here at home, especially with the little ones, to always give a hug—special hug we call it—on a daily basis to reinforce we're not here, no guarantees, tomorrow. The positive from that is not to take each other for granted. The minor things, the coffee cup left on the table, it doesn't matter, it's no big issue. We could be here today

and gone tomorrow. With J's death, there isn't anything that can hurt me; no one, nothing can ever hurt me like that. I'm not laughing at fate, but the idiots that we have in this world can't hurt me after watching him disappear, disintegrate in front of me. One of the words to use is "unconditional." You go through life with conditions, boy you're setting yourself up for big disappointments. You have to come from the heart, unconditional. Nothing was going to keep me from him. That gave me the edge to deal with the taboos, what people thought. So I have empowered myself to feel like walking on air sometimes. We went through the whole way together. It was great. (Ginny, 45, who lost her 36-year-old brother to AIDS)

I probably take a lot shorter-term view of what's going on. I think there's a lot more of NOW than there ever was before. I think we all tend to respond that way to things—you know, we've got plenty of time, and things will take care of themselves. I've said things to people, and asked people to do things that I'd no more have done six months ago than fly. I came from a family, hell, everybody lived into their nineties . . . If there's anything I want to do, don't put it off, is the whole thing I'm saying. (Keith, 61, whose 67-year-old wife died of ovarian cancer)

When I saw her die, [I was] such an angry and upset person. This cancer does affect the brain. I saw her in this state, and I started my goal to live completely every day of [my] life that [I] have left, and not to fall into the same pitiful existence that she experienced (Joel, 48, whose 78-year-old mother died of pancreatic cancer)

I sit here alone in this big house, four or five empty bedrooms, R.'s empty bedroom, new kitchen, big yard, everything nice. No one here but me. I could have done with less. You know—less prosperous. Maybe only one car, less things. We could have enjoyed more together. Things we buy aren't important. Yes, enjoy life more, every minute in every day. (Raul, 65, whose 64-year-old wife died of brain cancer)

PERSONALITY CHANGES

Many people talked of positive changes in their personalities as a result of their loss. They often felt they had become more tolerant, more sensitive, more patient, and more loving with others. Some people described becoming less controlling and more willing to take life as it comes.

> I learned about compassion, I learned about suffering. Suffering leads to compassion. Compassion leads to beauty. . . . It was an opportunity to look at myself and to be non-complacent. I was always very complacent before. I thought I had it made. . . . I was stagnating. It opened my heart, my mind and my spirit. . . . I wish it had happened another way, but that's the way it happened. (Arnold, 50, whose 70-year-old mother died of breast cancer)

> I think I somehow learned by going through two years of this experience to be a bit more laid back about things—when you can't control them, to not worry that you can't control them. Up until that time I would try my best to control them, and if I couldn't control them, I would worry like heck because I couldn't. I think now, having gone through it and having come out on the other side, I see it's OK not to worry about it. I see it's OK to do what you can do, and it's ok to forget it when you can't do any more. (Millie, 46, whose 83-year-old father died of cancer)

> Throughout this whole thing there developed a softness in me, and a greater sense of my vulnerable side. An inner peacefulness [exists] that I have felt. Now I can always recognize (people who have gone through this)—they have a softness to them, a side of

> life that many people do not see, and then once they see, a lot of them have a real sense of compassion. That's what I felt that I didn't have before—this sensitivity. (Lee, 50, whose 74-year-old father died of cancer)

> His illness was for me to learn something. I learned patience. I learned compassion. I learned forgiveness. I learned that my priorities were worthless. And I learned that, no matter how bad things can be, there's still love and humor in the world. (Angel, 60, whose 64-year-old husband died of AIDS)

REALIZING PERSONAL STRENGTH

Although people often experienced their loss as challenging their coping skills and pushing them to the limit of their strengths, they also talked about realizing personal strengths that they previously had not discovered, or developing new strengths (for similar findings, see Calhoun & Tedeschi, 1989; Lund, Caserta, & Dimond, 1993). Those who had been caregivers to their loved ones before the death described engaging in activities they would not have believed they could perform—providing nursing care, being assertive in interactions with physicians, hospitals, and insurance companies.

> Watching Richard die was horrible, but even that was—I got something from that, even. I learned how much I can put up with. I learned there's nothing to be feared in life. Even, I could lose this house and live on the street, and I know I could do it. There's nothing I couldn't do. (Nora, 46, whose 46-year-old husband died of AIDS)

> I found personal growth. And I saw myself acting in a role of competence where I had to pull on all my resources just to get through sometimes. I would have to be directing the medical people about what I wanted to do. A person like me hates show-

> ing anger and can't stand conflict. I would have to stand and demand care from the nursing home, and it was necessary and I did it. So I came away with a feeling of competence and strength and gratitude. (Martha, 46, whose 83-year-old father died of cancer)

> There were plenty of positive things. In fact I'm still feeling—I felt a lot of "Gee, I didn't know that I could be this tough. I didn't know." But even on a day to day basis right now, I feel a lot stronger and a lot more capable of dealing with life in general and the sadness. Life is sad. Life is joyous and life is sad. Instead of getting depressed and overwhelmed by its sadness, I'm able to put it in what for me is its proper perspective. (Nora, 46, whose 46-year-old husband died of AIDS)

> Part of me didn't know that I had the strength for this. If you had asked me ten years ago, could I have gotten through this and still be sitting and talking, I would have said, "Not on your life!" But it's amazing what you *can* do when you have to. Maybe that's one of the ways I've been able to live with myself, because I did all I could. The other thing is, I did reprioritize my life to a great degree after the death. I had been a workaholic, not really available to my children; I was very much career oriented. I started to freelance from the house so I would be more available. (Cara, 45, whose 76-year-old mother died of lung cancer)

Some women who lost their husbands said that, although they missed their husbands, they had found strength and tremendous personal growth in the freedom they now had to make their own decisions and to live the lifestyles they wished.

> I think that when you lose a loved one, it's a rebirth for yourself. You can't always dwell on the loss of the loved one. You have to look forward to what you are going to do with your life now—who you are as a single person, which is very disturbing.

> Many people have been married much longer than I was, and they have to find out who they are. And it's a whole new experience, learning who you are, knowing who you are as a single person. That's one of the hard parts about being a widow or widower. A lot of people don't have time to think of who they are, because they're always attached to someone. And it's exciting. I mean, it's not bad, but it's exciting and it's also a little fearful to have to do that. Every day's a little learning experience for myself, of doing new things and learning new things as a single person. (Joy, 48, whose 49-year-old husband died of colon cancer)

> I really am stronger than I thought I was, and I thought I was pretty strong, but I'm stronger even than that. Not having the relationship of a husband, a close relationship like that, is—this sounds terrible, maybe—I find that I can do what I want, without hurting anybody, without asking anybody. I can just make decisions on my own, and take credit or blame for the results; and I'm ready to do that. (Paula, 56, whose 62-year-old husband died of lung cancer)

Those who had not been caregivers described their expectation that they would "fall apart" upon the death of their loved one, but instead found strength to cope very effectively with their loss. Others described how they changed their usual coping strategies from maladaptive ones to adaptive ones following the loss.

REALIZING THE IMPORTANCE OF RELATIONSHIPS

One of the most common "wake-up calls" that the loss provided to people in our study was the realization of the importance of their relationships in their lives (see also Calhoun & Tedeschi, 1989, 1990; Malinak, Hoyt, & Patterson, 1979; Zemore & Shepel, 1989). Rather than expecting always to have enough time to show love and concern to family members and friends, they now realized that loved ones could be gone with a moment's notice. As a result, they were now actively expressing how they felt to others, spending time with others, and generally valuing their relationships a great deal more.

> I learned that when you love someone, the relationship is so important. It's enhanced my relationship with other people because I realize that time is so important, and you can waste so much effort on small, insignificant events or feelings. I feel that in my present relationship I'm better able to be a real good friend, and I don't take things so personally. I don't feel that someone's got to fill me up. I can fill myself. I feel stronger as a person. I have more confidence in myself. (Karen, 47, whose partner died of cancer)

> I hold onto the fact that when we learned he was sick, we got to know our son better than parents ever know their children. We got way past parent-child syndrome, able to show love. [It's] very unusual to get past roles. We totally accepted him, he knew it, and we appreciated his honesty. Our love for him was limitless. He showed us what life was all about. (Al, 54, whose 31-year-old son died of AIDS)

RESOLVING FAMILY CONFLICTS

Although families often comfort and support each other after a loss, it can also bring family conflicts to the surface and exacerbate them. In some families, these conflicts are never resolved and the family is torn apart. In other families, however, these conflicts are confronted and resolved, leading individual family members to feel relieved of the burden of the conflicts and consequently, become closer to other family members than they may ever have been before.

> Most of all, he helped to bridge—he came to grips—he finally encountered with my Mom all the problems that we'd had during my growing-up years. And he validated me as a person. And was able to say to my mother that she was wrong. So my Dad

> healed me. And he completed me, my social growth. And yet, I did the same for him. Because I know that I gave him the strength and gave him the ability to see and to finally acknowledge the problems that had gone on for years and years. And once he was able to do that, during this period of talking things out and not bottling all this anger and frustration up, he was able to get stronger. He physically became stronger and emotionally became stronger. And I think, then, [in] this period of his illness we finally had a chance to do a father and daughter relationship, and a friend and friend relationship, with his living here. And he was happy—it gave me a great deal of happiness, and he was happy. I feel like we were blessed. (Judith, 33, whose 74-year-old father died of pancreatic cancer)

In some cases, the conflicts may have been with the family member who died. The fact that the death was anticipated allowed some family members to resolve their conflicts with the dying family member. The surviving family members then often felt a tremendous weight had been lifted, and they could continue with their lives after the death occurred.

> During the last years of her life my Mom stopped drinking, so I came to know her in way that I was unable to when I was growing up. I learned a lot about the reasons why my parents did some of the things they did, felt some of the ways they felt, and acted some of the ways they acted. It did not exactly reconcile me to the situation, but it's sort of a balance. . . . I carried around a lot of resentment for my older brother who kind of divorced himself from family proceedings as early as possible. . . . I never appreciated how scared he was at the time. . . . I seem to have gotten a lot of the "screwiness" out of my system in one real acute, nasty episode of time. (Will, 42, whose 80-year-old mother died of pancreatic cancer)

> I was able to experience my mother in a positive way—[through] the stories at her funeral [and] going through her personal papers. When you're dealing with a frail, elderly person

> who is so needy, on top of that an alcoholic, . . . it's very scary to be around them, because they keep almost sucking your lifeblood, they keep taking from you. Once they're dead, the threat is gone. You feel safe, and then you can open up. It's safe to . . . pull in all the good stuff about them. And to forgive, and accept healing. And for me, death had to precede all that. (Nellie, 44, whose 78-year-old mother died of lung cancer)

LOSING THE FEAR OF DEATH

Finally, many participants in our study said that they had always believed they could not face death and had feared both the death of loved ones and their own death. But the experience of watching a loved one die and subsequent coping with that loss had erased their fear of death. They no longer saw death as frightening or horrible. Instead, many people were intrigued by the mystery of death and more peaceful about their own deaths.

> We grow in hard times. I've been more available to joy and loving than before. I'm not afraid of death as I was before. I embrace life more—a powerful reminder to live well. (Attie, 30, whose 30-year-old friend died of AIDS)

> Death is a part of life but we don't talk about it, we don't want to think about it. It's sort of like a dirty word or something. I think most of us are so unprepared for dealing with a loved one and our own death. I just think it needs to be more out in the open. We need to talk about it, we need to teach classes about it. It needs to be not such a dirty word, because we all act as if it's not going to happen, and it's going to happen to all of us. I think we all spend our time burying our heads in the sand. I think part of the reason it's so terrifying is because we know so little about it. (Jenna, 48, whose 45-year-old friend died of AIDS)

WHAT DOES IT MEAN TO FIND SOMETHING POSITIVE?

Researchers have disagreed on the meaning of finding something positive in a trauma. Tedeschi and Calhoun (1996) distinguish between theories that view finding something positive as a way of *coping* with the trauma and those that view it as part of a true *transformation* that occurs within individuals in the wake of a trauma.

The theories that target coping note that learning about one's strength in the face of adversity, or gaining insight into the meaning of life, or the importance of relationships, may help to mitigate the feelings of loss or helplessness at the passing of a loved one. This may help to preserve or restore the idea that one's own life has purpose and worth, which may be critical to well-being (Antonovsky, 1987; Frankl, 1984; Janoff-Bulman, 1992; Taylor, 1983; Thompson & Janigian, 1988). Taylor (1983, 1989; Taylor & Armor, 1996) has argued that threats to one's sense of self are often diminished by perceiving the event as a "wake-up call" that one's priorities and goals are not as they should be. The reordering of priorities and the revision of life goals constitute part of a reappraisal of the event as an opportunity for growth, rather than only as a loss (Park, Cohen, & Murch, 1996; Tedeschi & Calhoun, 1996); and this reappraisal may be a coping strategy that helps to shore up self-esteem (Taylor & Armor, 1996).

Others have contended, however, that traumatic events such as loss can create true developmental change by confronting people with new situations and issues they have never faced before (Baumeister, 1989; Frankl, 1963; Thompson, 1991; Thompson & Janigian, 1988). Major roles may change—a woman may perceive she is no longer her husband's wife or mother's daughter. People who lose their parents may now perceive themselves as the "head of the family" or "the last one left in their generation." Young widowhood may mean being thrust abruptly and involuntarily into single parenthood. This shift in roles and in self-perceptions can lead to major developmental changes. Observing yourself doing things you never thought possible, certainly, can also lead to growth and change in self-perceptions.

FINDING SOMETHING POSITIVE AND PSYCHOLOGICAL ADJUSTMENT

Whether finding something positive is simply a cognitive coping strategy or a true growth experience, people who do so might be expected to adjust better to their loss. Several previous studies have found associations between finding something positive (or finding some meaning) in a trauma and in adjustment (e.g., Aldwin, Levenson, & Spiro, 1994; Curbow et al., 1993; McIntosh, Silver, & Wortman, 1993; Silver, Boon, & Stones, 1983; Taylor, Lichtman & Wood, 1984).

In our study, people who reported something positive in their loss by six months post-loss showed lower levels of distress on a combined measure of anxiety and depression at six, thirteen, and eighteen months post-loss, than those who reported no positive dimension by six months post-loss (see figure 6.1). This result held true even after we statistically controlled for how distressed people were at the beginning of the study (see Davis, Nolen-Hoeksema, & Larson, 1999).

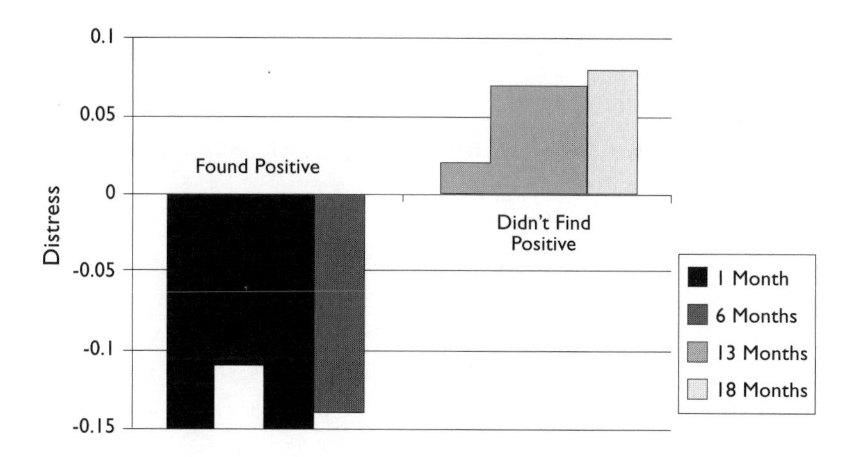

Figure 6.1. Differences between people who found something positive and those who did not in psychological distress at 1, 6, 13, and 18 months.

None of the specific themes described earlier were more strongly associated with adjustment than another. Simply finding something positive was related to better adjustment, regardless of what it was. Other studies suggest that it is not how many positive things people find following a loss, or what specifically they find positive that predicts adjustment, but simply whether or not they can find anything positive (Davis, Lehman, & Wortman, 1997).

We might expect that losses violating the natural order and our most basic assumptions would present survivors with the most difficulty in finding anything positive. Yet, in our study, parents who lost a child (usually an adult child) were not less able than other family groups to find something positive in their loss. Indeed, the parents seemed to be striving to instill some positive meaning in their loss, more than any other family group, perhaps because they needed this to overcome the sense of injustice they felt at having lost a child.

> I learned a lot about myself and my son. We were very close. We always were very close, but the past three years have [developed] a real deepening of our understanding of each other. He taught me a lot. That's why I talk to his picture, because I want to continue to remember what he taught me. (Penny, 62, whose 32-year-old son died of AIDS)

According to our research, the family group least able to find something positive in their loss was bereaved spouses.

> I frankly can find no good has come out of death. My situation has improved over what it would have been were she alive. . . . I wouldn't own a house, I wouldn't have $50,000 in the bank . . . honestly, I'd prefer not to have that and to have her alive. (Charles, 62, whose 52-year-old wife died of liver cancer)

> No, [there was] nothing positive. It's just very cruel, very hard, very wrong. (Randolph, 65, whose 60-year-old wife died from a brain tumor)

For people who lose their spouses, the changes in their roles are often seen only as negative—they feel alone, isolated, and without their lifelong companion and helpmate. It can be very difficult for them to see any positive benefit to these role changes. Many older people who lost their spouses expressed bitter disappointment that their expectations for living the "golden years" with their mates had now vanished. They may have saved and planned for decades, now only to have lost the one person with whom they wanted to live out these years.

People who had lost their parents or a sibling were especially likely to mention changes in their own self-perceptions, life goals, and priorities as a result of their loss (see also Scharlach & Fredriksen, 1993). Their priorities had changed; consequently, they decided to make a career change or spend more time with their families. Frequently, they tried to improve their health habits and re-established religious ties, perhaps because of a greater sense of their own mortality.

> I found many gifts from it. It has shaken me to rethink living—and looking at her life in terms of my life. I'm aware, in a different way, of life's tentativeness. So I'm trying to be more appreciative and active in my own life. So I'm trying to be more involved with the kids and their lives. This shaking has provided me with a chance to look at that stuff. (Sallie, 45, who lost her 70-year-old mother to cancer)

Also, a number of bereaved adult children and siblings commented on how family members rallied and grew closer around the loss, providing something positive.

> We definitely learned a lot about ourselves and about each other within the family circle. There was a rallying of support, and a camaraderie that I think only shows itself, truly shows itself, when something like this occurs. I think you always assume that it's there, but it was tested, and we were pleasantly surprised, very pleased with how each one took his or her role, and no one was ever left to feel abandoned. There was a lot of support, a lot of physical and mental support. (Gil, 40, whose mother, 68, died of a brain tumor)

When we examined the coping strategies that people used following their losses, we found that those who had found something positive in their losses were using different coping strategies than those who had not. People who had found something positive pursued more reappraisal coping mechanisms—they purposely tried to reappraise their loss in positive terms. In addition, they were more likely than those who had not found something positive to engage in active problem-solving, by seeking social support, by expressing their emotions to others, and by participating in positive distractions, such as hobbies or exercise. People who found something positive in their losses were not more likely to be engaging in avoidance coping—denying the importance of the loss or engaging in maladaptive behaviors to distract themselves from the loss, such as excessive alcohol use. This suggests that seeking something positive in a loss does not simply constitute a form of defensiveness or denial.

People who sought something positive in their losses tended to be dispositional optimists. Indeed, we found that dispositional optimism predicted finding something positive in the loss better than any of the other variables we have discussed thus far, and better than any sociodemographic variables, even after controlling for how distressed people were (Davis, Nolen-Hoeksema, & Larson, 1999). Other studies also maintain that dispositional optimists are more likely to perceive benefits or report positive life changes following a trauma (Affleck & Tennen, 1996; Park, Cohen, & Murch, 1996; Tedeschi & Calhoun, 1996).

A MODEL OF SIGNIFICANT PATHS

Finally, we conducted path analyses to investigate the relationships among optimism, coping, and finding something positive. In these analyses, one-month post-loss scores on optimism and coping were used to predict finding something positive at six, thirteen, and eighteen months post-loss, while statistically controlling for one-month distress scores. Figure 6.2 shows the paths that were statistically significant in these analyses. Optimism contributed to more adaptive coping strategies, namely more positive reappraisal, more problem-solving coping, and more use of positive distractions (e.g., hobbies and exercise). These coping strategies were then associated with a greater likelihood of finding something positive at six, thirteen, and eighteen months post-loss.

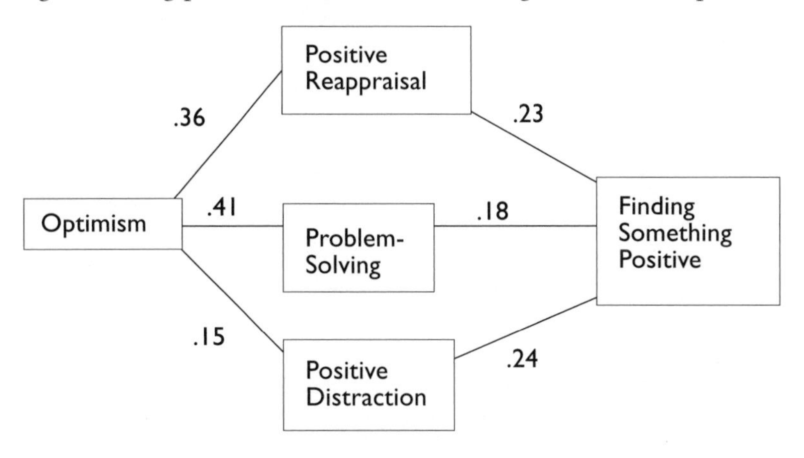

Figure 6.2. Significant paths after accounting for one-month distress scores.

CONCLUSIONS

Although the loss of a significant loved one can be a highly distressing experience, the majority of bereaved people report finding something positive in their loss experiences. Common positive themes included having a sense of personal growth and personality change, a realization of personal strengths, a reprioritizing of life goals, a greater appreciation of relationships, and a diminished sense of fear about death. Being an optimist not only seemed to contribute to engaging in more positive coping strategies, but also to finding something positive in the loss. In turn, people who found something positive in their losses showed better psychological adjustment to the loss, both shortly after the loss and long afterward.

The results of this study and several others suggest that traumas need not be debilitating to everyone, and indeed that most people are resilient and even grow in the wake of traumas. Understanding the sources of this resilience and growth will help psychologists foster the strengths of the people they serve.

REFERENCES

Affleck, G., & Tennen, H. (1996). Construing benefits from adversity: Adaptational significance and dispositional underpinnings. *Journal of Personality, 64,* 899–922.

Aldwin, C.M., Levenson, M.R., & Spiro, A. (1994). Vulnerability and resilience to combat exposure: Can stress have lifelong effects? *Psychology and Aging, 9,* 34–44.

Antonovsky, A. (1987). *Unraveling the mystery of health.* San Francisco: Jossey-Bass.

Baumeister, R.F. (1989). The problem of life's meaning. In D. M. Buss & N. Cantor (Eds.), *Personality psychology: Recent trends and emerging directions* (pp. 138–148). New York: Springer-Verlag.

Calhoun, L.G., & Tedeschi, R.G. (1989). Positive aspects of critical life problems: Recollections of grief. *Omega: Journal of Death and Dying, 20,* 265–272.

Collins, L.G., Taylor, S.E., & Skokan, L.A., (1990). A better world or a shattered vision? Changes in life perspective following victimization. *Social Cognition, 8,* 263–285.

Curbow, B., Somerfield, M.R., Baker, F., Wingard, J.R., & Legro, M. (1993). Personal changes, dispositional optimism, and psychological adjustment to bone marrow transplantation. *Journal of Behavioral Medicine, 16,* 423–443.

Davis, C.G., Lehman, D.R., & Wortman, C.B. (1997). Finding meaning in loss and trauma: Making sense of the literature. Unpublished manuscript, University of Michigan.

Davis, C., Nolen-Hoeksema, S., & Larson, J. (1999). Making sense of loss and benefiting from the experience: Two construals of meaning. *Journal of Personality and Social Psychology, 75,* 561–574.

Frankl, V.E. (1963). *Man's search for meaning: An introduction to logotherapy* (3rd ed.). New York: Vintage Books.

Janoff-Bulman, V.E. (1992). *Shattered assumptions: Towards a new psychology of trauma.* New York: Free Press.

Laerum, E., Johnsen, N., Smith, P., & Larsen, S. (1987). Can myocardial infarction induce positive changes in family relationships? *Family Practice, 4,* 302–305.

Lehman, D.R., Davis, C.G., DeLongis, A., Wortman, C.B., Bluck, S., Mandel, D.R., & Ellard, J.H. (1993). Positive and negative life changes following bereavement and their relations to adjustment. *Journal of Social and Clinical Psychology, 12,* 90–112.

Lund, D.A., Caserta, M.S., & Dimond, M.F. (1993). The course of spousal bereavement in later life. In M.S. Stroebe, W. Stroebe, & R.O. Hansson (Eds.), *Handbook of bereavement* (pp. 240–254). Cambridge: Press Syndicate of the University of Cambridge.

Malinak, D.P., Hoyt, M.F., & Patterson, V. (1979). Adults' reactions to the death of a parent: A preliminary study. *American Journal of Psychiatry, 136,* 1152–1156.

McIntosh, D.N., Silver, R.C., & Wortman, C.B. (1993). Religion's role in adjustment to a negative life event: Coping with the loss of a child. *Journal of Personality and Social Psychology, 65,* 812–821.

Michela, J.L. (1987). Interpersonal and individual impacts of a husband's heart attack. In A. Baum (Ed.), *Handbook of psychology and health: Vol. 5: Stress* (pp. 255–301). Hillsdale, NJ: Lawrence Erlbaum Associates, Inc.

Miles, M.S., & Crandall, E.K.B. (1983). The search for meaning and its potential for affecting growth in bereaved parents. *Health Values, 7,* 19–23.

Nolen-Hoeksema, S., & Larson, J. (1999). *Coping with loss.* Mahwah, NJ: Lawrence Erlbaum Associates.

Park, C.L., & Cohen, L.H. (1993). Religious and nonreligious coping with the death of a friend. *Cognitive Therapy and Research, 17,* 561–577.

Park, C.L., Cohen, L.H., & Murch, R.L. (1996). Assessment and prediction of stress-related growth. *Journal of Personality, 64,* 71–105.

Scharlach, A.E., & Fredriksen, K. (1993). Reaction to the death of a parent during midlife. *Omega: Journal of Death and Dying, 27,* 307–319.

Silver, R.L., Boon, C., & Stones, M.H. (1983). Searching for meaning in misfortune: Making sense of incest. *Journal of Social Issues, 39,* 81–102.

Taylor, S.E. (1983). Adjustment to threatening events: A theory of adaptation. *American Psychologist, 38,* 1161–1173.

Taylor, S.E. (1989). *Positive illusions: Creative self-deception and the healthy mind.* New York: Basic Books.

Taylor, S.E., & Armor, D.A. (1996). Positive illusions and coping with adversity. *Journal of Personality, 64,* 873–898.

Taylor, S.E., Kemeny, M.E., Reed, G.M., & Aspinwall, L.G. (1991). Assault on the self: Positive illusions and adjustment to threatening events. In J. Strauss & G.R. Goethals (Eds.), *The self: Interdisciplinary approaches* (pp. 239–254). New York: Springer-Verlag.

Taylor, S.E., Lichtman, R.R., & Wood, J.V. (1984). Attributions, beliefs about control, and adjustment to breast cancer. *Journal of Personality and Social Psychology, 46,* 489–502.

Tedeschi, R.G., & Calhoun, L.G. (1996). The Posttraumatic Growth Inventory: Measuring the positive legacy of trauma. *Journal of Traumatic Stress, 9,* 455–471.

Thompson, S.C. (1991). The search for meaning following a stroke. *Basic and Applied Social Psychology, 12,* 81–96.

Thompson, S.C., & Janigian, A.S. (1988). Life schemes: A framework for understanding the search for meaning. *Journal of Social & Clinical Psychology, 7,* 260–280.

Zemore, R., & Shepel, L.F. (1989). Effects of cancer and mastectomy on emotional support and adjustment. *Social Science and Medicine, 28,* 19–27.

ACKNOWLEDGMENTS

The study was made possible by U.S. Public Health Grant l Rol 43760 to Susan Nolen-Hoeksema. I wish to thank the following hospices and home health care agencies for recruiting participants into this study: Hospice of Contra Costa, Hospice Caring Project of Santa Cruz County, Hospice of Marin, Hospice of the Valley, Lifesource of Larkspur and Mountain View, Mills-Peninsula Hospital, Mission Hospice, Vesper Hospice, Visiting Nurse Association of San Jose, and Visiting Nurses and Hospice of San Francisco. I also thank Dr. Judith Larson for running this study, Dr. Louise Parker for her contributions to the early phases of this study, Drs. Sarah Erickson, Peter Goldblum, and Claire Costello for their contributions to the AIDS-related interviews, and Dr. Christopher Davis for statistical advice.

✦ CHAPTER 7 ✦

The Hope Mandala: Coping with the Loss of a Loved One

C. R. Snyder

A FRAMEWORK FOR UNDERSTANDING BEREAVEMENT

SUSAN NOLEN-HOEKSEMA'S summary (see Chapter 6) of her work on the bereavement process illustrates many important positive human characteristics. Bereavement by its nature suggests that the surviving person had established a strong attachment to the deceased individual. Indeed, if we did not bond with another, there should be no need to mourn our loss. In addition to mourning the loss, of course, the bereaved person also is coping. Although we may know people who totally cease to cope effectively when a loved one dies, such responses are extreme, and this important caveat becomes apparent in the Nolen-Hoeksema findings. Indeed, general coping processes are effective in enabling most survivors to continue their life activities with some degree of satisfaction (see Davis, Nolen-Hoeksema, & Larson, in press; Frankl, 1992; Nolen-Hoeksema & Larson, 2000; Snyder, 1996, 1998). Metaphorically, the black shroud of bereavement is supplanted with a more brightly colored garment that is appropriate for getting on with the tasks of life. In this chapter, I will suggest that a new theory of hope provides a means for understanding the adaptive emergence from the mourning processes described by Nolen-Hoeksema.

A NEW THEORY OF HOPE: AGENCY AND PATHWAYS GOAL-DIRECTED THINKING

Hope is a thinking process that taps a sense of agency and pathways for one's goals (Snyder, 1994). In more specific terms, hope is defined as "a reciprocally derived sense of successful (a) agency (goal-directed determination) and (b) pathways (planning of ways to meet goals)" (Snyder et al., 1991, p. 571). This definition ties hopeful thinking expressly to goals. By focusing on goal objects, we are able to respond effectively to our surrounding environment. Compared to the vague and ambiguous nature of the goals for low-hope people, high-hope persons are more likely to clearly conceptualize their goals (Snyder et al., 1991). Goals as the mental targets of human action are shown in the protagonist of figure 7.1.

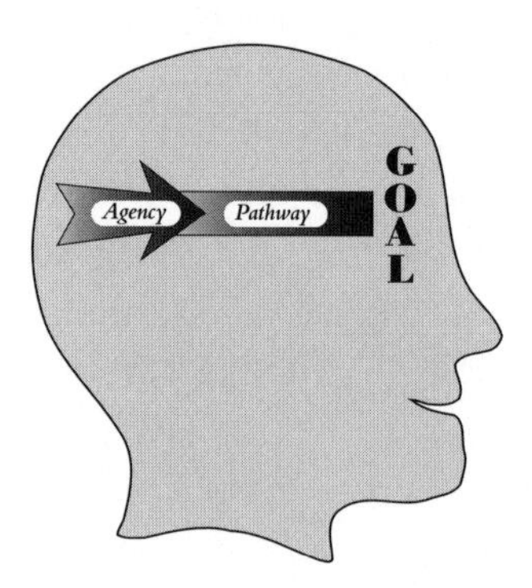

Figure 7.1. Schematic of hope, including agency and pathway thinking toward goals.

Two related crucial thoughts are aimed at goals. First, there is pathway thinking, which reflects the routes that people produce in relation to goals. Pathway thought involves the perceived capacity to come up with mental road maps to reach goals. Usually, the protagonist thinks about one primary pathway, (see figure 7.1) although alternate ones also may exist. Second, the individual thinks about his or her perceived capability to move along the selected pathway to the goal. Agency thought mobilizes the person to use given pathways (see figure 7.1). Again returning to our protagonist, we can see that the agentic thought is applied to a goal pathway. In summary, hope reflects a thinking process in which the protagonist perceives that he or she can produce the pathway(s) to reach the goal, as well as the agency to actually use the existing pathway(s). As such, both the agentic and pathway goal-related thoughts are necessary to yield hope.

It is important to keep in mind that hope theory is built upon goal pursuit thinking. As such, blockages to either pathway or agency thought may impact coping. Thus, unimpeded goal pursuit results in positive emotions; conversely, goal blockages produce negative feelings. Research conducted within my laboratory indicates that goal blockages elicit negative emotions (Snyder et al., 1996). Similarly, research in other laboratories reveals that problems encountered in pursuing goals undermine well-being (e.g., Little, 1989).

High- as compared to low-hope people do not experience, however, the same debilitating emotions when confronting impediments. In part, this adaptive coping reflects the fact that high- as compared to low-hope people generate alternative paths, especially when the original path is blocked (Irving, Snyder, & Crowson, 1998; Snyder et al., 1991). Equally important in terms of actual outcomes, however, are the findings that high- as compared to low-hope people have coping advantages when their goal pursuits are unimpeded, as well as when they are impeded (for reviews, see Snyder, 1994; Snyder, Cheavens, & Michael, 1999).

LOSS OF DESIRED RELATIONAL OBJECT

Using hope theory as a framework, the loss of a loved one produces two principal blockages. I realize that I run the risk of dehumanizing interpersonal relationships by describing them as "commodities" with goal properties, but I think that it would be absurd to somehow artificially exclude from analyses one type of goal-related activity—namely, those pertaining to intimate relationships. Indeed, I would argue that having a significant other is a desired goal in the very best sense of this concept. With a brief example tracing the early stages of an intimate relationship, the reader may more readily see how a significant other can be construed as a goal object. Thus, I would ask the reader to turn back the hands of time to those early moments when he or she "fell" in love. During that time, it is as if one's mate subsumes all of one's thinking, and that mate quite literally becomes the goal superseding all others. Indeed, our friends jokingly may ask us whether we have forgotten about them. In fact, we construct our lives so that we can spend more of our time thinking about the coveted loved one. We find ways to be near him or her (pathway thinking), and we are highly motivated to use those pathways (agency thinking) to achieve the relationship goals of having more interaction.

As time goes on, we continue our goal-related thinking toward a loved one. Such thinking may not have the burning consciousness that characterized the early stages of ardor, but it nevertheless is operative. Although I have used the example of a romantic relationship, any interpersonal relationship (e.g., parents, friends, etc.) that is a valued one may entail similar goal-related thought processes.

As can be seen in the mind of a person experiencing a loss in figure 7.2, the object of one's attentions—the loved one—is no longer there in physical reality (i.e., the "X" through the goal). To the person mourning such a loss, it is amazing how frequently the awareness turns to the perception that the desired person is "gone."

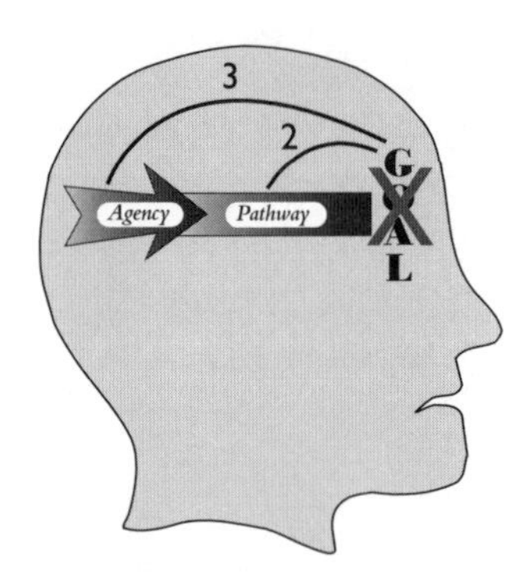

Figure 7.2. Schematic of loss in the context of hope, including the blockages produced by loss on agency and pathway thinking.

Pathway Blocks

A loss, however, involves more than just the sense that a loved one is no longer "with us." Another major aspect of such a loss is that the normal pathway thinking in relation to one's significant other is blocked. As the loss continues over time, survivors become more aware of the routes that they *cannot* take to their usual relationship goal partner. As shown by Point #2 in figure 7.2, the surviving protagonist's pathway thinking centers upon realizations that he or she cannot successfully use the avenues previously leading to interactions with the loved one. Simply put, a major part of the perceived loss when a loved one dies is that the survivor no longer can engage in cherished activities with that partner. Survivors miss such activities not only for their familiarity, but for the relational pleasures that they previously brought. In relationships, for example, talking is crucial for attaining shared goals. Additional examples of interference with pathways thinking are almost endless, but the new contribution offered by hope theory is that the previous pathways-related activities no longer are available to the survivor.

Agency Blocks

The loss of a loved one also can block agentic thinking (see Point #3 in figure 7.2). Thus, the loss undermines the surviving person's previous mental energy for using the favored pathways. From the perspective of a bereaving person, it is typical to feel drained of "energy." Not only is physical energy lost, but there also is a lack of psychological willfulness. Further, given the vivid reality that the departed loved one is not "coming back," the survivor may find it difficult to apply him- or herself, not only to the previously favored paths, but to any paths. In this sense, the bereaving person is similar to the low-hope person with an ongoing "I can't!" internal dialogue (see Snyder, LaPointe, Crowson, & Early, 1998). Lacking mental vigor, one's usual goal pursuit activities are shut down.

Double the Trouble

Unfortunately, the survivor's sense of loss is not constrained to just the pathways *or* agency thinking. More often, the loss serves to block *both* the pathways and agency thoughts. Likewise, when the survivor thinks about one of these two components, he or she often will think of the other component, as well as the inability to find another acceptable goal.

HOPING THROUGH THE MOURNING PROCESS

As I have reasoned previously, hopeful thinking is intimately linked to the sense of blockage encountered in grieving for a lost loved one. I will turn to the clinical and research lessons that I have learned concerning the revival of the grieving person's hope. Research suggests that both optimistic and hopeful people have coping advantages when dealing with both psychological and physical problems (Scheier & Carver, 1992; Snyder, 1996, 1998; Snyder, Sympson, Michael, & Cheavens, in press). What can we discern from high-hope people as they confront the blockages in their lives? Contrary to the view that high-hope persons have led lives of relative ease, I have found that they have encountered impediments to the same degree as have low-hope people. (Nolen-Hoeksema makes a similar point in that the resilience of survivors emerges in the stressful context of bereavement.) What differentiates these high-hopers, however, is that they learn to anticipate these difficulties as a natural part of life (Irving, Snyder, and Crowson, 1998).

In the present section, I will use the goal-, pathway-, and agency-thinking components of hope theory in order to make suggestions for facilitating the grieving process.

Goal Thinking

High-hope people are willing to embrace substitute goal objects when it is apparent that the original goal is lost (Snyder, 1994, 1996). High-hope people have multiple goals and, as such, can focus their attentions on another goal when they have lost a loved one. It is not that the grieving person immediately should be encouraged to produce a new love object (indeed, this may backfire), but rather there may be some other life goals involving work, recreation, and the like that distract the grieving person from focusing solely on the lost loved one. It is important to add the cautionary note, however, that the person should not throw her- or himself so pervasively into activities that the processing of the loss is avoided.

Attention to alternative life goals may be facilitated during the very time that the person is grieving. Perhaps an example may clarify this point. I once worked in psychotherapy with a woman who could not stop thinking about her departed husband. Unable to shake her constant thoughts of him, she was mired in a depression that transcended the normal period of time for mourning. Instead of attempting to have her lessen her time in such thoughts about her husband, I asked her to enumerate the other worthwhile goals in her life. She immediately offered her grandchildren. With this clue, we then established a program where she would take care of these two children for one and then two nights weekly. Once she was spending time with her grandchildren, I asked her to consider another goal. She came up with the idea of getting a part-time job. Accordingly, she found a volunteer job for several hours each week at the local hospital. Throughout this process, we talked about how satisfying these experiences were to her. Slowly, she began to supplant her constant thoughts of her deceased husband with thoughts about her grandchildren and volunteer work. The final part of this hopeful "regoaling" involved her imagining what her departed husband would want to say to her. She imagined him telling her to get out more. During one such imagined interchange with her husband, she laughed. Surprised, I asked her what had happened. She informed me, with a smile, that her husband had told her to "Get a life!" By this point, she was again reengaged in the day-to-day necessity of establishing meaningful life goals.

If the grieving person continues to focus on the lost loved one, the psychological pain and suffering also will continue. It is the hopeful person, however, who often comes to appreciate a previous loved one along with the understanding that she or he is truly gone. As I have noted earlier, such hopeful mourning allows the person to focus on goal pursuits in other life arenas. Additionally, over time, a new loved one may occupy the attentions of the hopeful person who is moving out of the mourning process. I would emphasize again, however, that it is inappropriate to encourage the partner to begin dating again immediately. Such input can solidify the surviving partner's thinking that "there will never be another one like her." Over time, however, the survivor may slowly attend to possible new love interests. Just as one took time initially to fall in love, so too does it take time to attach one's attentions to a new loved one. Likewise, even though the survivors may not "regoal" in terms of finding a new mate, it is reasonably certain that they can find other satisfying life goals. In this regard, Nolen-Hoeksema (see Chapter 6) reports that two adaptive bereavement responses are to (1) rethink one's goals so as to focus more on the here and now life events, and (2) value important interpersonal relationships. We have found that these two goal foci also characterize high-hope people (Snyder, Cheavens, & Sympson, 1997).

Pathway Thinking

As noted previously, part of mourning is that the survivor misses the usual pathway activities related to the departed person. One counterproductive type of mourning involves catastrophizing, in which the survivor conjures that all meaningful pathways are now blocked. In other words, the loss of the loved one spreads to cast a sense of blockage to all planned thought. The person thus entertains the existential question, "What can I possibly do with myself now?" For those who are dealing with this aspect of the grieving, I would suggest allowing the survivor a little time to "wallow" in such total goal blockage thoughts. With time, however, such "wallowing" needs to be lessened via pathway thinking. Although there are many pathway type activities related to the departed person that simply cannot be reinstated, there are still some pathways that can be pursued. Likewise, some of the same goals (as when the departed person was alive) may be pursued, but the survivor needs new pathway thinking. The surviving person may need tips about the activities that can be undertaken, and this may flow from considering other goals that still are worth pursuing (see previous section).

Perhaps another case history may illustrate how such pathways thought can be taught. Several years ago, a young couple who had lost their 10-year-old daughter in an automobile accident joined a psychotherapy group that I was leading. This man and woman kept talking about all the fun things they missed doing with their departed daughter. They spoke with heartfelt emotions about how they would take their daughter fishing, and the joy that this brought her. In the group, it was suggested that *they* should go fishing together. They had not done this since their daughter had died and, in fact, they had thrown away their rods and reels. The couple agreed to go fishing, and they took their younger daughter (age 7). To their surprise, they still greatly enjoyed fishing, and they learned that their younger daughter was an excellent angler. Slowly, with encouragement, this couple undertook other activities that they had discontinued since their older daughter had died. Such pathway thinking fed upon itself and, over time, the couple found that they no longer were as preoccupied with the death of their daughter. They not only reestablished old and satisfying routines, but they were freed to establish new ones for themselves and their younger daughter.

Another pathway lesson that I have borrowed from research on high-hope people is the observation that they naturally break big goals into small subgoals (Snyder, 1994). For the mourning person, this means that the survivor need not undertake pathway thought all at once. Rather, the mourning person can be encouraged to move very slowly to reestablish activities previously undertaken with a loved one. If the survivor engaged in these activities previously, those avenues may have some intrinsic satisfaction. Anything that can be done to encourage the survivor to slowly restart old and cherished activities may allow that person to rediscover the satisfaction in such pathway thinking.

Agentic Thinking

The survivor also may feel drained of mental energy, and perceive that "Nothing seems worth the effort." My advice is to give the person some time to recharge. If the survivor continues in this malaise, however, there are some alternatives for enhancing the agentic thought. First, I would suggest what I call the "voices in the mind" exercise. This approach stems directly from my laboratory findings showing that high-hope people have an ongoing self dialogue of energizing and affirming statements such as "I'll make it," "I can," and "I won't give up" (Snyder et al., in press). Thus, I encourage people to actively practice saying such affirming statements. These "voices in the mind" can help the survivor to get out and do things. Sometimes, I also will teach the mourners how to "contain" the negative voices (e.g., "I can't") by having 5-minute time periods where they actively practice such energy-robbing thoughts. This latter exercise helps to reduce the time spent on negative thoughts during the rest of their lives.

People who are in mourning also do not feel like doing much physically. Unfortunately, they may engage in fewer physical activities than they did previously in their lives, and they may sit (or stay in bed) thinking about how tired they are (one refrain here is "Life is no longer worth living"). Our research, however, suggests that exercise is related to higher agentic thought (Snyder, 1994). In this regard, the person may undertake any one of several possible exercise routines to enliven agentic thinking.

Another means of enhancing agentic thinking is to help the mourning persons to inject more humor into their daily routines. Obviously, this is not appropriate for the person who is in the early throes of the grieving process, but eventually humor becomes more fitting. Whenever mourners can adopt an existential perspective about the sometimes ridiculous and precarious nature of life, they then may attain a mental lift. Likewise, I have asked survivors to consider whether their departed partners would want them to live humorless lives. The answer always has been "No."

One final point is that family members unwittingly can lessen the agency of the mourning individual by being overly solicitous and protective. This solicitousness only reinforces the grieving person's perceived lack of mental energy. Sometimes, therefore, family members need to be apprised of their counterproductive roles. Once this pattern is made more obvious to everyone involved, each person can interact so as to foster the survivor's activity rather than inactivity.

The Hope Mandala

In this chapter, I have used hope theory as a framework for understanding bereavement. Hope provides an explanation that parallels many of the points made in the Nolen-Hoeksema chapter. First, Nolen-Hoeksema suggests that optimists are most likely to navigate successfully the mourning process (see Davis, Nolen-Hoeksema, & Larson, in press; Chapter 6). On this point, we have found that optimism and hope are highly and positively correlated (for review see Snyder, Sympson, Michael, and Cheavens, in press). Second, Nolen-Hoeksema's findings show that positive reappraisal, problem-solving, and positive distraction are mediating variables that drive the relationship between optimism and finding benefits in the mourning process. In this regard, higher hope persons also use these positive reappraisal, problem-solving, and positive distraction processes to deal with a variety of life stressors (see Snyder, 1994; Snyder, Cheavens, & Michael, 1999). Third, Nolen-Hoeksema (see Chapter 6) reports that those persons who used positive reappraisals of their losses were not more likely to use avoidance coping, denial, and drug usage (alcohol) strategies; similarly, my research shows that the high- as compared to low-hope persons are not drawn to these same maladaptive coping strategies (Snyder, 1994; Snyder et al., 1991). For these three reasons, Nolen-Hoeksema's important work on the positive emergence from bereavement appears to bear many similarities to hope theory.

Whether it is the researcher striving to understand bereavement, a therapist treating it, or a friend helping a loved one to deal with the mourning process, hope theory offers three touchstones. First, the survivor may establish new goals that bring meaning to his or her daily life. Second, the mourner can attend to pathway thoughts about how to get to those goals. Third, this individual may become energized to use the pathways for the new goals. Slowly, without trying to hurry this process, the bereaving person rejoins the "goal game" of life. Little by little, the very pathway and agency thoughts about the deceased loved one that defined the nature of the mourning process are supplanted by new hopeful thoughts.

In this process, it is important to emphasize that *any one* of the three components of hope theory may serve as a catalyst to help the mourning person. Above, I have described the scenario wherein the mourning person establishes new goals, and the associated pathways and agency thoughts naturally follow. Just as likely, however, the mourner may obtain a surge of agentic thought, and by necessity this mental energy will have goals as its target, as well as the requisite pathways to get to those goals. Or, the mourning person may achieve heightened pathway thinking, which also must be attached to a goal, and will need to be fueled by agentic thought. My point is that the three components of hopeful thinking—goals, agency, and pathways—are so intertwined that the elicitation of any one should ignite the entire process of hopeful thought (see Snyder, 1994, for further discussion of this "ripple effect").

As the adaptive forces of hopeful thought increasingly fill the mind of the mourning person, it is only a matter of time until that person will pass out of the bereavement stage and reinitiate the activities of life. Just as it is natural to shut down the hopeful thinking during the early stage of the bereavement process, so too is it likely that hopeful thoughts eventually will re-emerge. Nolen-Hoeksema's findings (see Chapter 6) eloquently make this latter point. Elsewhere, I have written that, "There is an ebb and flow to hopeful thinking. We live in cycles where we hope, experience a loss or losses of some magnitude, and then over time raise our hopeful thinking once again. . . . This cycle mirrors the message in the Egyptian mythology of the phoenix. This legendary bird was said to live for years flying over the Arabian Desert, whereafter it crashed to the ground consumed by flames, only to rise again from its own ashes" (Snyder, 1996, p. 15). As such, bereavement is not a maladaptive process to be ignored or hurried. Instead, it is a crucial process that prepares people to hope again. Indeed, Nolen-Hoeksema's take-home message is that most persons come out of the bereavement process as stronger, more resilient people. In this spirit, I would close with a hope mandala: "Loss is our lot, but endless agony is not."

REFERENCES

Davis, C.G., Nolen-Hoeksema, S., & Larson, J. (In press). Making sense of loss and growing from the experience: Two construals of meaning. *Journal of Personality and Social Psychology.*

Frankl, V.E. (1992). *Man's search for meaning: An introduction to logotherapy* (4th ed.). Boston: Beacon.

Irving, L.M., Snyder, C.R., & Crowson, J.J., Jr. (1998). Hope and the negotiation of cancer facts by college students. *Journal of Personality, 66,* 198–214.

Little, B.R. (1989). Personal projects analysis: Trivial pursuits, magnificent obsessions, and the search for coherence. In D.M. Buss & N. Cantor (Eds.), *Personality psychology: Recent trends and emerging directions* (pp. 15–31). New York: Springer-Verlag.

Nolen-Hoeksema, S., & Larson, J. (2000). *Coping with loss.* Mahwah, NJ: Erlbaum.

Scheier, M.F., & Carver, C.S. (1992). Effects of optimism on psychological and physical well-being: Theoretical overview and empirical update. *Cognitive Therapy and Research, 16,* 201–228.

Snyder, C.R. (1994). *The psychology of hope: You can get there from here.* New York: Free Press.

Snyder, C.R. (1996). To hope, to lose, and hope again. *Journal of Personal and Interpersonal Loss, 1,* 3–16.

Snyder, C.R. (1998). A case for hope in pain, loss, and suffering. In J.H. Harvey, J. Omarzu, & E. Miller (Eds.), *Perspectives on loss: A sourcebook* (pp. 63–79). Washington, DC: Taylor & Francis, Ltd.

Snyder, C.R., Cheavens, J., & Michael, S.T. (1999). Hoping. In Snyder, C.R. (Ed.), *Coping: The psychology of what works* (pp. 205–231). New York: Oxford University Press.

Snyder, C.R., Cheavens, J., & Sympson, S. (1997). Hope: An individual motive for social commerce. *Group Dynamics: Theory, Research, and Practice, 1,* 1–12.

Snyder, C.R., Harris, C., Anderson, J.R., Holleran, S.A., Irving, L.M., Sigmon,

S.T., Yoshinobu, L., Gibb, J., Langelle, C., & Harney, P. (1991). The will and the ways: Development and validation of individual differences measure of hope. *Journal of Personality and Social Psychology, 60,* 570–585.

Snyder, C.R., LaPointe, A.B., Crowson J.J., Jr., & Early, S. (1998). Preferences of high- and low-hope people for self-referential feedback. *Cognition and Emotion, 12*(6), 807–823.

Snyder, C.R., Sympson, S., Michael, S., & Cheavens, J. (In press). The optimism and hope constructs: Variants on a positive expectancy theme. In E.C. Chang (Ed.), *Optimism and pessimism.* Washington, DC: American Psychological Association.

Snyder, C.R., Sympson, S.C., Ybasco, F.C., Borders, T.F., Babyak, M.A., & Higgins, R.L. (1996). Development and validation of the State Hope Scale. *Journal of Personality and Social Psychology, 2,* 321–335.

ACKNOWLEDGMENTS

Thanks are extended to Jennifer Cheavens, Beth Dinoff, Jane Gillham, and Susie Sympson for comments on an earlier version of this manuscript.

Section C. Physical Health

✦

✦ CHAPTER 8 ✦

Optimistic Explanatory Style and Health

Christopher Peterson

FOR TWENTY YEARS, my work as a psychologist has been guided by the attributional reformulation of the learned helplessness model, as proposed by Abramson, Seligman, and Teasdale (1978). Although Seligman's learned helplessness tradition began with an interest in how people and animals respond to uncontrollable aversive events, its significance lies in the light shed on failures of adaptation involving passivity. Like any fruitful perspective, this research has led us to ask questions not originally envisioned. I would like to focus specifically on investigating how and why an optimistic view of the causes of bad events is associated with good health and long life.

GENERAL ISSUES

First, I would like to address some issues of definition, measurement, and research design. None of these matters is cut and dried, and the validity of my conclusions rests on the convergence of studies that resolved these matters in somewhat different ways.

Defining Health and Illness

Physical health and illness prove as difficult to define and thus to measure as the most diffuse of psychological constructs. No single and simple definition of physical well-being is adequate. Rather, a number of factors counts toward the judgment of whether or not an individual is ill, but most are neither necessary nor sufficient:

- general complaints about feeling ill
- specific symptoms such as shortness of breath
- identifiable damage to the body
- presence of germs
- impairment of daily activities
- a short as opposed to a long life

These factors may not coincide with one another. Someone might feel fine but harbor all sorts of germs; another might be free of germs but feel poorly; and yet another might live a long but impaired life or a short but vigorous one.

In making sense of health psychology research, we must understand just how physical health and illness are measured. A tendency exists to regard "hard" measures of health and illness—those based on physical tests—as the most valid, but this bias is not warranted. Biological measures of illness, such as the presence of germs, are no more basic than psychological measures, such as a person's general sense of well-being or the degree to which he or she can lead an active life.

Designing Studies

The ideal investigation of the psychological precursors of health and illness, including optimism, should satisfy procedural criteria such as these:

1. *The research design must be longitudinal.* Research participants must be followed over time. Merely showing a contemporaneous association between psychological states and physical well-being leaves the direction of the implied effect unanswered. It may be that illness or health determines the psychological state. Or perhaps another factor gives rise to both the psychological state and health status.

2. *The longitudinal design must span enough time for changes in health to take place.* This may require several years or even decades, and because we are exploring new territory, the right time frame remains uncertain. We must, therefore, be leery of researchers who report "no results" from their studies when trying to link psychological states with health and illness. The researchers may have simply overlooked the optimal time span.

3. *The initial health status of the research participants must be known when the investigation begins.* It is not interesting to demonstrate that sick people stay sick, while healthy people stay healthy. Many researchers start with participants' current health status and then try to work backwards to reconstruct what they were like in the first place. This constitutes a reasonable procedure if the distant past can be reconstructed with fidelity—unfortunately, that is not always the case. People distort their past, innocently or otherwise, and may retrospectively make better sense of what ensued than the facts warrant. Sick people may tell a story that rationalizes their sickness, as healthy people may rationalize their health. When we see a story about a centenarian, the person always attributes his or her longevity to something: eating yogurt, drinking cranberry wine, or staying busy. While these are pleasing accounts, they hardly represent scientific explanations.

4. *An adequate number of research participants must be studied.* Links between psychological states and illness, if and when they exist, are apt to be subtle in nature and modest in strength. Only with a large number of research participants can patterns be discerned and potential confounds ruled out. Case studies of single individuals, no matter how striking, can be ambiguous precisely on this score.

5. *The psychological states of interest must be well-defined and able to be measured in a reliable and valid fashion.* Researchers should avoid, in particular, measures that are contaminated by a person's health status, which means they use one aspect of a participant's health to predict another aspect. As a result, the measures will be related but prove nothing. This

problem appears in stress research, for instance, where "illness," considered a stressful life event, usually predicts subsequent illness.

6. *Objective measures of health and illness must be made when an investigation begins, as the study proceeds, and at the time it ends.* Health and illness may seem easy for a researcher to ascertain, but remember the ambiguity of health status. Knowing that no criterion of well-being is foolproof, researchers, nonetheless, must settle on a strategy for measuring it. As already emphasized, the various criteria of illness do not perfectly agree. One of the best established findings in twentieth-century epidemiology demonstrates that morbidity and mortality do not perfectly line up once we look separately at males and females: Women have more illnesses than men, but they also live longer (Verbrugge, 1989).

OPTIMISTIC EXPLANATORY STYLE AND HEALTH

To date, there exist several dozen studies that have attempted to establish a correlation between optimism, rendered as explanatory style (measured with the Attribution Style Questionnaire [ASQ] or the Content Analysis of Verbatim Explanations [CAVE]), and physical well-being. The detailed description of two such studies follows.

Establishing the Link

The first substantive investigation studied 172 undergraduates at Virginia Tech (Peterson, 1988). These individuals completed the ASQ at one point in time, along with a baseline measure of physical health (i.e., the number of days during the past month in which at least one symptom of illness had been experienced) and the Beck Depression Inventory (BDI). Thirty days later, 170 of these subjects again completed the measure of health. And one year later, 146 of these subjects reported how many doctor visits they had made during the previous twelve months for diagnosis or treatment of an illness.

The vast majority of subjects who fell ill reported cold or flu symptoms. Pessimistic explanatory style predicted both the numbers of days ill (after thirty days) and the number of doctor visits (after twelve months). These correlations held when the baseline measure of illness was statistically controlled, and when scores on the BDI were held constant. Explanatory style was related to health, and in this study, several likely third variables were ruled out, notably depressive symptoms.

Next we undertook a 35-year longitudinal study, assessing with content analysis the explanatory style of ninety-nine men who completed open-ended questionnaires in 1946 about their difficult war-time experiences (Peterson, Seligman, & Vaillant, 1988). At that time, the subjects were approximately 25 years of age. Available for each subject, at subsequent five-year intervals, were ratings of overall health, based on a physician's exam abetted with medical tests.

Pessimistic explanatory style predicted poor health from ages 45 through 60, even when initial measures of physical health and emotional well-being (taken at age 25) were held constant. The most robust correlation occurred at age 45, suggesting that in middle adulthood psychological factors from earlier life most critically determine someone's physical well-being. This conclusion, strengthened by more detailed analyses, shows that explanatory style predicted worsening of health for subjects between ages 40 and 45. Finally, the data indicated that the smoking habit was more likely among pessimists than optimists, suggesting one plausible link between explanatory style and poor health.

Taken together, the results of these and subsequent investigations of explanatory style and health converge impressively (see reviews by Michaels, Michaels, & Peterson, 1997; Peterson, 1995, 1999; Peterson & Bossio, 1991, 1993, in press; Peterson, Maier, & Seligman, 1993; Peterson & Seligman, 1987). Optimism predicts good health operationalized in a number of ways: from self-report to physician ratings of general well-being, to doctor visits, to survival time following a heart attack, to immunological efficiency, to successful completion of rehabilitation programs, and finally to longevity. Usually stability and globality of explanatory style relate to measures of health, not internality.

Questions about the Link

How strong is the association between optimism and good health? Most of the relevant studies report correlation coefficients in the .20 to .30 range, which are moderate in size and typical of correlations in psychological research. Research participants included not only males and females, some initially healthy and others initially quite ill, but also adults across the life span. Many of these studies were longitudinal, spanning mere weeks to almost five decades. And at least some of these longitudinal studies statistically controlled for initial levels of health and potential confounds involving tendencies to complain.

Optimism apparently can impact health at a number of junctures. It can make the initial onset of illness less likely; it can minimize the severity of illness; it can speed recovery; it can make relapse less likely. Most of the relevant studies, however, by virtue of rather stark correlational designs, do not allow exact conclusions about when health is impacted. Perhaps the cognates of optimism affect different aspects of physical well-being. Certainly, future investigations of a more fine-grained nature are indicated.

To date, research raises several critical questions. First, can a lifetime of good health be encouraged by the early cultivation of optimism? Gillham, Reivich, Jaycox, and Seligman (1995) have begun an intervention program that involves teaching grade school children to be more optimistic. Results to date suggest that optimism training makes subsequent episodes of depression less likely, and work in progress is investigating whether such training also affects physical well-being.

Research raises a second critical question: Will optimistic ways of thinking, acquired once an individual falls ill, boost good health? Again, studies of optimism and depression suggest that this question is worth pursuing. Cognitive therapy that targets negative ways of thinking alleviates depression and prevents its recurrence (Seligman et al., 1988). By implication, cognitive therapy for the seriously ill might pay health dividends.

Certainly, the most basic question that arises from research into optimism and health involves the mechanisms linking the two. In earlier writing, I suggested that the link is overdetermined and sketched a number of plausible routes (Peterson & Bossio, 1991). For example, there may be an *immunological pathway*. Kamen-Siegel, Rodin, Seligman, and Dwyer (1991) showed that optimism correlates positively with a vigorous immune system response to an antigen challenge. And several other researchers have looked at how explanatory style is linked to the progression of AIDS. Results here are mixed, but indications are that optimism predicts survival time, and that this effect is mediated, in part, by immunological factors (e.g., Blomkvist et al., 1994; Caumartin, Joseph, & Gillespie, 1993; Rabkin, Remien, Katoff, & Williams, 1993; Tomakowsky, Lumley, Markowitz, & Frank, 1996; but see Bofinger, Marguth, Pankofer, Seidl, & Ermann, 1993; Chuang, Jason, Pajurkova, & Gill, 1992).

There may also be an *emotional pathway* between optimism and health. An extensive research literature has shown optimism to be incompatible with depression (Sweeney, Anderson, & Bailey, 1986), and other studies have linked depression to poor health and early death. At least part of this latter path may be immunological (Schleifer, Keller, Siris, Davis, & Stein, 1985), and we begin to see the complexity involved in explaining why optimism and health are associated.

Probably several *cognitive pathways* exist between optimism and health as well. Optimism does not constitute an isolated belief like an obscure theology, but rather comprises part of a complex knowledge system that can impact physical well-being in numerous ways. Dykema, Bergbower, and Peterson (1995), for example, showed that individuals with an optimistic explanatory style see the world as less hassle-filled than do their pessimistic counterparts; this tendency, in turn, is linked to better health.

Peterson and de Avila (1995), for another example, found that an optimistic explanatory style is associated with the belief that good health can be "controlled" (i.e., maintained and promoted). Indeed, their research showed that an optimistic explanatory style correlates positively with what has been called an optimistic bias: seeing oneself as less likely than others to fall (Weinstein, 1989). However, this correlation was accounted for by the belief that one was able to do things to reduce risk.

Another explanation of why optimistic thinking relates to physical well-being points to a *social pathway*. People with a pessimistic explanatory style are often socially isolated (Anderson & Arnoult, 1985), and social isolation is a consistent predictor of poor health (Cobb, 1976). In general terms, the individual's social context can set the stage for the optimism-health link. Sagan (1987) formulated the intriguing argument that the dramatic increase in life expectancy, present in the Western world over the centuries, was due not to breakthroughs in medical or public health practices, but instead to cultural diffusion of the originally radical notion that an individual is a discrete self, who is able to affect the world. Once the idea of individual agency was invented, legitimized, and disseminated, the findings discussed here became possible.

Although I believe that the link between optimism and health is complexly determined, the most typical and most robust mechanism is a mundane *behavioral pathway*. Peterson (1988) found that an optimistic explanatory style was associated with a variety of "healthy" practices: exercising, drinking in moderation, avoiding fatty foods, and the like. Lin and Peterson (1990) and Peterson, Colvin, and Lin (1992) similarly found that people with an optimistic explanatory style were more likely than those with a pessimistic explanatory style to respond to colds with appropriate actions: staying home, resting, and consuming fluids.

Our most recent study of optimistic explanatory style and physical well-being investigated these variables among participants in the Terman Life-Cycle Study (Peterson, Seligman, Yurko, Martin, & Friedman, 1998). This investigation began in 1921–1922, when most of the 1,528 participants were in public school. The average birth date for children in the sample was 1910, with a standard deviation of 4 years. Most of the children were preadolescents when first studied; those still living are now in their eighties. Data were collected prospectively, without any knowledge of eventual health or longevity. The original sample has been followed ever since, with attrition (except by death) of less than 10%. For most of those who have died (about 50% of males and 35% of females as of 1991), year of death and cause of death are known.

In 1936 and 1940, the participants completed open-ended questionnaires about difficult life events. Their responses included causal explanations, which we content analyzed for explanatory style with the CAVE technique. We determined the associations between dimensions of explanatory style on the one hand and time of death and cause of death on the other.

Among the 1,182 participants for whom explanatory style scores were available, mortality information was known for 1,179. Among this group, the numbers of deaths as of 1991 were 148 from cancer (85 men, 63 women); 159 from cardiovascular disease (109 men, 50 women); 57 from accidents or violence (40 men, 17 women); 87 from other (known) causes (50 men, 37 women); and, 38 from unknown causes (24 men, 14 women).

To investigate the association between the dimensions of explanatory style and mortality (through 1991), Cox Proportional Hazards regression analyses were used and checked with logistic regression analyses. When all three attributional dimensions were examined simultaneously, only globality was significantly associated with mortality risk. Results from the logistic regressions (predicting a dichotomous variable of survival to at least age 65 versus dying before age 65) similarly found that only the odds ratio for globality was significant.

Next we investigated whether globality was differentially related to specific causes of death by comparing Gompertz models. When comparing a model with both sex and globality as predictors, but constraining the effects of globality to predict equally across all causes of death with an unconstrained model (in which globality was allowed to predict differentially to separate causes of death), we found that the unconstrained model fit better than the constrained model. This finding was also obtained when participants who did not survive until at least 1945 were eliminated.

A closer examination revealed that globality best predicted deaths by accident or violence, and those from unknown causes. The risk ratios associated with other causes were greater than one, but not significantly above chance. As we have argued, globality taps a style of catastrophizing about bad events, expecting them to occur across diverse situations. Such a style can be hazardous, as the present results show, presumably because of its association with passive coping, social estrangement, and risky decision-making (Peterson et al., 1993). Deaths by accident or violence may result from a fatalistic lifestyle, one more likely to be followed by males than by females. Perhaps deaths due to unknown causes may similarly reflect an incautious lifestyle.

Accidental deaths like these are not random. "Being in the wrong place at the wrong time" may be the result of an incautious and fatalistic lifestyle, entwined not only with pessimism but also with the male gender role. This study did not indicate what our deceased research participants were doing when they died accidentally or violently, yet we strongly suspect that their behavior was somehow implicated, if only by affecting the settings they habitually entered or not (Buss, 1987).

Explanatory Style and Accidents

I have recently conducted three studies, more modest in scope, that follow up on the implications of the Terman investigation (Peterson et al., 1998). Can explanatory style be linked not only to fatal "accidents" but to more mundane mishaps as well? In the first study, 140 college students at Virginia Tech completed the ASQ and a measure of depressive symptoms; they returned four weeks later, when they described the four worst events that had happened to them in the past month. The vast majority of the students reported disappointing grades on tests and papers or romantic frustrations and difficulties. But 10% of the research participants described traumatic accidents—sprained ankles, poked eyes, motor vehicle collisions, and the like.

Individuals with an optimistic explanatory style (those who favored unstable and specific explanations for bad events) were less likely to be among the "accident" group than were individuals with a pessimistic explanatory style. These results held even when initial depression scores were held constant statistically, suggesting that the accident reports were not just a by-product of dysphoric complaining.

In the second study, 440 introductory psychology students at the University of Michigan completed a variety of questionnaires the first day of class, including the question: "How many accidents have you experienced in the past 24 months that required medical attention?" (This is standard phrasing from epidemiological surveys of traumatic accidents.) In addition, they completed an abbreviated version of the ASQ, asking them how they usually explained bad events: with stable (versus unstable) causes and with global (versus specific) causes. Because these ratings were entwined, they were combined into a single hopelessness score. Also available for the research participants was information pertinent to other variables previously linked to accident-proneness: gender, ethnicity, handedness, depression, anger, and impulsivity.

These variables were not only included in a multiple regression formula to predict the number of reported mishaps, but also were entered in blocks, with the composite explanatory style score as the final predictor examined. The zero-order correlations were modest but more or less replicated what is known about risk factors for so-called accidents. Explanatory style remained a significant predictor even when all the other variables had been entered. In essence, individuals who explained bad events in a pessimistic fashion were more likely to have experienced recent accidents requiring medical attention.

These two studies are consistent with the Terman study, suggesting that explanatory style is a risk factor for mundane mishaps. By extension, a lifetime of mishaps puts someone at risk someday for a lethal accident. The final investigation in this series attempted to discern possible mediators between explanatory style and traumatic injuries. The research participants were fifty-nine male students from introductory psychology classes at the University of Michigan. They completed the ASQ, the BDI, and reported on the number of accidents they had experienced in the past twenty-four months that required medical attention. Also included among the questionnaires were measures of neuroticism, extraversion, and sensation seeking, which some researchers have linked to accident-proneness.

Individuals who favored unstable and specific explanations for bad events were less likely to have experienced recent accidents, and these results held even when the other variables were controlled. In searching for possible mediators leading from explanatory style to accidents, I realized that the sensation-seeking measure, as a whole, was probably *not* useful for this purpose. Arguably, it mixed items that put individuals at risk for mishaps (like a preference for driving fast or drinking) with items that clearly do not (like a preference for crunchy foods). As a result, I created a new measure by choosing just the former items; the resulting scale can be identified as a "preference for dangerous activities" measure, which, in effect, taps an individual's desire to do all the things that our mothers warned us not to do.

A path analysis revealed that this factor mediated the link between explanatory style and accidents. Individuals with an optimistic explanatory style had a preference for a prudent lifestyle and, in turn, experienced few traumatic mishaps. Their pessimistic counterparts preferred a more dangerous lifestyle and then paid the price in the form of accidental injuries.

This I believe to be an interesting finding, but a puzzling one nonetheless. "Pessimism" as we usually conceive it entails passivity and indifference. One might conclude that a pessimistic person would be unlikely to get out of harm's way, but this finding suggests something additional —that pessimists might actively seek out situations in which danger lurks. Why this is the case seems unclear, but I am reminded of Baumeister's (1990) argument that unhappy individuals are motivated to "escape from the self," and perhaps our pessimistic research participants did so by putting themselves in the fast lane and thereby overwhelming their self-awareness.

In retrospect, I wish females had been included in the sample, along with measures of additional strategies that people use to cloud awareness. Pessimistic males may "escape" by drinking and engaging in other blatantly dangerous activities, whereas pessimistic females may do so by eating too much or not at all—alternatively, pessimistic females may ruminate and become depressed (Nolen-Hoeksema, 1987). A more general issue here focuses on explanatory style that has been linked to a variety of outcomes—like depression, illness, and accidents—that show marked sex differences in prevalence, yet there is no satisfactory evidence that men and women differ, on average, with respect to explanatory style. Theory and research, to date, have not grappled with the possibility that optimistic and pessimistic explanatory styles set into operation different psychological cascades for men versus women.

Psychology knows a great deal about what can be termed intentional trauma: people perpetrating injuries, psychological and physical, upon other people (cf. Herman, 1992). However, the psychological investigation of unintentional trauma remains relatively neglected, even though "accidents" are the leading cause of death in the United States today among individuals under the age of 45. They comprise the third leading cause of overall death, trailing only heart disease and cancer, but even in comparison to these illnesses, which afflict mainly an older population, unintentional trauma results in more years of lost productivity. It would seem that any interventions that can decrease the likelihood of unintentional trauma would be immensely valuable, to individuals and society alike. For example, Shatté, Gillham, and Reivich (see Chapter 11) present a program of optimism training for school children. Although designed to prevent depression, this program might additionally prevent traumatic mishaps by encouraging young people to decatastrophize.

CONCLUSIONS

Optimistic thinking is linked to good health, but two important conditions must be satisfied. First, a person's optimism must lead him or her to act in a vigorous and sustained fashion: behavior constitutes a critical link in the process of attaining and sustaining physical well-being. Second, the behavior encouraged by optimism must have a realistic link to health. A casual reading of the popular literature on health and optimism might lead one to conclude that good health exists exclusively in the mind, but thoughts and beliefs must be situated within the person, and the person must be situated within the world (cf. Chopra, 1993; Cousins, 1981; Peale, 1952; Siegel, 1988).

Modern medical practice has become so specialized and so narrowly biological that patients feel dealt out of the process of maintaining their own health. No wonder alternative medicine is thriving in the United States today (Eisenberg et al., 1993), just as it did about a century ago when conventional medicine was in a similar crisis (Weil, 1988). Alternative approaches address the whole person: thoughts, feelings, and behaviors. They allow the person to exercise choice and to sustain hope. Conventional medicine, in contrast, dismisses the role of psychological factors in health as placebo (that is, not real).

Many health professionals (myself included) tend to focus on the quantity of life: how long people live and the degree to which they are free from disease. The quality of life—how people live for as long or as short as they do—is surely as important. Living well is sometimes referred to as wellness, a concept that cannot be captured by longevity or freedom from disease (Barsky, 1988). Wellness involves a zest for ongoing life, a fulfilling career, and satisfactory relationships with family members and friends. When we consider psychological influences on health, we should examine how psychology can enrich our quality of life (Seeman, 1989). Attention to optimism certainly ensures a significant way to do so.

REFERENCES

Abramson, L.Y., Seligman, M.E.P., & Teasdale, J.D. (1978). Learned helplessness in humans: Critique and reformulation. *Journal of Abnormal Psychology, 87,* 49–74.

Anderson, C.A., & Arnoult, L.H. (1985). Attributional style and everyday problems in living: Depression, loneliness, and shyness. *Social Cognition, 3,* 16–35.

Barsky, A.J. (1988). *Worried sick: Our troubled quest for wellness.* Boston: Little, Brown.

Baumeister, R.F. (1990). Suicide as escape from self. *Psychological Review, 97,* 90–113.

Blomkvist, V., Theorell, T., Jonsson, H., Schulman, S., Berntorp, E., & Stiegendal, L. (1994). Coping style in relation to the consumption of factor concentrate in HIV-infected hemophiliacs during the years after their infection became known. *Psychotherapy and Psychosomatics, 61,* 205–210.

Bofinger, F., Marguth, U., Pankofer, R., Seidl, O., & Ermann, M. (1993). Psychosocial aspects of longterm-surviving with AIDS. *International Conference on AIDS, 9,* 878.

Buss, D.M. (1987). Selection, evocation, and manipulation. *Journal of Personality and Social Psychology, 53,* 1214–1221.

Caumartin, S.M., Joseph, J.G., & Gillespie, B. (1993). The relationship between social participation and AIDS survival in the Chicago MACS/CCS cohort. *International Conference on AIDS, 9,* 886.

Chopra, D. (1993). *Ageless body, timeless mind.* New York: Harmony Books.

Chuang, H.T., Jason, G.W., Pajurkova, E.M., & Gill, M.J. (1992). Psychiatric morbidity in patients with HIV infection. *Canadian Journal of Psychiatry, 37,* 109–115.

Cobb, S. (1976). Social support as a moderator of life stress. *Psychosomatic Medicine, 38,* 300–314.

Cousins, N. (1981). *The anatomy of an illness.* New York: Norton.

Dykema, J., Bergbower, K., & Peterson, C. (1995). Pessimistic explanatory style, stress, and illness. *Journal of Social and Clinical Psychology, 14,* 357–371.

Eisenberg, D.M., Kessler, R.C., Foster, C., Norlock, F.E., Calkins, D.R., & Delblanco, T.L. (1993). Unconventional medicine in the United States: Prevalence, costs, and patterns of use. *New England Journal of Medicine, 328,* 246–252.

Gillham, J.E., Reivich, K.J., Jaycox, L.H., & Seligman, M.E.P. (1995). Prevention of depressive symptoms in schoolchildren: Two-year follow-up. *Psychological Science, 6,* 343–351.

Herman, J. (1992). *Trauma and recovery.* New York: Basic Books.

Kamen-Siegel, L., Rodin, J., Seligman, M.E.P., & Dwyer, J. (1991). Explanatory style and cell-mediated immunity. *Health Psychology, 10,* 229–235.

Lin, E.H., & Peterson, C. (1990). Pessimistic explanatory style and response to illness. *Behaviour Research and Therapy, 28,* 243–248.

Michaels, C.E., Michaels, A.J., & Peterson, C. (1997). Motivation and health. In P. Pintrich & M. Maeher (Eds.), *The psychology of motivation* (Vol. 10, pp. 339–374). Greenwich, CT: JAI Press.

Nolen-Hoeksema, S. (1987). Sex differences in unipolar depression: Theory and evidence. *Psychological Bulletin, 101,* 259–282.

Peale, N.V. (1952). *The power of positive thinking.* Englewood Cliffs, NJ: Prentice-Hall.

Peterson, C. (1988). Explanatory style as a risk factor for illness. *Cognitive Therapy and Research, 12,* 117–130.

Peterson, C. (1995). Explanatory style and health. In G.M. Buchanan & M.E.P. Seligman (Eds.), *Explanatory style* (pp. 233–246). Hillsdale, NJ: Erlbaum.

Peterson, C. (1999). Personal control and well-being. In D. Kahneman, E. Diener, & N. Schwarz (Eds.), *Well-being: The foundation of hedonic psychology* (pp. 288–301). New York: Russell Sage.

Peterson, C., & Bossio, L.M. (1991). *Health and optimism.* New York: Free Press.

Peterson, C., & Bossio, L.M. (1993). Healthy attitudes: Optimism, hope, and control. In D. Goleman & J. Gurin (Eds.), *Mind/body medicine: How to use your mind for better health* (pp. 351–366). Yonkers, NY: Consumer Reports Books.

Peterson, C., & Bossio, L.M. (in press). Optimism and physical well-being. In E.C. Chang (Ed.), *Optimism and pessimism.* Washington, DC: American Psychological Association.

Peterson, C., Colvin, D., & Lin, E.H. (1992). Explanatory style and helplessness. *Social Behavior and Personality, 20,* 1–14.

Peterson, C., & de Avila, M.E. (1995). Optimistic explanatory style and the perception of health problems. *Journal of Clinical Psychology, 51,* 128–132.

Peterson, C., Maier, S.F., & Seligman, M.E.P. (1993). *Learned helplessness: A theory for the age of personal control.* New York: Oxford University Press.

Peterson, C., Moon, C.H., Michaels, C.E., Bishop, M.P., Smith, J.S., & Michaels, A.A. (1998). *Explanatory style as a risk factor for traumatic mishaps.* Unpublished manuscript, University of Michigan.

Peterson, C., & Seligman, M.E.P. (1987). Explanatory style and illness. *Journal of Personality, 55,* 237–265.

Peterson, C., Seligman, M.E.P., & Vaillant, G.E. (1988). Pessimistic explanatory style is a risk factor for physical illness: A thirty-five year longitudinal study. *Journal of Personality and Social Psychology, 55,* 23–27.

Peterson, C., Seligman, M.E.P., Yurko, K.H., Martin, L.R., & Friedman, H.S. (1998). Catastrophizing and untimely death. *Psychological Science, 9,* 127–130.

Rabkin, J.G., Remien, R., Katoff, L., & Williams, J.B. (1993). Resilience in adversity among long-term survivors of AIDS. *Hospital and Community Psychiatry, 44,* 162–167.

Sagan, L.A. (1987). *The health of nations: True causes of sickness and well-being.* New York: Basic Books.

Schleifer, S.J., Keller, S.E., Siris, S.G., Davis, K.L., & Stein, M. (1985). Depression and immunity. *Archives of General Psychiatry, 42,* 129–133.

Seeman, J. (1989). Toward a model of positive health. *American Psychologist, 44,* 1099–1109.

Seligman, M.E.P., Castellon, C., Cacciola, J., Schulman, P., Luborsky, L., Ollove, M., & Downing, R. (1988). Explanatory style change during cognitive therapy for unipolar depression. *Journal of Abnormal Psychology, 97,* 13–18.

Siegel, B.S. (1988). *Love, medicine, and miracles.* New York: Perennial.

Sweeney, P.D., Anderson, K., & Bailey, S. (1986). Attributional style in depression: A meta-analytic review. *Journal of Personality and Social Psychology, 50,* 974–991.

Tomakowsky, J., Lumley, M.A., Markowitz, N., & Frank, C. (1996). The relationships of optimistic explanatory style and dispositional optimism to health in HIV-infected men. Unpublished manuscript, Wayne State University.

Verbrugge, L.M. (1989). Recent, present, and future health of American adults. *Annual Review of Public Health, 10,* 333–361.

Weil, A. (1988). *Health and healing* (Rev. ed.). Boston: Houghton Mifflin.

Weinstein, N.D. (1989). Optimistic biases about personal risks. *Science, 246,* 1232–1233.

✦ CHAPTER 9 ✦

What I *Do* Know Won't Hurt Me: Optimism, Attention to Negative Information, Coping, and Health

Lisa G. Aspinwall and Susanne M. Brunhart

Do optimistic beliefs help or hurt people who are confronted with negative events and information? That is, does optimism help people manage their problems, or does it lead people to ignore or minimize their problems, putting them at risk for worse problems over time? This chapter reviews a program of research designed to answer this question. We begin with an introduction to dispositional optimism and a brief review of its prospective link to good mental and physical health. We then consider several alternative explanations for these benefits, as well as some hypothesized liabilities of optimistic beliefs. In the body of the chapter, we focus on three studies designed to test the benefits of optimism and to rule out some of these alternative explanations and potential liabilities. The chapter concludes with a discussion of the functional implications of optimism for coping with stress, as well as other kinds of problem solving.

INTRODUCTION TO DISPOSITIONAL OPTIMISM

Generalized Positive Expectancies and the Life Orientation Test

Unlike optimistic explanatory style, which refers to typical ways of understanding the causes and implications of events (Gillham, Shatté, Reivich, & Seligman, in press; Peterson & Seligman, 1984), dispositional optimism refers to people's generalized positive expectancies about events in the future (Scheier & Carver, 1985). Such expectancies are measured with the Life Orientation Test (LOT), which consists of eight items, such as "In uncertain times, I usually expect the best," and "If something can go wrong for me, it will" (Scheier & Carver, 1985; see Scheier, Carver, & Bridges, 1994, for a revised 6-item version). It is important to note that such items refer to people's expectations about future events in general, not in such specific domains as health, wealth, or romance. Domain-specific beliefs—optimism about one's health, for example—have been increasingly studied (Aspinwall & Brunhart, 1996; Taylor et al., 1992; see Armor & Taylor, 1998, for a comprehensive review), but will not be considered in detail here.

Optimism is sometimes confused with beliefs about personal control or agency. A belief in personal control or agency typically refers to a person's beliefs that he or she can bring about desired outcomes through his or her own efforts (see Bandura, 1986, and Skinner, 1996, for reviews), whereas optimism is simply the belief that good future outcomes will occur (Carver & Scheier, 1990). Optimism may, therefore, have many sources. It may be based on one's sense of competence or learned ways of coping (see related work on hope, Snyder, 1994), but it may also be based in spiritual beliefs, religious faith, and other beliefs in powers outside the self.

As a widely used measure of dispositional optimism, the LOT has been subjected to several tests of discriminant validity, test-retest reliability, and internal structure. While there is some disagreement about whether optimism and pessimism are endpoints of a single continuum or two separate constructs with distinct effects (see Marshall, Wortman, Kusulas, Hervig, & Vickers, 1992; Scheier et al., 1994), there is increasing consensus about the relation of dispositional optimism to other constructs. Specifically, the LOT has been shown to have good discriminant validity with respect to constructs such as locus of control, psychological adjustment, self-esteem, neuroticism, and concurrent positive and negative mood (Scheier & Carver, 1985; Scheier et al., 1994; see also Aspinwall & Taylor, 1992).

The Role of Optimism in Self-Regulation

Self-regulation is the process through which people control and direct their own actions in the service of meeting their goals (Fiske & Taylor, 1991). Optimism plays a central role in current theories of self-regulation. According to Carver and Scheier (1981, 1990), optimism influences self-regulation when people encounter difficulties in making progress toward their goals. When their progress is impeded, people reassess their expectations of meeting their goals. If their expectations are favorable, people usually continue their goal-directed efforts. If their expectations are unfavorable, they are predicted to disengage from the goal. Depending on the situation, disengagement can be behavioral (the person leaves the situation) or mental (the person gives up the goal and stops thinking about it, even if he cannot physically leave the situation).

Dispositional optimism is thought to play a central role in decisions about persistence versus disengagement, because people who are optimistic typically make more favorable appraisals of their expected success at meeting goals and so are more likely to persist in pursuit of their goals. In this way, optimism plays a critical role in the initiation and maintenance of goal-directed behavior. Although this tendency to see things favorably has led some researchers to speculate that optimists may be vulnerable to persisting on lost causes, there is increasing evidence that optimists may be more adept at deciding which goals are worth their effort and which are not (see Aspinwall & Richter, 1999; Aspinwall, Richter, & Hoffman, in press, for discussion).

Benefits of Dispositional Optimism

Like optimistic explanatory style, dispositional optimism has an impressive track record in predicting good psychological and physical health outcomes (for reviews, see Chang, in press; Scheier & Carver, 1992; Scheier, Carver, & Bridges, in press; Taylor & Aspinwall, 1996). Increasing evidence from prospective studies suggests that the psychological benefits associated with dispositional optimism may be mediated by more active and less avoidant ways of coping with stress (Aspinwall & Taylor, 1992; Carver et al., 1993). That is, optimists report more active efforts to solve their problems and report fewer efforts to avoid thinking about or confronting their problems. Such effects have been obtained for a wide range of stressors, including adjustment to college (Aspinwall & Taylor, 1992), recovery from surgery (Carver et al., 1993), and emigration from East to West Germany (Jerusalem, 1993).

Thus far, these results may be easily understood in terms of the self-regulatory processes described earlier. Optimists, because they typically have more favorable expectations of success, pursue their goals more actively. Such persistence is likely to pay off in terms of better outcomes in most cases. This line of reasoning suggests that optimistic beliefs should be adaptive most of the time. There are, however, two major challenges to this conclusion that served as the impetus for the present research. First, there are several alternative explanations for the benefits of optimism, most of which cannot be adequately tested in self-report studies of coping and well-being. Second, there may be some potential liabilities of optimistic beliefs, especially when people encounter situations they cannot change or situations that are doomed to failure, no matter what their efforts. We will consider these two possibilities in some detail because they raise fundamental questions about the nature of optimism and its relation to good mental and physical health. We will then describe a program of research devoted to examining these alternative explanations and gaining further insight into the role optimism may play in coping with negative events and information.

ALTERNATIVE EXPLANATIONS FOR THE BENEFITS OF DISPOSITIONAL OPTIMISM

In this section, we will describe several potential alternative explanations for the benefits of optimism. Our focus will be on the challenge of developing ways to test how optimism "works" while reducing or eliminating some of these alternative explanations. We should note that many of the alternative explanations considered here apply to many other individual difference variables implicated in coping with stress; however, there are some concerns that are particularly acute for the study of optimism.

Positivity Bias: Optimism is "Yay-Saying"

The simplest alternative explanation of the benefits of optimism is that optimists' self-reports of better adjustment may represent "yay-saying." That is, some critics suggest that it should not be surprising that people who report favorable expectations about the future also report good psychological adjustment, because favorable responses to questionnaires would be positively correlated with each other among people who are predisposed to respond affirmatively. In this view, the benefits of optimism are not real, but instead a reflection of a *positivity bias* in reporting. Unfortunately, even the most rigorous prospective study of people coping with chronic illness, surgery, or other stressors cannot muster evidence against this alternative explanation because most measures in a typical study are self-reports of adjustment, distress, and the like, which are inherently subject to positivity and other reporting biases. It is possible to use measures of positive mood or social desirability to control statistically for the influence of such biases on the relation between optimism and some other measure (see, e.g., Scheier & Carver, 1985), but it is impossible to rule out such reporting biases completely when all critical study outcomes are self-reported.

One solution to this problem has been to examine the relation of optimism to more objective measures of health and adjustment, such as the number of days to return to work and other activities following surgery. To date, the results of studies using these more objective outcomes have been consistent with those of self-report measures of adjustment (see, e.g., Scheier et al., 1989; Taylor & Aspinwall, 1996).

Differences in the Objective Life Experience of Optimists and Pessimists

A second possibility is that the reported benefits of optimism may be due to *differences in objective life experience*. In this view, optimists may report better outcomes, not because they cope better, but because their problems were less severe from the start. If optimists are usually better off to start with, their superior outcomes at some later point do not provide useful information (see Dohrenwend, Dohrenwend, Dodson, &

Shrout, 1984, and Rhodewalt & Zone, 1989, for discussion). If this is the case, optimistic beliefs may simply be a marker or proxy for favorable life experiences or good prior health, and thus can tell us little about adjustment to adversity.

This argument is difficult to refute on the basis of correlational survey studies of adjustment to stress, because there is no way to prove that all respondents experienced the same stressful event or experienced it to the same degree. Because it would be unethical to subject research participants to a major life stressor as part of an experiment, a definitive causal answer to the question of how optimists and pessimists may differ in their approaches to major life stressors remains out of reach. At present, the best evidence against the hypothesis that optimists report better adjustment because they have easier lives comes from research examining the role of optimism in coping with life-threatening illnesses, such as HIV infection, breast cancer, and heart disease (Carver et al., 1993; Taylor et al., 1992; Scheier et al., 1989). In these studies, optimists who are in the midst of or recovering from an extremely stressful life event or chronic stressor report superior coping and adjustment. These findings present a convincing argument against the "easy-life" hypothesis; however, they are not, as we will review shortly, immune to other alternative explanations of the benefits of optimism.

Negative Affectivity: The Benefits of Optimism Are Due to the Absence of Negative Emotions

A third alternative explanation concerns the possibility that the "active ingredient" in optimism is not the presence of positive beliefs about the future or the typically positive state that accompanies optimism, but the absence of negative beliefs or states. That is, there may be no benefits to positive thinking; instead, there may be substantial costs of negative thinking. According to this argument, optimism is not the real variable of interest in understanding psychological well-being and physical health; instead, it is a marker for the lack of negative states that are really responsible for these effects. One particular set of negative tendencies has received extensive research attention. *Negative affectivity*, which is the propensity to experience negative emotions such as anxiety, hostility, and depression (Watson & Clark, 1984), consistently shows a strong inverse relation to dispositional optimism and has been identified by some researchers as the real active ingredient in the relation of optimism to better self-reported health. In some studies, when measures of negative affectivity are considered in the analyses, the predictive relation between optimism and self-reported physical symptoms disappears, and the relation between negative affectivity and symptoms remains robust (Smith, Pope, Rhodewalt & Poulton, 1989; Scheier et al., 1994). These findings have led some people to suggest that optimism has no distinct effects apart from its association with negative affectivity. It is important to note, however, that the link between optimism and other kinds of outcomes, such as coping and well-being, does not appear to be similarly confounded (Scheier et al., 1994; see Taylor & Aspinwall, 1996, for discussion). That is, there appear to be some outcomes that are associated with optimism that cannot be explained by the presence or absence of negative states.

These conflicting findings highlight the importance of determining which benefits of optimism are due to the presence of positive beliefs and which are due to the absence of negative beliefs (see Aspinwall, 1998, and Marshall et al., 1992, for discussion). Finally, it is important to emphasize that all individual differences measures, including negative affectivity, share this interpretational difficulty; that is, it is always possible that their effects are due to their association with some other, unmeasured variable that is also correlated with the outcomes of interest. In the present studies, we will examine the relation of optimism to outcomes, while statistically controlling for negative affectivity, but it is important to note that such controls are inherently imperfect for two reasons. One can never be sure one has controlled for all potential confounds in the relation of optimism to outcomes, and one's ability to control for such confounds is limited by the reliability of the measures used.

Optimism in the Face of Adversity Represents Denial and Other Defensive Processes

A final alternative explanation—and one that is particularly acute in the study of optimism—is *denial*. We mentioned earlier that optimists report coping better with life-threatening illnesses, such as HIV infection and cancer. These reports can be interpreted as denial; that is, when optimistic people report adjusting well to life-threatening illnesses, they may simply be denying the gravity of their situations. In this case, optimists' self-reports of superior psychological adjustment in the face of adversity may not only be false, but they may also be potentially dangerous because they may be the product of defensive processing of negative events and information. Denial has been linked to poor long-term adjustment to illness (see Taylor & Aspinwall, 1990, for review), and is also likely to compromise one's ability to anticipate and prepare for incipient stressors (Aspinwall & Taylor, 1997; Perloff, 1983; Weinstein, 1984). Additionally, people who deny the reality of their situations may be especially devastated by negative events when they do occur, because they did not expect them and did not adjust their views of themselves and the world to allow for negative outcomes (Janoff-Bulman & Frieze, 1983; Tennen & Affleck, 1987). In sum, many researchers fear that optimistic beliefs hurt people by giving them a false sense of security and by interfering with the acquisition of useful risk information.

The denial explanation is difficult to refute on the basis of self-report data concerning adjustment and health, because one can always suggest that superior self-reports of adjustment represent wishful thinking at best and outright denial at worst.[1] For example, studies examining the link between dispositional optimism and self-reported coping consistently find that optimism predicts lower self-reports of denial and disengagement (Carver et al., 1993; Scheier, Weintraub, & Carver, 1986). However, these self-reports are themselves vulnerable to the denial explanation because it is impossible to obtain purely objective measures of these outcomes. In sum, even the best prospective correlational research on self-reported coping and adjustment simply cannot definitively establish whether optimists' reports of better outcomes are real or whether they represent denial or other defensive processes.

OPTIMISM AND ATTENTION TO THREATENING HEALTH INFORMATION: AN EXPERIMENTAL PARADIGM

The alternative explanations and potential liabilities we have just reviewed present a substantial challenge to the view that optimistic beliefs are adaptive as people confront negative events and information. Of these explanations, the denial explanation is perhaps the most pernicious because it suggests that optimists are deluding themselves and may suffer deleterious consequences at some later point. To refute the denial explanation, it will be necessary to demonstrate that optimistic beliefs predict good outcomes that are not self-reports of behavior, health, or psychological adjustment. It will also be important to demonstrate that optimistic beliefs are *prospectively*, rather than retrospectively, linked to constructive responses to negative events and information. In retrospective studies examining the correlation between optimism and the processing of negative information, it is impossible to tell whether optimism leads people to use negative information constructively, or whether people who are able to use negative information constructively become more optimistic (see Tennen & Affleck, 1987, and Weinstein & Nicolich, 1993, for discussion). For this reason, it is important to examine how optimistic beliefs, once they are in place, are related to the processing of *subsequent* information.

In light of the interpretational difficulties inherent in most widely used methods, we set out to devise a new method of testing whether optimism functions like denial or other defensive processes. We began with the idea that we would test the prospective relation of optimistic beliefs to attention to threatening health information in an experimental setting. We would expose research participants to health-risk information that varied in its severity, relevance to the self, and other properties. Participants would be instructed to read as much or as little of the information as they wished, and measures of reading time and recall for the target information would be collected. If, as the level of threat conveyed by the information increased, optimists' attention to and recall of the information decreased, this would provide some objective, prospective evidence for a denial-like process. In contrast, if optimists' attention to such information increased as a function of increasing threat, this would provide evidence that optimism does not function like denial and may instead facilitate attention to negative information.

This design allowed us to address the other alternative explanations of the benefits of optimism, as well. The use of reading time and recall as outcome measures would eliminate self-report and positivity biases, because these measures would be collected via computer or scored by objective raters. Additionally, social desirability concerns would be reduced, because participants would not know they were being timed and would not be told in advance about the recall task that followed exposure to the information. Concerns about differences in exposure to objective life stressors would be reduced, as all participants would be exposed to the same set of negative stimulus materials and their responses compared. Finally, the design allowed us to control statistically for negative affectivity and experience with illness as potential confounds in the relation of optimism to the processing of information about health risks.

Why Use Health-Risk Information?

We chose health-risk information as our primary source of stimulus materials for several reasons. First, health risks are real and involving to participants, and there are some potential benefits to be gained from attention to information about them. While the desirability of employing materials that are useful and involving to participants may seem obvious, it is important to note that many studies testing the relation of positive beliefs and states to the processing of negative information have used stimulus materials of low personal relevance to research participants (see Aspinwall, 1998; Isen, 1993; and Smith & Shaffer, 1991, for reviews and discussion). If negative information is irrelevant to one's current goals, health, or well-being, there is little reason to attend to it, and it is difficult to argue that inattention to such information is maladaptive. To test how optimists in our college student samples would respond to negative information that was clearly useful and relevant to them, we created stimulus materials containing medical information about illnesses of young adulthood.

A second reason for focusing on health-risk information is that the availability of such information to the public has mushroomed in the last decade. New research findings concerning etiology, treatment, and prevention of disease are disseminated rapidly through the Internet and other media. Given the incredible amount of information available, it would be impossible for anyone to process all that is potentially relevant to him or her. Therefore, understanding how and why people attend to some kinds of information, as opposed to others, is a potentially important theoretical and practical question. As we will describe, the computer-based menus we have used to present health information in our various studies are quite similar in design to the web pages of several national health foundations, in that visitors to such sites may select information pertaining to symptoms, causes, risk factors, and treatments of various illnesses from a menu of topics.

In addition to our desire to test the relation of optimism to attention to negative information in a situation with high external validity, we focused on health-risk information because it provides a convenient way of manipulating theoretically meaningful parameters of threatening information (see Paterson & Neufeld, 1987, for review). Factors such as the severity or self-relevance of the information are relatively easy to vary experimentally. For example, one may vary the threat-level of the information within-subjects or between-subjects by presenting people with information about mild, moderate, and severe threats to health, or by manipulating whether the information is of high or low personal relevance to participants. The systematic variation of such factors allows us to test whether, as the health-risk information becomes more serious and more personally relevant, optimists respond with increased or decreased attention to that information. In this way, we can test whether optimism functions like denial.

Study 1: Optimism and Attention to Severe Health Threats

Method

Our first study simply tested the relation of optimism to attention to information about illnesses that varied in severity. Young adult college students (n = 34; 17 men, 17 women; ages 18–21) participated in a study of health decisions for credit in their introductory psychology course. The study took place in two sessions. During an initial mass testing session, participants completed questionnaires assessing dispositional optimism, experience with illness, and negative affectivity. During a second session approximately two weeks later, participants were asked to read information about illnesses common to young adults. Participants were told that because prior studies concerning health decisions had used illnesses typically experienced in later life, little was known about the judgment processes for illnesses common to young adults. These comments were made in order to increase the perceived relevance of the stimulus materials.

The information was presented via computer, using an index card metaphor (Silicon Beach Software, Inc., 1989) to present detailed, graphic information about the symptoms, causes, and treatments of six target illnesses. As a manipulation of illness severity, two illnesses were mild, two moderate, and two severe. Participants were told that each "card" was color coded for severity in a manner analogous to a traffic light, such that green cards indicated illnesses of low severity (athlete's foot, wart); yellow cards, medium severity (kidney infection, stomach ulcer); and red cards, high severity (brain tumor, tuberculosis). The illnesses were presented in alphabetical order for all participants. Each card contained fifty words of text written at the tenth grade level and an equal number of independent facts. Participants were instructed to read at their own pace and were not given the opportunity to reread previous screens. Reading time for each card was measured unobtrusively by the computer. At the end of the session, participants were presented with a surprise recall task and asked to recall as many facts as possible about each illness.

Reading time and recall were analyzed as a function of optimism, illness severity, and information type (symptoms, causes, treatments). All analyses statistically controlled for participants' grade point averages (GPAs) in order to remove this potential confound from the measures of reading time and recall.

Results

On the basis of the large number of studies relating optimism to good outcomes, we predicted that optimistic beliefs would facilitate, rather than inhibit, attention to threatening information as the severity of the health threat increased. This prediction was supported for information about the symptoms of the target illnesses. Specifically, a significant Optimism × Illness Severity × Information Type interaction (F [4, 29] $= 5.13, p < .003$) indicated that optimism was positively related to reading time for the symptoms of the severe illnesses and negatively related to reading time for the symptoms of the less severe illnesses. This relation is shown in figure 9.1. This pattern of results was unique to symptoms, as there were no significant differences in reading time for the causes and treatments of illness as a function of optimism and illness severity. The surprise recall test revealed no significant effects of optimism.

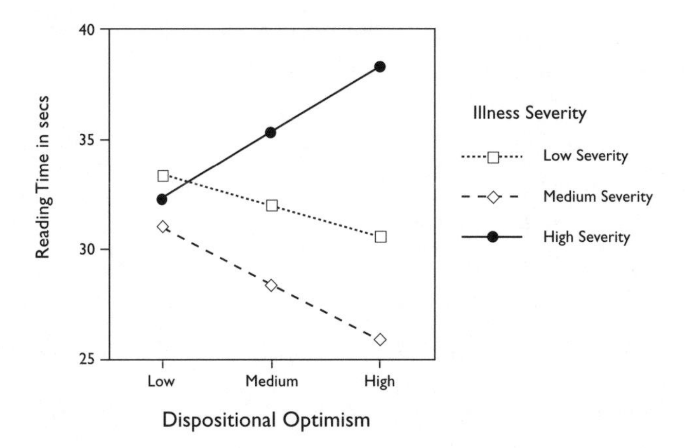

Figure 9.1. The relation of dispositional optimism to predicted reading times for information about symptoms as a function of illness severity in Study 1.

In light of concerns that the effects of optimism may be due to other factors, such as low levels of negative affectivity or differences in life experience, we tested whether such factors could account for this pattern of results. When the effects of negative affectivity were statistically controlled, the interaction among optimism, illness severity, and type of information remained significant. Similarly, the inclusion of measures of prior personal experience with the target illnesses and the incidence of the illnesses among friends or family members did not affect this pattern of results.

Discussion

The results of our first study provided preliminary evidence that optimism may facilitate attention to some kinds of threatening health information. Specifically, dispositional optimism predicted increased attention to the symptoms of highly severe illnesses compared to other kinds of health information, and this relation remained significant when the effects of negative affectivity and experience with illness were statistically controlled. These findings, though preliminary, are inconsistent with the idea that optimism functions likes denial and other defensive processes.

Why did optimists attend only to the symptoms of severe illnesses? There are several possible explanations, none of which may be definitively endorsed from the results of Study 1 alone. First, attention to symptoms may indicate that optimists are interested in the early detection and management of illness. Second, optimists may have been using information about symptoms of severe illnesses to make a determination about the personal relevance of the target illnesses—that is, to determine whether they had been experiencing any such symptoms. Once such a determination had been made (which would likely be negative, given that the two high severity illnesses are uncommon), optimists may have been less interested in the information about causes and treatments that followed. Finally, it is possible that the generality of the findings concerning optimists' attention to symptoms, as opposed to causes and treatments, may be limited by the particular illnesses used in the stimulus set. In particular, the illnesses in Study 1 were mostly viral or bacterial, and so may not have provided participants with much in the way of useful preventive or causal information.

Two other factors made the results of this initial study difficult to interpret. First, the set of six target illnesses differed not only in their rated severity, but also in the body systems they affected, their prevalence, their preventability, and other factors, making it difficult to explain differences in reading time for the severe illnesses solely in terms of the severity of the illnesses. A potentially more serious limitation was that the stimulus materials did not create a strong test of the denial hypothesis because they addressed illnesses fairly remote to the lives of young adults and so were unlikely to trigger defensive reactions to the information. Accordingly, a second study was conducted to test the relation of optimism to attention to health-risk information that was more directly relevant to participants' own health behaviors.

Study 2: Optimism and Attention to Self-Relevant Risk Information

Method

To create a stronger test of the relation of optimism to attention to threatening information, we presented optimists with medically accurate and potentially threatening information about the risks of their own health behavior. Attention to such information was then analyzed as a function of the degree to which participants practiced the behavior in question. If optimism functions like denial, attention to risk information should decrease as that information becomes more relevant to one's own health behavior. In contrast, if optimism is useful in managing negative information, attention to risk information should increase as a function of its relevance to one's own behavior.

To ensure that all participants would be exposed to some information that was relevant to their behavior and some information that was not relevant to their behavior (so we could test whether optimists differed in their attention to the two kinds of information), we chose two health behaviors that are common among college students: vitamin use and tanning (either through sunbathing or the use of tanning booths). We excluded from the study respondents who reported moderate to high levels of both behaviors or low levels of both behaviors on the screening questionnaire (see Aspinwall and Brunhart, 1996, for a complete description of the participant selection procedure and results of this study). This procedure yielded a sample of 57 college students (20 men, 37 women; ages 18–40) who reported either regular vitamin use or regular UV exposure, but not both. These students were then invited to participate in our study of health decisions for extra credit in their psychology class.

As in Study 1, participants were presented with computer-based menus of health information. This time, the menus contained 100-word passages about the risks and benefits of vitamin use, as well as neutral information. For example, risk topics for vitamin use were "vitamin supplements can have harmful interactions" and "vitamins can hide serious illnesses." Our intent in providing participants with risk, benefit, and neutral information was to test whether optimists' attention to risk information was distinct from more general interest in self-relevant health information. It was also important to test whether optimists, when presented with information about their own health behavior, choose to read only favorable information about it. The computer program was modified to allow participants to read the information in any order they wished, to return to previous passages, and to skip any or all of the passages. These modifications created a better test of the denial hypothesis, in that participants would be free to skip all information related to the risks of their own behavior. Finally, all participants completed two surprise recall tests, the first following the presentation of the stimulus materials and the second in a follow-up session one week later.

To extend our consideration of the relation of optimistic beliefs to attention to health-risk information, we considered both dispositional and health-related optimism. Drawing from prior research (Taylor et al., 1992), we developed a 16-item inventory of favorable beliefs about one's ability to prevent and to withstand illness. Sample items are "positive thinking can prevent illness from occurring" and "if I had a serious illness, I could cure myself if I wanted to" (1 = strongly disagree, 7 = strongly agree). It is important to note that some of these optimistic beliefs about health may be unwarranted given current medical knowledge. This measure, which proved to be reliable (alpha = .85), was scored such that higher scores indicated more favorable beliefs. Health-related optimism and dispositional optimism (the LOT) were significantly positively correlated in the sample ($r = .59, p < .0001$).

Results

We first examined reading time and recall for risk, benefit, and neutral information about the two behaviors, as a function of whether people practiced the behavior and their degree of either dispositional or health-specific optimism. Our first analysis tested whether optimists[2] attended to risk information more than to other kinds of information. As shown in figure 9.2, participants who were optimistic about their health were more likely to read risk information than benefit or neutral information. This pattern of results was also obtained for dispositional optimism.

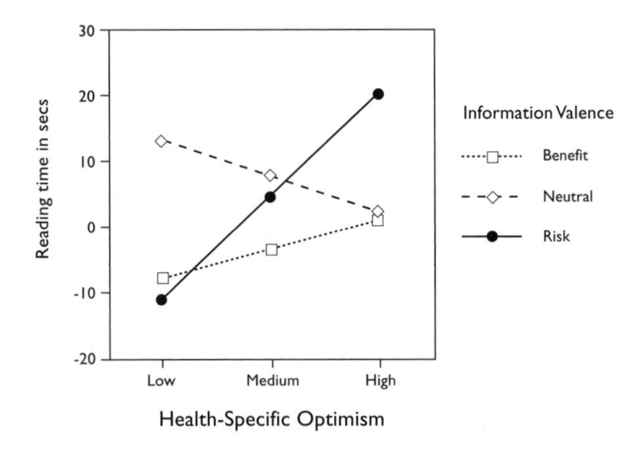

Figure 9.2. The relation of health-specific optimism to predicted reading times for risk, benefit, and neutral information in Study 2. Figure reprinted from Aspinwall and Brunhart (1996), Personality and Social Psychology Bulletin, *22(10), p. 997, copyright © by Lisa G. Aspinwall and Susanne M. Brunhart. Reprinted by permission of Sage Publications, Inc.*

Consistent with these findings, the results of the surprise recall tests revealed that participants who were optimistic about their health remembered more information overall. Of particular interest was the finding that participants who were optimistic about their health were especially likely to recall risk information, compared to participants who were low in optimism. No results linking dispositional optimism to recall were found in this first set of analyses.

To test whether optimists' attention to the risks of their own behavior increases or decreases as their practice of the behavior increases, we conducted a second set of analyses examining optimists' reading time and recall for the information as a function of participants' lifetime practice of each behavior (see Aspinwall & Brunhart, 1996, for details regarding the lifetime behavior measures). These analyses were designed to provide an especially stringent test of whether optimism functions like denial, because we would be testing optimists' attention to risk information as a function of their lifetime practice of the particular behavior.

The analyses of reading time for information about vitamins revealed several interesting findings. First, there was an overall trend for participants who were long-term vitamin users to read less of the risk information, a finding that would typically be taken to indicate defensive processing of self-relevant risk information. However, participants who were optimistic about their health were the exception to this pattern. As shown in the top half of figure 9.3, optimists who were long-term vitamin users paid greater attention to risk information about vitamin use. In contrast, as shown in the bottom half of figure 9.3, optimism was not associated with increased reading time for risk information among participants who did not take vitamins. Finally, there was no relation of health-specific optimism to reading time for neutral or benefit information at any level of vitamin use, indicating that optimists' elevated reading time was specific to self-relevant risk information.

When we repeated these analyses using dispositional optimism as a predictor, we did not find a significant relation of dispositional optimism to reading time as a function of lifetime vitamin use. However, the analyses of the surprise recall test indicated that dispositional optimism predicted somewhat greater recall for all types of information at the follow-up session among participants high in vitamin use, relative to those low in vitamin use. A similar trend suggesting higher recall for health information as a function of increasing vitamin use was found for health-specific optimism.

We also examined reading time and recall for information about tanning as a function of lifetime tanning behavior. Contrary to our predictions, neither measure of optimism was related to reading time or

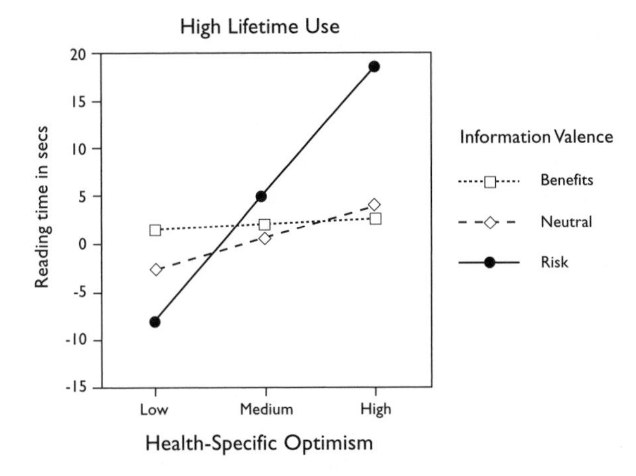

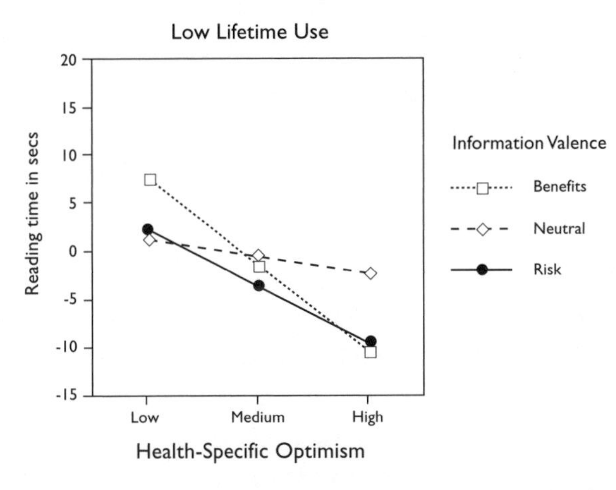

Figure 9.3. The relation of health-specific optimism to predicted reading time for risk, benefit, and neutral information about vitamins as a function of lifetime vitamin use in Study 2. Figure reprinted from Aspinwall and Brunhart (1996), Personality and Social Psychology Bulletin, *22(10), p. 998, copyright © by Lisa G. Aspinwall and Susanne M. Brunhart. Reprinted by permission of Sage Publications, Inc.*

recall for this information when lifetime ultraviolet (UV) exposure was considered.

Finally, to examine whether these results were confounded by negative affectivity, we repeated the analyses, controlling for negative affectivity and its interaction with other predictors. Although the inclusion of negative affectivity as a predictor did weaken the results for dispositional optimism, most of the results reported for health-specific optimism remained significant. Additionally, negative affectivity was not itself a significant predictor of reading time or recall in any analysis, suggesting that the presence or absence of negative emotional states does not account for the results of this study (see Aspinwall & Brunhart, 1996, for discussion).

Discussion

The results of this second study provide stronger evidence that optimism predicts increased attention to and recall for health-risk information, especially when that information is relevant to participants' own behavior. These results were obtained for both dispositional and health-specific measures of optimism. With respect to the health-specific measure, it is interesting to note that, although some of the positive beliefs assessed (such as the strong belief one could cure oneself of serious illness through positive thinking) are likely to be incorrect given current medical knowledge, they did not interfere with the acquisition of health-risk information. Instead, they seemed to facilitate it. Finally, although both measures of optimism were related to greater attention to risk information overall, it is important to note that our predictions about increased attention to health-risk information as a function of lifetime behavior were supported for information about vitamin use, but not for information about UV exposure. However, it is also important to note that no evidence was found to support the idea that either measure of optimism predicted decreased attention to health-risk information for either target behavior.

Thus far, the results of these first two studies suggest that optimism does not function like denial or other defensive processes. Specifically, people who were optimistic (dispositionally or about their health) differentially attended to and recalled threatening health information, especially when the information was self-relevant or severe. What has yet to be established, however, is that optimists' greater attention to threatening health risk information is in the service of careful, veridical processing of such information. That is, although optimism appears to be linked to greater reading time and recall for self-relevant health-risk information, it is possible that optimists are devoting extra processing efforts to refute the threatening information and its implications. To examine this issue, we conducted a third study to test whether optimistic beliefs promoted veridical or defensive processing of self-relevant risk information.

Study 3: Optimism and Elaborative Processing of Health-Risk Information

Method

The primary goal of Study 3 was to examine what optimists were doing with the threatening health information: were they taking the information to heart, or were they working hard to refute the information and its implications for their own health and behavior? In the design of Study 3, we drew on a large literature on the defensive processing of threatening health information, which suggests that people frequently distort unfavorable information about their health or health behavior (Jemmott, Ditto, & Croyle, 1986; Liberman & Chaiken, 1992; see Croyle, 1992, for review). These comforting distortions may be accomplished in many ways, for example, by questioning the validity of a diagnostic test that suggests one is at risk for illness, by downplaying the seriousness of an illness for which one is at risk, or by questioning the quality of the medical evidence linking one's behavior to poor health outcomes. In Study 3, we used a stimulated recall interview to obtain self-report measures of people's thoughts as they were reading health-risk information and examined whether these thoughts represented attempts to counterargue or otherwise minimize the information.

A second goal of Study 3 was to understand why the results of Study 2 concerning optimists' increased attention to self-relevant risk information were found for vitamin use, but not for UV exposure. We were concerned about two potentially serious alternative explanations. The first was that optimism promoted attention to relatively mild health threats (e.g., those stemming from the misuse of vitamins), but not to severe ones (e.g., skin cancer). Participants' comments during the debriefing conducted at the end of the follow-up session, however, suggested a different explanation for their lack of attention to information about the risks of UV exposure. Several participants indicated that they thought that skin cancer was a relatively mild condition because it could be treated easily and successfully. They also thought that skin cancer would not affect them until much later in life.

A second alternative explanation for the results of Study 2 involved our procedure for selecting participants. By selecting participants who were either 1) high in vitamin use and low in tanning, or 2) low in vitamin use and high in tanning, it is possible that we had confounded health-consciousness with the relevance of the health information. That is, people who use vitamins and who avoid UV exposure are likely to be more health-conscious than people who sunbathe frequently and who don't take vitamins. Thus, the results of the analyses of each behavior as a function of lifetime practice may not really be comparable, as people who are long-term vitamin users are likely different in many respects from those who are long-term tanners.

The design of Study 3 addressed these issues in a number of ways. First, we included for study only participants who were regular tanners. All participants were young adult women (n = 41; ages 18–21) who reported moderate to high levels of weekly UV exposure, either through sunbathing or the use of tanning booths. Second, we took several steps to make the information about UV exposure more self-relevant and threatening (see Aspinwall & Brunhart, 1998, for a complete description of methods and results). Instead of using the generic term "skin cancer," we focused on the link between UV exposure and a potentially fatal kind of skin cancer, malignant melanoma. We also restricted the stimulus set to include only materials about UV exposure. In this way, all of the information presented would be highly relevant and threatening to all participants. Finally, in response to participants' comments that they did not pay much attention to the risks of tanning because they thought skin cancer would not affect them until later in life, we told half the participants that the average melanoma patient was a 25-year-old woman (proximal threat condition) and told the other half that the average patient was a 55-year-old woman (distal threat condition). Thus, all participants were regular tanners, and half of them were given reason to believe that tanning posed an immediate threat to their health. The design of Study 3, therefore. allowed us to test the effects of threat proximity on optimists' attention to risk information about potentially life-threatening consequences of their tanning behavior.

As in our previous studies, participants were given the opportunity to read risk, benefit, and neutral information about tanning and were instructed to read as much or as little as they wished. The stimulus materials addressed both medical and cosmetic aspects of tanning. For example, the risk information consisted of two passages entitled "Medical Risks of Tanning" and "Cosmetic Risks of Tanning." The computer-based portion of the session was videotaped. To examine what optimists were doing with the risk information, we conducted a stimulated recall interview immediately following the on-line session. A second experimenter, who was unaware of participants' assignment to experimental condition (proximal versus distal threat), level of optimism, or prior responses, conducted the interview.

Participants were shown a videotape of their on-line session in which they could clearly see the text on the screen, their mouse movements, and their answers to various questions. Participants were told that we were "interested in what went through their minds as they went through the computer segment of the study." Each time the videotape showed some response on the part of the participant, such as choosing a different topic from the menu or answering a question, the experimenter stopped the tape and asked a series of questions, such as "How did you select this passage?" and "What thoughts and feelings, if any, did you experience while you were reading?" To reduce demand, the instructions to participants emphasized that it was okay to report feelings that were irrelevant to the materials, such as fatigue, boredom, or hunger.

We then subjected the interview transcripts to a cognitive response analysis (Cacioppo & Petty, 1981). From each participant's transcript, we derived sum scores for two kinds of statements about the risks of UV exposure. Elaboration refers to statements that indicate that a participant was thinking about the information and its relation to her own behavior in ways that supported the idea that tanning posed health risks. Elaborative statements were taken to indicate participants' veridical processing of the risk information and its relevance to their own behavior and health. *Counterarguing* refers to statements in which a participant questioned the validity of the risk information and/or its relevance to her own behavior and health. Statements that downplayed the risks of UV exposure were also coded as instances of counterarguing. The transcripts were coded by two independent raters with 80% agreement.

Results

Sum scores for elaboration and counterarguing of risk information about UV exposure were analyzed as a function of dispositional optimism and threat proximity, statistically controlling for participants' current reported weekly level of UV exposure. As predicted, a significant

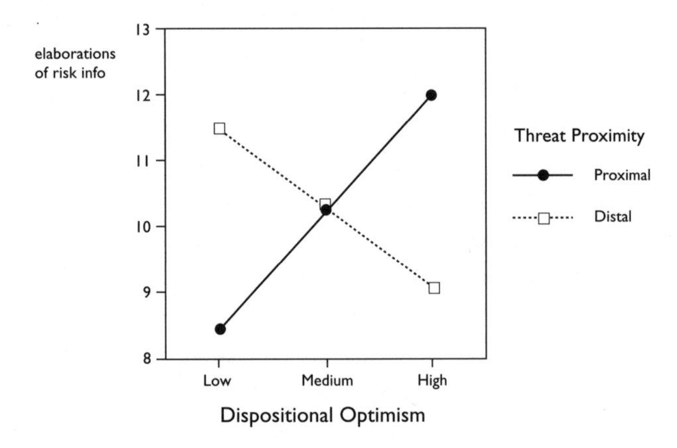

Figure 9.4. The relation of dispositional optimism to predicted scores for cognitive elaboration of risk information about UV exposure as a function of threat proximity in Study 3.

Optimism × Threat Proximity interaction (F [1, 36] = 4.61, $p < .04$) revealed that dispositionally optimistic participants were more likely to elaborate risk information in the proximal threat condition than in the distal threat condition. As shown in figure 9.4, when melanoma was said to affect women close to their age, young adult women who were optimists were more likely to discuss the risk information and its relation to their own behavior in ways that supported its riskiness.

Table 9.1 presents examples of elaborative statements made by optimists in the proximal threat condition. As these examples illustrate, optimists in the proximal threat condition were clearly cognizant of physical damage caused by UV exposure, its cumulative nature, and its relation to their own level of tanning. No evidence was found to suggest that optimists were more likely to generate counterarguments in response to the risk information.

Table 9.1

Examples of Elaboration of Risk Information in Study 3

"I kind of already knew the risks of tanning, but not to the certain extent that they were talking about: flaky, bleeding skin and lumpiness, and so it just made me more aware of what ultraviolet rays can do."

"I didn't know that it [skin damage] was cumulative. That kind of scared me, because I tan a lot. So I got a little more information on that."

"This is interesting, I thought, because it talks about when your tan fades, it [the effect/damage] stays there. Because I do tan a decent amount of time, so it made me think a little bit. You forget it's so risky because I am young now."

Note. All examples are from optimists in the proximal threat condition.

Discussion

These results supplement and extend those of the first two studies by demonstrating that optimistic beliefs are associated with more reported thoughts consistent with health-risk information about participants' own behavior. For health threats said to be proximal, optimists responded with greater elaboration of self-relevant risk information. Although the exact mechanism has yet to be elucidated, these results suggest that optimism may confer an advantage not only in attending to, but also in expanding on threatening information and linking it to one's own behavior and health. No evidence was found to suggest that optimists were more likely to question or minimize such information. These results suggest that optimists' greater attention to threatening health information is not in the service of refuting or counterarguing that information and its implications for the self, but may instead be associated with greater elaborative processing of such information.

GENERAL DISCUSSION

In three studies using different manipulations, materials, and measures, we have demonstrated that optimistic beliefs are linked to greater, not lesser, processing of health-risk information as the level of threat or self-relevance increases. The results of these studies have several implications for understanding the nature of optimism and the mechanisms through which it may promote better outcomes. We will discuss each in turn, and then consider the implications of these results for understanding the role of optimism in coping with stress and other problem-solving activities.

Optimism Does Not Appear to Function Like Denial

We believe these results present a strong challenge to the idea that optimism functions like denial. Although optimism has been characterized as "blind," "naive," or defensive in the face of threatening information, we find no evidence that optimists maintain their positive beliefs by tuning out negative information. Instead, optimists appear to devote more attention to severe than mild illnesses, to self-relevant than to irrelevant health risks, and to proximal rather than distal threats to health. These results lend support to correlational studies that find that optimism predicts lower levels of self-reported denial, avoidant coping, and disengagement among people coping with stressful events (Aspinwall & Taylor, 1992; Carver et al., 1993; Scheier et al., 1986).

These findings also have implications for the ongoing debate concerning the nature and adaptiveness of positive beliefs (see Colvin & Block, 1994; Taylor & Brown, 1988, 1994). The crux of this debate is whether favorable beliefs, especially those that may be unrealistically favorable, are responsive to negative information. That is, some researchers have been concerned that some kinds of positive beliefs may prevent people from obtaining useful information that challenges their favorable beliefs. Over time, resistance to such information would lead to beliefs and behaviors that correspond poorly to reality and to subsequent problems in self-regulation. The results of the present studies, along with several studies of the role of positive beliefs in adaptation to life-threatening illness and other negative life events, suggest that such fears may not be warranted in the case of optimism (see Taylor & Aspinwall, 1996; Armor & Taylor, 1998; and Aspinwall, 1998, for reviews). Instead, to the extent that optimists attend to self-relevant risk information and elaborate, rather than downplay, its riskiness, they may be said to be realistic rather than unrealistic in their approach to useful negative information.

The Benefits of Optimism Do Not Appear to Be Explained by Other Factors

The results of the present studies are also inconsistent with several other alternative explanations of the benefits of optimism. Specifically, the findings that optimists read, remember, and elaborate more *negative* information cannot be taken as evidence of a positivity bias and, in fact, are highly inconsistent with such a bias (see Aspinwall, 1998, for discussion). Additionally, each of the present studies examined participants' reactions to a common set of stimulus materials to reduce the influence of differences in exposure to negative events and information between optimists and pessimists. Such differences in objective experience were also statistically controlled through measures of experience with the target illness in Study 1 or practice of the target behavior in Studies 2 and 3. In no case were the results for optimism found to be attributable to these factors. Instead, the results of Study 2 suggest that, as participants' practice of the behavior increased, optimism showed an even stronger relation to attention to risk information. As we note below, the correlational design of these studies does not allow all potential confounds to be eliminated, but the evidence to date is inconsistent with the idea that optimists report better outcomes because they have less experience with illness or other negative life events. Finally, in Studies 1 and 2, we tested whether the results for optimism could be attributed to participants' lack of negative affectivity and found little to no support for this alternative explanation. In sum, although no study using a measured individual difference predictor such as optimism can rule out all potential confounds, we believe we have produced evidence against the most likely candidates.

Limitations of the Present Studies

Although we have suggested that these results argue against the major alternative explanations for the benefits of optimism, it is important to note some limitations of the present studies. The most important limitation is that no causal conclusions can be drawn, because optimistic beliefs were measured rather than manipulated. In light of this inherent limitation in the study of naturally occurring differences in optimism, we have recently developed a completely experimental paradigm to test the relation of induced positive beliefs and states to the processing of self-relevant negative information. To date, our results are highly consistent with those reported here (Reed & Aspinwall, 1998).

A second limitation is that we can currently offer no evidence that optimists' increased attention to health-risk information will result in lower levels of risky health behavior or higher levels of health-promoting behaviors. Because of an ethical responsibility to debrief participants as soon as possible after the presentation of threatening health information, we have not studied people over long periods of time to assess changes in behavior following exposure to health-risk information. For example, although it would be interesting to know whether optimists who were told that the average melanoma patient was a 25-year-old woman subsequently decreased their UV exposure, we were ethically obligated to tell participants that the 25-year figure was incorrect and had been presented for research purposes.

Finally, we have not tested whether our findings will generalize to other samples that vary in age, health status, and other potentially important factors. All of the current studies were conducted with relatively healthy young adult college students. Although the generality of these results to other groups, such as older adults and people with chronic illnesses, remains an open question, we wish to note that getting healthy young people to attend to risk information is an important element of (and frequently a major stumbling block in) health promotion efforts and therefore worthy of study in its own right. Nonetheless, it will be important in future research to see if optimism functions the same way in other populations and to see whether the results of studies using paradigms like the one we have presented here are consistent with the results of the large number of studies of optimism among people with chronic or life-threatening illnesses.

IMPLICATIONS FOR COPING AND HEALTH

We conclude with a discussion of the potential implications of our findings for understanding the role of optimism in coping with threats to health and well-being and for understanding the role of positive beliefs in self-regulation more generally.

Does Optimism Help or Hurt People as They Confront Negative Events and Information?

At the outset of this chapter, we noted that optimism was consistently associated with more adaptive ways of coping and better outcomes among people facing a wide range of stressors. The results of the present studies suggest that the ability to attend to and process negative information is one potential mechanism through which optimists may attain such outcomes. Specifically, the ability to attend to and process negative information, especially self-relevant information, is likely to confer several advantages in coping with potential and actual stressors. First, attention to negative information should facilitate the detection of negative events early in their course, a phenomenon we have termed "proactive coping" (Aspinwall & Taylor, 1997). For example, the person who notices troubling physical symptoms and keeps an eye on them may be more successful in obtaining treatment early in the course of an illness. Proactive coping may allow people to tackle incipient problems before they develop into big ones, thus preserving mental and physical health and other coping resources. Second, optimists' ability to attend to and process negative information is likely to prove to be just as important in other parts of the coping process, such as tracking the development of potential and actual stressors and modifying one's coping efforts.

These potential effects of optimism on different parts of the coping process are diagramed in figure 9.5, which has been adapted from Aspinwall and Taylor's (1997) model of proactive coping. The first two stages in the figure refer to the activities of screening the environment for danger (Attention/Recognition) and making initial appraisals of what a potential stressor is and what it is likely to become (Initial Appraisal). As shown in Feedback Loop 1, the Attention/Recognition and Initial Appraisal stages are reciprocally related as people track the development of incipient stressors and modify their appraisals accordingly. If optimists are able to maintain attention to negative information and to elaborate on it, their appraisals of actual and potential stressors may correspond more closely to the objective features of such stressors. For example, the person who fears a layoff at work but who can maintain attention to this threatening information may be able to learn more about whether the layoff is likely to affect him or her.

As shown in Feedback Loop 2, optimism may also assist people in detecting whether they are using the right kinds of coping and problem-solving strategies for a particular stressor. As shown in the figure, appraisal processes may be reciprocally related to the last two components of the model, preliminary coping efforts and the elicitation and use of feedback about the success of one's efforts in addressing the problem. If optimists are more likely to undertake active, as opposed to avoidant, preliminary coping efforts, they may become better informed about the stressful situation because active efforts are generally more likely than avoidant ones to elicit information about a stressor. For example, the person who fears layoffs and who copes actively with these fears by arranging an informal lunch to discuss this possibility with fel-

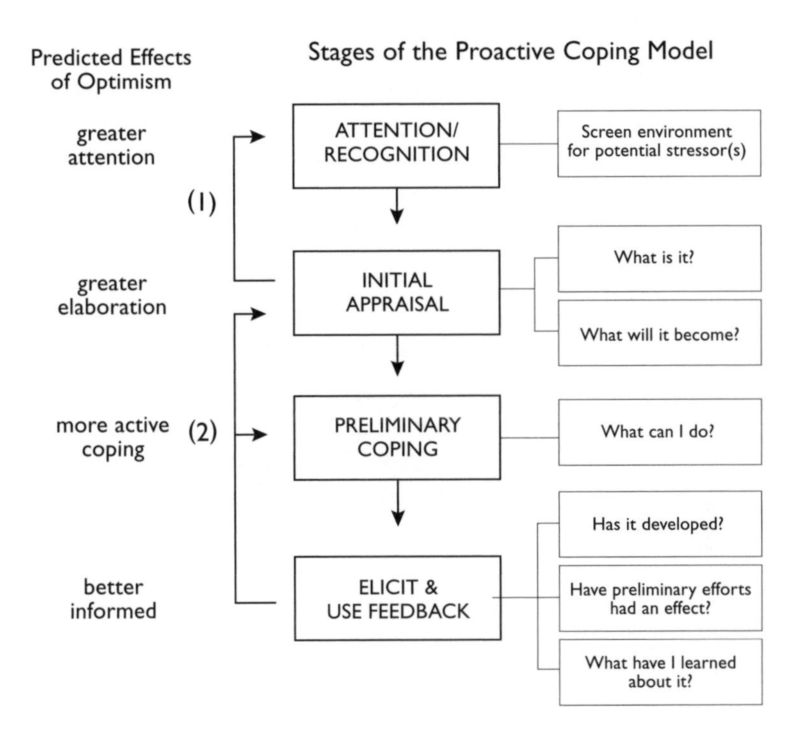

Figure 9.5. The predicted relation of dispositional optimism to four stages of Aspinwall and Taylor's (1997) model of proactive coping and the potential feedback loops among the stages as people detect, manage, and monitor potential stressors. Feedback Loop 1 represents the reciprocal relation between attention to potential stressors and appraisals of them. Feedback Loop 2 represents the reciprocal relations among appraisals of potential problems, preliminary coping efforts, and feedback elicited by those efforts. An initial stage of the model, "Resource Accumulation," is not shown for convenience of presentation. Figure adapted with permission, copyright American Psychological Association and Lisa G. Aspinwall and Shelley E. Taylor (1997).

low co-workers or her supervisor is more likely to learn useful information than the person who avoids discussing the situation. This information may, in turn, inform his or her subsequent coping efforts (applying for other jobs, acquiring marketable new skills, making sure the person making the layoff decisions has a copy of his or her most recent performance review, etc.).

An important aspect of Feedback Loop 2 and the model more generally is that feedback from active coping efforts may work in tandem with optimists' ability to attend to and elaborate negative information, such that optimists are better able to use this information to revise their appraisals and coping strategies. Over time, such information may lead optimists to become more informed about particular stressors and to undertake coping efforts that correspond well to the nature of the particular problem. This information may also serve to build procedural knowledge about different kinds of stressors and the coping strategies they require. This procedural knowledge may then inform subsequent coping efforts and may explain some of the beneficial effects associated with optimism (see Aspinwall, 1997; Aspinwall, Richter, & Hoffman, in press; Aspinwall & Taylor, 1997).

SUMMARY AND CONCLUSION

Optimistic beliefs have an impressive track record in predicting physical health and psychological well-being. In the past few years, several studies have demonstrated that much of dispositional optimism's association with good outcomes may be due to optimists' more active coping efforts and lower levels of avoidant coping. The results of our series of studies suggest that optimistic beliefs may play an especially important and beneficial role in earlier stages of the coping process, namely in maintaining attention to negative information, especially to negative information that is severe, self-relevant, and/or proximally threatening. Optimists' ability to attend to and elaborate self-relevant negative information, working in conjunction with their more active coping efforts, may explain some of the impressive prospective benefits of optimistic beliefs in coping with a wide range of stressors.

NOTES

1 Outright denial of fact is only one kind of defensive processing (Breznitz, 1983; Lazarus, 1983). For example, one might accept that an event occurred, but deny its negative implications for the self. It is important to note that the present studies test only a subset of the full range of defensive processes that may result from exposure to negative information about the self. In our subsequent research, we have examined the relation of positive states to some of these other kinds of defensive processing, such as the evaluation of the strength of arguments suggesting that one's health behavior is harmful. To date, we have obtained results highly consistent with those reported here (Reed & Aspinwall, 1998; see Aspinwall, 1998, for a review).

2 Throughout the chapter, the term "optimist" or "participants high in optimism" refers to participants with scores 1.0 *SD* or more above the sample mean on the particular optimism scale (either the LOT or the health-specific measure). The designations "medium" and "low" optimism correspond to participants with scores at the mean or 1.0 *SD* or more below the mean, respectively.

REFERENCES

Armor, D.A., & Taylor, S.E. (1998). Situated optimism: Specific outcome expectancies and self-regulation. In M.P. Zanna (Ed.), *Advances in experimental social psychology* (Vol. 30, pp. 309–379). New York: Academic Press.

Aspinwall, L.G. (1997). Where planning meets coping: Proactive coping and the detection and management of potential stressors. In S.L. Friedman & E.K. Scholnick (Eds.), *The developmental psychology of planning: Why, how, and when do we plan?* (pp. 285–320). Hillsdale, NJ: Erlbaum.

Aspinwall, L.G. (1998). Rethinking the role of positive affect in self-regulation. *Motivation and Emotion, 22,* 1–32.

Aspinwall, L.G., & Brunhart, S.M. (1996). Distinguishing optimism from denial: Optimistic beliefs predict attention to health threats. *Personality and Social Psychology Bulletin, 22,* 993–1003.

Aspinwall, L.G., & Brunhart, S.M. (1998). *Optimism and attention to proximal threats to health*. Manuscript in preparation.

Aspinwall, L.G., & Richter, L. (1999). Optimism and self-mastery predict more rapid disengagement from unsolvable tasks in the presence of alternatives. *Maturation and Emotion, 23,* 221–245.

Aspinwall, L.G., Richter, L., & Hoffman, R.R. (in press). Understanding how optimism "works": An examination of optimists' adaptive moderation of belief and behavior. In E.C. Chang (Ed.), *Optimism and pessimism: Theory, research, and practice.* Washington, DC: American Psychological Association.

Aspinwall, L.G., & Taylor, S.E. (1992). Modeling cognitive adaptation: A longitudinal investigation of the impact of individual differences and coping on college adjustment and performance. *Journal of Personality and Social Psychology, 63,* 989–1003.

Aspinwall, L.G., & Taylor, S.E. (1997). A stitch in time: Self-regulation and proactive coping. *Psychological Bulletin, 121,* 417–436.

Bandura, A. (1986). *Social foundations of thought and action: A social cognitive theory*. Englewood Cliffs, NJ: Prentice-Hall.

Breznitz, S. (1983). The seven kinds of denial. In S. Breznitz (Ed.), *The denial of stress* (pp. 257–280). New York: International Universities Press, Inc.

Cacioppo, J.T., & Petty, R.E. (1981). Social psychological procedures for cognitive response assessment: The thought-listing technique. In T.V. Merluzzi, C.R. Glass, & M. Genest (Eds.), *Cognitive assessment* (pp. 309–342). New York: Guilford Press.

Carver, C.S., Pozo, C., Harris, S.D., Noriega, V., Scheier, M.F., Robinson, D.S., Ketcham, A.S., Moffat, F.L., Jr., & Clark, K.C. (1993). How coping mediates the effect of optimism on distress: A study of women with early stage breast cancer. *Journal of Personality and Social Psychology, 65,* 375–390.

Carver, C.S., & Scheier, M.F. (1981). *Attention and self-regulation: A control-theory approach to human behavior.* New York: Springer-Verlag.

Carver, C.S., & Scheier, M.F. (1990). Principles of self-regulation: Action and emotion. In E.T. Higgins & R.M. Sorrentino (Eds.), *Handbook of motivation and cognition,* (Vol. 2, pp. 3–52). New York: Guilford Press.

Chang, E.C. (in press). *Optimism and pessimism: Theory, research, and practice.* Washington, DC: American Psychological Association.

Colvin, C.R., & Block, J. (1994). Do positive illusions foster mental health? An examination of the Taylor and Brown formulation. *Psychological Bulletin, 116,* 3–20.

Croyle, R.T. (1992). Appraisal of health threats: Cognition, motivation, and social comparison. *Cognitive Theory and Research, 16,* 165–182.

Dohrenwend, B.S., Dohrenwend, B.P., Dodson, M., & Shrout, P.E. (1984). Symptoms, hassles, social supports, and life events: Problems of confounded measures. *Journal of Abnormal Psychology, 93,* 222–230.

Fiske, S.T., & Taylor, S.E. (1991). *Social cognition* (2nd ed.). New York: McGraw-Hill.

Gillham, J.E., Shatté, A.J., Reivich, K.J., & Seligman, M.E.P. (in press). Optimism, pessimism, and explanatory style. In E.C. Chang (Ed.), *Optimism and pessimism: Theory, research, and practice.* Washington, DC: American Psychological Association.

Isen, A.M. (1993). Positive affect and decision making. In M. Lewis & J.M. Haviland (Eds.), *Handbook of emotions* (pp. 261–277). New York: Guilford Press.

Janoff-Bulman, R., & Frieze, I.H. (1983). A theoretical perspective for understanding reactions to victimization. *Journal of Social Issues, 39,* 1–17.

Jemmott, J.B., III., Ditto, P.H., & Croyle, R.T. (1986). Judging health status: Effects of perceived prevalence and personal relevance. *Journal of Personality and Social Psychology, 50,* 899–905.

Jerusalem, M. (1993). Personal resources, environmental constraints, and adaptational processes: The predictive power of a theoretical stress model. *Personality and Individual Differences, 14,* 15–24.

Lazarus, R.S. (1983). The costs and benefits of denial. In S. Breznitz (Ed.), *The denial of stress* (pp. 1–30). New York: International Universities Press, Inc.

Liberman, A., & Chaiken, S. (1992). Defensive processing of personally relevant health messages. *Personality and Social Psychology Bulletin, 18,* 669–679.

Marshall, G.N., Wortman, C.B., Kusulas, J.W., Hervig, L.K., & Vickers, R.R. (1992). Distinguishing optimism from pessimism: Relations to fundamental dimensions of mood and personality. *Journal of Personality and Social Psychology, 62,* 1067–1074.

Paterson, R.J., & Neufeld, R.W.J. (1987). Clear danger: Situational determinants of the appraisal of threat. *Psychological Bulletin, 101,* 404–416.

Perloff, L.S. (1983). Perceptions of vulnerability to victimization. *Journal of Social Issues, 39*(2), 41–61.

Peterson, C., & Seligman, M.E.P. (1984). Causal explanations as a risk factor for depression: Theory and evidence. *Psychological Review, 91,* 347–374.

Reed, M.B., & Aspinwall, L.G. (1998). Self-affirmation reduces biased processing of health-risk information. *Motivation and Emotion, 22,* 99–132.

Rhodewalt, F., & Zone, J.B. (1989). Appraisal of life change, depression, and illness in hardy and nonhardy women. *Journal of Personality and Social Psychology, 56,* 81–88.

Scheier, M.F., & Carver, C.S. (1985). Optimism, coping and health: Assessment and implications of generalized outcome expectancies. *Health Psychology, 4,* 219–247.

Scheier, M.F., & Carver, C.S. (1992). Effects of optimism on psychological and physical well-being: Theoretical overview and empirical update. *Cognitive Therapy and Research, 16,* 201–228.

Scheier, M.F., Carver, C.S., & Bridges, M.W. (1994). Distinguishing optimism from neuroticism (and trait anxiety, self-mastery, and self-esteem): A re-evaluation of the Life Orientation Test. *Journal of Personality and Social Psychology, 67,* 1063–1078.

Scheier, M.F., Carver, C.S., & Bridges, M.W. (in press). Optimism, pessimism, and psychological well-being. In E.C. Chang (Ed.), *Optimism and pessimism: Theory, research, and practice.* Washington, DC: American Psychological Association.

Scheier, M.F., Matthews, K.A., Owens, J., Magovern, G.J., Sr., Lefebvre, R.C., Abbott, R.A., & Carver, C.S. (1989). Dispositional optimism and recovery from coronary artery bypass surgery: The beneficial effects on physical and psychological well-being. *Journal of Personality and Social Psychology, 57,* 1024–1040.

Scheier, M.F., Weintraub, J.K., & Carver, C.S. (1986). Coping with stress: Divergent strategies of optimists and pessimists. *Journal of Personality and Social Psychology, 51,* 1257–1264.

Silicon Beach Software, Inc. (1989). Super Card v1.6. San Diego, CA.

Skinner, E.A. (1996). A guide to constructs of control. *Journal of Personality and Social Psychology, 71,* 549–570.

Smith, S.M., & Shaffer, D.R. (1991). The effects of good moods on systematic processing: "Willing but not able, or able but not willing?" *Motivation and Emotion, 15,* 243–279.

Smith, T.W., Pope, M.K., Rhodewalt, F., & Poulton, J.L. (1989). Optimism, neuroticism, coping, and symptom reports: An alternative interpretation of the Life Orientation Test. *Journal of Personality and Social Psychology, 56,* 640–648.

Snyder, C.R. (1994). *The psychology of hope: You can get there from here.* New York: Free Press.

Taylor, S.E., & Aspinwall, L.G. (1990). Psychosocial aspects of chronic illness. Presented as a Master Lecture at the American Psychological Association annual meetings, New Orleans, LA (1989, August). Reprinted in P.T. Costa, Jr. & G.R. VandenBos (Eds.), *Psychological aspects of serious illness: Chronic conditions, fatal disease, and clinical care* (pp. 3–60). Washington, DC: American Psychological Association.

Taylor, S.E., & Aspinwall, L.G. (1996). Mediating and moderating processes in psychosocial stress: Appraisal, coping, resistance and vulnerability. In H.B. Kaplan (Ed.), *Psychosocial stress: Perspectives on structure, theory, life-course, and methods* (pp. 71–110). San Diego, CA: Academic Press.

Taylor, S.E., & Brown, J.D. (1988). Illusion and well-being: A social psychological perspective on mental health. *Psychological Bulletin, 103,* 193–210.

Taylor, S.E., & Brown, J.D. (1994). Positive illusions and well-being revisited: Separating fact from fiction. *Psychological Bulletin, 116,* 21–27.

Taylor, S.E., Kemeny, M.E., Aspinwall, L.G., Schneider, S.C., Rodriguez, R., & Herbert, M. (1992). Optimism, coping, psychological distress, and high-risk sexual behavior among men at risk for AIDS. *Journal of Personality and Social Psychology, 63,* 460–473.

Tennen, H., & Affleck, G. (1987). The costs and benefits of optimistic explanations and dispositional optimism. *Journal of Personality, 55,* 378–393.

Watson, D., & Clark, L.A. (1984). Negative affectivity: The disposition to experience aversive emotional states. *Psychological Bulletin, 96,* 465–490.

Weinstein, N.D. (1984). Why it won't happen to me: Perceptions of risk factors and susceptibility. *Health Psychology, 3,* 431–457.

Weinstein, N.D., & Nicolich, M. (1993). Correct and incorrect interpretations of correlations between risk perceptions and risk behaviors. *Health Psychology, 12,* 235–245.

ACKNOWLEDGMENTS

The authors wish to acknowledge the Department of Psychology and the General Research Board of the University of Maryland for their support of this work. The second author was also supported in part by an Undergraduate Apprenticeship in Research and Scholarship sponsored by the Office of Undergraduate Studies and the University Honors Program.

We also wish to thank Ben Harper of Caffeinated Concepts Group for the design of the stimulus presentation and data collection programs and Tynette Galltin, Allyson Leven, Wendy Hess, and Gretchen Lichtner for their assistance in the conduct and analysis of Study 3.

✦ CHAPTER 10 ✦

On the Mechanisms by Which Optimism Promotes Positive Mental and Physical Health: A Commentary on Aspinwall and Brunhart

Lauren B. Alloy, Lyn Y. Abramson, and Alexandra M. Chiara

RESEARCH AND THEORY on optimism are notable for the variety of conceptualizations of this personality variable. Interestingly, most studies coincide in documenting a positive association between physical and psychological well-being and optimism, whether the construct of optimism is operationalized in terms of positive expectations for the future (Scheier & Carver, 1985), adaptive attributions (Abramson, Metalsky, & Alloy, 1989; Peterson & Seligman, 1984), self-enhancement (Greenwald, 1980; Weinstein, 1980), or illusions of personal control (Alloy & Abramson, 1979; Langer, 1975). The systematic and elegant research conducted by Aspinwall and Brunhart (see Chapter 9) was designed to define the parameters and elucidate the processes underlying this well-established link, with a specific focus on the mechanisms underlying the association between positive expectations for the future and health. In striving toward these goals, Aspinwall and Brunhart (see Chapter 9) address many key issues in the literature and suggest compelling avenues for future exploration.

Despite many research findings indicating that optimism confers positive effects on physical health and psychological adjustment, various theoretical contributions suggest that optimism may actually have a detrimental impact on health (Baumeister, 1989; Goleman, 1989; Janoff-Bulman, 1989). Specifically, it has been proposed that self-enhancing biases may predispose optimists to disregard potential risks and unwittingly place themselves in danger by failing to take preventive action (Perloff, 1983; Weinstein, 1980, 1984, 1987). It has also been suggested that optimists are less likely to acknowledge mistakes or accept limitations, thus failing to modulate their efforts according to situational demands (Colvin & Block, 1994). When blatant difficulties or threats are recognized, the impact of disconfirmation of positive expectations may be greater for optimists (Janoff-Bulman & Frieze, 1983). Compromised resilience may lead to loss of self-esteem and disillusionment, resulting in chronic emotional or physical problems.

Theorists who emphasize the negative consequences of optimism maintain that optimistic biases serve a defensive function, sheltering individuals from accepting personal imperfections and the unpredictability of life (Schwarzer, 1994). While dispositional optimism may be associated with the need to maintain beliefs about a benevolent world, illusions of control and enhancing attributions may serve to reassure optimists of the predictability and manageability of their circumstances (Perloff, 1983). Different aspects of optimism such as positive attributions and self-enhancing biases may protect self-esteem through denial, fulfilling the need to view oneself in a positive light (Weinstein, 1982, 1987). When difficult situations challenge these beliefs and call for a realistic appraisal of resources and possible responses, it is this very denial that may place optimists at risk.

Although the denial notion is consistent with prevailing views of mental health that emphasize contact with reality (Beck, 1967; Jahoda, 1958), it is contradicted by naturalistic research showing dispositional optimists' greater use of flexible coping when faced with experiences as varied as a diagnosis of breast cancer (Carver et al., 1993), adjusting to college (Aspinwall & Taylor, 1992), and coronary bypass surgery (Scheier et al., 1989). Prospective studies with different samples have demonstrated the positive association between optimism and psychological adjustment (Taylor et al., 1992), physical well-being (Shepperd, Maroto, & Pbert, 1996), and health-protective behavior (Robbins, Spence, & Clark, 1991).

In order to directly test the hypothesis that optimism functions like denial, Aspinwall and Brunhart (1996; see Chapter 9) chose an information-processing approach that would permit a microanalysis of attention to and recall of threatening information. The ingenious within-subjects design built upon previous research through the use of an Internet paradigm to present threat information in a naturalistic fashion, the inclusion of both general and specific optimism measures (expectations of the future), and the manipulation of threat valence and relevance. Other strengths included the focus on process and the analysis of information processing variables.

Aspinwall and Brunhart (1996; see Chapter 9) proposed that a negative correlation between attention and threat would provide evidence of denial in optimistic individuals. Their results suggested that optimists actually attended to information about risks for severe illnesses more than pessimists did and that optimists showed a trend for better recall of the threatening information at a one-week interval in one of two studies (Study 2). The pattern of increased attention to threatening information was particularly marked when the risk information presented pertained directly to behaviors that optimists themselves engaged in. Optimists' failure to exhibit reduced attention, elaboration, and memory as the valence and relevance of the illness threat increased provided further evidence that optimists did not deny risk, but actively engaged in thinking about it.

This conclusion contrasts with at least one study that examined a dimension of optimism distinct from outcome expectancies. In our research on possible information processing mechanisms by which attributional optimism protects people against depression, nondepressed individuals exhibiting either an optimistic or pessimistic inferential style (style for inferring causes, consequences, and self-implications of negative life events) completed a self-referent information processing task battery (Alloy, Abramson, Murray, Whitehouse, & Hogan, 1997). The battery consisted of four tasks that yielded five dependent measures. Each task utilized four types of adjectives, matched for word length and frequency, representing a 2 (valence) x 2 (content) design: these types consisted of positively and negatively valenced adjectives that were either relevant or irrelevant to a depressive self-concept (e.g., incompetent is a negative, depression-relevant adjective; effective is a positive, depression-relevant adjective; examples of depression-irrelevant adjectives are polite or rude). In Task 1, participants were presented with trait adjectives (of each of the four types) on a computer monitor and were asked to judge whether each was self-descriptive or not. Response times for making these judgments were also recorded without the awareness of the participants. In Task 2, participants received a booklet containing three adjectives of each of the four types. For each adjective they judged to be self-descriptive, they were asked to provide specific evidence of their own past behaviors that indicated why the adjective described them. For example, if a participant believed that he or she was incompetent, he or she had to provide specific examples of his or her past incompetent behaviors. The dependent measure was the number of behavioral examples provided for each of the four types of adjectives. In Task 3, participants read twenty-four statements describing hypothetical behaviors from each of the four content × valence domains. They were asked to judge the probability (0–100%) that they would behave or react in the way described if they were in that situation in the future. Task 4 was an incidental free recall test for the adjectives participants had judged as self-descriptive or not in Task 1. The free recall test followed Task 1 with a delay of two hours.

Consistent with Aspinwall and Brunhart's (1996; see Chapter 9) results, Alloy and colleagues (1997) found enhanced processing of self-relevant information among participants with optimistic inferential styles. However, this was only apparent when participants were presented with favorable information about themselves. When faced with negative self-referent information (e.g., worthless), optimists exhibited less endorsement, and given endorsement, slower response times, less elaboration (i.e., fewer past behavioral examples and lower future probability judgments), and poorer recall of the threatening information than did pessimistic individuals. This suggests that under certain conditions, optimists appear to exhibit denial relative to pessimists.

Both the research of Aspinwall and Brunhart and the study of Alloy and colleagues (1997) emphasize the information processing correlates of optimism. The paucity of research in this area indicates the need for replication studies and suggests that the current results should be interpreted with caution. Nonetheless, there are various preliminary explanations for the finding that optimism can lead to both heightened and inhibited processing of threat information. One possibility is that the discrepant findings stem from the focus on two different aspects of the optimism construct. Aspinwall and Brunhart (see Chapter 9) operationalized optimism in terms of positive expectations for the future (in general, and specifically for one's health), whereas Alloy and colleagues (1997) studied inferential style, identifying optimism in terms of people's inferences about the causes, consequences, and self-implications of events that already occurred. Whereas dispositional optimism is considered to be independent of control expectancies, these represent an essential aspect of attributional style. In our exploration of the distinct and overlapping features of four types of optimism, we found that both dispositional and attributional optimism were related to enhanced well-being (Chiara & Alloy, 2000). However, each loaded onto its own factor in a factor analysis and correlated differently with self-report measures of depression, anxiety, mania, and physical health complaints. This suggests that different dimensions of optimism may be linked to health through distinct mechanisms, with pathways involving separate patterns of information processing.

Another source of the discrepancy between the results of Aspinwall and Brunhart (see Chapter 9) and those of Alloy and colleagues (1997) may be the nature of the threat presented. In Aspinwall and Brunhart's studies, participants responded to future hazards to their physical health; in the study by Alloy and colleagues, they faced current threats to their self-image. Optimists exhibited increased attention and elaboration of the threat in the former condition, where there were clear external sources of threat and ways in which risk could be minimized (i.e., by eliminating unhealthy habits and incorporating sound ones). Conversely, information about negative characteristics that challenged optimists' sense of self-worth and may have seemed difficult to modify may therefore have resulted in relatively poorer attention, elaboration, and recall by this group.

One way in which this paradox may be resolved is to consider the theme of self-preservation in both sets of findings. One benefit of being optimistic may lie in the ability to successfully protect oneself from whatever threat is present. When the danger is actual physical harm to one's body, rapid orientation and problem-focused coping with that threat is most adaptive. However, when what is at risk is one's self-esteem and immediate change may seem impossible or too daunting to entertain, the most appropriate solution may be to protect oneself by selectively attending to threatening information. Maintaining one's positive view of oneself in the face of threats to the self-concept may result in appropriate modulation of negative affect, thereby increasing the likelihood of eventual acceptance of negative information and subsequent self-improvement. Although vigilance to external threat information is undoubtedly essential for survival, self-esteem preservation is key if an individual is to thrive through perseverance and learn from experience. Well-being broadly defined entails not only the avoidance of danger, but also the achievement of desired personal goals, and these needs should not be considered incompatible. Individuals who value themselves are more likely to take precautions to guarantee their future well-being, and in so doing may reinforce their sense of positive self-esteem.

The apparently contradictory findings linking optimism to both better and worse processing of threat may therefore reflect the multiple functions of optimism, which result in different patterns of processing as circumstances and threat vary. When threat is imminent, attention to environmental cues will ideally take precedence over buffering one's self-esteem. Appropriate regulation of information processing may allow optimists to attend to threat cues without becoming hypervigilant. The simultaneous ability to manage anxiety and distress may render optimists better able to consider options, mobilize resources, and follow through with solutions than realistic or pessimistic peers. Optimistic attributions, elevated control beliefs, and an enhanced sense of competence may increase self-efficacy, thus contributing to well-being by promoting consistent implementation of health-protective behaviors and avoidance of dangerous activities (Ajzen & Madden, 1986).

In addition to increasing the likelihood of an adaptive response to threat, optimism may positively affect striving toward goals and the likelihood of achieving them. In their expectancy-value theory, Carver and Scheier (1990) emphasized not only the self-protective effects of optimism, but also the motivational effects of believing that things will turn out well. They proposed that optimists will persevere more than individuals who fail to view challenging goals as attainable. However, this does not imply that optimists persist even when outcomes are clearly unattainable and perseverance would be futile. The finding that optimists are actually quicker to disengage from unsolvable laboratory tasks suggests that optimism allows individuals to adaptively judge when they have exerted sufficient effort in trying to achieve a goal (Janoff-Bulman & Brickman, 1982). Again, other dimensions of optimism may also have an impact on efforts to either achieve a desirable goal or to avoid a disagreeable outcome. Perseverance and an increased likelihood of success may be facilitated by self-enhancing biases for traits or the future, elevated control beliefs, and optimistic attributions for positive and negative events.

Coping style is one variable that has been proposed as a mediator of the relationship between dispositional optimism and well-being (Cozzarelli, 1993; Scheier, Weintraub, & Carver, 1986). A growing body of research has corroborated that optimism predicts active coping, as well as lower levels of denial, avoidant coping, and disengagement from stressful situations (Aspinwall & Taylor, 1992; Carver et al., 1993; Stanton & Snider, 1993). Unfortunately, interest in coping and dispositional optimism has not extended to studies on other dimensions of optimism and, therefore, little is known about the relation between avoidant or active coping and attributional style, illusions of control, or self-enhancement. Another possible mediator of positive associations between optimism and health that warrants further study is social support (Aspinwall & Taylor, 1997). Although extreme optimism may irritate others, it is likely that optimists' positive attitudes and generally better adjustment to life make them attractive associates for peers, thus increasing their access to social support when identifying, appraising, and responding to threatening situations (Aspinwall & Taylor, 1997). Information and material assistance from others can improve problem-focused coping, while emotional support may encourage adaptive responses focusing on affect. Optimists' ability to create personal environments conducive to social support may be an influential factor in explaining the better adjustment and general well-being of this group.

The small body of research that exists on information processing and optimism suggests many fruitful avenues for future exploration. The most obvious priority should be to increase the number of sound experimental and naturalistic studies designed to address the information processing effects of optimism, so that laboratory findings could be linked to actual behavior and well-being. Concurrent designs involving different samples and a variety of threats to self-esteem and health should be complemented by longitudinal, prospective studies. The examination of changes in information processing over time would be of great utility in determining whether optimism is a flexible characteristic (Armor & Taylor, 1997) that allows individuals to maximize success while minimizing deleterious outcomes. These studies could also serve to elucidate the role of coping, social support, and other relevant variables.

Given that various dimensions of optimism have been associated with increased levels of adjustment and health, studies should expand their scope to include measures of self-enhancement, attributions, and the illusion of control. Aspinwall and Brunhart's (see Chapter 9) use of general and health-specific dispositional optimism yielded different effects on attention to threatening information about health risks, indicating the utility of addressing this distinction further in examining the distinct and overlapping information processing features of other conceptualizations of optimism. In addition, researchers should continue to utilize threat information that is relevant to samples, while exploring the role of other characteristics of the threat such as proximity and lethality. A clearer understanding of the mechanisms by which different forms of optimism contribute to positive physical health and psychological adjustment is essential to the development of maximally effective interventions for the promotion of health. The work of Aspinwall and Brunhart presented in this volume takes an important step in this direction.

REFERENCES

Abramson, L.Y., Metalsky, G.I., & Alloy, L.B. (1989). Hopelessness depression: A theory-based subtype of depression. *Psychological Review*, 96, 358–372.

Ajzen, I., & Madden, T.J. (1986). Prediction of goal-directed behavior: Attitudes, intentions, and perceived behavioral control. *Journal of Experimental Social Psychology, 22,* 453–474.

Alloy, L.B., & Abramson, L.Y. (1979). Judgment of contingency in depressed and nondepressed students: Sadder but wiser? *Journal of Experimental Psychology: General, 108,* 441–485.

Alloy, L.B., Abramson, L.Y., Murray, L.A., Whitehouse, W.G., & Hogan, M.E. (1997). Self-referent information-processing in individuals at high and low cognitive risk for depression. *Cognition and Emotion, 11,* 539–568.

Armor, D.A., & Taylor, S.E. (1997). Situated optimism: Specific outcome expectancies and self-regulation. In M.P. Zanna (Ed.), *Advances in experimental social psychology* (Vol. 30). New York: Academic Press.

Aspinwall, L.G., & Brunhart, S.M. (1996). Distinguishing optimism from denial: Optimistic beliefs predict attention to health threats. *Personality and Social Psychology Bulletin, 22,* 993–1003.

Aspinwall, L.G., & Taylor, S.E. (1992). Modeling cognitive adaptation: A longitudinal investigation of the impact of individual differences and coping on college adjustment and performance. *Journal of Personality and Social Psychology, 63,* 989–1003.

Aspinwall, L.G., & Taylor, S.E. (1997). A stitch in time: Self-regulation and proactive coping. *Psychological Bulletin, 121,* 417–436.

Baumeister, R.F. (1989). The optimal margin of illusion. *Journal of Social and Clinical Psychology, 8,* 176–189.

Beck, A.T. (1967). *Depression: Clinical, experimental, and theoretical aspects.* New York: Harper & Row.

Carver, C.S., Pozo, C., Harris, S.D., Noriega, V., Scheier, M.F., Robinson, D.S., Ketcham, A.S., Moffat, F.L., & Clark, K.C. (1993). How coping mediates the effect of optimism on distress: A study of women with early stage breast cancer. *Journal of Personality and Social Psychology, 65,* 375–390.

Carver, C.S., & Scheier, M.F. (1990). Origins and functions of positive and negative affect: A control-process view. *Psychological Review, 97,* 19–35.

Chiara, A.M., & Alloy, L.B. (2000). *Optimistic illusions and well-being: A longitudinal analysis of mental and physical health using multiple measures of optimism.* Philadelphia: Temple University.

Colvin, C.R., & Block, J. (1994). Do positive illusions foster mental health? An examination of the Taylor and Brown formulation. *Psychological Bulletin, 116,* 3–20.

Cozzarelli, C. (1993). Personality and self-efficacy as predictors of coping with abortion. *Journal of Personality and Social Psychology, 65,* 1224–1236.

Goleman, D.J. (1989). What is negative about positive illusions? When benefits for the individual harm the collective. *Journal of Social and Clinical Psychology, 8,* 190–197.

Greenwald, A.G. (1980). The totalitarian ego: Fabrication and revision of personal history. *American Psychologist, 35,* 603–618.

Jahoda, M. (1958). *Current concepts of positive mental health.* New York: Basic Books.

Janoff-Bulman, R. (1989). The benefits of illusions, the threat of disillusionment, and the limitations of inaccuracy. *Journal of Social and Clinical Psychology, 8,* 130–157.

Janoff-Bulman, R., & Brickman, P. (1982). Expectations and what people learn from failure. In N.T. Feather (Ed.), *Expectations and actions: Expectancy-value models in psychology* (pp. 207–237). Hillsdale, NJ: Erlbaum.

Janoff-Bulman, R., & Frieze, I.H. (1983). A theoretical perspective for understanding reactions to victimization. *Journal of Social Issues, 39,* 1–17.

Langer, E.J. (1975). The illusion of control. *Journal of Personality and Social Psychology, 32,* 311–328.

Perloff, L.S. (1983). Perceptions of vulnerability to victimization. *Journal of Social Issues, 39,* 41–61.

Peterson, C., & Seligman, M.E.P. (1984). Causal explanations as a risk factor for depression: Theory and evidence. *Psychological Review, 91,* 347–374.

Robbins, A.S., Spence, J.T., & Clark, H. (1991). Psychological determinants of health and performance: The tangled web of desirable and undesirable characteristics. *Journal of Personality and Social Psychology, 61,* 755–765.

Scheier, M.F., & Carver, C.S. (1985). Optimism, coping and health: Assessment and implications of generalized outcome expectancies. *Health Psychology, 4,* 219–247.

Scheier, M.F., Matthews, K.A., Owens, J.F., Magovern, G.J., Sr., Lefebvre, R.C., Abbott, R.A., & Carver, C.S. (1989). Dispositional optimism and recovery from coronary artery bypass surgery: The beneficial effects on physical and psychological well-being. *Journal of Personality and Social Psychology, 57,* 1024–1040.

Scheier, M.F., Weintraub, J.K., & Carver, C.S. (1986). Coping with stress: Divergent strategies for optimists and pessimists. *Journal of Personality and Social Psychology, 51,* 1257–1264.

Schwarzer, R. (1994). Optimism, vulnerability, and self-beliefs in health-related cognitions: A systematic overview. *Psychology and Health, 9,* 161–180.

Shepperd, J.A., Maroto, J.J., & Pbert, L.A. (1996). Dispositional optimism as a predictor of health changes among cardiac patients. *Journal of Research in Personality, 30,* 517–534.

Stanton, A.L., & Snider, P.R. (1993). Coping with a breast cancer diagnosis: A prospective study. *Health Psychology, 12,* 16–23.

Taylor, S.E., Kemeny, M.E., Aspinwall, L.G., Schneider, S.C., Rodriguez, R., & Herbert, M. (1992). Optimism, coping, psychological distress, and high-risk sexual behavior among men at risk for AIDS. *Journal of Personality and Social Psychology, 63,* 460–473.

Weinstein, N.D. (1980). Unrealistic optimism about future life events. *Journal of Personality and Social Psychology, 39,* 806–820.

Weinstein, N.D. (1982). Unrealistic optimism about susceptibility to health problems. *Journal of Behavioral Medicine, 5,* 441–460.

Weinstein, N.D. (1984). Why it won't happen to me: Perceptions of risk factors and susceptibility. *Health Psychology, 3,* 431–457.

Weinstein, N.D. (1987). Unrealistic optimism about susceptibility to health problems: Conclusions from a community-wide sample. *Journal of Behavior Medicine, 10,* 481–500.

ACKNOWLEDGMENTS

Preparation of this chapter was supported by National Institute of Mental Health grants MH 48216 to Lauren B. Alloy and MH 43866 to Lyn Y. Abramson.

Section D. Promoting Optimism and Hope

✦

✦ CHAPTER 11 ✦

Promoting Hope in Children and Adolescents

Andrew J. Shatté, Jane E. Gillham, and Karen Reivich

THE PREVALENCE of depression has reached epidemic proportions. One in ten children experiences clinical depression before age 14 (Garrison, Schluchter, Schoenbach, & Kaplan, 1989). As many as one in five adolescents suffers a major depressive episode before the end of their high school years (Lewinsohn, Hops, Roberts, & Seeley, 1993). For many depressed youth, the future seems foreshortened and bleak—a pervasive sense of hopelessness is a prominent symptom of their major depressive disorder.

Suicide is the ultimate expression of this hopelessness. Suicide is the default option when all other courses of action have been eliminated as futile. Tragically, many of our youth do come to feel so profoundly hopeless. More than 8% of high school students in this country attempt suicide each year (Center for Disease Control, 1991). Each year, approximately 13 in every 100,000 American adolescents aged 15 through 19 take their own lives (Lewinsohn, Rohde, & Seeley, 1996). Paradoxically, this occurs against a backdrop of unprecedented opportunity for social and economic advancement.

This chapter examines the Penn Optimism Program—a depression prevention initiative for children developed at the University of Pennsylvania. There are two major components of the Penn Optimism Program (POP), which together instill a sense of hope in children at risk for depression; the first is predominately cognitive and the second is largely behavioral. In the cognitive module, children learn to challenge their overly pessimistic attributions and predictions. Through this process participants learn to generate problem-solving options that were previously unavailable to them. The behavioral component equips participants with the skills to act on these options.

HOPE AND HOPELESSNESS

Clinical psychologists have traditionally adopted a disorder-oriented approach to personality, emphasizing the remediation of negative characteristics over and above promotion of the positive. Consequently, substantially more research attention has been paid to the etiology of hopelessness than to understanding the development of hope.

Abramson, Metalsky, and Alloy have developed one of the most comprehensive models of the etiology of hopelessness and have proposed a corresponding hopelessness subtype of depression (Abramson, Metalsky, & Alloy, 1989). According to their theory, hopelessness is a proximal sufficient cause of depression, and the final common pathway for all other, more distal, causes of the subtype (Metalsky, Joiner, Hardin, & Abramson, 1993). They characterize hopelessness as the "expectation that highly desired outcomes will not occur or that highly aversive outcomes will occur, with the further expectation that nothing is going to change this situation for the better" (Metalsky et al., 1993, p. 101). The critical risk factor for hopelessness depression is a cognitive diathesis—the tendency to attribute negative life events to stable and global causes.

Snyder and his colleagues conceptualize hope as a journey, requiring a destination, a map, and a means of transportation. That is, a child preparing for such a journey needs well-defined goals, knowledge of how to achieve those goals, and the determination and energy to act (Snyder, McDermott, Cook, & Rapoff, 1997). They emphasize that this journey of hope "lives first and foremost in our minds" (Snyder et al., 1997, p. 3).

The theories of Snyder and Abramson and colleagues intersect at the realm of cognitions. For Abramson and colleagues, attributions and expectations of negative valence are focal to hopelessness. For Snyder and colleagues, hopefulness is the product of the synergy between mental representations of goals, pathways to goals, and mental energy (Snyder et al., 1997, p.7). It seems clear then that any program designed to promote hope and prevent hopelessness and depression should address cognitions, and the first half of POP is devoted to cognitive restructuring. But is this sufficient?

We contend that two conditions must be satisfied to foster hope in children. First, the child's cognitive style must allow that, to a threshold degree, her situation is changeable, her goals are clear, and that desirable outcomes can be achieved. Second, the child must be equipped with the behavioral skills to successfully accomplish her goals. Neither condition is sufficient. If the at-risk child perceives that she can improve her life, but does not have the skills to act on that perception, then the window of hope will close. If the child believes that the causes of her problems will be around forever and will ruin everything she attempts, then she will feel helpless and hopeless whether or not she in fact has the social, academic, or introspective skills to advance her life.

In this chapter we examine how POP aims to promote hope in children through training in cognitive and behavioral techniques.

THE PENN OPTIMISM PROGRAM

POP is a 12-week (24-hour), school-based intervention (see table 11.1). It is delivered in groups of eight to twelve children by a trained leader. POP is a manualized protocol in which the principles of cognitive-behavioral therapies have been calibrated for the appropriate developmental age and recast in a preventive mode. Key aspects of cognitive theory are taught in brief didactic sections. Most of the session is devoted to scripted activities in which the participants try out the new skills.

Sessions 1 through 5 represent the cognitive component. In Sessions 6 through 9 we teach more behaviorally-oriented skills. Sessions 10 and 11 combine these skills with more hopeful thinking in a comprehensive problem-solving strategy.

Table 11.1

The 12-Session POP Agenda

Session #	Cognitive/Behavioral Content
Session 1:	The ABC Model
Session 2:	Explanatory Style
Session 3:	Generating Alternatives and Evaluating Evidence
Session 4:	Decatastrophizing
Session 5:	The ABC's of Family Conflict and Rapid-Fire Thought Disputing
Session 6:	Assertiveness and Negotiation
Session 7:	Relaxation and Other Coping Strategies
Session 8:	Dealing with Procrastination and Social Skills
Session 9:	Decision Making
Session 10:	Problem Solving
Session 11:	Problem Solving
Session 12:	Review and Farewell Party

THE COGNITIVE ELEMENTS OF POP

There is now considerable research evidence indicating that children are vulnerable to the same cognitive distortions as adults, and that these cognitions are causal in the development of childhood and adolescent hopelessness and depression (e.g., Hammen, 1988; Kaslow, Rehm & Siegel, 1984). Many of the children who enter POP have cognitive styles that restrict their behavioral options and hamper their problem solving.

The cognitive component introduces the participants to five skills designed to increase cognitive flexibility, expand the arena of possible solutions, and thereby maximize hopefulness: the ABC model, explanatory style, disputing of causal beliefs, decatastrophizing, and rapid-fire disputing.

Cognitive Skill #1: The ABC Model

Session 1 encapsulates the focal role of cognitions in mood under the rubric of Ellis's ABC model (Ellis, 1962; Ellis & Grieger, 1977). Ellis recognized that our lay understanding is that activating events (As) have direct emotional and behavioral consequences (Cs). For example, Tom fails to make the cut in the school baseball tryouts (A), feels depressed (emotional C), and never again tries for another sporting team (behavioral C). However, Ellis proposed that a mediating individual difference variable must be added to the model to explain why different people react differently to what is ostensibly the same event. For example, Linda's failure to make the cut for baseball, rather than leading her to give up on sports, inspires her to train harder for track. According to Ellis, our beliefs (Bs) about the event and the meaning we attach to it directly cause what we feel and what we do (i.e., A→B→C). It is not the activating event per se, but rather Tom's belief, "I'm a terrible athlete," that causes him to avoid all future tryouts. Conversely, Linda's belief that she missed the baseball cut because "I didn't train hard enough" is energizing. Causal attributions (Session 2) and catastrophizing (Session 4) are important belief subsets of ABC.

We convey the ABC skill to participants using cartoons in three panels, representing activating events, beliefs, and emotional consequences (see figure 11.1). The children are taught to describe objectively the activating event pictured in Panel A, providing only the facts of the situation without the actor's interpretation (e.g., "he missed the cut for the baseball team" rather than "he messed up again" or "he's a terrible athlete"). Participants label the emotion on the face in Panel C and estimate its intensity. Finally, the children fill in the thought bubble with a belief that will make sense of the emotion, given the activating event.

Figure 11.1. The ABC skill with 3-panel cartoons.

We believe that the skill is best internalized if the children practice it on situations in their own lives. For this reason we devote considerable class time to eliciting activating events from the children (e.g., "My dad yelled at me when I broke the vase"), delineating the emotional consequences ("I felt really sad"), and identifying the causal belief ("I always mess up"). The group leader helps the participants "tune in" to their automatic thoughts—the "self talk in their heads." We utilize the group setting to spotlight the power of the model in explaining how different Bs lead to different Cs (e.g., "I wouldn't have felt sad. I would have been angry, because he shouldn't yell at you if it's an honest mistake").

After several iterations most of the children learn the logic of the B-C connection, the link between their thoughts and their feelings. They become adept at identifying Bs that can explain their Cs. This is an essential skill. It is their cognitions that lead to helplessness, hopelessness, and depression. These cognitions are often inaccurate. Only by learning to identify their beliefs can they hold them up to empirical scrutiny.

Cognitive Skill #2: Explanatory Style

We are predisposed to explain the adversities that bombard our lives. We generate beliefs about their causes, and from these attributions we make predictions about our future. For both the hopelessness theory of depression (Abramson, Metalsky, & Alloy, 1989) and the reformulated learned helplessness model (Abramson, Seligman, & Teasdale, 1978), our habitual manner of explaining negative events, or explanatory style, is a significant causal risk factor for hopelessness and depression. Imagine a child who fails to make the school baseball team. Any belief she has about why she failed can be coded on three dimensions. First, causal explanations are relatively internal or external; that is, she will attribute the failure either to herself or to another person or circumstance (e.g., "I'm not good at baseball" versus "the coach has it in for me"). Second, she will attribute the failure to relatively permanent or temporary causes (e.g., "I don't have good hand-eye coordination" versus "I wasn't focused enough"). Third, the cause she infers will be relatively pervasive or specific, undermining everything she does or affecting only her baseball standing (e.g., "I'm such a loser" versus "I'm no good at ball games").

Pessimists are those who, in the wake of adversity, tend to infer internal, permanent, and pervasive causes. Conversely, optimists tend to generate external, temporary, and specific causal explanations. Each of the three characteristics of causal beliefs is dimensional, and any given causal belief can be located in this three-dimensional space. Over time we come to inhabit an idiosyncratic area in attributional space, and respond reflexively with causal beliefs that reflect this explanatory style. There is some research evidence that our style crystallizes by about age nine and, without intervention, remains stable across the life span (Burns & Seligman, 1989; Nolen-Hoeksema, Girgus, & Seligman, 1986; Peterson, Seligman, & Vaillant, 1988).

Our perception of the controllability of adversity is represented across the three dimensions. External attributions indicate less control than internal beliefs, holding permanence and pervasiveness constant. Attribution to permanent causes indicates uncontrollability across time, while pervasiveness suggests uncontrollability across life domain (see Shatté,

Reivich, Gillham, & Seligman, 1998). Helplessness derives from the belief that we currently have no control over an adversity. We feel hopeless when we believe that we will never be able to gain that control.

Many of the children who enter POP are reflexive pessimists. They automatically apply an internal, permanent, pervasive "cookie cutter" to the world whenever adversity strikes. "I didn't make the team because I have no athletic ability" (internal, permanent, pervasive across sports). "She doesn't like me because I'm just not good with people" (internal, permanent, pervasive across interpersonal situations). "I failed the history class because I'm just plain stupid" (internal, permanent, pervasive across intellectual pursuits). In some cases, their attributions may reflect a reality. There are innate abilities and temperaments, normally distributed, which partially determine athletic and intellectual ability and interpersonal skill. But in many cases their pessimistic attributions are either inaccurate, or present only part of the causal picture (c.w., "I'm not the best athlete in the school by any stretch of the imagination, but I didn't practice that much before the tryouts either").

In Session 2 of POP, we liken the concept of explanatory style to an individual's fashion style—a habitual way of thinking just as we have habitual ways of dressing. We focus on the internal and permanent dimensions since they are easier constructs for the children to grasp. We introduce two cartoon characters to represent pessimism and optimism (Gloomy Greg and Hopeful Holly) and the children act out several skits depicting each until they are confident using the two dimensions. We guide the children to an understanding of their own style as well as the recognition that any causal explanation is merely one view of the world—one possible belief in response to that adversity.

Cognitive Skill #3: Disputing Causal Beliefs

Adversities typically are multifactorially caused. To the extent that we obstinately endorse the causal explanation derived from our explanatory style, we will fail to recognize the richness of the causal picture. Since we use our beliefs about the cause of our problems to generate possible solutions, our problem-solving options will also be restricted. The first step in disputing, then, is to generate alternative causal explanations.

Figure 11.2. Generating alternatives using 3-panel cartoons.

We begin teaching the requisite cognitive flexibility in Session 2, again using cartoons (see figure 11.2). We present children with an adversity in Panel A and with either a highly internal or permanent thought in Panel B. The participants are expected to describe the logical behavioral and emotional consequences of the pessimistic causal belief, generate a more optimistic alternative, and delineate how the initial and new behavioral and emotional responses differ. Participants are encouraged to generate four or five alternatives that span the three explanatory style dimensions. In the 'sister' example presented above, some 'temporary me' alternatives to the actor's initial 'permanent me' explanation (i.e., "I'm a terrible sister") could include "I'm sometimes careless with my sister's things," or "I don't pay attention to when she's about to get angry," or "this time I took something she really cares about." At other times we may encourage the children to generate external causes, as counterpoint to the extreme pessimism of the initial belief (e.g., "she gets so angry over nothing"). Returning to our baseball tryout example, if the child's initial beliefs are reflexively optimistic, he is taught to generate less optimistic beliefs that indicate some responsibility for the adversity (e.g., "maybe I didn't train hard enough").

The next step in disputing is the skill of evaluating evidence—adducing evidence from one's life to determine the accuracy of the initial and alternative causal beliefs. Cognitive therapists often compare this to the scientific process—generating several hypotheses and testing each against the available empirical evidence. In POP we use a detective analogy. A good detective, like Sherlock Holmes, comes up with a full list of suspects (initial belief plus alternatives) and looks for clues (evaluates evidence). Some suspects, it will be discovered, have a convincing alibi. This process is comparable to disproving a causal belief ("well I guess it's not true that I have no athletic ability, because I do ok at tennis and that takes athletic ability too"). Bad detectives conclude that the first suspect that popped into their heads (initial belief) must be guilty, without checking on the suspect's whereabouts on the night in question (evaluating evidence).

The process of generating alternatives and evaluating evidence taps into the complexity of adversity. Many factors contribute to problems in varying degrees. The alternatives and evidence process helps children analyze the relative importance of several candidate causal explanations. POP participants are taught through a series of activities to incorporate the results of their search for alternatives and evidence into a pie chart, in which each piece of pie corresponds to a causal belief, and with the size of each slice reflective of causal significance (see figure 11.3).

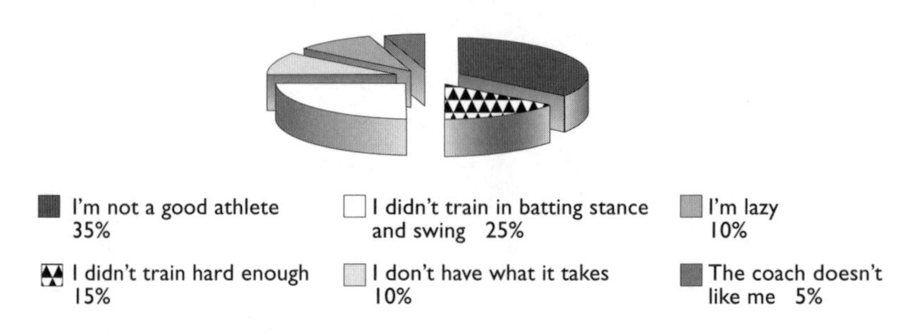

Figure 11.3. The pie chart maps the relative contribution of all causes.

A highly pessimistic belief, such as "I have no athletic ability," is a road block to problem solving and hope. As an initial belief, it represents

100% of the problem. Only after generating plausible alternatives and evaluating evidence is its true contribution revealed. Disputation may determine that a lack of athletic ability indeed explains a considerable portion of the variance in who made the cut and who did not. However, only through disputing can the child recognize the role of physical conditioning and batting practice—two causes over which the child can exert some control. As such, disputing is a skill that offers children hope for the future.

Cognitive Skill #4: Decatastrophizing

Implicit in any causal attribution is a prediction about the future role of the adversity. Highly permanent attributions indicate that the problem will continue to affect the person's life for a substantial time period. If combined with a high degree of pervasiveness, then helplessness and hopelessness are likely outcomes.

Pessimistic thoughts about the future tend to come in a catastrophic chain, the first link of which is an adversity that the child explains pessimistically. The following example represents an amalgam of anecdotes from our experiences implementing POP.

> Josh has noticed that his parents have been arguing more and more over the last six months. Every day now they seem to fight, shouting at each other and slamming doors. Recently he even heard his mother cry out, making him wonder if his dad had hit her. Today his mother yelled out to his dad, "You're a rotten father." His father had forgotten to pick him up after practice and Josh had to take a bus home—and this is not the first time. Josh thinks, "It's all my fault. I'm so messed up even my dad doesn't want to hang out with me. My dad's going to leave because he can't stand being with me. I'll never see him again. My mom won't be able to take care of all us kids. I'll probably end up in a foster home. If that happens I'll have to run away. I know what happens to kids like that. They end up on the streets and go to prison."

This tendency to catastrophize can be countered by using the skill of generating the worst case, best case, and most likely scenarios. The first step is to flesh out the entire causal chain, from current events through to the child's worst fears—the worst case scenario. For Josh, the chain is:

> Arguing → divorce → absent father → financial hardship → foster home → runaway → prison

Second, we estimate the likelihood of the final link in the chain, that Josh will end up in prison. Children, and adults, with pessimistic styles will tend to inflate the probability, perhaps giving estimates of one in ten or even one in three. The link to link nature of the chain of beliefs contributes to the tendency to exaggerate the probability of the catastrophic outcome. The step from the present reality to the final belief is enormous; imagine how our prisons would fill if we were imprisoned because our parents argue. However, the step from arguing to divorce is not absurd, nor is that between runaway status and prison. Nevertheless, catastrophic chains are a string of conditional probabilities—the probability that Josh's parents will get divorced *given* their arguing, the probability that Josh will never see his father again or get financial support *given* a divorce, and the probability that Josh would run away *given* his being sent to a foster home, etc. Therefore, the probability that the entire chain will play out is calculably small.

The next step in the skill of decatastrophizing is to generate some best case scenarios of similar probability (e.g., "his parents will never fight again because their struggles have caused them to bond more closely"). Best case scenarios provide a positive anchor to the negativity of the catastrophic chain. Finally, using worst and best as balances, we teach the children to generate most likely outcomes and devote most of their problem-solving resources to what is most probable, rather than what is most feared.

The skill of decatastrophizing provides children with a method of evaluating the accuracy of their expectations that "highly aversive outcomes will occur" (Metalsky et al., 1993). By so doing it provides a direct challenge to hopelessness.

Cognitive Skill #5: Rapid-Fire Disputing

The effectiveness of the cognitive skills in preventing depression and hopelessness is contingent upon their utility. If the children cannot employ the skills when most needed, then the hope they offer will soon fade. Specifically, they must be effective in the real world, outside of POP, away from worksheets and supportive leaders. When pessimistic thoughts assail us they are fast and reflexive. In order to repel them successfully, the cognitive skills must operate *as* fast and reflexively. When negative thoughts arise, the child must be able to respond immediately with an alternative, some counter-evidence, or decatastrophizing. This skill is called rapid-fire disputing.

We teach this skill in POP using a game called the Hot Seat. The children are presented with a hypothetical adversity (e.g., "It's the first day of junior high and you don't feel like anybody likes you"). The leader reads a list of negative thoughts to the children and asks them to dispute on-line (e.g., "I'll never have any friends." "nobody likes me because I'm too boring," "If I were better looking, people would like me," "I'm going to be lonely for the rest of the year"). From its introduction in Session 4, rapid-fire disputing is practiced in every session.

THE BEHAVIORAL ELEMENTS OF POP

As stated earlier, while the cognitive skills afford the child the hope that change is possible, they do not provide the skills required to effect that change. In the second half of the program, POP participants receive training in some action-oriented, behavioral skills that are an essential part of many problem-solving strategies, including assertiveness and negotiation, countering procrastination, and decision making. We illustrate the additive nature of the cognitive and behavioral aspects of POP in the following three scenarios.

Scenario #1: Disputation and Assertiveness

Becky and her friend Debra have plans to meet at the mall after

> school, but Debra fails to show for the third time this month. Becky feels very sad for the next few days and avoids Debra at school.

Becky uses the ABC technique to identify her initial belief that "people just don't like me because I'm boring" and to help understand why she has been feeling so depressed. Next, she generates some alternatives to her initial causal belief, including "Debra doesn't like me," "She's not good at keeping dates with anyone," "She's very forgetful," "Some people find me boring," and even "Debra's a jerk," She uses evidence and the pie chart to determine that while Debra can be inconsiderate, the biggest slices of pie correspond with her forgetfulness, especially when it comes to appointments.

Since this is a more external and specific attribution, the disputing work is likely to alleviate Becky's sad mood. In addition, it offers greater opportunity for change, since forgetfulness, even on the part of another, is more easily remedied than being unlovable. But as effective as this cognitive technique is, the problem with Debra remains. Indeed, reattributing to an external cause will likely give rise to mild anger or frustration. Clearly, Becky must do something more than clarify her perception of the adversity and its causes. She must do something about the adversity itself, that is, Debra's pattern of standing her up. She can achieve this by talking assertively with her and negotiating a mutually agreed upon plan of action for the future.

Scenario #2: Disputing and Procrastination

> Jimmy's teachers know he's a pretty bright kid, but it almost never shows in his grades. His biggest problem is getting written assignments turned in on time. Getting him started on those essays is like pulling teeth. He'll even clean his room to avoid writing that paper.

Procrastination is a behavioral consequence of maladaptive beliefs. When Jimmy applies the ABC model with the help of his POP leader, he identifies several beliefs that cause him to avoid getting started. When he has a paper to write, he often thinks "I have to get this just right to get a good grade." In combination with his recurring beliefs that "I'm a terrible writer" and "this project is just too big for me to get through," the situation seems hopeless. Using disputing he comes to realize that he could get a good grade even if the paper isn't perfect. But he still has trouble believing that the assignment is manageable. The behavioral skill of the graded task is valuable here. In the graded task, the child learns to break the entire project into ten or so meaningful and manageable chunks. For Jimmy, these may include "go to the library and check out some relevant books," "read the first book," "write a brief summary of it," "read the second book," "write a brief summary," "make a page by page outline for the essay," "write the introduction," "write section 1," "write section 2," "write the conclusion," and "turn in the paper." At the successful completion of each subtask, Jimmy has a reward planned for himself—two hours of TV, a movie, or a computer game.

Scenario #3: Decatastrophizing and Decision Making

> Lisa saw two classmates cheating during her science exam. She is currently on the B/C grade boundary, and this was her last chance for the semester to improve her grade. She knows that her sixth-grade science teacher grades on a curve. She has to decide whether or not to tell the teacher. If she does, the other kids may find out. But, if she keeps it to herself her grade could suffer.

Lisa clearly faces a dilemma. She uses decatastrophizing to more accurately determine the probable outcomes of each option. In so doing, she realizes that if she were to tell, she would probably have a tough time interpersonally. However, she now recognizes that it is highly unlikely that no one will ever be her friend again, which was her worst fear. Her analysis also indicates that her catastrophic belief that she will fail the course were she to keep the information to herself is also improbable. This cognitive work has eased her anxiety considerably, but she still faces a tough choice.

POP Session 9 teaches the children a systematic approach to decision making. In the case of a binary choice, participants draw up a simple two-by-two table and list the costs and benefits of pursuing each course of action under consideration. They weight those outcomes that are particularly salient to them—perhaps due to their ethics. In a future-oriented version of the pie chart, Lisa can estimate the probability of each outcome (the group leader's approach to this activity is more directive with younger children). She can also flag any especially desirable or aversive outcomes.

THE PROBLEM-SOLVING PROCESS

In this chapter we have presented snapshots of the cognitive and behavioral skills taught in POP, and how they combine to foster hope and prevent depression and hopelessness. Of course, these do not capture the true iterative nature of problem solving. For any adversity, the participants learn to follow a multi-step process. First, they apply ABC—objectively describing the adversity, identifying the beliefs, and understanding the effect of these beliefs on their emotions and behaviors. Second, if their negative thoughts are beliefs about cause, they generate alternatives, evaluate evidence, and determine the relative contribution of each causal factor. The skill of decatastrophizing is applied to beliefs about future implications. Third, they use their more accurate beliefs about the causes of events as the basis for generating possible problem-solving strategies. Fourth, they use decision-making skills to prioritize their plan of action, based on the changeability of the causes, their degree of contribution, and the likely outcomes of pursuing that plan. Fifth, they enact the plan using the behavioral skills of POP—social skills, assertiveness and negotiation, or the graded task. Sixth, they evaluate the success of the strategy in achieving their goals, and modify and reenact when necessary. This final step reflects the iterative nature of real-world problem solving. It requires resilience in the face of setbacks and disappointments, which in turn requires a sense of hope that the cognitive skill of disputing provides.

THE EFFECTIVENESS OF POP

In the first empirical test of POP, 140 children in fifth and sixth grade were assigned either to POP or a no-intervention control (Jaycox, Reivich, Gillham, & Seligman, 1994). The children were selected as at risk for depression due to their self report of depressive symptomatology and their perception of family conflict and cohesion at home. They completed the Children's Depression Inventory (Kovacs, 1985) every six months for two years following the final session of the 12-week program (see figure 11.4). The final sample numbered 118.

Children in POP experienced significantly fewer symptoms of depression than their control group counterparts across the 2-year evaluation period (Gillham, Reivich, Jaycox, & Seligman, 1995). Analysis of the proportion of children experiencing moderate to severe levels of depressive symptoms indicates that POP halved the rate of depression in at-risk children.

	Prevention	Control
Screen	11.7	11.1
Pre	9.1	10.1
Post	7.6	8.9
6 Month	7.8	9.9
12 Month	6.4	9.5
18 Month	7.3	12.4
24 Month	9.1	13.3

Figure 11.4. Depressive symptoms (mean CDI) by prevention condition and time.

Furthermore, children in POP remained significantly more optimistic than controls. These findings suggest that POP fostered a sense of hope, which buffered these children against the adolescent increase in risk for depression.

Since this study, our research attention has focused on two corollary issues—dissemination and active ingredients. We have developed a protocol for training educators and counselors as POP leaders. In order to examine the change process, we designed a specific-component control, an alternative, affective-interpersonal intervention called the Penn

Enhancement Program, or PEP. Early empirical indications are that middle school teachers can be trained to be effective implementers of POP. Our initial research with PEP has raised treatment specificity questions—girls seem to benefit more from PEP than POP. Our research agenda continues to isolate and test process hypotheses involving issues of program content and group dynamics.

We believe that both the cognitive and behavioral skills in POP are active ingredients of the observable changes in helplessness, hopelessness, and depression. The cognitive elements instill hope in the child who once believed that the problems in her life were caused by uncontrollable permanent and pervasive factors. The behavioral component equips the child with the resources to act on that hope. If these newly acquired skills fail her at first, she has the cognitive tools to challenge the beliefs about failure that previously led to helplessness and hopelessness. She has a resilience that comes from hope.

REFERENCES

Abramson, L.Y., Metalsky, G.I., & Alloy, L.B. (1989). Hopelessness depression: A theory-based subtype of depression. *Psychological Review, 96,* 358–372.

Abramson, L.Y., Seligman, M.E.P., & Teasdale, J.D. (1978). Learned helplessness in humans: Critique and reformulation. *Journal of Abnormal Psychology, 87,* 49–74.

Burns, M.O. & Seligman, M.E.P. (1989). Explanatory style across the life span: Evidence for stability over 52 years. *Journal of Personality and Social Psychology, 56,* 471–477.

Center for Disease Control (1991). Attempted suicide among high school students-United States. 1990. *Morbidity and Mortality Weekly Report, 40,* 633–635.

Ellis, A. (1962). *Reason and Emotion in Psychotherapy.* New York: Lyle Stuart.

Ellis, A., & Grieger, R. (1977). *Handbook of Rational-Emotive Therapy.* New York: Springer.

Garrison, C.Z., Schluchter, M.D., Schoenbach, V.J., & Kaplan, B.K. (1989). Epidemiology of depressive symptoms in young adolescents. *Journal of the American Academy of Child and Adolescent Psychiatry, 28(3),* 343–351.

Gillham, J.E., Reivich, K.J., Jaycox, L.J., & Seligman, M.E.P. (1995). Prevention of depressive symptoms in schoolchildren: Two-year follow-up. *Psychological Science, 6(6),* 343–351.

Hammen, C. (1988). Self-cognitions, stressful events, and the prediction of depression in children of depressed mothers. *Journal of Abnormal Child Psychology, 16(3),* 347–360.

Jaycox, L.H., Reivich, K.J., Gillham, J.E., & Seligman, M.E.P. (1994). Prevention of depressive symptoms in school children. *Behaviour Research and Therapy, 32(8),* 801–816.

Kaslow, N.J., Rehm, L.P., & Siegel, A.W. (1984). Social-cognitive and cognitive correlates of depression in children. *Journal of Abnormal Child Psychology, 12(4),* 605–620.

Kovacs, M. (1985). The Children's Depression Inventory (CDI). *Psychopharmacology Bulletin, 21,* 995–1124.

Lewinsohn, P.M., Hops, H., Roberts, R., & Seeley, J. (1993). Adolescent psychopathology: I. Prevalence and incidence of depression and other DSM-III-R disorders in high school students. *Journal of Abnormal Psychology, 102,* 110–120.

Lewinsohn, P.M. Rohde, P. and Seeley, J.R. (1996) Adolescent suicidal ideation and attempts: Prevalence, risk factors, and clinical implications. *Clinical Psychology: Science and Practice, 3,* 25–46.

Metalsky, G.I., Joiner, T.E., Hardin, T.S., & Abramson, L.Y. (1993). Depressive reactions to failure in a naturalistic setting: A test of the hopelessness and self-esteem theories of depression. *Journal of Abnormal Psychology, 102,* 101–109.

Nolen-Hoeksema, S., Girgus, J.S., & Seligman, M.E.P. (1986). Learned helplessness in children: A longitudinal study of depression, achievement, and explanatory style. *Journal of Personality and Social Psychology, 51,* 435–442.

Peterson, C., Seligman, M.E.P., & Vaillant, G. (1988). Pessimistic explanatory style as a risk factor for physical illness: A 35-year longitudinal study. *Journal of Personality and Social Psychology, 55,* 23–27.

Shatté, A.J., Reivich, K., Gillham, J.E., & Seligman, M.E.P. (1998). Learned optimism in children. In C.R. Snyder (Ed.), *Coping in Children.* New York: Oxford University Press.

Snyder, C.R., McDermott, D., Cook, W., & Rapoff, M.A. (1997). *Helping Children Through Good Times and Bad.* Boulder: Westview Press.

ACKNOWLEDGMENT

The work described in this chapter was supported by a National Institute of Mental Health Grant (MH52270).

✦ CHAPTER 12 ✦

Discussion of the Penn Optimism Program: Recognizing Its Strengths and Considerations for Enhancing the Program

Kevin D. Stark and Janay Boswell

THE OBJECTIVE OF THIS CHAPTER is to discuss the results of the Penn Optimism Program (POP) as reported in the previous chapter by Shatté, Gillham, and Reivich (chapter 11). The therapeutic objective of POP is to teach youngsters a more realistic cognitive style, which will be a more optimistic one, and a number of coping skills that are listed in Table 12.1. The authors of POP are to be commended for developing a creative and engaging program that helps youngsters acquire cognitive and social problem-solving skills through an interactive medium. This aspect of the program is important for its success as engagement in treatment is one of the predictors of therapy outcome for children.

Table 12.1

Skills Trained During the Penn Optimism Project

1. A more flexible and realistic attributional style.
2. Thinking is tied to behavior and in particular to the notion of the self-fulfilling prophecy.
3. Problem-solving skills are taught and these skills are tied to making accurate attributions.

4. Errors in social cognition—more specifically hostile attributions—are identified and altered.

5. Cognitive skills training is supplemented with behavioral skills training, including assertiveness, negotiation, relaxation, anger and sadness control, dealing with procrastination, social skills, and decision making.

POP has been compared to a control condition in which there was a focus on interpersonal relationships. While only preliminary findings have been reported to date, the results of the evaluation of the effectiveness of POP are impressive. To summarize, children who participated in POP scored significantly lower on the Children's Depression Inventory (CDI: Kovacs, 1981) at each assessment point, including a two-year follow-up. This finding was especially pronounced for boys. Fewer of POP participants relative to the controls (12% versus 38%) scored greater than 18, the recommended clinical cut-off on the CDI. Furthermore, these improvements were associated with a change in attributional style. If the results of the other outcome measures including measures of cognition, problem-solving, self-perception, and general psychological adjustment parallel those reported to date, POP will give school practitioners, parents, and mental health professionals hope for a brighter future. Thus, the following discussion is offered in the hope of enhancing the evaluation effort and as a reminder of the importance of remaining rooted in relevant developmental literature.

ENHANCING THE EVALUATION COMPONENT

To date, the primary instruments used to evaluate POP are self-report paper-and-pencil measures. The primary outcome measure that has been reported thus far has been the CDI. The CDI is best conceptualized as a measure of psychological distress rather than a measure of depression in children (Reynolds, 1994). Given the limitations of this measure, it is not possible to determine whether fewer youngsters develop depressive disorders due to participation in POP. However, it is possible to say that youngsters who participated in POP reported less distress and fewer depressive symptoms. A diagnostic interview would have to be used to determine whether the prevention program was successful at reducing the number of youths who experienced a depressive disorder. It would be extremely interesting and methodologically useful to include a semi-structured diagnostic interview of participants in POP at multiple assessment points so that the program's ability to prevent the development of depressive disorders and other psychiatric disorders can be evaluated. Given the large number of participants in this prevention project (which is another strength of the project), it would not be practical to have every participant complete a diagnostic interview, but it would be possible to interview a large sample of randomly selected participants.

In a similar vein, if a primary objective of the prevention program is a reduction in the number of cases of depressive disorders, best practices for the assessment of depression suggest that it is important to include ratings of depression that are completed by significant others (Reynolds, 1994). While teacher-completed measures have their problems, it would be possible for teachers to complete the Child Behavior Checklist (Achenbach & Edelbrock, 1982) or some other behavior rating scale since POP is conducted in schools. In addition to teacher ratings, it would be useful to have parents rate their children's depressive symptoms on a relevant measure. Inclusion of such measures would ensure that youths who participate in POP or other experimental conditions are not reporting improvements due to the demand characteristics of the study.

The investigators are to be commended for building into the design a method for evaluating the possible psychological process that could be producing the improvements in the adjustment of participants. To date, results have been reported for one process measure: The Children's Attributional Style Questionnaire. It is assumed that future manuscripts will report the changes in other process variables such as depressive thoughts, and a measure of the children's sense of self. From a theoretical perspective, these different cognitive constructs are linked, and changes in one should have an impact on the others. Thus, it would be very interesting to determine the extent to which each one predicts severity of depressive symptoms.

Current results suggest that the improvement in adjustment is attributable in part to the change in attributional style that results from participation in POP. This finding is both impressive and somewhat curious. These results suggest that adjustment as measured by the CDI is associated with change toward a more optimistic attributional style. These results also raise a number of questions as attributional retraining was limited to the dimensions of stability and internality. Training in the global dimension was too conceptually complex for the youngsters. Thus, one is left wondering what produced the improvement in attributional style? Was it the direct attributional retraining? Was it produced through other experiences within POP, or was it due to nonspecific changes in the group or in the interactions of the children with each other and with the teacher? For example, as the teacher and group members talk with a youngster about his or her distressing situation, one of the messages could be "It is not your fault." Such discussions along with others that more accurately identify the source of a problematic situation could, over time, lead to a change in attributional style. Could the improvements be due to other intrapsychic changes such as an improvement in problem-solving skills, reduction in information processing errors, or an improvement in self-schema or self-efficacy? As the other outcome measures are analyzed, it may be possible to better understand the process that leads to the development of an optimistic attributional style.

Since POP is school-based, it would be very interesting to evaluate its impact on academic performance. Are there additional practical benefits from participation such as improvement in school attendance, engagement in extracurricular activities, and improvements in interpersonal relationships? In our previous outcome studies, we found that children who had attendance problems tended to attend school on the days when they would meet with their treatment group. In some cases, attendance appeared to improve. In the long-run, do fewer POP participants drop out of school? What is the impact on the special education program? Do fewer youngsters who participate in POP need services for the severely emotionally disturbed as they matriculate through school? Do fewer POP participants need more restrictive services such as placement in self-contained classrooms or alternative learning centers? It may not be fair to expect or ask for such far-reaching effects from a one shot prevention program. It may be necessary to infuse some of the middle school and high school curriculum with developmentally appropriate refresher materials. This would seem desirable given the numerous changes youngsters experience in the course of their development through high school.

Thus far, evaluation of POP has overlooked the impact on the teachers who implement the prevention program. Teachers learn a number of helpful skills that they can apply to their own lives. Do they apply these skills to their own lives, and if so, do they benefit from them? Is the teachers' adjustment positively affected by leading POP groups? Most teachers truly enjoy children and care about their welfare. Thus, the opportunity to provide children with some useful life skills may lead them to find their jobs more satisfying. Do teachers in the POP program experience an improvement in job satisfaction? Teachers often lead a very isolated professional existence as they have little adult contact at work. Do they benefit from the training and other planning meetings that are conducted with other teachers and the counseling staff? If they are more satisfied and more capable of coping with their own distress, is this having an impact on their classrooms in a positive way? Is teacher participation affecting their interactions with children, which may influence the youngsters' cognitive style? For example, are the teachers who are participating in POP more positive in their interactions with students than those that don't participate, and if so, does this lead to the development of a positive sense of self in all of the students in the classroom? Do teachers who participate in POP model conflict resolution skills rather than rely on punitive procedures to manage conflict in the classroom? It appears as though there would be some benefits for the teachers who participate in POP. It is important to evaluate these benefits and their impact on the teachers and consequently, their classrooms and students.

Twelve percent of the youngsters who participated in POP reported elevated symptoms of depression on the CDI. Shatté, Gillham, and Reivich have noted that the overall benefits of the program are greater for boys than for girls. Are the majority of the non-responders girls? In a later section, we offer a number of thoughts relevant to this gender issue. While recognizing that most of the youngsters responded to POP, it is important for future prevention efforts to identify variables that could maximize the impact of POP and minimize the number of non-responders. Were the non-responders reacting to an acute stressor? For example, a youngster's parents might have been in the process of splitting up while the youngster was a participant. Did the non-responders learn the skills but forget how to apply them over time? Did they fail to acquire the skills? Are there any variables that predict who will be non-responders? For example, longitudinal research is revealing variables that predict the duration of an episode of depression (Kovacs, Obrosky, Gatsonis, & Richards, 1997). These same variables might have an impact on the overall efficacy of an intervention or prevention program. Do non-responders report more severe levels of depressive symptoms at the initial assessment (McCauley, Myers, Mitchell, Calderon, Schloredt, & Treder, 1993)? Did these youngsters come from more disturbed family environments (McCauley et al., 1993)? Did they have more pessimistic cognitive styles prior to POP? It is important to determine whether there are any variables that can be used to predict responders and non-responders to the intervention. Answers to these questions may lead to the development of alternative prevention or intervention strategies that might help this group.

DEVELOPMENTAL ROOTS

Cognition

POP has its theoretical base in the learned helplessness/hopelessness model of depression (Abramson, Seligman, & Teasdale, 1978; Abramson, Metalsky, & Alloy, 1989), which has proven to be one of the most useful heuristics in the study of depression in adults and has garnered a remarkable amount of empirical support as evident in the chapters in this text. In the learned helplessness/hopelessness model (Abramson et al., 1978, 1989), the individual who is prone to the development of depression has a trait-like tendency to attribute the cause of negative events to internal, stable, and global causes, and positive events to external, unstable, and specific causes. Attributional style is hypothesized to be a stable variable, which serves as a filter for processing information. This model was initially developed on, and applied to, depressed adults. Given the developmental differences in cognition and cognitive abilities between children and adults, it may not be possible to directly apply the model to youths. If the objective of POP is to help youngsters to develop a more optimistic cognitive style, it is important to empirically determine that they process information in a similar fashion to adults and that this model applies to youths. Consequently, it may be useful to look at relevant developmental research to determine the appropriateness of the model that serves as the basis for POP. To do this, we will first review basic research on the form of children's cognition. Then, we review research on children's ability to experience helplessness, and finally, we review the investigations that have addressed the applicability of the learned helplessness model to childhood depression.

Many investigators have assumed that children's cognition is similar in form to cognition in adults. For example, it has been assumed that children, like adults, ask themselves why an event has occurred and that this cognition takes on the form of an attribution, which is reflective of a more encompassing attributional style. This assumption of developmental similarity has been empirically evaluated with mixed results. Consistent with the adult literature, negative cognitions can be divided into two categories (outlook and attributions) that assess different aspects of the cognitive functioning of adolescents (Gotlib, Lewinsohn, Seeley, Rohde, & Redner, 1993). In contrast, Garber, Weiss and Shanley (1993) did not find a separation of adolescent cognition into outlooks and attributions. Their results identified one factor of negative cognitions that included both expectations and attributions. Thus, the age at which children's cognitions assume the form of an attribution similar to that in adults is not clear from an empirical standpoint. Youngsters in middle childhood may not be developmentally ready to participate in attributional retraining, which could explain why children have so much difficulty understanding the concept of globality. In our own intervention efforts with youngsters of a similar age (Stark, Reynolds, & Kaslow, 1987; Stark, 1990) we found that children had great difficulty understanding the three dimensions of attributional style so we abandoned this in our latest treatment program (Stark & Kendall, 1996). Earlier, we asked the question about why children would report changes in attributional style when the training was only conducted in two dimensions. It is possible that the improvements stem from this developmental limitation. Their cognitive processes may not be mature enough to be differentiated into more than a single dimension of negative cognitions. Thus, a more general change of global optimism may occur.

Additional research has begun to apply developmental principles to the evaluation of the appropriateness of cognitive theories of depression for children. Based on Piaget's theory of cognitive development, Moilanen (1993) hypothesized that children need to be at least to the formal operations stage of reasoning (12+), where they can think about the future and the hypothetical, before they can experience hopelessness and severe depression. However, contrary to this hypothesis, younger children who were in the concrete operations level actually were more depressed and experienced greater hopelessness than the children who had reached formal operations. Rholes, Blackwell, Jordan, and Walters (1980) investigated children's susceptibility to learned helplessness with the utilization of hidden figures problems with repeated success or failure feedback. It was hypothesized that younger children (kindergarten and first graders) would experience less helplessness than older children (third and fifth graders) because of developmental differences in causal attributions. This hypothesis was supported in that younger subjects showed no evidence of helplessness on the hidden figures tasks while the fifth grade children who failed appeared to be more helpless in both persistence and performance on the hidden figures. The authors concluded that younger children were relatively less susceptible to learned helplessness, perhaps because they did not make the same types of attributions as older children when confronted with repeated failure. Consistent with this research and other research within developmental psychology, children begin to be able to make negative evaluations around 8 years old, and it is at this age that their sense of self, future, and causality develop (Garber, 1992).

It is obvious that a paucity of relevant developmental research exists. While it has been hypothesized that children older than eight would have the cognitive ability to benefit from participation in POP, the empirical basis for this assumption is mixed. It is not clear that cognitions of children of the targeted age for POP are differentiated into attributions and expectations. This may be due to a lack of metacognitive abilities or to a developmental difference in which their cognitions are not yet differentiated into attributions, expectations, and evaluations. It is clear that additional basic research on cognition in children needs to be conducted and results of this research could be used to guide prevention and intervention efforts.

Applicability of the Attributional Model

Results of early studies that evaluated the reformulated model of learned helplessness depression, while mixed, were generally supportive as children who self-reported symptoms of depression also reported a more depressogenic attributional style. Specifically, these children reported internal, stable, and global attributions for negative events and external, unstable and specific attributions for positive events although the results for the positive events were not as strong (Asarnow & Bates, 1988; Kaslow, Rehm, Siegel, 1984; Seligman et al., 1984). Recent research also provides support for the basic tenets of the model with youths (Cole & Turner, 1993; Garber et al., 1993; Tems, Stewart, Skinner, Hughes, & Emslie, 1993).

The aforementioned early research that evaluated the applicability of the attributional model to depressed youths did not address the specificity of negative attributional style to depressive disorders by including a psychiatric control group. Thus, it was not possible to determine whether the helpless attributional style was specific to depression. Cole and Turner (1993) addressed this limitation and reported that the attributional style of depressed youngsters did not differ from the attributional style of a group of youngsters with a variety of other psychiatric disorders. Thus, a negative attributional style was not specific to depressive disorders in this study but was nonspecific to psychopathology in general. These results suggest that POP and its attributional retraining component, or a revised attributional retraining component, might be helpful for children who develop a variety of emotional disorders.

A number of investigators have attempted to conduct a more complete evaluation of the attributional model of depression by looking at the interaction of stress and attributional style as they predict depressive symptoms (Cole & Turner, 1993; Dixon & Ahrens, 1992; Hammen, Adrian, & Hiroto, 1988; Nolen-Hoeksema, Girgus, & Seligman, 1986). Nolen-Hoeksema and her colleagues (1986) followed school children over a year to evaluate the interactive effect of stress and attributional style on depressive symptoms. Major life events, attributional style, and depressive symptoms were assessed five times producing four intervals. Results indicated that attributional style alone predicted change in depressive symptoms during two intervals. The stress attributional style interaction significantly predicted change in depressive symptoms in one of the other intervals, while it marginally predicted change in the remaining interval. Among at-risk populations, Dixon and Ahrens (1992) reported that attributional style did not predict depressive symptoms while a measure of daily hassles did. The interaction of daily hassles and attributional style significantly increased the predictive power of depression scores. Secondary analyses revealed that the effect of stress on depression was greatest for those who had a negative attributional style. In a study that included children of depressed parents, the interaction effect of stress (major life events) and attributional style failed to predict depression 8.4 months later (Hammen et al., 1988).

While the results of research into the applicability of the attributional model of depression for children have been mixed, it is clear that stress is related to depressive disorders in youths and that the combination of stress with a depressogenic attributional style is more predictive of depression than either alone. Thus, if a prevention program is going to be effective, it must include training in coping skills that will help the participants manage stress and it should be directed at reducing the stressors within the youngsters' environment. POP is designed to teach the youngsters coping and problem-solving skills to help them manage stress. Furthermore, the problem-solving skills may help them to manage or eliminate the stressors in their environment. In addition, since social support is one of the most powerful buffers against the deleterious effects of stress, an effective component of a prevention program may be the building of social support networks.

Coping Skills

As noted in the previous section, depressed youths experience greater stress and may not have the coping strategies necessary for dealing with it. POP teaches youngsters a number of coping skills. How were these specific coping skills chosen and are they appropriate for the developmental status of the target child population? A common assumption is that children can, and naturally do, employ the same coping and emotional regulation strategies as adults. Owing to a variety of developmental differences, this may not be a valid assumption. Rather than looking at the adult treatment models for guidance about which coping strategies should be taught to children, it may be more beneficial to determine which coping strategies are naturally employed by well-adjusted children. Unfortunately, this literature is sparse. Recently we surveyed three hundred middle school students and asked them to tell us about the problems they faced over the past week, and what they did to cope with sadness and anger. The results were fascinating. Seven of the ten most frequently faced problems were interpersonal in nature and involved some form of conflict. These results suggest that intervention and prevention programs may have to direct their efforts at the cognitive, emotional, and interpersonal skills that enable youngsters to successfully avoid and resolve interpersonal conflict. One of the most common strategies for teaching individuals to avoid conflict is to teach them how to be assertive. However, traditional forms of assertiveness training may not be developmentally appropriate for children and adolescents, who commonly say, "I can't use this assertiveness stuff that you're trying to teach me. If I said that, they'd laugh at me." Either the language has to be adapted for the specific population or the process needs to be altered to be appropriate for the age and culture of the children.

It would be helpful to incorporate findings from research on the affect-regulation strategies used by well-adjusted children and youngsters who have demonstrated resiliency. The strategies that they use may be helpful for children who are experiencing difficulties managing their moods. Youngsters in our survey reported using a variety of active coping strategies, such as doing something fun, talking to a friend on the phone, watching television, distracting themselves by listening to music, and withdrawing to their bedrooms when angry. In addition, they reported using cognitive strategies such as trying to look at it in a different way and trying to think about positive things. More so than adults, these youngsters reported that they rely very heavily on others to cheer them up. In fact, they seek out other people who they know are in a good mood or they call a friend to talk about what is bothering them. It appears to be beneficial to invest more effort in identification of the strategies of youngsters who effectively manage their moods and successfully resolve conflict. Such research could direct the choice of coping strategies taught in prevention and intervention programs.

One of the coping skills that is taught as part of POP is problem solving. Meta-analytic research on problem-solving training indicates that children can learn problem solving and that it contributes to healthy adjustment. However, these positive effects are achieved after thirty-nine one-hour training sessions. This begs the question: Are children really mastering problem-solving skills in the three sessions that directly focus on problem solving in POP? A related concern is the nature in which we teach depressed youths to use problem-solving strategies. We have to address the cognitions that surround the use of problem solving. The youngster must believe that it will be helpful—that it actually works. It may be important to spend a number of sessions dealing directly with these negative thoughts and helping the children to identify ways that they can get, and remain, psyched-up for using problem-solving skills in the face of depressed mood and repeated exposure to stressors.

FAMILY INFLUENCES

Family Environment

While it is generally recognized that the family plays an influential role in the psychological and psycho-social adjustment of children, this very significant aspect of a youngster's psycho-social development has been, to date, overlooked by POP and by most other prevention and intervention programs. This is unfortunate as results of this research could guide prevention programs. Evidence from clinical observations and research indicates that many depressed youngsters come from disturbed families (for reviews see Burbach & Borduin; 1986; Stark & Brookman, 1992). Early reports provided evidence for the existence of disturbances within the families of depressed youths, but they did not identify the specific nature of the disturbances. For example, Kaslow, Rehm, and Siegel (1984) reported greater general dysfunction among the families of children who had elevated scores on the CDI (Kovacs, 1981), relative to normal controls. Asarnow and colleagues (Asarnow, Carlson, & Guthrie, 1987) also reported disturbances in the perceived family environments of depressed children, but these disturbances were nonspecific to psychopathology. Additional research suggests that the families of depressed youths are characterized by greater chaos, abuse and neglect (Kashani, Ray, & Carlson, 1984), conflict (Forehand, Brody, Slotkin, Fauber, McCombs, & Long, 1988), a critical, punitive and belittling, or shaming parenting style (e.g., Arieti & Bemporad, 1980; Poznanski & Zrull, 1970), communication difficulties (Puig-Antich, Lukens, Davies, Goetz, Brennan-Quattrock, & Todak, 1985), lower activity level (Puig-Antich et al., 1985), and structural disturbances (Grossman, Poznanski, & Banegas, 1983). In addition, when affection is expressed, it is contingent upon behavior that is consistent with parental expectations (Grossman et al., 1983). Furthermore, the tone of the mother-child, and to a somewhat lesser extent the father-child relationship, was characterized as cold, hostile, tense, and at times rejecting (Puig-Antich et al., 1985). In one of our own studies, an attempt was made to evaluate mothers' and depressed children's perceptions of their family milieu by using a measure that assessed a breadth of characteristics of family functioning (Stark, Humphrey, Crook, & Lewis, 1990). Results of the investigation of the family milieu indicate that there appears to be a unique pattern of disturbances in the families of depressed, anxious, and comorbid depressed anxious children.

Results of the aforementioned research have implications for the design of a parent component that would supplement the existing child component of POP. Children are placed at risk for the development of a depressive disorder by stressors within the family environment. The extent to which these environmental disturbances precede the child's depressive disorder or result from the depressive disorder is not clear. While conflict is consistently found to be related to children's depression in the literature, the sources of conflict have not been identified. It is possible that the conflict is between the marital partners, a parent and the depressed child, the depressed child and siblings, or some other combination of family members. Nevertheless, it is clear that conflict within the family should be a target of prevention efforts. This aspect of the prevention program may be directed toward the entire family or a depressed parent. While clinical observations indicate that parents of depressed youngsters use critical and punitive parenting techniques, research has yet to validate this observation or to elucidate the specific behaviors. If these results are supported in future research, then prevention efforts should be directed at teaching parents more positive and adaptive methods for managing their children's behavior. The failure of the family to participate in pleasant activities may stem from a variety of factors, perhaps even the conflict and punitive parenting tactics. Prevention efforts may need to be directed at teaching families how to engage in more pleasant activities. Involvement in pleasant activities is a powerful tool for regulating mood and a source of distraction from worries and stress.

Inclusion of a family component in prevention efforts seems highly desirable. However, adolescents and parents find traditional forms of family therapy to be aversive. Consequently, they avoid this form of treatment. As cognitive-behavioral therapists, we have to be concerned with the thoughts, beliefs, emotions, and behaviors that cause this reticence. How can we alter the nature of the family intervention component to increase the likelihood that the family will engage in the process and remain involved until the therapeutic objectives have been reached?

Development of Depressive Cognitive Style

As noted above, disturbances in cognition are associated with depression. The critical question for prevention researchers are (1) how do these disturbances in cognition develop and (2) how are they maintained? Beck (Beck, Rush, Shaw, & Emery, 1979), as well as others (e.g., Freeman, 1986), hypothesize that a cognitive disturbance, more specifically depressive schema, is formed through early learning experiences, especially those within the family. Cole and Turner (1993) believe that repeated exposure to negative life events, stressors, or specific forms of pathogenic feedback to the child lead to the internalization of negative cognitions and the eventual development of dysfunctional schemata. In addition, they note that at certain developmental periods youngsters actively seek information from daily experiences and from their peers about their own competencies, which they use to construct their sense of self. Young (1991) hypothesizes that maladaptive schemata could be the result of inadequate parenting or ongoing aversive experiences within the family milieu such as repeated criticism or rejection. From the social learning perspective (Bandura, 1977), it also is possible that cognitive disturbances could be learned vicariously through parental modeling.

Consistent with theoretical predictions, maladaptive interactions between parent and child have been implicated in the development of depressogenic cognitive processes. Mothers' negatively toned comments contribute to the development of a negative self-schema in their children (Radke-Yarrow, Belmont, Nottelmann, & Bottomly, 1990). Jaenicke and colleagues (1987) reported that mothers' self-critical statements were unrelated to their children's self-criticism; however, a significant relationship was found between mothers' verbal criticism of their children and their children's tendency to make self-blaming attributions for negative events. In one of the authors' investigations, perceived parental messages about the self, world, and future were predictive of severity of depressive symptomatology and the children's sense of self, world, and future (cognitive triad); (Stark, Schmidt, & Joiner, 1996). The relationship between perceived parental messages and depression was completely mediated by children's cognitive triads and this relationship was specific to depressive versus anxious symptoms. In a more recent investigation, we (Stark, Schmidt, & Joiner, 1998) found that negative messages from fathers were significantly related to daughters' depressive thinking and that negative messages from mothers were related to both daughters' and sons' depressive thinking. Together, these findings suggest that the psycho-social context within which children develop may influence their cognitive processes. More specifically, negative verbal communications and/or messages communicated through actions, from parents to children, may influence children's maladaptive information processing and especially their sense of self.

The aforementioned results suggest that prevention and intervention efforts should be directed at parent-child interactions that may lead to the development and maintenance of a depressogenic style of thinking. Parents may need to be taught to identify and to change maladaptive interactions that lead to the development of depressive styles of thinking. The actual procedure for accomplishing this may be complex and require some individual work with the families and possibly intervention with the parents. If a parent does not have an adaptive cognitive style, then the parent may not be able to communicate positive and adaptive messages.

GENDER AND DEPRESSION

During early adolescence, the prevalence of depressive disorders among females increases faster than for boys (Nolen-Hoeksema, 1995). Girls begin to report more severe levels of depressive symptoms and a different symptom picture including lower self-esteem (Allgood-Merten, Lewinsohn, & Hops, 1990), poor body image (Baron & Joly, 1988), hopelessness (Boggiano & Barrett, 1992), and appetite and weight disturbances (Baron & Joly, 1988). It is important for prevention researchers to consider the following question. With what do we equip girls in order to inoculate them against developing depression? As noted in the chapter by Shatté, Gillham, and Reivich (chapter 11), POP has been compared to an alternative treatment that has an interpersonal focus (PEP) and has been designed to control for peer support, adult attention, and other non-specific treatment factors. The authors reported that a gender effect was evident in the initial results, with girls benefiting less from both programs at posttreatment, but benefiting more from participation in PEP. Research suggests that we can equip boys with methods for enhancing or protecting their sense of self and this may help inoculate them against the development of a depressive disorder. Girls may require a different approach since they appear to experience a more ruminative style of processing information and coping that may put them at risk for the development of depression (Nolen-Hoeksema, 1987). It has been hypothesized that girls get stuck in the decision making part of problem solving (Nolen-Hoeksema, 1987). They don't make it beyond the stage of identifying information that will enable them to make a safe decision. They seem to keep looking for more and more information. What might be the most effective method for helping them to take a more active approach to coping? It may be important for girls to be taught to take a break, and then complete the problem-solving process while keeping in mind that they can evaluate their plan as it unfolds and modify it as they go along. How can we best help them develop a positive self-image, a positive body image? Perhaps it would be helpful to borrow some procedures from the adolescent eating disorders programs.

Research suggests that adolescent girls turn more to their families for support during times of stress while adolescent boys turn to their peers (Kavanaugh & Hops, 1994). At the same time that girls are turning to their parents for support, a growing body of evidence suggests that they are more adversely impacted by negative paternal behaviors (Petersen, Sarigiani, & Kennedy, 1991). Can this be addressed within POP, or is it necessary to intervene directly with the family in order to achieve the desired improvements? Do parents have to be taught how to be more supportive of their teenage daughters? Many questions remain to be answered regarding the most effective methods for helping girls to inoculate themselves against the development of depressive disorders.

SUMMARY

In summary, POP appears to incorporate solid theory and innovative practice to help prevent depressive symptoms and enhance optimistic thinking in school-age children. This program is especially promising due to its delivery in schools. This aspect of POP curriculum makes the program available to a large number of children across many communities. Although there are no published data available on the secondary outcomes of POP, there are many exciting avenues to explore. As POP research continues to develop, it could potentially benefit the field of resiliency research in several ways. First, family variables are an important aspect of a child's life, which could be incorporated into POP intervention. Optimism and family relationships are likely an integral part of developing and maintaining an optimistic thinking style in children. Further investigation of this area appears highly important for resilience and prevention research. It will be interesting to examine the secondary outcomes of academic performance and achievement. In addition, the potential effects on behavior, especially in boys, will be crucial to examine in ways other than self-report measures. The prevention efforts may be targeting depression, but the potential to prevent additional behavior difficulties is perhaps equally important. All in all, POP offers a promising curriculum that benefits children, their families, and their communities. As the effects of decreasing depressive symptoms are shown to last over time, it is especially important to develop ways that POP can be modified for specialized target populations and cultures. It is with anticipation and optimism that we will await future findings of the POP research team.

REFERENCES

Abramson, L.Y., Metalsky, G.I., & Alloy, L.B. (1989). Hopelessness depression: A theory-based subtype of depression. *Psychological Review, 96,* 358–372.

Abramson, L.Y., Seligman, M.E.P., & Teasdale, J. (1978). Learned helplessness in humans: Critique and reformulation. *Journal of Abnormal Psychology, 87,* 49–74.

Achenbach, T., & Edelbrock, C. (1982). *Manual for the child behavior checklist and child behavior profile.* Burlington: Department of Psychiatry, University of Vermont.

Allgood-Merten, B., Lewinsohn, P.M., & Hops, H. (1990). Sex differences and adolescent depression. *Journal of Abnormal Psychology, 99,* 55–63.

Arieti, S., & Bemporad, J.R. (1980). The psychological organization of depression. *American Journal of Psychiatry, 137,* 1360–1365.

Asarnow, J.R., & Bates, S. (1988). Depression in child psychiatric inpatients: Cognitive and attributional patterns. *Journal of Abnormal Child Psychology, 16,* 601–615.

Asarnow, J.R., Carlson, G.A., & Guthrie, D. (1987). Coping strategies, self-perceptions, hopelessness, and perceived family environments in depressed and suicidal children. *Journal of Consulting and Clinical Psychology, 55,* 361–366.

Bandura, A. (1977). *A social learning theory.* Englewood Cliffs, NJ: Prentice-Hall.

Baron, P., & Joly, E. (1988). Sex differences in the expression of depression in adolescents. *Sex Roles, 18,* 1–7.

Beck, A.T., Rush, A.J., Shaw, B.F., & Emery, G. (1979). *Cognitive therapy of depression.* New York: Guilford Press.

Boggiano, A.K., & Barrett, M. (1992). Gender differences in depression in children as a function of motivational orientation. *Sex Roles, 26,* 11–17.

Burbach, D.J., & Borduin, C.M. (1986). Parent-child relations and the etiology of depression: A review of methods and findings. *Clinical Psychology Review, 6,* 133–153.

Cole, D., & Turner, J., Jr. (1993). Models of cognitive mediation and moderation in child depression. *Journal of Abnormal Psychology, 102,* 271–281.

Dixon, J.F., & Ahrens, A.H. (1992). Stress and attributional style as predictors of self-reported depression in children. *Cognitive Therapy and Research, 16,* 623–634.

Forehand, R., Brody, G., Slotkin, J., Fauber, R., McCombs, A., & Long, N. (1988). Young adolescent and maternal depression: Assessment, interrelations, and predictors. *Journal of Consulting and Clinical Psychology, 56,* 422–426.

Freeman, A. (1986). Understanding personal, cultural and family schema in psychotherapy. In A. Freeman, N. Epstein, & K.M. Simon (Eds.), *Depression in the family* (pp. 79–100). New York: The Haworth Press.

Garber, J. (1992). Cognitive models of depression: A developmental perspective. *Psychological Inquiry, 3,* 235–240.

Garber, J., Weiss, B., & Shanley, N. (1993). Cognitions, depressive symptoms, and development in adolescents. *Journal of Abnormal Psychology, 102,* 47–57.

Gotlib, I.H., Lewinsohn, P.M., Seeley, J.R., Rohde, P., & Redner, J.E. (1993). Negative cognitions and attributional style in depressed adolescents: An examination of stability and specificity. *Journal of Abnormal Psychology, 102,* 607–615.

Grossman, J.A., Poznanski, E.O., & Banegas, M.E. (1983). Lunch: Time to study family interactions. *Journal of Psychosocial Nursing and Mental Health Services, 21,* 19–22.

Hammen, C., Adrian, C., & Hiroto, D. (1988). A longitudinal test of the attributional vulnerability model in children at risk for depression. *British Journal of Clinical Psychology, 27,* 37–46.

Jaenicke, C., Hammen, C., Zupan, B., Hiroto, D., Gordon, D., Adrian, C., & Burge, D. (1987). Cognitive vulnerability in children at risk for depression. *Journal of Abnormal Child Psychology, 15,* 559–572.

Kashani, J.H., Ray, J.S., & Carlson, G.A. (1984). Depression and depressive-like states in preschool-age children in a child development unit. *American Journal of Psychiatry, 141,* 1397–1402.

Kaslow, N.J., Rehm, L.P., & Siegel, A.W. (1984). Social-cognitive and cognitive correlates of depression in children. *Journal of Abnormal Child Psychology, 12,* 605–620.

Kavanaugh, K., & Hops, H. (1994). Good girls? Bad boys? Gender and development as contexts for diagnosis and treatment. In T.H. Ollendick & R.J. Prinz (Eds.), *Advances in clinical child psychology* (pp. 45–78). New York: Plenum Press.

Kovacs, M. (1981). Rating scales to assess depression in school aged children. *Acta Paedopsychiatrica, 46,* 305–315.

Kovacs, M., Obrosky, D.S., Gatsonis, C., & Richards, C. (1997). First-episode major depressive and dysthymic disorder in childhood: Clinical and sociodemographic factors in recovery. *Journal of the American Academy of Child and Adolescent Psychiatry, 36,* 777–784.

McCauley, E., Myers, K., Mitchell, J., Calderon, R., Schloredt, K., & Treder, R. (1993). Depression in young people: Initial presentation and clinical course. *Journal of the American Academy of Child and Adolescent Psychiatry, 32,* 714–722.

Moilanen, D.L. (1993). Depressive experiences of nonreferred adolescents and young adults: A cognitive-developmental perspective. *Journal of Adolescent Research, 8,* 311–325.

Nolen-Hoeksema, S. (1987). Sex differences in unipolar depression: Evidence and theory. *Psychological Bulletin, 101,* 259–282.

Nolen-Hoeksema, S. (1995). Epidemiology and theories of gender differences in unipolar depression. In M.V. Seeman (Ed.), *Gender and Psychopathology* (pp. 63–87). Washington, DC: American Psychiatric Press.

Nolen-Hoeksema, S., Girgus, J.S., & Seligman, M.E.P. (1986). Learned helplessness in children: A longitudinal study of depression, achievement, and explanatory style. *Journal of Personality and Social Psychology, 51,* 435–442.

Petersen, A.C., Sarigiani, P.A., & Kennedy, R.E. (1991). Adolescent depression: Why more girls? *Journal of Youth and Adolescence, 20,* 247–271.

Poznanski, E.O. & Zrull, J. (1970). Childhood depression: Clinical characteristics of overtly depressed children. *Archives of General Psychiatry, 23,* 8–15.

Puig-Antich, J., Lukens, E., Davies, M., Goetz, D., Brennan-Quattrock, J., & Todak, G. (1985). Psychosocial functioning in prepubertal major depressive disorders: I. Interpersonal relationships during the depressive episode. *Archives of General Psychiatry, 42,* 500–507.

Radke-Yarrow, M., Belmont, B., Nottelmann, E., & Bottomly, L. (1990). Young children's self-conceptions: Origins in the natural discourse of depressed and normal mothers and their children. In D. Cicchetti & M. Beeghly (Eds.), *The self in transition: Infancy to childhood.* (pp. 345–361). Chicago: University of Chicago Press.

Reynolds, W.M. (1994). Assessment of depression in children and adolescents by self-report questionnaires. In W.M. Reynolds & H.F. Johnston (Eds.), *Hand-*

book of depression in children and adolescents (pp. 209–234). New York: Plenum Press.

Rholes, W., Blackwell, J., Jordan, C., & Walters, C. (1980). A developmental study of learned helplessness. *Developmental Psychology, 16,* 616–624.

Seligman, M.E.P., Peterson, C., Kaslow, N.J., Tanenbaum, R.L., Alloy, L.B., & Abramson, L.Y. (1984). Attributional style and depressive symptoms among children. *Journal of Abnormal Psychology, 93,* 235–238.

Stark, K.D. (1990). *Childhood depression: School-based intervention.* New York: Guilford Press.

Stark, K.D., & Brookman, C. (1992). Childhood depression: Theory and family-school intervention. In M.J. Fine & C. Carlson (Eds.), *Family-school intervention: A systems perspective* (pp. 247–271). Needham Heights, MA: Allyn & Bacon.

Stark, K.D., Humphrey, L.L., Crook, K., & Lewis, K. (1990). Perceived family environments of depressed and anxious children: Child's and maternal figure's perspectives. *Journal of Abnormal Child Psychology, 18,* 527–547.

Stark, K.D., Reynolds, W.M., & Kaslow, N.J. (1987). A comparison of the relative efficacy of self-control therapy and a behavioral problem-solving therapy for depression in children. *Journal of Abnormal Child Psychology, 15,* 91–113.

Stark, K.D., Schmidt, K., & Joiner, T.E. (1996). Depressive cognitive triad: Relationship to severity of depressive symptoms in children, parents' cognitive triad, and perceived parental messages about the child him or herself, the world, and the future. *Journal of Abnormal Child Psychology, 24,* 615–631.

Stark, K.D., Schmidt, K., & Joiner, T.E. (1998). Gender differences in the relationship between perceived parental messages, cognitive triad, and depressive symptoms. Manuscript submitted for publication.

Tems, C., Stewart, S., Skinner, J., Jr., Hughes, C., & Emslie, G. (1993). Cognitive distortions in depressed children and adolescents: Are they state dependent or trait like? *Journal of Clinical Child Psychology, 22,* 316–326.

Young, J. (1991). *Cognitive therapy for personality disorders: A schema-focused approach.* Sarasota, FL: Professional Resource Exchange, Inc.

Section E. Discussions of Part II

✦

✦ CHAPTER 13 ✦

Commentary: New Directions for Study

Stanley Rachman

DR. SELIGMAN'S WORK is intentionally provoking, and as is evident in the literature and this compendium, it has provoked. The range of the research arising from his writings is impressive. It is deep, broad, and moving along steadily and successfully.

The quality of the work is exceptionally fine. To take one example, the high-risk strategy for investigating depression is powerful, and Alloy, Abramson, and Chiara (see chapter 10) have splendidly illustrated how the method is being used to address some of the key questions in depression. Why do some people get depressed and many others, the majority, not get depressed even though they experience a comparable amount of stress? The recurrence of depressive affect is also an extremely important, indeed central feature of this phenomenon, and is open to investigation using their research strategy.

These two major questions, among others, were tacked by Dr. Seligman in his original writings, and it is gratifying to see them explored so effectively and in so direct and enlightening a fashion. It is inevitable that this research into the nature and causes of depression has led to progressive attempts to anticipate and prevent the occurrence of depression, particularly in young people and the new findings are the most encouraging to date. The application of Dr. Seligman's ideas to the modification of depression has however been oddly slow. More direct and concerted efforts are needed here; the Seligman theory can be and should be translated into therapy.

I will not go into the questions of the relationship between optimism and explanatory style. It is a complex relationship, and I will use the term optimism in a broad sense. Optimism has of course had a great press, particularly in these proceedings. But let me put in a word for its darker cousin, pessimism. Within our clinical practices and in our research, it is fitting that we should favor optimism. It is positive, constructive, motivating, and strong. But I think a case can be made for an association, even a causal relationship, between certain kinds of pessimistic outlook, negative explanatory style, and creativity. Consider the triumphs of Russian literature; no one could claim that the Russian writers were brimming with optimism, but their contributions are monumental. Similarly, the works of Kafka, Beckett, Chekhov—and many other writers, painters, musicians—were the product, in part, of their pessimism. Here we might consider the connections between pessimism and creativity, especially artistic creativity.

There is a connection between optimism and the concept of resiliency. One of the great attractions of Dr. Seligman's work is his ability to see strength where there is weakness, to see hope in the face of helplessness. He has shown how we can take what are common and serious problems, turn them around and impose on them an intellectual structure and understanding that enables us to view them in a freshly positive way. Some years ago, I experienced this type of turnaround when conducting research on fear. For a number of years we had been heavily involved in researching fear, and the modification of fear, in the early days of behavior therapy. Slowly it dawned on me that we had become immersed in a major paradox. These frightened patients were in need of considerable help and we learned that the most effective way of assisting them to overcome their fears was to encourage them gradually and progressively to encounter and to confront their feared situations over and over again. With few exceptions they succeeded in these encounters and benefited.

The paradox was that these significantly frightened people were encouraged to behave courageously, and they did so. As a consequence, our thinking on the subject shifted. We moved from considering courageous actors to considering, instead, courageous *acts*. Even the most frightened can behave courageously. This turn of events stimulated our interest in courage rather than fear, but to my dismay when we looked into the research, to the published literature on courage, we found in a single year over two thousand references to fear and less than two hundred to courage.

Is this a common human attribute? Are we more often and more easily drawn to negatives where positives are equally available? Be that as it may, we became interested in the nature of courage and spent about eight years studying the development of courageous behavior. We studied courageous competence in bomb-disposal operators of the Royal Army working in Northern Ireland, young soldiers being trained for parachute duties, and infantrymen (Rachman, 1990). It proved to be an enlightening experience. Most of the work focused on the bomb-disposal operators of the Royal Army. They produce remarkably competent operators, extraordinarily brave, and we were fascinated to know how they do it. We were trying to learn how it is possible to carry out this work, work in which you cannot make errors and survive. If you make one significant error, you are dead.

At the worst of times, these operators dealt with several improvised explosive devices each week, and did so with remarkable skill. The casualty rate was high at the start of the bombing campaign, but with experience and improved techniques, it was reduced to virtually zero. We learned a great deal in those eight years, but I can summarize it in two main conclusions: Training and cohesion combined to promote courageous and then fearless conduct. The bomb-disposal groups were organized into small groups of four operators each and they lived and worked together constantly. They were like close family. The training was excellent and realistic. In a matter of six months a qualified ammunitions technician was transformed into a first class bomb-disposal operator acting under stressful, highly dangerous conditions. They went from confidence levels of about 50% at the beginning of training to about 90% at the end of their training. And then they progressed from 90% to virtually 100% within two weeks on operational duty. Courageous conduct was promoted and sustained (Rachman, 1983).

The background to these remarkable achievements was critical. The commanding officers were skilled, experienced, and optimistic. They were confident in their soldiers and in their training procedures, and conveyed a sterling optimism about both, and about their unit's ability to deal with explosive devices. Doubt, hesitation, and pessimism were not seen. And rightly so. It requires no effort to calculate the effects of pessimism, or doubt, when called upon to deal with an improvised explosive device.

Our shift in interest from fear to courage was deliberate and enlightening. It is of course in keeping with Dr. Seligman's insistent urging in this volume and elsewhere that we introduce a preferable and more wholesome balance into modern psychology, and that we balance our preoccupation with misery and disaster with a comparable regard for positive psychology. There is fear and depression and rage, yes, but equally there is courage, compassion, accomplishments, creativity, generosity, inventiveness, loyalty, affection, originality, perseverance, honesty, kindness, happiness, and optimism. These human attributes are no less deserving of attention and certainly no less interesting.

REFERENCES

Rachman, S. (Ed.) (1983). Fear and courage in military bomb-disposal operators. *Advances in Behaviour Research and Therapy, 4,* 99–165.

Rachman, S. (1990). *Fear and Courage: Second Edition.* New York: Freeman.

CHAPTER 14

How Negative Psychology Is Integral To Positive Psychology

Robert J. DeRubeis

I would like to summarize some of the important lessons from the work described in the preceding papers. In so doing, I hope as well to integrate the findings of Alloy, Abramson, Aspinwall, and Shatté, which deal at least in part with the negative side of mental life, with the theme of this volume, optimism and positive psychology.

The most recent work of Alloy and Abramson answers definitively and in the affirmative the question of whether explanatory style is a risk factor for depression. This group is to be commended for the care, thoroughness, and thoughtfulness of their research. But as is true of any superlative research program, it raises as many questions as it answers. In particular, it raises the causal question: Where does a negative explanatory style come from?

If there are people who possess a thinking style that makes them vulnerable to depression in the face of negative life events, it is likely that both genetic (see Schulman, Keefe, & Seligman, 1993) and environmental factors play a role in the development of that style. The recent findings reported by Garber and Flynn (1998) suggest that a relative absence of maternal acceptance, and the presence of maternal psychological control, are associated with the development of thinking styles characteristic of persons at risk for depression. These findings accord with the observation that depressed adults report having experienced a parental style of affectionless control (Parker, 1992). Behavior genetic research designs, such as adoption studies, will be required to test between two possibilities: (1) that these parenting styles are associated with increased risk for depression in offspring irrespective of the genetic relation between parent and child; or (2) that these styles serve as a marker of genetic loading, which the parents pass on to their children. The first possibility can be further broken down into two causal hypotheses: (a) that parents determine the style of parenting, which then affects risk of depression in their adopted children; or (b) that children evoke specific parenting styles, such that children who are at genetic risk for depression bring out a parenting style of affectionless control. To make this distinction, comparisons will be needed of the parenting styles of adoptive parents toward adopted siblings who become depressed versus those who do not. If the adoptive parents engage in more affectionless control with adoptees who eventually become depressed than they do with their adopted siblings, it would point to possibility "b"—that children vulnerable to depression evoke the parenting style of affectionless control. This kind of research will be important as psychologists continue their attempts to characterize the genetic and environmental inputs that result in pessimism and depression on the one hand, and optimism and optimal functioning on the other.

The work of Aspinwall raises other causal questions that become interesting once it is understood that there is a connection between explanatory style and optimism, and between optimism and positive adaptation. In particular, Aspinwall's work suggests that optimism can have profound effects on one's behavior and, as a consequence, on one's future environment. When one has an optimistic outlook, perhaps the most important consequence is that possibilities are opened up—possibilities one may not otherwise even see, much less act upon. To be optimistic, then, is in part to be ready for opportunities, to be prepared to engage in specific behaviors that might improve one's circumstances. One might think of this as the "active" side of optimism, where the "passive" side is faith in the idea that the future is bright. Passive optimism might improve one's mood, but if it is not accompanied by active optimism, it may be associated with maladaptation (see Frese, 1992; Isaacowitz & Seligman, 1998). Active optimism may also entail the conviction that, even if one has not yet grasped the full nature of a particular predicament, one will develop an appropriate plan that will resolve current dilemmas; such a plan will become clear when uncertainties in the environment are resolved. A comprehensive characterization of an adaptive—or positive—optimism is essential. It will be important to distinguish such a positive optimistic mindset from blind optimism, both in our theories and in our measures of optimism.

Yet another causal question is addressed in the work of Shatté and colleagues: How can an explanatory style that has already developed in a maladaptive direction be changed to a more adaptive one? My own work addresses this question in the context of treatment of depressed adults who have already suffered the consequences of a negative outlook (e.g., DeRubeis, Hollon, Evans, Garvey, Grove, & Tuason, 1990). The work of Shatté and colleagues examines this problem from a prevention perspective. Their findings have led to an interest in applying such prevention programs as part of school curricula. This is a most noteworthy development; surely the kinds of life skills taught in the Penn Optimism Program, as beneficial as they might be, will have greater impact if young people are exposed to them repeatedly over years of schooling.

The findings of Shatté and colleagues also raise challenging questions about the best means of teaching optimistic life skills to young students. Will it be necessary to separate boys from girls in order for girls to benefit from the program as much as boys do? Will implementers of these programs need to conduct them differently for boys and girls? If so, this should shed more light on sex differences in social and emotional development in pre-adolescence and early adolescence.

An important theoretical question raised by depression prevention programs concerns the place of these programs in discussions of "positive psychology." The short shrift given to positive emotions and positive mind-sets is a major theme in the present volume. Yet the Penn Optimism Program, and others like it, do not use positive psychology methods. Rather, the methods they use are meant to limit or reduce negative and maladaptive emotions and behaviors rather than to promote positive emotions and behaviors per se. That is, these programs teach people to pay attention to negative emotions, so that they may rid themselves of unnecessarily or excessively negative reactions to life's obstacles. This is a noble goal, yet it is one that focuses on the negative side of mental life, with the purpose of limiting its effects.

If this analysis is correct—that even prevention programs aim primarily to limit the negative rather than enhance the positive—one can ask: Are there any institutions in society that focus on the positive, especially on the positive emotions? One answer to this that I would like to propose begins with the assumption that a focus on the positive very often involves a focus on learning to do things, or learning to do things well. It seems that the act of accomplishing, or of becoming accomplished, is an essential element in the pursuit of a positive psychology. This is of course the domain, broadly speaking, of education. Becoming skilled at and benefiting from engagement in reading, mathematics, and playing a musical instrument all fall into this category. Enhancing one's cultural or aesthetic sense, as happens when one learns to appreciate fine music or wine, is also an example. As psychologists attempt to define the domain of positive psychology, the pursuit and enjoyment of knowledge, skill, and refined aesthetic sense will likely figure prominently in the definition.

If the definition of a positive psychology is broadened to include not just the enhancement of positive states, but also the pursuit of and engagement in the good life, then negative psychological elements must be considered. Indeed, much of what is considered good character and adaptive living involves the inhibition of negative or maladaptive mental states and behaviors. As examples, maturity, courage, and self-regulation, all of which are positive goals, require the inhibition of undesirable states or motives. One is considered mature, in part, because one inhibits childish impulses. Courage involves overcoming (inhibiting) selfish or maladaptive fear. Self-regulation is primarily about monitoring negative or maladaptive thoughts and impulses and overcoming them. Thus, any attempt to enhance positive features of mental life and of living will also include substantial efforts to control or curtail the negative, which Shatté and colleagues are engaging in so admirably in their prevention programs.

I discovered an interesting parallel to this distinction between the positive and the negative in a magazine article on Sir John Templeton's approach to identifying profitable mutual funds. It turns out that the Templeton Fund was begun with a strategy to look for "points of maximum pessimism," to find those industries or nations whose prospects outpaced the public's (pessimistic) perception of them. Through this process of identifying problems (in this case inaccurate pessimistic assessments), growth occurred, and wealth was achieved. The growth of the Templeton Fund is certainly a positive development, especially for the Fund and its investors, but it derives from an acute capacity to detect, and act upon, inappropriate negativity. This is how many prevention programs and other self-improvement efforts work. We become better people by identifying our foibles and mistakes, and by learning ways to correct or inhibit them.

The overarching theme of this volume, that there should be a renewed focus on the positive side of psychology, is an exciting one. It is indeed true that psychologists have not been as careful or persistent in the characterization of positive states, or in developing methods to enhance them, as they have been in their attempts to limit negative or pathological states. But even in the pursuit of the positive, it would be a mistake to disparage the approach taken in prevention programs such as the program of Shatté and colleagues. Psychologists may want to increase their efforts to promote positive states per se, but efforts to correct problems are no less noble, and no less critical to the enhancement of positive functioning. Indeed, I would submit, it is not possible to optimize the positive without careful attention to, and methods to deal with, the negative aspects of living.

REFERENCES

DeRubeis, R.J., Hollon, S.D., Evans, M.D., Garvey, M.J., Grove, W.M., & Tuason, V.B. (1990). How does cognitive therapy work? Cognitive change and symptom change in cognitive therapy and pharmacotherapy for depression. *Journal of Consulting and Clinical Psychology, 58,* 862–869.

Frese, M. (1992). A plea for realistic pessimism: On objective reality, coping with stress, and psychological dysfunction. In L. Montada, S-H Filipp, &

M.J. Lerner (Eds.), *Life crises and experience of loss in adulthood* (pp. 81–94). Hillsdale, NJ: Lawrence Erlbaum Associates.

Garber, J., & Flynn, C. (1998). Origins of the depressive cognitive style. In D.K. Routh & R.J. DeRubeis (Eds.), *The science of clinical psychology: Accomplishments and future directions* (pp. 53–93). Washington, DC: American Psychological Association.

Isaacowitz, D.M., & Seligman, M.E.P. (1998). Is pessimism a risk factor for depression in old age? Manuscript submitted for publication.

Parker, G. (1992). Early environment. In E.S. Paykel (Ed.), *Handbook of affective disorders* (2nd ed., pp. 171–183). New York: The Guilford Press.

Schulman, P., Keith, D., & Seligman, M.E.P. (1993). Is optimism heritable? A study of twins. *Behaviour Research and Therapy, 31,* 569–574.

Part III

✦

Optimism in Families and Cultures

Section A. Optimism in the Family

CHAPTER 15

Optimism and the Family

Frank D. Fincham

In *Anna Karenina* Tolstoy notes that "All happy families resemble one another; every unhappy family is unhappy in its own way." Psychologists appear to have accepted Tolstoy's observation and focused their research efforts on understanding "unhappy" families, assuming perhaps that "happiness" in families is either self-evident or does not require examination. Seligman's call for a psychology that embraces the study of human strength and resiliency (see Seligman, Chapter 25) clearly runs counter to the relative lack of attention given to positive aspects of marital and familial functioning. What remains perhaps less obvious is that Seligman's work has already profoundly influenced the study of marriage, an extremely important relationship for the physical and psychological well-being of spouses and their children (see Burman & Margolin, 1992; McAllister, 1995; Grych & Fincham, 1990). As I have noted previously (e.g., Fincham, 1991; see also Doherty, 1981), Seligman's work contributed to the shift from a purely behavioral account of marriage to a more complete one that includes cognitive processes; Abramson, Seligman, and Teasdale's (1978) seminal paper informed initial studies of cognition in marriage, and the research that subsequently emerged from these roots constitutes, by far, the largest portion of the marital cognition literature (see Fincham, 1994; 1998).

Using research on marital cognition as a starting point, this chapter explores the role of optimism in family relationships. The exploration is structured in terms of three questions: What have we learned about optimism in marriage? How can this knowledge be used to inform understanding of optimism in other family relationships? What challenges lie ahead? Before turning to these questions, two themes that permeate the answers to them are briefly outlined. These themes concern language use and cross fertilization across different research domains. Each is addressed in turn.

TWO THEMES

Language Matters

A search for journal articles on optimism and marriage published in the last twenty-three years (*PsychLit:* 1974 to 1997) yields only twelve articles. Does this contradict the earlier observations about the impact of Seligman's work? In essence, as one might guess, the language of many of the studies relevant to understanding optimism do not use this term. Peterson, Maier, and Seligman (1993) accord choice of the terms "learned helplessness," "explanatory style," and "optimism" an important role in their brief history of learned helplessness research: "Everything we have learned about helplessness is something we have learned about optimism and vice versa" (p. 303). Assuming Peterson and colleagues (1993) are correct, and the refutation of the Sapir-Whorf hypothesis that language influences thought notwithstanding (by now most of us know that Eskimos do not have numerous words for snow, even though this remains an attractive way to present the Sapir-Whorf hypothesis, [Pullum, 1991]), the linguistic lens used by researchers can have profound effects. From this perspective, the present volume provides a powerful new lens through which marital and family researchers may examine their subject.

An example illustrates this point. Because marital research focuses on the attributional analysis associated with "helplessness" and because attributions tend only to occur for negative events (we seldom seek to explain our good fortune; see Weiner, 1985), marital research has focused heavily on pessimistic explanations for negative events and their sequelae. Thinking in terms of "optimism" frees us from focusing on the negative and reminds us of positive aspects of marital and family relationships. Does this matter?

Yes. There are at least two cogent reasons why it matters. First, marital health and family health are not simply the absence or mirror image of dysfunction (Kelly & Fincham, 1998; Weiss & Heyman, 1997). Currently, what little we know about functional marriages and families comes from research designed to investigate dysfunction. Typically, studies compare functional and dysfunctional marriages/families on variables that might elucidate dysfunctional relationships. For example, some 30 years of observational research has investigated the conflict behavior of distressed and nondistressed couples; little attention has been given to observing behavior that promotes positive relationship functioning (e.g., how spouses provide support to each other). However, if we are to promote marital and family well-being, we need to understand healthy, functioning marriages and families as an end in their own right and not simply in relation to dysfunction.

Second, recent evidence across several areas of psychology suggests that it is important to consider the relation between positive and negative aspects of human functioning. Like affect (Watson, Clark, & Tellegen, 1988) and attitudes (Thompson, Zanna, & Griffin, 1995), marital quality appears to comprise distinct and somewhat independent positive and negative dimensions (see Fincham & Linfield, 1997). Understanding positive and negative dimensions of relationships may require us to see helplessness and optimism differently—not as bipolar opposites on a single dimension but as unipolar, related dimensions each with its own probability of being activated. By thinking in bipolar terms and by using bipolar assessment scales, we have made an assumption about psychological structure relating to optimism and pessimism, and the time has come to examine this assumption.

Cross-fertilization: Differentiation and *Integration*

Although this chapter is not the place to explore the radical implications of such a conception, it draws attention to a second theme that permeates the chapter, namely, cross-fertilization. As noted earlier, the study of helplessness/optimism in the marital domain and more general research on this topic were initially closely linked, but their growth has since been characterized by increased differentiation. The process of differentiation rapidly resulted in two independent literatures. Research conducted in each domain seldom influenced research in the other; indeed, even referencing the other domain tends to be the exception rather than the rule.

In turning to explore the three questions posed in this chapter, I wish to complement the aforementioned differentiation by highlighting areas of cross-fertilization. As with the development of any biological system, development of understanding is best achieved through the complementary processes of differentiation *and* integration.

THREE QUESTIONS

What Have We Learned about Optimism from Marital Research?

This question explores the phenomenon that served as the genesis for research on explanatory style in marriage, considers some features of the research, and demonstrates why optimism is important in marriage.

Basic Phenomenon

The starting point for marital research relating to optimism has been marital quality, the most frequently studied construct in the marital literature (Glenn, 1990). Data relating to optimism focus on how spouses explain marital events and partner behavior. By now, well over forty studies document that a negative marital event (e.g., spouse unexpectedly arrives home late) that is explained using an optimistic explanatory style (e.g. "there was more traffic than usual") is associated with higher reported marital quality. What makes this explanation an "optimistic" one? Specifically, it does not locate the cause of the lateness in the spouse; it suggests that the cause is likely to change; it is specific to this situation; and, it does not blame the partner. The negative partner behavior is likely, therefore, to have minimal impact, which contrasts to the relatively greater impact that follows from a "pessimistic" or conflict promoting explanation (e.g., "she only thinks about herself and her work"). The association between explanatory style and marital quality represents, arguably, the most robust phenomenon documented in the marital literature.

Features of the Research

A few observations about the research documenting this phenomenon are apposite because they not only delineate differences between explanatory style, as studied in marital and nonmarital literatures, but also illustrate starkly the need for cross-fertilization.

First, optimistic explanatory style in the marital literature differs slightly from that in the broader literature on optimism—the stimulus event for attributions consists of a marital event or partner (not one's own) behavior. As a consequence, the locus causal dimension is assessed as a unipolar dimension and targets the partner as cause. Therefore, it avoids the ubiquitous problems posed by bipolar locus dimension assessment, a problem so acute that, at times, it has been dealt with by simply omitting the locus dimension from indices of explanatory style in the broader literature. Second, an additional set of attribution dimensions (intent, motivation, and blame) regarding responsibility are included in much marital research. This occurs because accountability of conduct is central in close relationships (see Fincham, 1985). Consequently, we are alerted to something rarely discussed, namely, that the implicit evaluative element of explanations may be what makes them so important (for an exception see Brewin, 1986).

Inclusion of additional attributional dimensions led to development of a relationship specific measure of optimistic explanatory style. Initially modeled on the *Attributional Style Questionnaire* (ASQ; Peterson, Semmel, von Baeyer, Abramson, Metalsky, & Seligman, 1982), used in the broader field of research on explanatory style (it was even named similarly—*Marital Attributional Style Questionnaire*, MASQ; Fincham, Beach, & Nelson, 1987), it evolved into a different, simpler form. Our experience has been that less educated persons find the ASQ somewhat confusing and abstract (e.g., we have sometimes found spouses rating causal dimensions in terms of the stimulus event rather than the cause they generated for the stimulus event). As a result we developed a simpler format for assessing attributions than used in the ASQ, and one that avoids the ambiguities we had encountered in the interpretation of responses. The resultant Relationship Attribution Measure (RAM; Fincham & Bradbury, 1992) provides a short, reliable assessment of explanatory style that makes fewer cognitive demands on respondents. Its format may be worth considering when assessing general explanatory style in samples that have difficulty with the ASQ. To facilitate comparison of the formats used in the RAM and ASQ, table 15.1 shows an item from each of the measures.

Thus far, I have mentioned three things about the marital domain that might be considered in the broader literature pertaining to optimism. I will now present two observations about the marital literature that call for cross-fertilization in the opposite direction. First, marital researchers have paid little attention to the diathesis-stress framework that has informed more general research on explanatory style. The paucity of research on explanatory style in the context of stress means that its role as a moderator variable remains unexplored in the marital domain. Both research on the role of explanatory style in moderating responses to negative events in the nonmarital domain (e.g., Metalsky, Halberstadt, & Abramson, 1987), as well as conceptual developments in this literature (e.g., Abramson, Metalsky, & Alloy, 1989), offer a great deal to relationship researchers, who seek to understand optimism in family relationships.

Second, marital researchers tend to have studied investigator solicited attributions. Although the explanatory style-marital quality link occurs also for unsolicited explanations (e.g., Holtzworth-Munroe & Jacobson, 1985, 1988), the study of unsolicited attributions is rare and restricted to analysis of material generated from thought listing techniques and marital/family discussions (e.g., Munton & Antaki, 1988; Stratton, Heard, Hanks, Munton, Brewin, & Davidson, 1986). Publicly communicated explanations have a different conceptual status to those that remain private, and the use of conversations between intimates for study generates many challenges (e.g., very low base rates of explanations possibly owing to implicit, shared understanding; see Bradbury & Fincham, 1988). The broader literature on explanatory style provides a good example of the creative use of content coding (see Peterson,

Table 15.1

Relationship Attribution Measure

	1	2	3	4	5	6
	DISAGREE Strongly	Disagree	Disagree Somewhat	Agree Somewhat	Agree	AGREE
YOUR SPOUSE CRITICIZES SOMETHING YOU SAY						
My spouse's behavior was due to something about him/her (e.g., the type of person he/she is, his/her mood).	1	2	3	4	5	6
The reason my spouse criticized me is *not* likely to change.	1	2	3	4	5	6
The reason my spouse criticized me is something that affects other areas of our marriage.	1	2	3	4	5	6
My spouse criticized me on purpose rather than unintentionally	1	2	3	4	5	6
My spouse's behavior was motivated by selfish rather than unselfish concerns.	1	2	3	4	5	6
My spouse deserves to be blamed for criticizing me.	1	2	3	4	5	6

Attribution Style Questionnaire

YOU HAVE BEEN LOOKING FOR A JOB UNSUCCESSFULLY FOR SOME TIME.

Write down one major cause ______________________________

Is the cause of your unsuccessful job search due to something about you or something about other people or circumstances?

Totally due to other people or circumstances	1	2	3	4	5	6	7	Totally due to me

In the future when looking for a job, will this cause again be present?

Will never again be present	1	2	3	4	5	6	7	Will always be present

Is the cause something that just influences looking for a job or does it also influence other areas of your life?

Influences just this particular situation	1	2	3	4	5	6	7	Influences all situations in my life

Schulman, Castellon, & Seligman, 1992) to analyze explanations in a wide range of contexts (see Satterfield, Chapter 21); marital and family researchers would profit from following this example.

A final feature of the marital research is the attention given to the possibility that the phenomenon studied is an artifact. Documentation of an association between an optimistic explanatory style and marital quality raises the question of why the association exists. Is it simply a spurious relationship that reflects the operation of third variables such as depression, negative affectivity, or violence, all of which are related to both attributions and marital quality? Several studies have examined these possibilities and the explanatory style–marital quality link does not appear to be an artifact (e.g., Fincham, Beach, & Bradbury, 1989; Fincham, Bradbury, Arias, Byrne, & Karney, 1997; Karney, Bradbury, Fincham, & Sullivan, 1994). Of course, third variable explanations for the association can never be ruled out as they are potentially infinite, but the attention given to this problem remains noteworthy and supports further investigation of optimism in marriage.

The Importance of Optimism in Marriage

There are two sets of findings that emphasize the crucial role of an optimistic explanatory style in marriage. The first concerns direction of effects. Optimism in marriage becomes more important if it can be shown that an optimistic explanatory style leads to higher marital quality rather than vice versa. In support of this view, the four available longitudinal studies suggest that earlier optimistic explanatory style predicts later marital quality (Fincham & Bradbury, 1987, 1993; Fincham et al., 1997, 1998) and offer little evidence of earlier marital quality predicting later optimism. Several considerations make these findings particularly noteworthy. First, because only the variance that explanations do *not* share with marital quality is used to predict changes in marital quality, it is difficult to account for significant findings by arguing that, as a self-report measure, explanatory style simply indexes marital quality (Weiss & Heyman, 1997). Second, the temporal lag studied was arbitrary and did not reflect any presumed causal lag between the two variables. Third, the result emerges across samples that differ in length of marriage and in established marriages where there is limited change in marital quality over time. Fourth, the longitudinal relation between an optimistic explanatory style and marital quality occurs independently of depressive symptoms and marital violence.

The most recent replication of this finding is illustrated in figure 15.1. This figure shows the results of structural equation modeling of the relation between the two constructs over an eighteen-month interval for 130 couples. The advantage of these results over previously published ones is that the parameters in the causal model are estimated simultaneously, and hence each parameter reflects an association controlling for all other associations in the model. Thus, each individual's attributions for partner behavior and marital satisfaction across time were expected to be a function of earlier measured, mutually associated, attributions and marital satisfaction, plus the stability of each measure. For both husbands and wives the model provides an excellent fit to the data. With regard to the cross-lagged parameters, it can be seen that significant effects were found between earlier measures of attributions for partner behavior and later marital satisfaction, but that no significant parameter estimates emerged for the cross-lagged effects between earlier marital satisfaction and later attributions.

What happens when we seriously consider what was discussed earlier about language use? Is any advantage gained when we free ourselves from the perspective of retrospection, inherent in making attributions, and explore the prospective dimension associated with optimism?[1]

Although marital cognition research has centered on expectations since its inception (e.g., Eidelson & Epstein, 1982), only belatedly has this core construct been investigated in relation to explanatory style. Theoretically, optimistic explanatory style should give rise to optimistic expectations, which should, in turn, lead to higher marital satisfaction. Consistent with these theoretical predictions, a measure of optimistic expectations was found to mediate the longitudinal relation between optimistic explanatory style and marital quality (Fincham et al., 1998). Figure 15.2 shows the results of adding optimistic expectations to the earlier described analysis and estimating indirect effects from attributions to marital satisfaction through this construct. The paths from Time 1

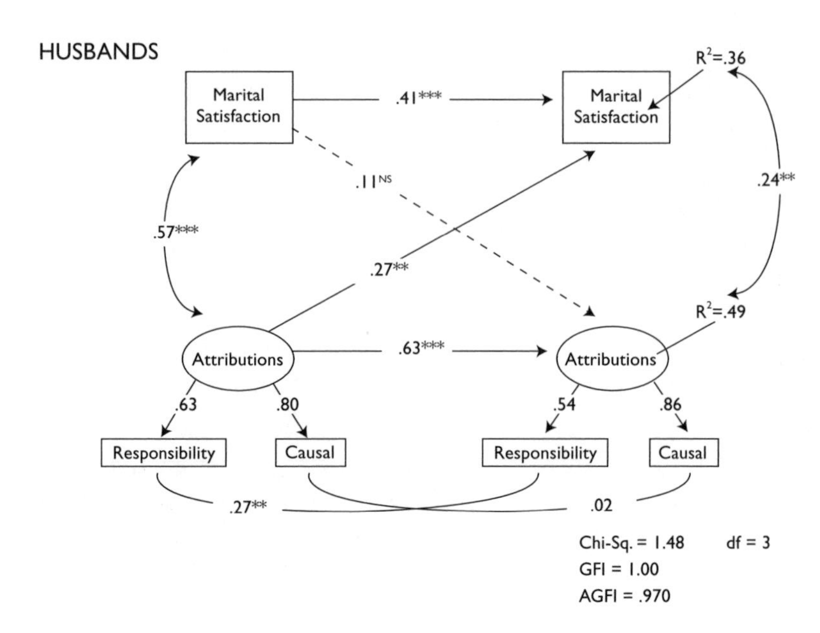

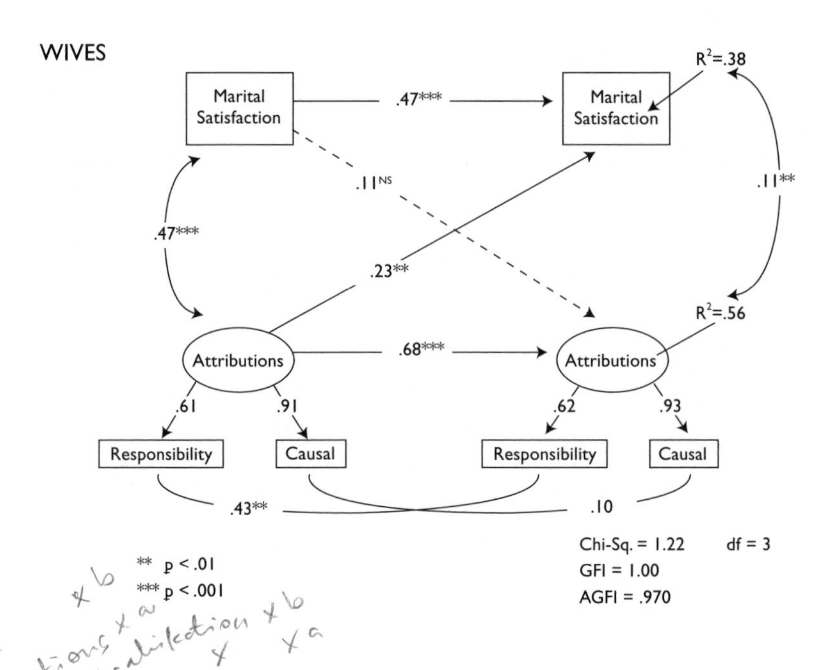

Figure 15.1 Model of relations between marital satisfaction and optimistic attributions at two time points.

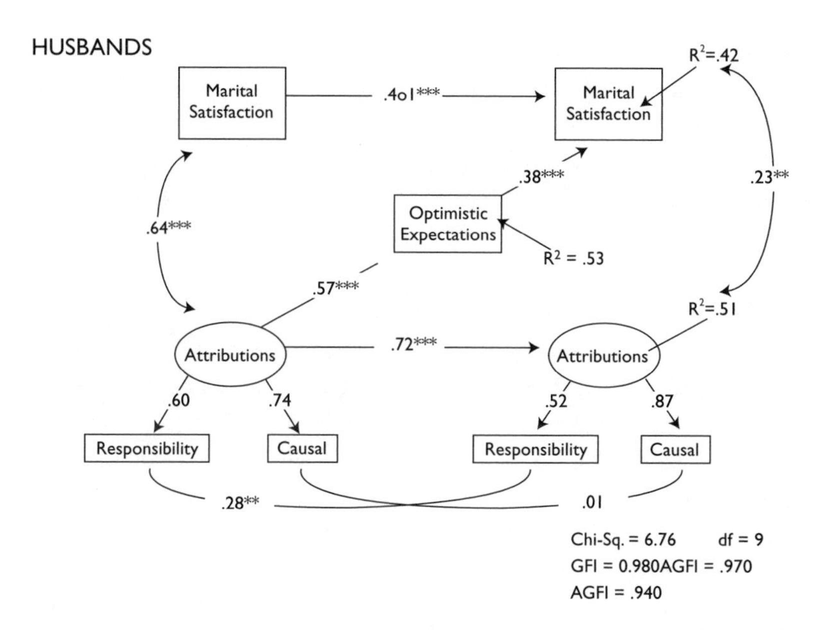

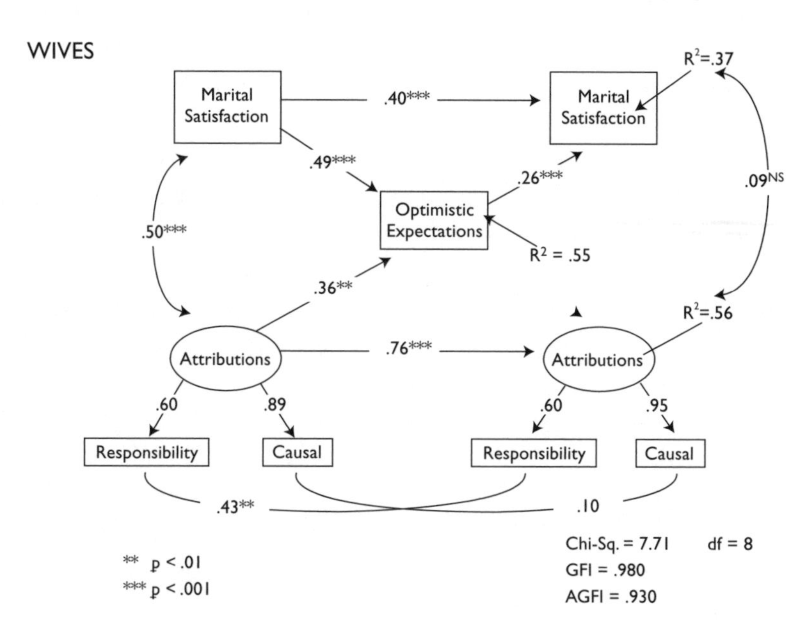

Figure 15.2. Optimistic expectations as a mediator of the relationship between optimistic attributions and marital satisfaction.

attributions to optimistic expectations and from expectations to marital satisfaction were significant. In separate analyses, it was also shown that the direct path from Time 1 attributions to Time 2 marital satisfaction became non-significant for both spouses when expectations were included in the analyses. These findings suggest that the effect between earlier attributions and later satisfaction is mediated by efficacy expectations.

Whether optimistic explanatory style effects marital quality directly or through expectations, a more complete understanding of its role in marriage must include consideration of spousal behavior. A second set of studies that emphasizes the importance of optimism in marriage therefore examines its impact on spousal behavior. Five studies demonstrate that optimistic explanatory style is associated with observed spousal behavior and, in fact, this association is independent of marital quality and of the co-morbidity of depression and marital quality (Bradbury & Fincham, 1992, Studies 1 & 2; Fincham & Bradbury, 1988; Miller & Bradbury, 1995; Bradbury, Beach, Fincham, & Nelson, 1996). Specifically, spouses with more optimistic explanatory styles show higher rates of positive behavior and lower rates of negative behavior; and for wives specifically, a lower probability of reciprocating negative partner behavior, the hallmark of a distressed marriage. These associations tend to occur most consistently for wives and for responsibility attributions. The only experimental study in the literature suggests that the association is a causal one in which explanatory style influences behavior (Fincham & Bradbury, 1988). Thus, there is both correlational and experimental evidence consistent with the view that spousal explanatory style influences marital behavior.

In sum, optimism appears to be rather important in marriage. It has both immediate and longer term implications. Its immediate effects are on ongoing behavior between spouses. In the longer term it appears to influence overall marital quality, something that has critical consequences for individuals, families, and society. If optimism is important in marital relationships might it be equally important in other family relationships? This brings us to the second question considered in this chapter concerning the implications of marital research on optimism for other family relationships.

How Can Marital Research Be Used to Inform Understanding of Optimism in Other Family Relationships?

In this section, I argue that the conceptual underpinnings and measurement technology that inform marital research on explanatory style can be profitably applied to other family relationships. Specifically, the marital literature provides a theoretical analysis of attributions in close relationships that can be a model for the study of all family relationships; in addition, the assessment of marital explanatory style can easily be generalized to provide comparable measures across different family relationships. This argument will be examined using the parent-child relationship as an illustration. In this illustration I focus on the child's perspective for two reasons. First, a body of knowledge has not yet emerged on children's explanations in family relationships. Second, reviews of work relevant to understanding parental explanations for child behavior are available elsewhere (e.g., Miller, 1995). Before turning to children's optimism in the parent-child relationship, we need to consider a broader literature on children's explanatory style, which brings us again to the theme of cross-fertilization.

Children's Explanatory Style

A robust literature exists on children's explanatory style and invites the question of whether there is anything to gain from examining the marital research described earlier. For example, the Children's Attributional Style Questionnaire (CASQ; Seligman et al., 1984) and CASQ-Revised (Kaslow & Nolen-Hoeksema, 1991) have been widely used to assess explanatory style. Meta-analyses show that a pessimistic explanatory style (internal, stable, and global attributions for negative events and external, unstable, and specific attributions for positive events) is associated with concurrent depressive symptoms and that a combined index for positive and negative events predicts future depressive symptoms (Gladstone & Kaslow, 1995; Joiner & Wagner, 1995). Although the original and revised CASQ include attributions for interpersonal events, these attributions tend *not* to be analyzed independently of attributions for achievement events (for an exception see Turner & Cole, 1994); and, in any event, concern those the child makes for his or her own behavior, rather than the behavior of a significant other.

Children's attributions have been examined in one interpersonal context, namely, peer relationships. In this domain, assessment of children's attributions has focused on a single attributional dimension, inferred hostile intent, for hypothetical, ambiguous peer behaviors. There is evidence that the tendency to infer hostile intent for hypothetical, ambiguous peer behaviors predicts retaliatory aggressive responses, later acts of aggression, and teacher ratings of reactive aggression (e.g., Crick & Dodge, 1996; Dodge, Bates, & Pettit, 1990). Although valuable, this research focuses on a single dimension and provides a limited view of explanatory style. In short, existing research on children's explanatory styles provides limited data on interpersonal relationships and does not specifically address family relationships. Does this matter?

In the absence of direct evidence, reference to marital research illustrates its potential utility for exploring optimism in family relationships. An answer to the current question is suggested by a marital study that speaks to the cross-fertilization mentioned earlier between general research on optimism and that conducted in the context of marriage. Reference to this study helps establish why my own energies have been devoted to developing a relationship specific measure of optimism for children modeled on the RAM.

Using a sample of 150 couples, Horneffer and Fincham (1995) assessed general (ASQ) and marital specific (RAM) explanatory styles and examined them in relation to the two major adaptations to which they have been related, namely, depressive symptoms and marital satisfaction. This study therefore combined examination of the two major constructs investigated in the general and marital literatures on explanatory style, respectively. It could be argued that an optimistic explanatory style in marriage simply reflects a more general explanatory style and that the relationship specific style is, therefore, redundant. From this perspective, only the more general optimistic style is needed to understand depressive symptoms and marital quality. This hypothesis was examined using structural equation modeling. Specifically, the restricted model shown in figure 15.3, which included only paths involving a general optimistic explanatory style, was tested to determine whether it was consistent with the data. However, this model did not fit the data for either husbands or wives.

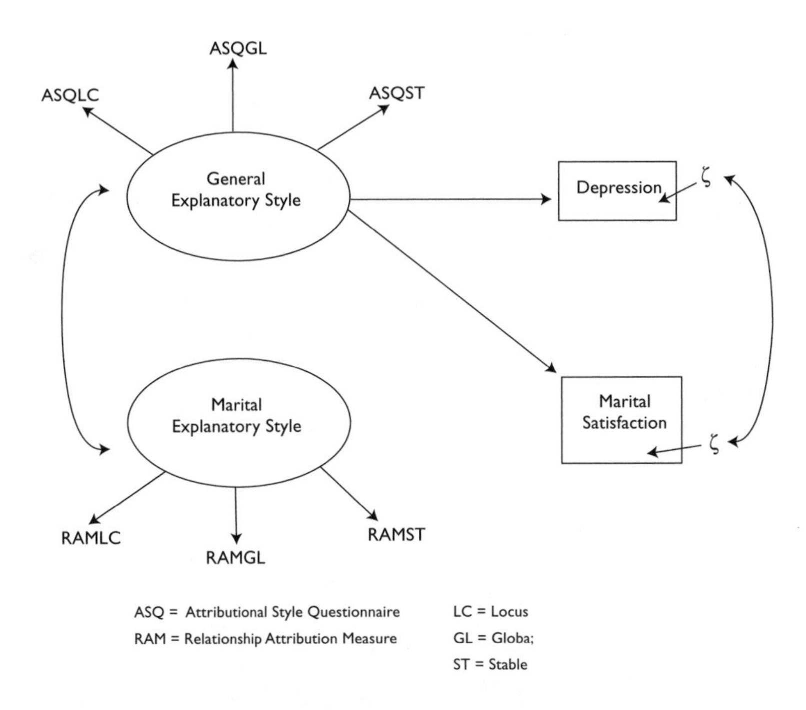

Figure 15.3. A restricted model where general explanatory style accounts for adaptational outcomes.

Findings obtained for the restricted model raise the question of whether a full model—that includes paths from marriage specific explanatory style to both adaptational outcomes—provides a better fit. When the restricted model was compared to this full model there was a significant improvement in fit. From the full model shown in figure 15.4, we can see that general and marriage specific measures of optimistic explanatory style both had direct effects; in essence, general optimism did not simply have indirect effects through marriage specific optimism. Thus, marital explanatory style supplies unique information in the prediction of depressive symptoms and marital satisfaction, and does not appear to be a subset of general explanatory style.

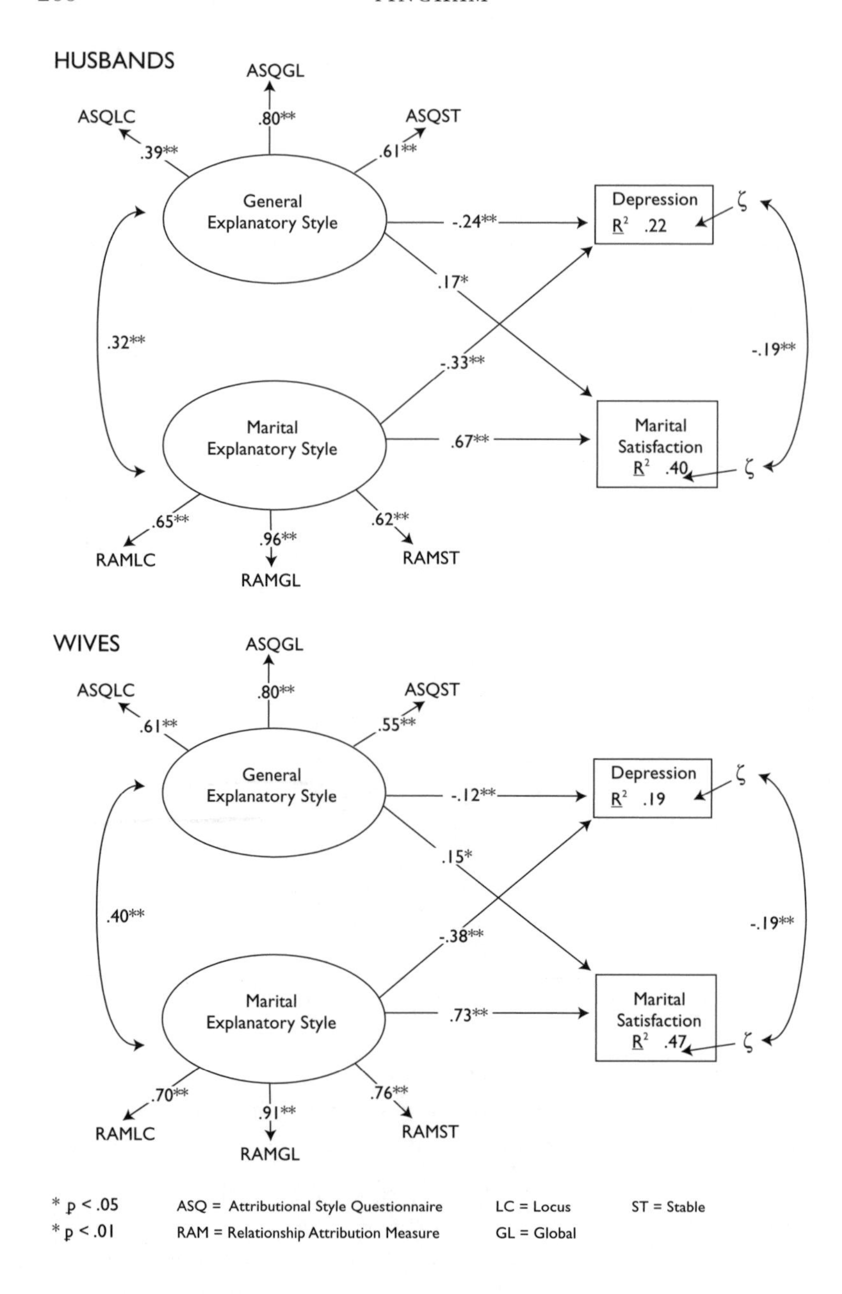

Figure 15.4. A full model where general and marital explanatory styles account for adaptational outcomes.

These findings, in turn, prompt a further question. Are general and marriage specific explanatory styles equally powerful in predicting depressive symptoms and in predicting marital distress? This question can be addressed first by creating a model in which paths linking both types of explanatory style to adaptational outcome are constrained to be equal to each other. Second, the reduced model can be compared to a model in which these paths are unconstrained. For both husbands and wives, when the paths from general and marital optimism to depressive symptoms were set to be equal, the resulting constrained model did not differ significantly from the unconstrained model. However, when analogous paths from explanatory style to marital distress were constrained in this manner, the reduced model did not fit as well as the full, unconstrained model. This suggests that the path coefficient linking general optimistic explanatory style to marital outcome differs significantly from the path coefficient linking martial optimism and marital satisfaction.

The goal in describing these data is to demonstrate that some purchase is gained by considering optimistic explanatory style as something that can vary in terms of the content domain examined. This is important because it returns us to our question of whether, in view of existing research on children's explanatory styles, there is anything to gain from examining the marital literature. Evidently, examination of this literature suggests that analyzing children's explanatory styles, in general terms, cannot be assumed to advance understanding of their family relationships. However, as any developmental psychologist will note, the differentiation of general and relationship specific optimism is likely to emerge with age. But until we identify the developmental stage at which general and family specific explanatory styles are differentiated, it is prudent to assume that we cannot generalize findings from one level of analysis to the other.

Optimism in the Parent-Child Relationship

What do we find when examining children's optimistic explanatory styles specifically in the context of the parent-child relationship? Is optimism important in this relationship? The marital research described earlier provides a useful starting point for addressing these questions.

Specifically, we can ask if the same kinds of findings emerge as those seen in marital relationships.

Data collected for Brody's Adolescent Development Research Project (University of Georgia) allow exploration of optimism in family relationships modeled on marital research. A sample of 230 children (10- to 12-year-olds), their parents, and siblings completed explanatory style measures modeled on the RAM in relation to each family member. Although this rich data set provides insight into a number of interesting questions about explanatory style in families, only children's explanations for parent behaviors are considered here.

Analysis of the structure that might underlie children's explanations for parent behavior yielded a single principal component (all items loaded .6 or higher). The resulting unidimensional scale had an internal consistency in excess of that recommended for research instruments (coefficient alpha > .75 for mother and father scales). This allowed for examination of whether children's explanatory style was related to the quality of the parent-child relationship. Table 15.2 shows that, consistent with findings in the marital domain, explanatory style for parent behavior was related to children's reports of the positive quality of the relationship with both their mothers and their fathers.

The second finding that emphasized the importance of optimism in marriage was the association between optimism and spousal behavior. The explanatory style-behavior association in the parent-child relationship was examined using self-reported conflict behavior with the parent and observed child behavior toward the parent. Observed behavior in this case was indexed by the preponderance of positive over negative behaviors and was simply the arithmetic difference between ratings of positive and negative behavior. As shown in Table 15.2, an association was found between optimistic explanatory style and behavior—except for girls' explanations for maternal behavior.

Following further the lead provided by marital research, one can ask whether the associations reported thus far are simply an artifact. In particular, the existence of an association between explanatory style and depressive symptoms raises the possibility that other associations found for children's explanatory style may simply constitute an artifact of depressive symptoms. In addition, childhood depression itself is related

Table 15.2

Correlations between child's optimistic explanatory style and perceived positivity of parent-child relationship and parent-child interaction.

	CHILD EXPLANATORY STYLE	
	Boys	
	Father	Mother
Relationship Positivity	.37**	.34**
Parent-child Interaction		
Ineffective Arguing	-.44**	-.27**
Positivity of Observed Interaction	.27**	.22**
	Girls	
	Father	Mother
Relationship Positively	.28**	.23**
Parent-child Interaction		
Ineffective Arguing	-33**	-.15*
Positivity of Observed Interaction	.22**	-.02 *

**p<.01, *p<.05

to family processes, including impairment of the parent-child relationship (Kaslow, Deering, & Racusin, 1994). It is, therefore, quite possible that the associations reported in table 15.2 simply reflect the association between children's explanatory style and reports of depressive symptoms. Importantly, when children's level of depressive symptoms was statistically controlled, these associations remained significant.

Although the work reported here is still quite preliminary, it suggests that the general framework used in marital research can be applied, with minor adaptations, to study optimism in different family relationships. This possibility raises some interesting challenges for the future.

WHAT CHALLENGES LIE AHEAD?

As this chapter demonstrates, the study of optimism in the family has received limited attention from researchers. The relative neglect of this topic is emphasized by its importance not only for understanding a variety of adaptational outcomes experienced by family members but also for understanding family relationships. The need to facilitate research on optimism in family relationships is apparent. However, a number of challenges need to be met in developing this field of inquiry. In this section, three of these challenges are briefly described.

Level of Analysis

Perhaps the most obvious challenge that arises in considering families is one that involves transcending the level of individual analysis. The study of dyads and families offers the possibility of studying optimism as a phenomenon that is greater than the sum of the characteristics of the individuals involved. How can we best investigate such a possibility? Too often we compute dyadic scores using responses obtained from each participant individually. However, as Broderick (1993) notes, "the average . . . represents an opinion that is held by neither participant and which is attributed to a social system that—like all social systems—is intrinsically incapable of any opinion at all" (p. 49). Assuming we successfully address this challenge in studying optimism, further questions arise. For example, are differences between families in an emergent optimism simply quantitative or do qualitative differences exist? What are the implications of an emergent family optimism for understanding individuals in the family?

Origins of Optimism

The importance of the first challenge is emphasized by the second—the study of families highlights the challenge of determining the origins of optimism. We already know: (a) that a parent's optimistic explanatory style correlates with that shown by their children (e.g., Seligman et al., 1984); (b) that mothers of children with optimistic and pessimistic explanatory styles display different behaviors toward their children during an achievement task (e.g., mothers who reassure children of their ability when they show helpless behavior, such as giving up on a task, tend to have more optimistic children; Hokoda & Fincham, 1995); and (c) that parents who explain their children's failures in terms of their children's ability tend to have children with a pessimistic explanatory style (e.g., Fincham & Cain, 1986). To obtain a more precise picture of the relationship between parental and child explanatory style and the mechanisms that account for it requires more research. For example, do children acquire an explanatory style (a) through observing parental explanations for other people's behavior, (b) through observing their parents' explanations for each other's behavior, or (c) through their experience of the parents' explanations for the child's behavior? What is the relative importance of each mechanism? What happens when parents have similar versus contrasting explanatory styles and so on?

What Is an Explanatory "Style"?

A third challenge confronts what is implicit in much research and clearly implied by the label "optimistic explanatory *style.*" The implication of an optimistic style can be explored at several new levels. For example, we can think about style in terms of response consistency, changing the focus from one of mean responses to variability in responses. Alternatively, style could denote patterns of responses across assessment dimensions, changing the focus from summated scores to the different patterns of responses across dimensions; different patterns can give rise to the same summated score. In either case, rigidity/flexibility in responses or patterns of responses may be just as important for understanding the consequences of optimism as mean scores. Both of these conceptions have been examined in the marital literature and have proved useful for understanding marital satisfaction (see Baucom, Sayers, & Duhe, 1989; Horneffer & Fincham, 1995).

A third possibility, mentioned earlier, is to think about styles in terms of responses across domains (e.g., affiliative, achievement) and across areas within domains (e.g., different relationships). Most research on optimistic explanatory style tends toward the most general level, but the marital work I have described illustrates the utility of considering optimism as domain specific. As we now move to examine optimism in different family relationships, and relationships more generally, there is the need to strike a balance between specificity and generality. Here the history of research on attitude-behavior relations helps to remind us of the importance of examining attitude (or optimism) and behavior (or the phenomenon related to optimism) at the same level of specificity. A critical consequence of taking the issue of domain specificity seriously is that it allows us to examine individual differences in optimism more systematically. For example, two individuals might have similar overall optimism scores but differ in how much optimism they show in different domains and, hence, potentially in domain specific functioning.

CONCLUSION

This chapter has explored marital research stimulated by learned helplessness through a new linguistic lens, and examined how marital research may provide a framework for studying other family relationships. In doing so, this discussion attempted to illustrate the value of cross-fertilization across two independent, but related, literatures. The focus on "optimism" challenges us to consider positive aspects of family relationships and to question whether an understanding of healthy relationship functioning will emerge from the study of relationship dys-

function. It seems unlikely that we will fully comprehend health or optimism through the mirror of ill health and pessimism. Rather, we must consider the possibility that health and dysfunction might be differently related to optimism and pessimism, respectively. This requires us to face fundamental questions such as: What is a healthy relationship and how does it function? How can we promote healthy family relationships? By focusing our attention on optimism and hope, the present volume takes us a step forward toward answering such questions.

NOTES

1 Focusing on expectations produces greater fidelity to theoretical writings prompted by dogs' observed failure to escape traumatic shock, the phenomenon that gave rise to later research on helplessness in humans. Expectations were central in explaining this initial phenomenon, and their centrality continued in theorizing about its human counterpart. It has always been a puzzle as to why expectations did not assume central stage in research on humans. There is a longstanding research tradition on expectancy-value theories of achievement motivation that seemed highly relevant for exploring human responses to noncontingent or uncontrollable outcomes. However, this literature does not appear to have had much of an impact and serves not only to underline the importance of cross-fertilization across different areas of psychology, but also to support the prominence given this theme in the present chapter.

REFERENCES

Abramson, L.Y., Metalsky, G.I., & Alloy, L.B. (1989). Hopelessness depression: A theory based subtype of depression. *Psychological Review, 96,* 358–372.

Abramson, L.Y., Seligman, M.E.P., & Teasdale, J.D. (1978). Learned helplessness in people: Critique and reformulation. *Journal of Abnormal Psychology, 87,* 49–74.

Baucom, D.H., Sayers, S.L., & Duhe, A. (1989). Attributional style and attributional patterns among married couples. *Journal of Personality and Social Psychology, 56,* 596–607.

Bradbury, T.B., Beach, S.R.H., Fincham, F.D., & Nelson, G.M. (1996). Attributions and behavior in functional and dysfunctional marriages. *Journal of Consulting and Clinical Psychology, 64,* 569–576.

Bradbury, T.N., & Fincham, F.D. (1988). Assessing spontaneous attributions in marital interaction: Methodological and conceptual considerations. *Journal of Social and Clinical Psychology, 7,* 122–130.

Bradbury, T.N., & Fincham, F.D. (1992). Attributions and behavior in marital interaction. *Journal of Personality and Social Psychology, 63,* 613–628.

Brewin, C.R. (1986). Internal attribution and self-esteem in depression: A theoretical note. *Cognitive Therapy and Research, 10,* 469–475.

Broderick, C.B. (1993). *Understanding family process: Basics of family systems theory.* Newbury Park, CA: Sage.

Burman, B., & Margolin, G. (1992). Analysis of the association between marital relationships and health problems: An interactional perspective. *Psychological Bulletin, 112,* 39–63.

Crick, N.R., & Dodge, K.A. (1996). Social information-processing mechanisms in reactive and proactive aggression. *Child Development, 67,* 993–1002.

Dodge, K.A., Bates, J.E., & Pettit, G.S. (1990). Mechanisms in the cycle of violence. *Science, 250,* 1678–1683.

Doherty, W.J. (1981). Cognitive processes in intimate conflict: II. Efficacy and learned helplessness. *American Journal of Family Therapy, 9,* 35–44.

Eidelson, R.J., & Epstein, N. (1982). Cognition and relationship maladjustment: Development of a measure of dysfunctional relationship beliefs. *Journal of Consulting and Clinical Psychology, 50,* 715–720.

Fincham, F.D. (1985). Attributions in close relationships. In J.H. Harvey & G. Weary (Eds.), *Attribution: Basic issues and applications* (pp. 203–234). New York: Academic Press.

Fincham, F.D. (1991). Understanding close relationships: An attributional perspective. In S. Zelen (Ed.), *New models—new extensions of attribution theory* (pp. 163–206). New York: Springer-Verlag.

Fincham, F.D. (1994). Cognition in marriage: Current status and future challenges. *Applied and Preventive Psychology: Current Scientific Perspectives, 3,* 185-198.

Fincham, F.D. (1998). Child development and marital relations. *Child Development, 69,* 543-574.

Fincham, F.D., Beach, S.R., & Bradbury, T.N. (1989). Marital distress, depression, and attributions: Is the marital distress-attribution association an artifact of depression? *Journal of Consulting and Clinical Psychology, 57,* 768–771.

Fincham, F.D., Beach, S.R., & Nelson. G. (1987). Attributional processes in distressed and nondistressed couples: 3. Causal and responsibility attributions for spouse behavior. *Cognitive Therapy and Research, 11,* 71–86.

Fincham, F.D., & Bradbury, T.N. (1987). The impact of attributions in marriage: A longitudinal analysis. *Journal of Personality and Social Psychology, 53,* 481–489.

Fincham, F.D., & Bradbury, T.N. (1988). The impact of attributions in marriage: An experimental analysis. *Journal of Social and Clinical Psychology, 7,* 147–162.

Fincham, F.D., & Bradbury, T.N. (1992). Assessing attributions in marriage: The Relationship Attribution Measure. *Journal of Personality and Social Psychology, 62,* 457–468.

Fincham, F.D., & Bradbury, T.N. (1993). Marital satisfaction, depression, and attributions: A longitudinal analysis. *Journal of Personality and Social Psychology, 64,* 442–452.

Fincham, F.D., Bradbury, T.N., Arias, I., Byrne, C.A., & Karney, B.R. (1997). Marital violence, marital distress and attributions. *Journal of Family Psychology, 11,* 367–372

Fincham, F.D. & Cain, K. (1986). Learned helplessness in humans: A developmental analysis. *Developmental Review, 6,* 301–333.

Fincham, F.D., Harold, G., & Gano-Phillips, S. (2000). The longitudinal relation between attributions and marital satisfaction: Direction of effects and role of efficacy expectations. *Journal of Family Psychology, 14,* 267-285.

Fincham, F.D., & Linfield, K.J. (1997). A new look at marital quality: Can spouses feel positive and negative about their marriage? *Journal of Family Psychology, 11,* 489–502.

Gladstone, T.R.G., & Kaslow, N.J. (1995). Depression and attributions in children and adolescents: A meta-analytic review. *Journal of Abnormal Child Psychology, 23,* 597–606.

Glenn, N.D. (1990). Quantitative research on marital quality in the 1980s: A critical review. *Journal of Marriage and the Family, 52,* 818–831.

Grych, J.H., & Fincham, F.D. (1990). Marital conflict and children's adjustment: A cognitive-contextual framework. *Psychological Bulletin, 108,* 267–290.

Hokoda, A., & Fincham, F.D. (1995). Origins of children's helpless and mastery achievement patterns in the family. *Journal of Educational Psychology, 87,* 375–385.

Holtzworth-Munroe, A., & Jacobson, N.S. (1985). Causal attributions of married couples: When do they search for causes? What do they conclude when they do? *Journal of Personality and Social Psychology, 48,* 1398–1412.

Holtzworth-Munroe, A., & Jacobson, N.S. (1988). Toward a methodology for coding spontaneous causal attributions: Preliminary results with married couples. *Journal of Social and Clinical Psychology, 7,* 101–112.

Horneffer, K.J., & Fincham, F.D. (1995). The construct of attributional style in depression and marital distress. *Journal of Family Psychology, 9,* 186–195.

Horneffer, K.J., & Fincham, F.D. (1996). Attributional models of depression and marital distress. *Personality and Social Psychology Bulletin, 22,* 678–689.

Joiner, T.E., & Wagner, K.D. (1995). Attributional style and depression in children and adolescents: A meta-analytic review. *Clinical Psychology Review, 15,* 777–798.

Karney, B.R., Bradbury, T.N., Fincham, F.D., & Sullivan, K.T. (1994). The role of negative affectivity in the association between attributions and marital satisfaction. *Journal of Personality and Social Psychology, 66,* 413–424.

Kaslow, N.J., Deering, C.G., & Racusin, G.R. (1994). Depressed children and their families. *Clinical Psychology Review, 14,* 39–59.

Kaslow, N.J., & Nolen-Hoeksema, S. (1991). Children's Attributional Style Questionnaire—Revised. Unpublished manuscript, Emory University, Atlanta.

Kelly, A.B., & Fincham, F.D. (1998). Marital health: Towards a more complete account of functional and satisfying couple relationships. *Encyclopedia of mental health.* New York: Academic Press.

McAllister, F. (1995). *Marital breakdown and the health of the nation* (2nd ed.). London: One Plus One.

Metalsky, G. I., Halberstadt, L.J., & Abramson, L.Y. (1987). Vulnerability to depressive mood reactions: Toward a more powerful test of the diathesis-stress and causal mediation components of the reformulated theory of depression. *Journal of Personality and Social Psychology, 52,* 386–393.

Miller, G.E., & Bradbury, T.N. (1995). Refining the association between attributions and behavior in marital interaction. *Journal of Family Psychology, 9,* 196–208.

Miller, S.A. (1995). Parents' attributions for their children's behavior. *Child Development, 66,* 1557–1584.

Munton, A.G., & Antaki, C. (1988). Causal beliefs among families in therapy: Attributions at the group level. *British Journal of Clinical Psychology, 27,* 91–97.

Peterson, C., Meier, S.F., & Seligman, M.E.P. (1993). *Learned helplessness: A theory for the age of personal control.* Cambridge: Cambridge University Press.

Peterson, C., Schulman, P., Castellon, C., & Seligman, M.E.P. (1992). The explanatory style scoring manual. In C.P. Smith (Ed.), *Handbook of thematic analysis* (pp. 383–392). New York: Cambridge University Press.

Peterson, C., Semmel, A., von Baeyer, C., Abramson, L.Y., Metalsky, G.F., & Seligman, M.E.P. (1982). The Attributional Style Questionnaire. *Cognitive Therapy and Research, 6,* 297–299.

Pullum, G.K. (1991). *The great Eskimo vocabulary hoax and other irreverent essays on the study of language.* Chicago: University of Chicago Press.

Seligman, M.E.P., Peterson, C. Kaslow, N.J., Tanenbaum, R.L., Alloy, L.B., & Abramson, L.Y. (1984). Attribution style and depressive symptoms among children. *Journal of Abnormal Psychology, 93,* 235–238

Stratton, P., Heard, D., Hanks, H.G.I., Munton, A.G., Brewin, C.R., & Davidson, C. (1986). Coding causal beliefs in natural discourse. *British Journal of Social Psychology, 25,* 299–31.

Thompson, M.M., Zanna, M.P., & Griffin, D.W. (1995). Let's not be indifferent about (attitudinal) ambivalence. In R.E. Petty & J.A. Drosnick (Eds.), *Attitude strength: Antecedents and consequences* (pp. 361–386). Hillsdale, NJ: Erlbaum.

Turner, J.E., & Cole, D.A. (1994). Developmental differences in cognitive diatheses for child depression. *Journal of Abnormal Child Psychology, 22,* 15–32.

Watson, D., Clark, L.A., & Tellegen, A. (1988). Development and validation of brief measures of Positive and Negative Affect: The PANAS scales. *Journal of Personality and Social Psychology, 54,* 1063–1070.

Weiner, B. (1985). "Spontaneous" causal search. *Psychological Bulletin, 97,* 74–84.

Weiss, R.L., & Heyman, R.E. (1997). A clinical-research overview of couple interactions. In W.K. Halford & H.J. Markman (Eds.), *The clinical handbook of marriage and couples interventions* (pp. 13–42). New York: Wiley.

✦ CHAPTER 16 ✦

Optimism: Definitions and Origins

Judy Garber

IN THE PAPER "Optimism and the Family," Frank Fincham raised several important issues concerning the definition and measurement of the construct of optimism. In addition, Fincham highlighted critical challenges to the field that provide directions for future research. The present paper has two purposes. First, three issues raised by Fincham regarding the definition of optimism are discussed: (a) Is optimism a unipolar or bipolar construct? (b) What is the distinction between causal attributions and expectancies about the future? and (c) Is there a difference between general and specific optimism? Second, we address Fincham's challenge regarding the origins of optimism.

DEFINITION OF OPTIMISM

Is Optimism a Unipolar or Bipolar Construct?

Fincham raised a very important question about whether optimism and pessimism are simply opposite ends of the same bipolar continuum or whether they are distinct, unipolar constructs that have different origins, structures, and relations with other constructs, such as health and maladjustment. That is, is there a substantive difference between optimism and pessimism, or is it simply linguistic?

There are other, related constructs for which this question also has been asked, including negative and positive affectivity (Watson & Tellegen, 1985), risk and protective factors (Rutter, 1990), competence and maladaptation (Masten & Coatsworth, 1995), social support and conflict (Barrera, Chassin, & Rogosch, 1993), and marital health and dysfunction (Kelly & Fincham, in press). Rutter (1990) asserted that even if the distinction is only linguistic, it still probably makes sense to use two different terms when referring to opposite poles of the same concept. That is, "up" and "down" is preferred to "up" and "not up" because each term emphasizes a different focus. Rutter stated that risk and protective factors are substantively distinct and reflect different mechanisms at opposite poles. Whereas risk mechanisms lead directly to disorders, protective factors have their effects only in interaction with other risk variables.

Watson and colleagues (Watson, Clark, & Tellegen, 1988; Watson & Tellegen, 1985) have shown that negative and positive affect are different dimensions with different structures and correlates. For example, whereas positive affect is related to social activity and shows significant diurnal variation, negative affect is significantly related to perceived stress and shows no circadian pattern (Watson et al., 1988). Finally, Barrera and colleagues (1993) noted that several studies have shown that the constructs of positive and negative social relationships are largely uncorrelated, and social support and conflict have different patterns of association with indicators of adjustment (e.g., Pagel, Erdly, & Becker, 1987; Sandler & Barrera, 1984). For example, the size of a conflicted social network was found to be positively associated with psychological distress, whereas unconflicted network size was unrelated (Sandler & Barrera, 1984). Thus, there are several different pairs of constructs that apparently are not simply different ends of a bipolar continuum because they are uncorrelated with each other and they relate differently to other variables (e.g., psychopathology).

Fincham suggested similarly that it might make sense to consider optimism and pessimism separately, particularly as they predict maladjustment and well-being. Thus, the opposite of optimistically expecting things to go well in the future is to not think that things will go well. This is different from having a pessimistic expectation that things are going to work out especially badly. For example, an individual can be optimistic about making a fortune in the stock market as opposed to not making much money. On the other hand, the pessimistic view would be that the person would lose a great deal of money. Each of these three outcomes is likely to be associated differently with moods as well as other symptoms.

The instruments used to measure the optimism/pessimism construct have limited the study of this issue. The Hopelessness Scale (Beck, Weissman, Lester, & Trexler, 1974) typically has been considered a measure of the single dimension of hopelessness, although it is possible to identify separate hopeless and hopeful items. Similarly, the Life Orientation Test (LOT; Scheier & Carver, 1985) yields a single factor such that optimism and pessimism generally have been treated as opposite poles of the same dimension.

However, Marshall, Wortman, Kusulas, Hervig, and Vickers (1992) conducted a factor analyses of the Hopelessness Scale and the LOT that yielded a two-factor model in which optimism and pessimism were correlated, but somewhat distinct, dimensions. Moreover, pessimism was primarily associated with neuroticism and negative affect, whereas optimism was principally associated with extroversion and positive affect (Marshall et al., 1992). Hence, there is at least some empirical support for the notion that optimism and pessimism are related, but are not necessarily unidimensional.

Thus, research examining the differentiability of optimism and pessimism has been constrained somewhat by the available measurement instruments. Further work needs to be conducted with regard to both the conceptual differentiation of these constructs as well as their measurement. Either current measures need to be revised or totally new and separate measures of optimism and pessimism need to be developed. Finally, such research also should pay attention to some of the more finely differentiated optimism-pessimism constructs that have been proposed, including defensive pessimism (Norem & Cantor, 1986) and naive optimism (Epstein & Meier, 1989).

Attributions and Expectancies

A second important point raised by Fincham was that the terms *pessimism, learned helplessness,* and *depressive attributional style* often have been used interchangeably to refer to the cognitive vulnerability that predisposes some individuals to becoming depressed under conditions of stress. However, attributions are distinct from expectations and they presumably play different roles in the onset of depression. Fincham noted this distinction and stated that "It has always been a puzzle as to why expectation did not assume central stage in research on humans" (see Chapter 15). Indeed, the concept of expectations was central to the original formulation of the learned helplessness theory (Seligman, 1975). The reformulation of the learned helplessness model of depression in humans (Abramson, Seligman, & Teasdale, 1978), however, made the concept of attributions more prominent. Moreover, with the development of the Attributional Style Questionnaire (ASQ; Seligman, Abramson, Semmel, & von Baeyer, 1979) the field seemed to focus more on the attributional component of the model rather than expectations.

The ASQ as well as the Children's Attributional Style Questionnaire (CASQ; Seligman, Peterson, Kaslow, Tanenbaum, Alloy, & Abramson, 1984) have now been used in hundreds of studies examining the relation between attributional style and depression (Gladstone & Kaslow, 1995; Joiner & Wagner, 1995; Sweeney, Anderson, & Bailey, 1986). It is not really clear, however, whether these measures assess attributions, expectancies, or both. The items on the ASQ ask questions about causality and then ask about the respondent's expectations regarding the identified cause. For example, one item on the ASQ is "You have been looking for a job unsuccessfully for some time." Respondents are then asked to indicate "*One* major cause" and whether this cause (a) is due to something about them or something about other people or circumstances, (b) will again be present in the future, and (c) is something that only influences this situation or influences other areas of their life. Thus, the ASQ explicitly assesses causal attributions about an event, indirectly assesses expectations about this cause, and asks nothing about expectations regarding possible future consequences of the event. The Children's ASQ also clearly measures attributions; expectancies are only inferred. Nevertheless, the ASQ and CASQ have been described as measures of optimism/pessimism, and results of studies utilizing these attribution measures have been used as evidence to support the link between optimism/pessimism and depression.

Despite this confusion in the empirical literature, theories about helplessness and depression have been clearer with regard to the distinction between attributions and expectancies. According to the reformulated learned helplessness model, after persons experience noncontingency "they attribute their helplessness to a cause" (Abramson et al., 1978, p. 49). This attribution then "*predicts* the recurrence of the expectations but the expectation *determines* the occurrence of the helplessness deficits" (Abramson et al., 1978, p. 59). Hollon and Garber (1980) similarly proposed a cognitive-expectancy theory of therapy in which they argued that whereas attributional processes might be central to the onset of depression, expectations play an equally large role in its maintenance, and "the explicit disconfirmation of those expectations provides the most efficient means of reversing all the dysfunctional cognitive processes" (p. 193). Hammen and colleagues (Hammen & Cochran, 1981; Hammen & deMayo, 1982) also suggested that cognitions about the consequences of events may be more important than beliefs about their causes in the development of depression. Finally, the hopelessness model (Abramson, Metalsky, & Alloy, 1989), which was a revision of the reformulated helplessness model, explicitly stated that whereas attributions were distal, contributing factors, negative expectations (i.e., hopelessness) were the proximal cause of depression.

Thus, although measures of attributional style have confused the distinction between attributions and expectancies, theories have been more explicit about their differences. A few empirical investigations have found some support for the role of expectations (i.e., hopelessness) as a mediator between attributions and depression. Metalsky and Joiner (1992) showed that the interaction of attributions and stress significantly predicted depressive symptoms and this relation was mediated by hopelessness. Fincham (see Chapter 15) similarly found in the domain of marriage that the relation between attributions and marital satisfaction was mediated by expectations.

In summary, there is a clear conceptual and empirical difference between attributions and expectations. The constructs are related, and attributions appear to predict expectations. Nevertheless, researchers should be careful to maintain this distinction in their writings and research with these constructs. Fincham noted that Peterson, Maier, and

Seligman (1993) stated that "Everything we have learned about helplessness is something we have learned about optimism and vice versa" (p. 303). However, the notion that helplessness, attributions, and optimism are all the same should be examined further. Future studies need to determine whether the Attributional Style Questionnaire (ASQ) actually measures attributions, expectations, or some combination of the two. Until then, caution should be used in referring to the ASQ as a measure of optimism-pessimism. Finally, further research that examines the temporal link between attributions and expectations as well as their respective relations with other constructs such as depression and adaptation is needed.

General Versus Specific Optimism

Fincham (Fincham, Beach, & Nelson, 1987; Fincham & Bradbury, 1992) has highlighted the importance of cognitions, particularly attributions, in the domain of marriage, and he has developed specific measures of attributions about the marital relationship. He raised an interesting question concerning whether individuals have a general cognitive *style* or whether their attributions and expectations are domain specific. Moreover, if there is domain specificity, to what extent do these cognitions relate differently to other constructs such as maladaptation and health?

Findings have been mixed in empirical examinations of the relation between general attributional style and attributions within specific domains (e.g., Garber & Flynn, in press; Horneffer & Fincham, 1996; Metalsky, Halberstadt, & Abramson, 1987). Metalsky and colleagues reported that students' general attributional styles for negative achievement events significantly predicted their specific attributions about a low midterm grade, whereas general attributional styles for interpersonal outcomes did not. Horneffer and Fincham (1996) reported a significant association between general attributional style and relationship specific attributions, although they found that the relationship attributions made a unique contribution to the prediction of both depressive symptoms and marital distress that did not appear to be a subset of general attributional style. Garber and Flynn (in press) examined mothers' general attributional styles in relation to their specific attributions about their children's behaviors and found that they were not significantly correlated.

It might be that there really is no general tendency to explain events the same way across a variety of contexts. This could partially account for the relatively low levels of internal consistency found for attributional style measures (Gladstone & Kaslow, 1995). Moreover, it appears that measures of domain specific cognitions have greater predictive validity than those that assess a general cognitive style. This would be consistent with specific vulnerability theories of depression (Abramson et al., 1989; Hammen, Marks, deMayo, & Mayol, 1985) that suggest that individuals who have depressive cognitions within a particular domain (e.g., academic, interpersonal) are more vulnerable to depression when they are faced with negative life events within that domain.

Studies are needed that explore the associations among individuals' cognitions about multiple domains (e.g., peers, family, school). Do people really have a general attributional style or pessimistic outlook, or do their attributions and expectations differ across contexts? Are some individuals more likely than others to have a consistent cognitive style, and what are the implications of this for their well-being? Are individuals who are chronically optimistic healthier than are those who are optimistic with regard to certain domains but not others? Does cognitive consistency across content domains reflect a cohesiveness or rigidity of thinking? For example, within the marital domain, Baucom, Sayers, and Duhe (1989) found that more consistent patterns of attributions about partner behaviors were more highly associated with marital discord. Baucom and colleagues noted that there was considerable variability in the extent to which individuals had a consistent attributional style, and that such consistency within the marital context can be maladaptive. Thus, important questions remain regarding the validity of the construct of cognitive style within and across content domains.

ORIGINS OF OPTIMISM

One of the challenges that Fincham identified for the field was to determine the origins of optimism. That is, what factors contribute to the development of optimism? Elsewhere, we (Garber & Flynn, 1998) have discussed some of the normative processes involved in the development of optimism/pessimism and attributional style. The experience of hopefulness and hopelessness involves the ability to think probabilistically about the future (Siomopolous & Inamdar, 1979). Causal thinking requires the ability to detect event sequences and to observe covariation (White, 1988). These skills tend to increase with cognitive development, although even young children have been found to be able to report optimism (Stipek, Lamb, & Zigler, 1981) and can engage in causal reasoning (Miller & Aloise, 1989).

Why do some children develop tendencies toward optimism whereas others tend toward pessimism and depressive explanatory thinking? Several processes have been proposed to account for these individual differences including genetics, attachment, social learning, and exposure to negative life events (Garber & Flynn 1998; Hammen, 1992; Kovacs & Beck, 1978; Rose & Abramson, 1992; Seligman, Kamen, & Nolen-Hoeksema, 1988). Garber and Flynn (in press) examined the latter two processes in relation to hopelessness and attributional style in young adolescents.

First, a simple social modeling perspective would suggest that there should be a relation between parents' and children's cognitions. According to Seligman and colleagues (1984) "We already know that parents' optimistic explanatory style correlates with that shown by their children." Other studies, however, have failed to find such a relation (Kaslow, Rehm, Pollack, & Siegel, 1988; Oliver & Berger, 1992) or have found it for one parent but not the other (Stark, Schmidt, & Joiner, 1996). Garber and Flynn (in press) also did not find a significant correlation between mothers' and children's general attributional styles or their reports of hopelessness. Similar to Fincham and Cain (1986) and Turk and Bry (1992), however, Garber and Flynn (in press) did find a significant relation between mothers' explanations for their children's behavior and children's attributional styles. Thus, children might not simply model their parents' cognitions in general, but rather they might learn to make causal attributions from observing their parents' explanations about the things that are particularly salient to them, such as their own behavior.

Second, children learn about themselves and their world from the social feedback they receive from important others including parents, teachers, and peers (Beck & Young, 1985; Bowlby, 1988). Children who are repeatedly exposed to parental criticism, rejection, intrusiveness, and excessive control are likely to develop negative attitudes about themselves, the world, and the future (Litovsky & Dusek, 1985; McCranie & Bass, 1984; Stark et al., 1996). Garber and Flynn (in press) examined the relation between parenting style as reported by mothers and children and children's cognitions. They found that high levels of maternal psychological control in the form of guilt-induction and love withdrawal significantly predicted a more depressive attributional style. Parenting did not significantly predict child hopelessness, however.

A third factor that has been hypothesized as influencing the development of attributions and expectations is the nature of the life events individuals experience. In particular, exposure to chronically aversive or major traumatic life events is likely to affect individuals' sense of themselves, their world, and their future (Janoff-Bulman, 1992) and result in cognitions of helplessness and hopelessness (Abramson et al., 1989). An association between negative life events and a depressive attributional style has been found in a cross-sectional study of adults reporting retrospectively about their childhoods (Rose, Abramson, Hodulik, Halberstadt, & Leff, 1994) and in a short-term longitudinal study of children (Nolen-Hoeksema, Girgus, & Seligman, 1992). Garber and Flynn (in press) similarly found that high levels of negative life events during the prior year significantly predicted a more depressive attributional style the following year. Moreover, the level of self-worth significantly interacted with life events to predict the level of hopelessness. That is, among children who had experienced higher levels of life events during the previous year, those with low self-worth had higher levels of hopelessness a year later. It might be that children who perceive themselves as being less competent are particularly vulnerable to becoming hopeless in the face of stressful life events (Stipek et al., 1981).

Thus, there are likely multiple pathways toward the development of optimism and pessimism and attributional style, including exposure to certain kinds of parenting styles and to stressful life events. One difficulty in conducting research on the development of such social cognitions concerns the issue of timing. It is likely that the working models (Bowlby,

1988) and cognitive schema (Beck, 1967) that underlie these cognitions are being formed very early in development. However, owing to children's cognitive and linguistic inability to report about optimism and causal attributions early in development as well as limitations in our measurement technologies, it is going to be difficult to assess the various precursors of the development of optimism and pessimism.

In summary, Fincham's paper raised several intriguing points that deserve further conceptual and empirical attention. Future research in the area of optimism should combine some of the issues raised in the present discussion. For example, are optimism and pessimism distinct constructs and are there separate pathways to their development? How are attributions and expectancies related to each other concurrently and over time? At what point in their development do children form attributions, and how might this have an impact on their ability to form expectations about the future? Is there a general optimistic/pessimistic or attributional style and when do children begin to manifest such tendencies? In addition to parenting and negative life events, what other factors contribute to the development of these cognitive styles? A clearer understanding of the processes involved in the development of optimism will provide directions for early interventions aimed at preventing the negative consequences of pessimistic thinking as well as increasing the positive outcomes associated with optimism.

REFERENCES

Abramson, L.Y., Metalsky, G.I., & Alloy, L.B. (1989). Hopelessness depression: A theory-based subtype of depression. *Psychological Review, 96,* 358–372.

Abramson, L.Y., Seligman, M.E.P., & Teasdale, J. (1978). Learned helplessness in humans: Critique and reformulation. *Journal of Abnormal Psychology, 87,* 49–74.

Barrera, M., Chassin, L., & Rogosch, R. (1993). Effects of social support and conflict on adolescent children of alcoholic and nonalcoholic fathers. *Journal of Personality and Social Psychology, 64,* 602–612.

Baucom, D.H., Sayers, S.L., & Duhe, A. (1989). Attributional style and attributional patterns among married couples. *Journal of Personality and Social Psychology, 56,* 596–607.

Beck, A.T. (1967). *Depression: Clinical, experiential, and theoretical aspects.* New York: Harper & Row.

Beck, A.T., Weissman, A., Lester, D., & Trexler, L. (1974). The measurement of pessimism: The Hopelessness Scale. *Journal of Consulting and Clinical Psychology, 42,* 861–865.

Beck, A.T., & Young, J.E. (1985). Depression. In D.H. Barlow (Ed.), *Clinical handbook of psychological disorders: A step-by-step treatment manual* (pp. 206–244). New York: Guilford Press.

Bowlby, J. (1988). Developmental psychiatry comes of age. *American Journal of Psychiatry, 145,* 1–10.

Epstein, S., & Meier, P. (1989). Constructive thinking: A broad coping variable with specific components. *Journal of Personality and Social Psychology, 57,* 332–350.

Fincham, F.D., Beach, S.R., & Nelson, G. (1987). Attributional processes in distressed and nondistressed couples: 3. Causal and responsibility attributions for spouse behavior. *Cognitive Therapy and Research, 11,* 71–86.

Fincham, F.D., & Bradbury, T.N. (1992). Assessing attributions in marriage: The Relationship Attribution Measure. *Journal of Personality and Social Psychology, 62,* 457–468.

Fincham, F.D., & Cain, K.M. (1986). Learned helplessness in humans: A developmental analysis. *Developmental Review, 6,* 310–333.

Garber, J., & Flynn, C. (1998). Origins of depressive cognitive style. In D. Routh & R.J. DeRubeis (Eds.), *The science of clinical psychology: Evidence of a century's profess* (pp. 53–93). Washington, DC: American Psychological Association.

Garber, J., & Flynn, C. (in press). Predictors of depressive cognitions in young adolescents. *Cognitive Therapy and Research.*

Gladstone, T.R.G., & Kaslow, N.J. (1995). Depression and attributions in children and adolescents: A meta-analytic review. *Journal of Abnormal Child Psychology, 23,* 597–606.

Hammen, C. (1992). Cognitive, life stress, and interpersonal approaches to a developmental model of depression. *Development and Psychopathology, 4,* 189–206.

Hammen, C., & Cochran, S.D. (1981). Cognitive correlates of life stress and depression in college students. *Journal of Abnormal Psychology, 90,* 23–27.

Hammen, C., & deMayo, R. (1982). Cognitive correlates of teacher stress and depressive symptoms: Implications for attributional models of depression. *Journal of Abnormal Psychology, 91,* 96–101.

Hammen, C., Marks, T., deMayo, R., & Mayol, A. (1985). Self-schemas and risk for depression: A prospective study. *Journal of Personality and Social Psychology, 49,* 1147–1159.

Hollon, S., & Garber, J. (1980). A cognitive-expectancy theory of therapy for helplessness and depression. In J. Garber & M.E.P. Seligman (Eds.), *Human helplessness: Theory and applications* (pp. 173–195). New York: Academic Press.

Horneffer, & Fincham, F. (1996). Attributional models of depression and mental distress. *Personality and Social Psychology Bulletin, 22,* 678–689.

Janoff-Bulman, R. (1992). *Shattered assumptions: Towards a new psychology of trauma.* New York: Free Press.

Joiner, T. E., & Wagner, K. D. (1995). Attributional style and depression in children and adolescents: A meta-analytic review. *Clinical Psychology Review, 15,* 777–798.

Kaslow, N.J., Rehm, L.P., Pollack, S.L., & Siegel, A.W. (1988). Attributional style and self-control behavior in depressed and nondepressed children and their parents. *Journal of Abnormal Child Psychology, 16,* 163–175.

Kelly, A.G., & Fincham, F.D. (in press). Marital health: Towards a more complete account of functional and satisfying couple relationships. *Encyclopedia of mental health.* New York: Academic Press.

Kovacs, M., & Beck, A.T. (1978). Maladaptive cognitive structures in depression. *American Journal of Psychiatry, 135,* 525–533.

Litovsky, V.G., & Dusek, J.B. (1985). Perceptions of child rearing and self-concept development during the early adolescent year. *Journal of Youth and Adolescence, 14,* 373–387.

Marshall, G.N., Wortman, C.B., Kusulas, J.W., Hervig, L.K., & Vickers, R.R. (1992). Distinguishing optimism from pessimism: Relations to fundamental dimensions of mood and personality. *Journal of Personality and Social Psychology, 62,* 1067–1074.

Masten, A.S., & Coatsworth, J.D. (1995). Competence, resilience, and psychopathology. In D. Cicchetti & D.J. Cohen (Eds.), *Developmental psychopathology Vol. II: Risk, disorder, and adaptation* (pp. 715–752). New York: John Wiley & Sons.

McCranie, E.W., & Bass, J.D. (1984). Childhood family antecedents of dependency and self-criticism: Implications for depression. *Journal of Abnormal Psychology, 93,* 3–8.

Metalsky, G.I., Halberstadt, L.J., & Abramson, L.Y. (1987). Vulnerability to depressive mood reactions: Toward a more powerful test of the diathesis-stress and causal mediation components of the reformulated theory of depression. *Journal of Personality and Social Psychology, 52,* 386–393.

Metalsky, G.I., & Joiner, T.E. (1992). Vulnerability to depressive symptomatology: A prospective test of the diathesis-stress and causal mediation components of the hopelessness theory of depression. *Journal of Personality and Social Psychology, 63,* 667–675.

Miller, P.H., & Aloise, P.A. (1989). Young children's understanding of the psychological causes of behavior: A review. *Child Development, 60,* 257–285.

Nolen-Hoeksema, S., Girgus, J., & Seligman, M.E.P. (1992). Predictors and consequences of childhood depressive symptoms: A 5-year longitudinal study. *Journal of Abnormal Psychology, 101,* 405–422.

Norem, J.K., & Cantor, N. (1986). Defensive pessimism: Harnessing anxiety as motivation. *Journal of Personality and Social Psychology, 51,* 1208–1217.

Oliver, J.M., & Berger, L.S. (1992). Depression, parent-offspring relationships, and cognitive vulnerability. *Journal of Social Behavior and Personality, 7,* 415–429.

Pagel, M.D., Erdly, W.W., & Becker, J. (1987). Social networks: We get by with (and in spite of) a little help from our friends. *Journal of Personality and Social Psychology, 53,* 793–804.

Peterson, C., Meier, S.F., & Seligman, M.E.P. (1993). *Learned helplessness: A theory for the age of personal control.* Cambridge: Cambridge University Press.

Rose, D.T., & Abramson, L.Y. (1992). Developmental predictors of depressive cognitive style: Research and theory. In D. Cicchetti & S.L. Toth (Eds.), *Rochester symposium on developmental psychopathology* (Vol. 4, pp. 323–349). Hillsdale, NJ: Erlbaum.

Rose, D.T., Abramson, L.Y., Hodulik, C.J., Halberstadt, L., & Leff, G. (1994). Heterogeneity of cognitive style among depressed inpatients. *Journal of Abnormal Psychology, 103,* 419–429.

Rutter, M. (1990). Psychosocial resilience and protective mechanisms. In J. Rolf, A.S. Masten, D. Cicchetti, K.H. Nuechterlein, & S. Weintraub (Eds.), *Risk and protective factors in the development of psychopathology* (pp. 181–214). Cambridge: Cambridge University Press.

Sandler, I.N., & Barrera, M. (1984). Toward a multimethod approach to assessing the effects of social support. *American Journal of Community Psychology, 12,* 37–52.

Scheier, M.F., & Carver, C.S. (1985). Optimism, coping, and health: Assessment and implications of generalized outcome expectancies. *Health Psychology, 4,* 219–247.

Seligman, M.E.P., (1975). *Helplessness: On depression, development, and death.* San Francisco: W.H. Freeman.

Seligman, M.E.P., Abramson, L.Y., Semmel, A., & von Baeyer, C. (1979). Depressive attributional style. *Journal of Abnormal Psychology, 88,* 242–247.

Seligman, M.E.P., Kamen, L.P., & Nolen-Hoeksema, S. (1988). Explanatory style across the life span. In E.M. Hetherington, R.M. Lerner, & M. Perlmutter (Eds.), *Child development in life-span perspective* (pp. 91–114). Hillsdale, NJ: Erlbaum.

Seligman, M.E.P., Peterson, C., Kaslow, N.J., Tanenbaum, R.L., Alloy, L.B., & Abramson, L.Y. (1984). Explanatory style and depressive symptoms among children. *Journal of Abnormal Psychology, 93,* 235–238.

Siomopolous, G. & Inamdar, S.C. (1979). Developmental aspects of hopelessness. *Adolescence, 14,* 233–239.

Stark, K.D., Schmidt, K.L., & Joiner, T.E. (1996). Cognitive triad: Relationship to depressive symptoms, parents' cognitive triad, and perceived parental messages. *Journal of Abnormal Child Psychology, 24,* 615–631.

Stipek, D.J., Lamb, M.E., & Zigler, E.F. (1981). OPTI: A measure of children's optimism. *Educational and Psychological Measurement, 41,* 131–143.

Sweeney, P.D., Anderson, K., & Bailey, S. (1986). Attributional style in depression: A meta-analytic review. *Journal of Personality and Social Psychology, 50,* 974–991.

Turk, E., & Bry, B.H. (1992). Adolescents' and parents' explanatory styles and parents' causal explanations about their adolescents. *Cognitive Therapy and Research, 16,* 349–357.

Watson, D., Clark, L.A., & Tellegen, A. (1988). Development and validation of brief measures of Positive and Negative Affect: The PANAS scales. *Journal of Personality and Social Psychology, 54,* 1063–1070.

Watson, D., & Tellegen, A. (1985). Toward a consensual structure of mood. *Psychological Bulletin, 98,* 219–235.

White, P.A. (1988). Causal processing: Origins and development. *Psychological Bulletin, 104,* 36–52.

ACKNOWLEDGMENTS

This work was supported in part by a grant (95070390) from the William T. Grant Foundation during completion of this work.

✦ CHAPTER 17 ✦

On Chaos, Fractals, and Stress: Response to Fincham's "Optimism and the Family"

Everett L. Worthington, Jr.

FINCHAM'S CHAPTER on "Optimism and the Family" presents a number of heuristic suggestions for family psychologists. I particularly appreciated the calls to (1) examine optimism at the (a) individual event, (b) generalized personal disposition, and (c) marriage-specific levels, (2) consider stress as a moderator in the study of attributions by married partners, and (3) explain why attributions about the partner are related to marital quality. I also appreciated Fincham's effort to do (1) and (3) in his chapter. Within the constraints of a brief response, I want to address two small points.

TROUBLED AND UNTROUBLED COUPLES, CHAOS, AND MATHEMATICS

Let us examine the two-wave structural linear model in which optimistic expectations were thought to be an interceding variable in the relationship between attributions and marital satisfaction for *happy couples*. In that model, when negative things happened—as they inevitably do in any relationship—the partners either accepted, ignored, or explained them away. Happy couples' attributions were positive when they attempted to explain the cause of negative events. Their expectations about the marriage were also positive, and positive expectations led to subsequent marital satisfaction. Besides having expectations and attributions that promote stability, happy marriages operate under the rules that I call *forbearing* and *forgiving*. Forbearance involves the acceptance of negative events and the absorption of the pain. Forgiveness involves the acknowledgment of the moral violation. It does not pretend no moral violation occurred. However, forgiveness combats the negativity of unforgiveness with an affiliative motive—reconciliation. Reconciliation might not be pursued because it might not be safe, prudent, or possible to reconcile. Nevertheless, forgiveness has within it an affiliative motive. Forgiveness goes beyond forbearance. Forgiveness offers a personal connection that might lead to implicit or explicit reconciliation.

Attitudes of forbearance, forgiveness, and reconciliation maintain positive attributions, expectations, and evaluation of marital quality. So, in Fincham's proposed model, I would suggest additional related predictors of marital satisfaction—forgiving, forbearing, and reconciling behavior. That is a model for satisfied or adjusted marriages.

Consider a hypothetical couple. Call them the Smiths. The Smiths were happy at time 1 (t1), but were divorced at time 2 (t2) in Fincham's study. They originally lived by forbearance, forgiveness, and reconciliation, but at some point they began to encounter what Gottman (1994) calls the four horsemen of the apocalypse. That is, their marriage degenerated dramatically and abruptly. The happy trinity of forbearance, forgiveness, and reconciliation gave sudden way to criticism, defensiveness, contempt, and stonewalling (or lack of feeling for each other). In short, love died. Death, of course, is a non-linear transformation. Death of a marriage, as Gottman (1994) pointed out, is similarly a non-linear transformation.

Structural linear equations that model processes in marriages and families—mathematical models that I personally use all the time—might not accurately capture what is going on in marriages that are undergoing a fundamental change. That is, the method of analysis imposes a structure on our interpretation of the phenomena in marriages that might yield modest path coefficients and R^2s for a combined sample that includes happy and troubled marriages. Structural equation modeling may obscure important differences between happy and troubled couples. In a uniform world, I assume that if I sample from a population, the results can be generalized to the whole population. That, of course, is not always a good assumption. With happy versus unhappy marriages, as Gottman (1994) has shown, that assumption of linear uniformity is probably not correct.

Thus, Fincham is very much on target with the thrust of the argument with which he begins and ends his presentation. Learning about distressed couples will not necessarily tell us about happy couples and learning about helplessness and pessimism will not necessarily tell us much about optimism and hope, either in general or specifically in marriage. However, perhaps we should be wary of structural linear models to analyze mixed samples of happy and troubled couples.

The psychological processes governing the two groups might be discontinuously dissimilar. This suggests two possibilities. First, we could make clear distinctions in choice of sample—either troubled or untroubled couples. Presumably, methods that assume linear changes (e.g., structural equations modeling, multiple regression) would reveal changes each group separately. Second, we could add to the type of mathematics with which we approach the study of marriages. For example, in addition to our present statistical methods, we could employ fractals, which are mathematical convolutions that have been developed to deal with non-linear change processes. Fractals can model many naturalistic systems. We find that at different levels of a system, patterns repeat. For example, the shape of a mountain is reflected in the shape of some of the hills and gullies on the mountain, which in turn is reflected by the shape of some of the rocks, which in turn is reflected by the physical shape of some of the molecules that make up the particular rocks in the mountain. Fractals have another property: patterns within apparently random processes often show repeating regularities. Fractals are mathematical methods especially applicable to the science of chaos or complexity (Butz, 1997). The science of chaos describes systems that move from linear to non-linear patterns. Such systems are often extremely sensitive to initial (or boundary) conditions. For example, when drops drip from a faucet at a slow rate, their pattern is regular and even. As the rate of flow is increased, the drip rate increases linearly. At some point, though, a small increase in flow rate causes a non-linear transformation in the pattern of drips. They become almost random (within limits).

Another example is heart rate. Exercise increases heart rate linearly. But at some given work load on the heart, the heart might fibrillate (e.g., beat irregularly), with disastrous consequences. The pattern can work in reverse. Brain waves as measured by EEG are random (within limits). An epileptic seizure, a transformation in brain activity, occurs often with little apparent provocation. Brain waves become synchronous and regular, with disastrous effects. The science of chaos and complexity has been applied to these non-linear transformations as has mathematical modeling using fractals.

I am making an analogy. The deterioration of marriage from untroubled to troubled (see Gottman's [1994] four horsemen of the apocalypse) is like having a heart attack or seizure. Gottman has shown that the transformation is non-linear and chaotic, but he is not specific about where the non-linear transformation actually occurs. That is, at what point does an "untroubled couple" who have some troubles become a (nonlinearly different) "troubled couple"? Monitoring partners' attributions might reveal where the transformation occurs. When attributions for negative events shift from largely unstable, external, and specific (untroubled couples) to stable, internal, and global (troubled couples), that is the cusp of the transformation. However, consistent with the science of chaos, the cusp is extremely sensitive to initial conditions.

To use a simple illustration, a raindrop that falls one-half inch to the west of the Continental Divide will eventually flow into the Pacific Ocean. A raindrop that falls one-half inch to the east of the Continental Divide will eventually flow into the Atlantic Ocean. The difference of one inch in initial conditions will result in a 3,000-mile separation at the drops' eventual destinations.

Consider, for instance, a mate's discovery of a spouse's affair that occurs on a day when the mate had a terrible experience at work. Conceivably, the initial negativity of the bad day at work could lead to the mate being extremely hateful and abusive. The mate might shout, hit, or even shoot the spouse, thus creating experiences that could eventually lead the couple to divorce. On the other hand, if the same affair had been discovered on the mate's good-events day, the progression of events—while providing a rocky time for the couple—might nonetheless have eventually resulted in reconciliation. The initial conditions would be critical to whether a non-linear transformation in the marriage occurred after the discovery of the affair.

Applying fractals and the science of complexity and chaos to marriage and family systems, especially to the degeneration of troubled marriages, might provide a new and exciting avenue into understanding couples who change from untroubled to troubled or vice versa. It might also help unify behavioral and social learning approaches, which have been empirically heuristic, with family systems theory, which has been conceptually focused but relatively unproductive empirically.

STRESS

Fincham recommended that stress be considered as a moderator between explanatory style and marital adjustment. I heartily agree that stress in marriage is understudied and should be studied more. Yet I would add that stress must be coupled with coping as moderators.

Pargament (1997) has argued that people's first-line coping efforts are usually conservative. That is, people attempt to deal with stress in ways that maintain their current view of life (or in our case, their current view of the marriage). When conservative coping strategies are judged to be inadequate, people only then engage in transformative coping strategies. Transformative coping strategies radically alter either one's circumstances (e.g., a person moves out of a marriage) or one's view of the situation (e.g., one decides a marriage cannot be saved).

Drawing on my earlier discussion, one's change in coping strategies from conservative to transformative is a chaotic non-linear change in the relationship. As such, a couple's use of conservative or transformative coping strategies might be extremely sensitive to initial conditions (of perceived initial stress, among other variables). For example, when negative relationship events occur, partners who are untroubled will generally employ conservative coping strategies to strive to maintain their sense of a good relationship. Those conservative coping strategies might include forbearance and forgiveness and might involve making unstable, specific, and external attributions for those negative events. What might induce an untroubled couple to flip-flop to a negative view of marriage (i.e., troubled-couple status)? The conditions might depend on subtle differences in many variables that together might eventually make a large difference in the relationship behaviors, affect, and cognition.

Similarly, troubled couples cope with stress by conserving their negative view of the relationship. The success of therapy, which attempts to help people employ transformative coping strategies and thus come to see their relationship as positive, will succeed or fail sometimes based on extremely small differences in initial conditions.

CLOSING

I apologize for extending my comments into areas that Fincham did not address, namely how to understand, detect, and deal with chaotic transformations from troubled to untroubled status and vice versa. I would plead your forbearance and forgiveness, and beg that you excuse my digression because Fincham's stimulating, provocative, and highly appropriate suggestions and analyses raise these questions, not about his paper, but about the field. His comments challenge us to ask whether (a) our sampling of couples is always appropriate, (b) our analyses (based on assumptions of linearity) are appropriate for our samples, and (c) we are asking the most interesting questions.

REFERENCES

Butz, M.R. (1997). *Chaos and complexity: Implications for psychological theory and practice.* Washington, DC: Taylor & Francis.

Gottman, J.M. (1994). *What predicts divorce? The relationship between marital processes and marital outcomes.* Hillsdale, NJ: Lawrence Erlbaum Associates.

Pargament, K.I. (1997). *The psychology of religion and coping: Theory, research, practice.* New York: Guilford.

Section B. Optimism and Faith

✦

CHAPTER 18

Hope and Happiness

David G. Myers

DURING MUCH of its first century, psychology has focused on negative emotions: on aggression more than love, on conflict more than peace, on fear more than courage. A PsycInfo electronic search of *Psychological Abstracts* since 1967 reveals 5,548 articles mentioning anger, 41,416 on anxiety, and 54,040 on depression, but only 415 on joy, 1,710 on happiness, and 2,582 on life satisfaction. In all, there are 21 articles on negative emotions for every article on positive emotions.

But the tide is changing. During the 1980s, articles mentioning well-being, life satisfaction, or happiness quadrupled from 200 to 800 annually. This new scientific pursuit of happiness and life satisfaction (together called "subjective well-being") has asked: How happy are people? And who is happy?

ARE ONLY A FEW PEOPLE HAPPY?

We are "not born for happiness," observed Samuel Johnson. Modern books for the would-be happy, written by clinicians who spend their days with the unhappy, agree. "One-third of all Americans wake up depressed every day," says Father John Powell in *Happiness Is an Inside Job*. Professionals estimate that only 10% to 15% of Americans think of themselves as truly happy. But when asked about their happiness, random samples of people paint a brighter picture. In National Opinion Research Center surveys, three in ten Americans say they are "very happy"; only one in ten say "not too happy"; and the rest, six in ten, describe themselves as "pretty happy." Diener (Myers & Diener, 1996) has assembled data from 916 surveys of 1.1 million people in 45 nations representing most of the human population. He recalibrated the self-reported well-being on a 0 to 10 scale (where 0 is the low extreme, such as reporting oneself "very unhappy" or "completely dissatisfied," 5 is neutral, and 10 is the high extreme). The average human, as shown in figure 18.1, responded at a moderately positive 6.75.

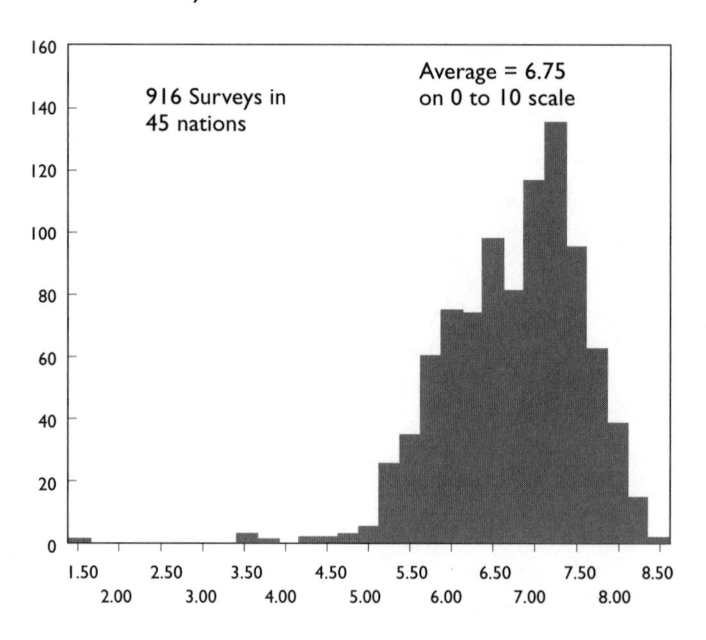

Figure 18.1. Subjective well-being, as self-reported in 916 surveys of 1.1 million people in 45 nations (with answers calibrated to a 0 to 10 scale, with 5 neutral). (From Myers & Diener, 1996.)

The set point for happiness, therefore, appears to be set slightly to the positive side of neutral. This serves to give the occasional stone in the emotional shoe signal value. When something goes awry, it alerts the organism to do something to alleviate the negative mood.

WHO IS HAPPY?

By searching for predictors of subjective well-being, psychologists and sociologists have exploded some myths. Consider some illustrative findings (see Myers, 1993, Myers & Diener, 1995, for further evidence).

Are There Happy and Unhappy Times of Life?

Many people believe so with the stress-filled teen years, the midlife crisis years, and the declining years brought on by old age representing major episodes. But as illustrated by one 16-nation survey of 170,000 people (figure 18.2), no time of life is notably happier and more satisfying. In every age group, there are many happy and some unhappy people.

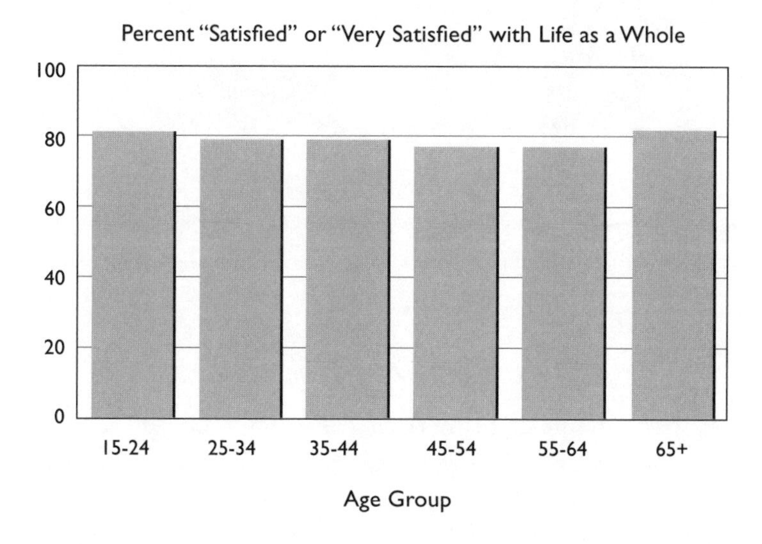

Figure 18.2. Age and well-being in 16 nations. Data are from 169,776 people representatively sampled from 1980 to 1986, as reported by Inglehart (1990).

Does Happiness Favor One Gender?

Are men happier, because of their greater incomes and social power? Are women happier because of their reportedly greater capacity for intimacy and social connection? Despite gender gaps in misery—women are much more vulnerable to disabling depression and anxiety, and men to alcoholism and antisocial personality disorder—gender gives no clue to subjective well-being. Men and women are equally likely to declare themselves "satisfied" or "very happy" (figure 18.3).

Figure 18.3. Gender and well-being in 16 nations. Data are from 169,776 people representatively sampled from 1980 to 1986, as reported by Inglehart (1990).

Does Money Buy Happiness?

In 1997, 74% of entering American collegians declared that a "very important" or "essential" life goal was "being very well off financially." As figure 18.4 shows, that was nearly double the 39% who said the same in 1970. Is wealth indeed linked with well-being, as these modern materialists believe?

More concretely, are rich people happier than the not-so-rich? Food, shelter, and safety are basic to well-being, which explains why satisfaction with finances is a moderate predictor of well-being in very poor countries, such as Bangladesh and India (Diener & Diener, 1995). But once able to afford life's necessities, people seem to adapt to increasing affluence. In North America and Europe, the income-happiness corre-

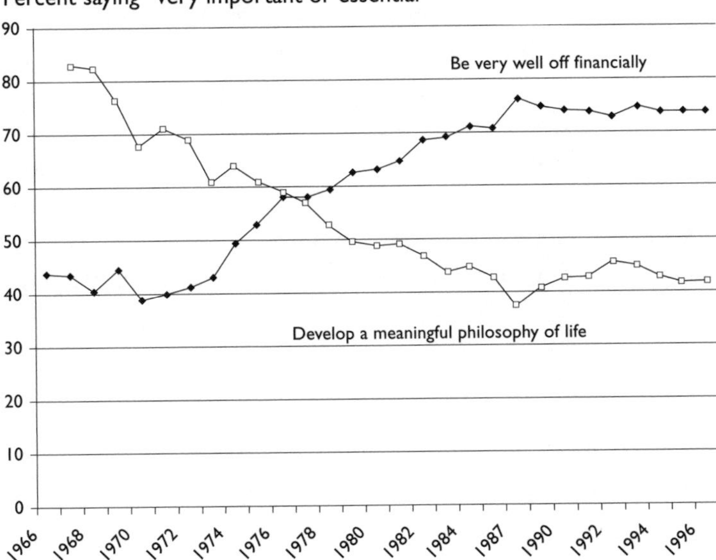

Figure 18.4. Changing materialism. Annual surveys of more than 200,000 entering American collegians revealed an increasing desire for wealth from 1970 to the late 1980s (Dey et al., 1991; Sax et al., 1997).

lation, though positive, has become "surprisingly weak (indeed virtually negligible)," reports Inglehart (1990, p. 242). Even the super rich and state lottery winners express only slightly greater than average happiness (Brickman, Coates, & Janoff-Bulman, 1978; Diener, Horwitz, & Emmons, 1985). Although its utter absence can breed misery, wealth does not guarantee happiness.

If even a *little* more money would buy a *little* more happiness, then has happiness grown over time as income has increased? In 1957, as economist John Galbraith was about to describe the United States as *The Affluent Society*, Americans' per person income, expressed in today's dollars, was about $9,000. Today, it is about $20,000, defining a doubly affluent society—with double what money buys. We own twice as many cars per person and eat out two and a half times as often. Home air conditioning, dishwashers, and clothes dryers have become commonplace instead of rare.

So, are we happier than forty years ago? Apparently, we are not. As figure 18.5 indicates, the percentage of Americans who report they are "very happy" has declined slightly since 1957, from 35% to 30%. Meanwhile, the divorce rate doubled. The teen suicide rate tripled. Arrests for juvenile crime quadrupled. Depression rates have soared. Much the same story can be told of many other industrialized nations. Although people in affluent countries enjoy better nutrition, health care, education, science—and are somewhat happier than people in very poor countries—increasing real incomes has not been accompanied by

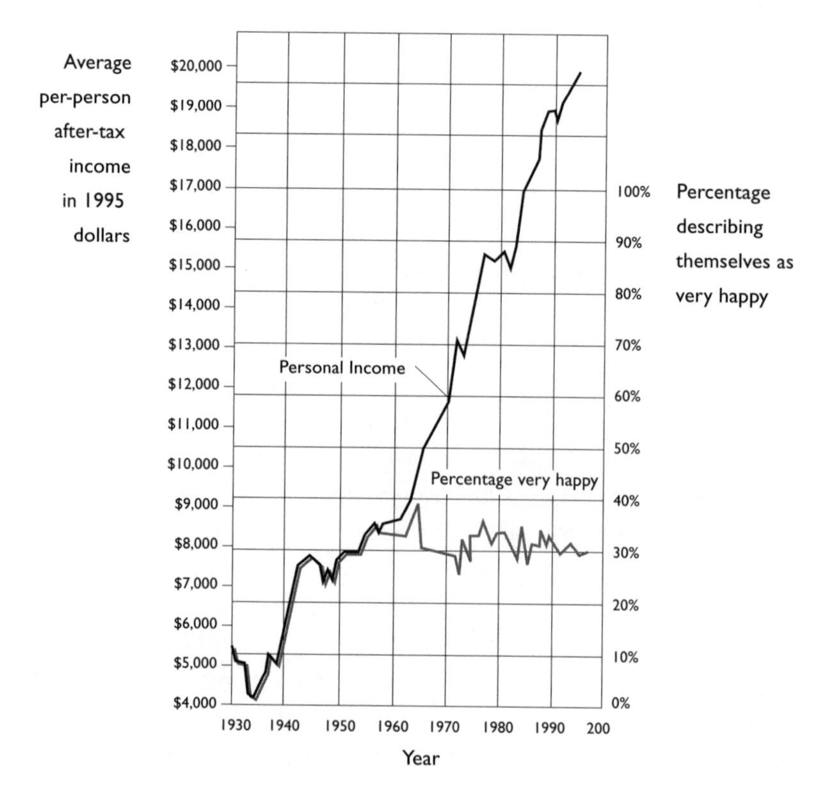

Figure 18.5. Does economic growth boost human morale? Inflation-adjusted income has risen, happiness has not. Income data from Bureau of the Census (1975) and Economic Indicators. Happiness data from the periodic General Social Survey, National Opinion Research Center, University of Chicago.

increasing happiness. Simply said, *economic growth in affluent countries has not boosted human morale.*

THE TRAITS OF HAPPY PEOPLE

If happiness is similarly available to those of any age or gender, and to people at all but the lowest income levels, then who are the very happy people? Through life's ups and downs, some people's capacity for joy persists. In one National Institute of Aging study of five thousand adults, the happiest of people in 1973 were still relatively happy ten years later, despite changes in their work, their residence, and their family status (Costa, McCrae, & Zonderman, 1987).

Across many studies, four positive traits have marked happy lives (Myers & Diener, 1995). First, happy people like themselves. Especially in individualistic countries, they exhibit high *self-esteem*, by agreeing with statements such as: "I'm a lot of fun to be with" and "I have good ideas." Perhaps not surprisingly, given the moderately happy human condition, most people do report positive self-esteem. They not only score above the scale midpoint on self-esteem tests, but also exhibit a self-serving bias, by believing themselves more ethical, intelligent, unprejudiced, sociable, and healthier than the average person (Myers, 1999).

Second, happy people tend to be *extroverted*. Although we might have expected that introverts would live more contentedly in the serenity of their unstressed contemplative lives, the consistent finding is that whether alone or with others, whether working in solitary or social occupations, extroverts are usually happier.

Third, happy people typically feel *personal control*. Feeling empowered rather than helpless, capable rather than victimized, they also perform better in school, achieve more at work, and cope better with stress. Deprived of control over one's life, as happens when in prison, in nursing homes, or when living under totalitarian regimes, people suffer lowered morale and worsened health. Severe poverty demoralizes people when it erodes their sense of control.

Fourth, happy people are commonly *optimistic*. One could reason that pessimists, whose low expectations are so often exceeded, would constantly be surprised by joy. "Blessed is he who expects nothing, for he shall never be disappointed," said Alexander Pope in a 1727 letter. Optimists, when undertaking something new, expect to succeed and thus tend to be more successful, healthier, and happier.

With each of these trait-happiness correlations, the causal traffic could go either way. Does optimism make people happier, or are happier people more optimistic? If the former (as suggested by other chapters in this volume), could people become happier by thinking, talking, and acting as if they had happiness-associated traits such as optimism?

Happiness, like cholesterol, seems variable but within the constraints of a genetic leash. This is partly because happiness-predicting traits such as extraversion are genetically predisposed. Thus, Lykken and Tellegen (1996) estimate from their study of 254 identical and fraternal twins that 50% of individual differences in happiness is heritable. Even identical twins raised apart often are similarly happy.

THE RELATIONSHIPS OF HAPPY PEOPLE

Close, supportive, committed relationships also mark happy lives. Despite Sartre's surmise that "Hell is other people," and despite all the stresses that mark our close relationships, those who can name several soul-mate friends are healthier and happier than those lacking such close relationships (Burt, 1986; Cohen, 1988; House, Landis, & Umberson, 1988). Our honoree, Martin Seligman (1991), contends that today's epidemic depression stems partly from impoverished social connections in increasingly individualistic Western societies. Individualistic societies offer personal control, harmony between the inner and outer person, and opportunity to express one's feelings and talents, but with the risks of a less embedded, more detached self.

For more than nine in ten people, one significant alternative to aloneness is marriage. Broken marital relationships are a source of much misery. Among Americans saying their marriage is "not too happy," a mere 3% live very happy lives (among 32,139 people sampled by the National Opinion Research Center since 1972). But among those in a "very happy" marriage, 57% declare their lives as "very happy." Most currently married people do report their marriages as happy, which helps explain why 40% of married adults, compared to 24% of never married adults, declare they are "very happy." Even slightly less happy are the divorced and separated (see figure 18.6).

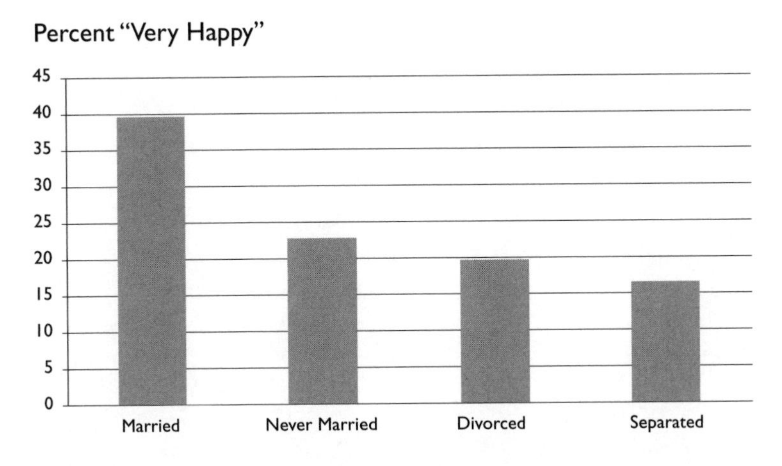

Figure 18.6. Marital status and happiness. Data from 32,139 participants in the General Social Survey, National Opinion Research Center, 1972 to 1994.

THE FAITH OF HAPPY PEOPLE

Although the accumulating studies of religiosity and happiness cannot speak to the truth of the claims of any religion, they do help us sort among conflicting opinions over whether religious faith is conducive or corrosive to a sense of well-being. Is religion, as Freud believed, an obsessional neurosis entailing guilt, repressed sexuality, and suppressed emotions? Or was C. S. Lewis right to presume that "Joy is the serious business of heaven"?

In Europe and North America, religiously active people report higher levels of happiness and satisfaction with life. Consider a Gallup Organization (1984) national survey. Those responding with the highest spiritual commitment (agreeing, for example, that "my religious faith is the most important influence in my life") were twice as likely, as compared to those lowest in spiritual commitment, to declare themselves "very happy" (figure 18.7). In National Opinion Research Center surveys of 32,000 Americans since 1972, religious attendance also predicts self-reported happiness. One meta-analysis of research on elderly people found that the two best predictors of life satisfaction were health and religiousness (Okun & Stock, 1987).

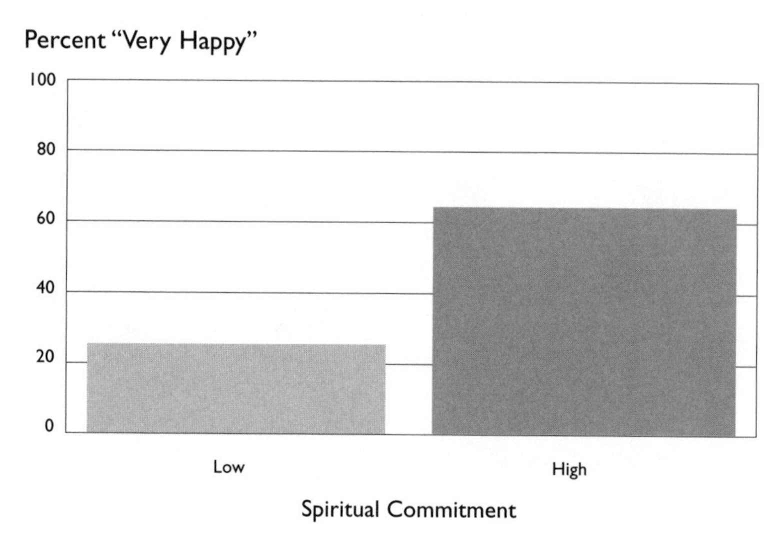

Figure 18.7. Spiritual commitment and happiness. Data from Gallup (1984).

Other studies have probed the connection between faith and coping with a crisis. Compared to religiously inactive widows, recently widowed women who worship regularly report more joy in their lives (Harvey, Barnes, & Greenwood, 1987; McGloshen & O'Bryant, 1988; Siegel & Kuykendall, 1990). Compared to irreligious mothers of disabled children, those with a deep religious faith are less vulnerable to depression (Friedrich, Cohen, & Wilturner, 1988). Those with a strong faith also recover greater happiness after suffering divorce, unemployment, serious illness, or bereavement (Ellison, 1991; McIntosh, Silver, & Wortman, 1993).

Researchers seek to explain these positive links between faith and well-being: Is it the supportive, close relationships often enjoyed by those in faith communities (of which there are some 350,000 in the United States alone)? Is it the sense of meaning and purpose that many people derive from their faith? Is it the motivation to focus beyond self (as reflected in the Gallup Organization's consistent finding of doubled rates of volunteerism and quadrupled rates of charitable giving among weekly church and synagogue attendees compared to nonattendees)?

Supportive evidence exists for each of these conjectures. Pertinent to this volume (and to my writing from a place called Hope), there remains also another possibility: that religious worldviews, by offering answers to some of life's deepest questions, encourage a more optimistic appraisal of life events; in addition, a sense of hope emerges when confronting what Solomon, Greenberg, and Pyszczynski (1991) call "the terror resulting from our awareness of vulnerability and death." Different faiths offer varied paths, but each offers its adherents a sense that they, or something meaningful in which they participate, will survive their deaths. Aware of the great enemies, suffering and death, religious faith offers a hope that in the end, the very end, "all shall be well and shall be well and all manner of things shall be well" (Julian of Norwich).

This hope-filled perspective on the fragility of life emboldens some to think that life has value. What is worth preserving, forever, must be of ultimate value. Moreover, a hope-filled utopian vision of peace, justice, and love can direct one's involvement in the here and now. It defines an ideal world—a back-to-the-present vision—and fuels courage to pursue it. Thus Martin Luther King (1964) could declare, "I have a dream," a vision of a future reality, of a world liberated from oppression, suffering, and death. With a dream worth dying for and a hope that even death could not kill it, he could also declare, "If physical death is the price I must pay to free my white brothers and sisters from a permanent death of the spirit, then nothing can be more redemptive." As Reubem Alves (1972) stated, "Hope is hearing the melody of the future. Faith is to dance to it."

REFERENCES

Alves, R. (1972). *Tomorrow's child: Imagination, creativity, and the rebirth of culture.* New York: Harper & Row.

Brickman, P., Coates, D., & Janoff-Bulman, R.J. (1978). Lottery winners and accident victims: Is happiness relative? *Journal of Personality and Social Psychology, 36*, 917–927.

Burt, R.S. (1986). *Strangers, friends and happiness.* GSS Technical Report No. 72. Chicago: National Opinion Research Center, University of Chicago.

Bureau of the Census (1975). *Historical abstract of the United States: Colonial times to 1970.* Washington, DC: Superintendent of Documents.

Cohen, S. (1988). Psychosocial models of the role of social support in the etiology of physical disease. *Health Psychology, 7*, 269–297.

Costa, P.T., Jr., McCrae, R.R., & Zonderman, A.B. (1987). Environmental and dispositional influences on well-being: Longitudinal follow-up of an American national sample. *British Journal of Psychology, 78*, 299–306.

Dey, E.L., Astin, A.W., & Korn, W.S. (1991). *The American freshman: Twenty-five year trends.* Los Angeles: Higher Education Research Institute, UCLA.

Diener, E., & Diener, M. (1995). Cross-cultural studies of life satisfaction and self-esteem. *Journal of Personality and Social Psychology, 68*, 653–663.

Diener, E., Horwitz, J., & Emmons, R.A. (1985). Happiness of the very wealthy. *Social Indicators, 16,* 263–274.

Ellison, C.G. (1991). Religious involvement and subjective well-being. *Journal of Health and Social Behavior, 32*, 80–99.

Friedrich, W.N., Cohen, D.S., & Wilturner, L.T. (1988). Specific beliefs as moderator variables in maternal coping with mental retardation. *Children's Health Care, 17*, 40–44.

Gallup, G., Jr. (1984, March). Commentary on the state of religion in the U.S. today. *Religion in America: The Gallup Report*, No. 222.

Harvey, C.D., Barnes, G.E., & Greenwood, L. (1987). Correlates of morale among Canadian widowed persons. *Social Psychiatry, 22*, 65–72.

House, J.S., Landis, K.R., & Umberson, D. (1988). Social relationships and health. *Science, 241*, 540–545.

Inglehart, R. (1990). *Culture shift in advanced industrial society*. Princeton, NJ: Princeton University Press.

King, M.L., Jr. (1964, June 6). I have a dream. *New York Times*, p. 10.

Lykken, D., & Tellegen, A. (1996). Happiness is a stochastic phenomenon. *Psychological Science, 7*, 186–189.

McGloshen, T.H., & O'Bryant, S.L. (1988). The psychological well-being of older, recent widows. *Psychology of Women Quarterly 12*, 99–116.

McIntosh, D.N., Silver, R.C., & Wortman, C.B. (1993). Religion's role in adjustment to a negative life event: Coping with the loss of a child. *Journal of Personality and Social Psychology, 65*, 812–821.

Myers, D.G. (1993). *The pursuit of happiness*. New York: Avon.

Myers, D.G. (1999). *Social psychology* (6th ed.). New York: McGraw-Hill.

Myers, D.G., & Diener, E. (1995). Who is happy? *Psychological Science, 6*, 10–19.

Myers, D.G., & Diener E. (1996, May). The pursuit of happiness. *Scientific American*, 54–56.

Okun, M.A., & Stock, W.A. (1987). Correlates and components of subjective well-being among the elderly. *Journal of Applied Gerontology, 6*, 95–112.

Sax, L.J., Astin, A.W., Korn, W.S., & Mahoney, K.M. (1997). *The American freshman: National norms for Fall 1997*. Los Angeles: Higher Education Research Institute, UCLA.

Seligman, M.E.P. (1991). *Learned optimism*. New York: Random House.

Siegel, J.M., & Kuykendall, D.H. (1990). Loss, widowhood, and psychological distress among the elderly. *Journal of Consulting and Clinical Psychology, 58,* 519–524.

Solomon, S., Greenberg, J., & Pyszczynski, T. (1991). A terror management theory of social behavior: The psychological functions of self-esteem and cultural worldviews. *Advances in Experimental Social Psychology, 24,* 93–159.

✦ CHAPTER 19 ✦

Intergenerational Transmission of Religion

Lisa Miller

I WOULD LIKE TO TELL A STORY, which I offer as a tribute to Marty Seligman.

I was waiting for the A-train at 168th Street in New York on a hot August day. It being a Sunday, the trains were infrequent, the wait typically crowded and unpleasant. Finally a packed train roared up to the platform, but to my surprise half of a car was empty. I boarded the empty car opting for a seat regardless of the broken air-conditioning. Abruptly I realized my mistake.

A homeless man boisterously confronted me. "Hey you," he said, pointing in my face. "Will you sit with me?" I walked away. He yelled, "Why won't you sit with me? How about some of my lunch? You want some of my lunch?"

"Then you there," he shouted at another passenger (I was off the hook). "How about you, will you sit with me?" Each successive passenger was assaulted in turn by the invitation of the homeless man. His hostile greeting was punctuated by his wild gesticulations, which were followed by greasy chicken bones dropping to the floor. His face shined with the remains of chicken. Yet, painfully enough, the desperation in his tone bespoke a plea for validation, possible even a query for a legitimation of his existence. By consensus of the passengers, pathos for his condition caved to fear of his irritable nature and foul habits. The ongoing flow of passengers backed off from his pointed finger and strode briskly toward the opposite end of the car.

We sped down the express track from 168th Street to 145th Street. Stomping his feet, the homeless man became progressively more agitated along the way. The passengers at the opposite end of the car huddled tightly against the rear door.

Then, at the 125th Street stop, the event worsened. The doors opened on an elegant couple: Grandmother and Granddaughter, a step behind, marched onto the train. The family of two were dressed in lace and pastels, carrying matched clutch purses; Grandmother was crowned by a pillbox hat. We all cringed in expectation of the inevitable welcome. The precipitous indignity against the royal couple seemed unbearable. Despite ourselves, we craned our necks to see the other side of the car.

As expected, in a particularly taunting tone he began, "Hey, you two. Lookin' good. You two, right there—want to sit with me?" Tension filled the car, followed by shock.

Without a pause or missed stride, Grandmother and Granddaughter faced each other, nodded, and sat down immediately next to the homeless man. In unison they looked him in the eye and acknowledged his invitation in a chorus "Thank you." The two again nodded to each other, settled in, and looked straight ahead.

The man was stunned; he looked back and forth at the members of the pair. As if to test reality, he bellowed, "You want some of my lunch?!" Food fell from his mouth. Grandmother and Granddaughter looked directly at him, in unison chimed "No, thank you," and then nodded at each other. Still seemingly incredulous, the homeless man asked the identical question three or four times more. Each time the pair responded politely (somehow as if having been asked for the very first time), nodded to each other, and then looked straight ahead.

The sentiment in the subway car had changed. Now the empty side was full. Those of us on the A-train had been thrown an abundant moment, but what did it mean? Grandmother and Granddaughter had gone far out of their way to dignify this man, to include him in humanity. Still there seemed to be something more to be deciphered in the lesson of the subway car.

Then I focused on the essential indicator—the nod. The nod meant that Grandmother was successfully teaching Granddaughter. What was being taught? Decency, dignity, respect, I philosophized. I queried my memory for psychological theories of parenting, moral development, group processes. Then it dawned on me. The day was Sunday, the pair was traveling between home and church. Passing from Grandmother to Granddaughter was the living enactment of creed. Teachings echoed in my head: "What you do to the least of me, you do to me." "You shall treat the stranger as yourself, for you too were once the stranger in the land of Egypt." Which lesson was it?

Then again I thought of the nod. A fierce intensity of understanding between Grandmother and Granddaughter seemed confirmed by the nod. It dawned on me that in the nod was transmitted time-honored instructions for living: it was the intergenerational transmission of religion. Grandmother was a religious teacher: she instructed through right living.

Every day I ride the A-train through the 125th Street stop, where often I remember the royal couple. Each day some passengers have brightness in their eyes, others glares of hostility. Somedays I feel loving toward strangers while other days I indulge my personal problems. I wonder why the royal couple had boarded the same car on the same day as that particular homeless man. Homeless men walk up and down the cars nearly every day asking for change. Yet none since that day has offered me his lunch.

✦ CHAPTER 20 ✦

The Role of Faith in Shaping Optimism

Rabbi Yechiel Eckstein

As a rabbi, and social activist, I approach the subject of the role of faith in fostering—or, as I will point out, diminishing—well-being more from a public policy and theological perspective than from a sociological or psychological one. But I have come to appreciate, and learn from, the outstanding trail-blazing work being done by Dr. Seligman and others contributing to this fertile area of endeavor.

I first became exposed to this whole field some twenty years ago while studying for my doctorate at Columbia University in the fields of religion and philosophy. The writings of William James and, particularly, Victor Frankl and his science of logotherapy, profoundly influenced my thinking. This was especially true regarding the correlation they posited between man's search for meaning (not necessarily his finding it) and his physical well-being. But while social psychologists insist that faith is a quantifiable discipline and empirically grounded science, for me, it remains, ultimately, in the realm of the ineffable—a matter that will forever elude our scientific grasp and transcend attempts to quantify or measure it with any degree of precision. Faith, for me, is not a "discipline" that we master, but a miracle that overpowers us. It is, by its very nature, beyond our mastering and dominating.

As a result of this fundamentally different way in which we approach the subject, the social psychologist is likely to find the theologian's views inadequate, while the latter is likely to accuse the social psychologist of incredible *hubris*. I trust, therefore, that anecdotal as my views may be, and as distant from the approach taken by others in this volume, they will be considered with the degree of earnestness this subject merits. Indeed, perhaps this paper can begin to build a bridge that will link the vast chasm currently existing between religion and science, faith and reason.

Last week, I flew to Washington on a 6:00 A.M. flight. As I went through the metal detector, I noticed that the woman in charge of security was smiling and clearly in a great mood. I asked her how she could be in such a good mood so early in the morning. Her response struck me. She told me she has to wake up at two o'clock every morning in order to make sure she has time to read the Bible and get to work by 5:00 a.m. "I'm a Christian," she explained, "and I start my day, every day, by reading the Bible. Before I do that, I'm grumpy. Afterwards, I'm fine and loving."

Ten years ago, I spent a month with my family in Israel. While in Jerusalem, in a very orthodox neighborhood called *Meah Shearim*, we visited a Hassidic uncle of mine who lost his leg in the 1967 Israeli-Arab war when he walked into a minefield to save a downed pilot and a landmine blew up under him. My uncle lived in abject poverty with his wife and ten children, in a home the size of our kitchen back home in America. My girls, who were then 11, 8 and 5, had never seen anything like that before, a man with a long beard and sidelocks—their relative, no less—living in such appalling conditions, hopping around the room without a leg. They were shocked and traumatized by the experience.

But what struck them most, was the clear sense of *joie de vivre* that exuded from this man's face, the sparkle of joy and contentment that radiated from his eyes, and the fact that he continuously invoked the verse from the Bible, *hodu lashem ki tov ki leolam chasdo*, "give thanks to the Lord for He is good, His mercy is upon us forever." My children walked away from that experience wondering how he could be so happy and grateful to God given his harsh and squalid circumstances. That visit had a profound and lasting effect on my children. It gave them a deeper appreciation of their own circumstances, a broader perspective of life, and a keener understanding of the true meaning of happiness and well-being.

I raise these two incidents because they shed light on the subject at hand. The scientific premise espoused by social psychologists in this volume is that optimism is intertwined with happiness which, in turn, is intrinsically linked to good health and physical well-being. These blessings, it is further maintained, are not consequences of external factors such as wealth, status, or age (as we might have expected), but are attributable to the conscious choices we make daily. Essentially, we *choose* to be happy; we *will* to have a rosy outlook on life.

Much like Solzhenitsyn, Scharansky, Mandela, and countless other dissidents who survived torture, incarceration, and years of solitary confinement but who felt inwardly *free,* so our happiness and disposition toward life are not shaped so much by external conditions as by internal factors. Indeed, characteristics like wealth and power can have the adverse effect of engendering feelings of grief and sadness as much as, if not more than, ones of happiness.

What is the primary factor guiding the correlation between optimism and well-being? A number of suggestions have been proffered in this volume, all of which are valid. And while the answer to this powerful question is, in all likelihood, "all of the above," two factors stand out as particularly significant—community and control.

People who both celebrate and mourn together with others, who have a shoulder to cry on and a friend to laugh with, a group of friends and acquaintances with whom they share a common vision, lifestyle, and values—these people are nurtured by community. Through it, they give and receive solace, comfort, and a sense of belonging. My own experience as a rabbi for twenty-five years, and my involvement with hospice programs, leads me to believe that people are not afraid so much of dying as they are of dying *alone.* It's not the pain of death that haunts them, nor what lies on death's other side, but the prospect of being alone in those final moments. The sense of community that religions tend to provide is a critical factor in the link between faith on the one hand, and optimism and well-being, on the other.

The second factor, control, is a more complicated and paradoxical one. Many social psychologists maintain that people who feel a sense of control over their lives also have a greater sense of optimism and psychological well-being. But the spiritual paradigm, in fact, teaches the opposite message. For at the core of religious faith is the concept of *surrender*

—surrendering our control to a higher authority, giving up *our* will for *His*. "Make God's will your own, and your own, God's," says the Talmud. Indeed, all three Western religions, as well as most Eastern traditions, focus on our duty to give up control in relation to God, to remember that we are not the masters of our destiny and that we ought to be subservient to God by sacrificing our ego for His and surrendering our life to Him.

There is a very real psychological danger that exists in such a doctrine. For surrender can destroy a healthy ego and identity, and lead the believer to face life with passivity and fatalism rather than with a go-getting, "I can shape my destiny" kind of attitude. And so, while faith may very well be a positive force for well-being, we should not lose sight of its potential dark side of being destructive and harmful to one's positive sense of worth, identity, overall ethos, and approach to life.

Similarly, while feeling "in control" may very well increase well-being, on the existential and spiritual levels, it needs to be broken down into its healthy versus deleterious dimensions, with clear parameters being set to avoid the latter. This subject clearly needs further exploration, particularly now, with the rise of religious fundamentalism and intolerance around the world, and the increasing role religion plays in shaping nations' public policies.

In the early 1960s, Glock and Stark, two sociologists at the University of California, wrote a book, *Christian Beliefs and Anti-Semitism*, which had a major impact on the Vatican II Council's declaration toward the Jews. (It should be noted that their study has since come under serious questioning by other social scientists.) This watershed Catholic document, which reversed a two-thousand-year history of negative Christian attitudes toward Jews, repudiated the deicide charge (the doctrine that Jews killed Christ and were, therefore, to suffer eternally for that). What Glock and Stark found was that there existed a correlation between fundamentalist faith and intolerance—the more fundamentalist one's Christian faith, the greater likelihood for that person to be anti-Semitic.

In short, we must never fail to remember that faith is not always positive and good. With all its fine features, and the fact that it can create happiness and well-being, we must never forget that faith can also have a very dark side, as history clearly attests. What needs to be explored are questions like, What are the optimal conditions for faith to be a positive force? Which aspects of faith and spirituality produce contentment and happiness and which, the reverse? If it is the sense of absolute certainty that is favorable, how shall we deal with its flip-side, namely, the fact that this often leads to narrowness, intolerance, and extremism?

Clearly, this whole field of study in which we attempt to gauge the impact religion and spirituality have in shaping optimism and contributing to well-being is in desperate need of further exploration. I encourage psychologists and other social science researchers to involve clergy and engage theologians and philosophers in their efforts, despite the differences in our approach—nay, *because* of them—as they explore these issues. This matter is far too important to leave to either discipline.

How can faith shape character and instill positive values in our children? This is but one more very critical question that, by itself, ought to compel us to do further research. It is but one of a number of important challenges facing us today—ones, I trust, theologians and social psychologists will address *together* in the years ahead.

REFERENCE

Glock, C., & Starck, R. (1996). *Christian beliefs and anti-semitism*. New York: Harper & Row.

Section C. Optimism and Culture

✦

✦ CHAPTER 21 ✦

Optimism, Culture, and History: The Roles of Explanatory Style, Integrative Complexity, and Pessimistic Rumination

Jason M. Satterfield

As evidenced by the impressive range of topics in this volume, explanatory style and learned helplessness theory have far surpassed their original applications to depression and mental health. The emotional and physical well-being of adults, children, couples, and families have all proven susceptible to the influence of explanatory style and malleable to subsequent preventive or treatment interventions (see Chapters 4, 8, 12, and 15). This chapter will further extend the range of explanatory style and optimism research into the realms of culture, political science, history, sociology, and economics. Predicting individual behavior will again prove important; however, the behavior of historically significant individuals and the behavior of the masses will likewise be examined. Attempts to enhance the specificity and predictive power of explanatory style by examining its interaction with other cognitive style variables will be introduced.

The chapter is composed of three sections. First, I will provide a broad survey of explanatory style research and potential mechanisms of action, including motivation, decision making, and coping. Two adjunctive cognitive style measures, integrative complexity and pessimistic rumination, are introduced and critiqued. Content analysis research methods for each cognitive style measure are briefly summarized. Second, I discuss the measurement of "cultural optimism" and its role in predicting the behavior of the masses. Third, I summarize research methods and results demonstrating the power of optimism and cognitive style in understanding politics and historical events by predicting the behavior of key political figures.

EXPLANATORY STYLE

Explanatory style, or an individual's habitual way of explaining why events occurred, has been shown to predict behavior in the face of aversive events and could influence decision making and a wide range of actions (Abramson, Seligman, & Teasdale, 1978; Seligman, 1991; Tennen & Herzberger, 1985). Individuals with a pessimistic explanatory style (who attribute the causes of negative events to internal, stable, and global factors) develop the helpless belief that their actions cannot change or alter the causes or consequences of an event, thereby decreasing their goal-directed behaviors. They give up in the face of failure or extreme challenge, display inadequate problem-solving and coping strategies, and become passive, indecisive, and depressed (e.g., Buchanan & Seligman, 1995; Peterson, Maier, & Seligman, 1993; Seligman, 1975, 1991; Sweeney, Anderson, & Bailey, 1986; Tennen & Affleck, 1987). Three of the possible pathways that lead from explanatory style to physical and psychological well-being are discussed below: motivation, decision making, and coping skills.

EXPLANATORY STYLE AND MOTIVATION

An individual with an optimistic explanatory style sees the causes of aversive events as changeable, controllable, and limited in scope. Greater motivation could arise from high expectancies of control or optimistic predictions of success. In Weiner's theory of motivation (1974, 1985), causal ascriptions and emotions play key roles. Beliefs regarding personal control and changeability are thought to be crucial in determining high expectancies for success while a high expectancy for success results in motivational gains. Research from other sources focusing on self-efficacy and helplessness also concur that a greater belief in control directly fosters higher levels of motivation (Bandura, 1977; Garber &

Seligman, 1980). Past work with explanatory style and helplessness suggests that optimists are more motivated to overcome the inertia of maintaining the status quo and might initiate more aggressive and perhaps risky actions (e.g., Satterfield, 1995; Satterfield & Seligman, 1994; Seligman, 1975; Weiner, 1985; Zullow, Oettingen, Peterson, & Seligman, 1988; Zullow & Seligman, 1990).

EXPLANATORY STYLE AND DECISION MAKING

Explanatory style could impact decision making by influencing the search and inference process. The search process could be impacted by biasing the search for alternatives and evidence used in evaluating potential courses of action. The inference process could be impacted by altering the estimations made about the probability of success or failure and the relative weighting of costs and benefits. It is likely that both the extreme optimist and the extreme pessimist engage in biased decision making; however, their biases have significantly different impacts on their subsequent behavior. The optimist might think of fewer alternatives, search only for limited supporting evidence, inflate probabilities of success, minimize perceived costs, and maximize perceived benefits. Goal-directed action is more likely. A pessimist might think only of evidence of failure, magnify costs, and minimize perceived benefits, making goal-directed action less likely.

An alternative view suggests the moderate pessimist might be a superior decision-maker depending on the needs of the situation. By definition, the pessimist is more concerned with how causes will affect future events (high stability scores) and is more concerned with the broad, interdimensional effects of a bad event (high globality). This seems more in keeping with a careful search for alternatives, a conservative cost-benefit analysis, and subsequent prudent action (Satterfield, Monahan, & Seligman, 1997). In a related vein, experimental studies with depressive realism suggest pessimists are more attuned to reality or could be more accurate thinkers (Ackerman & DeRubeis, 1991; Alloy & Abramson, 1979; Coyne & Gottlib, 1983; Lewinsohn, Mischel, Chaplin, & Barton, 1980; Ruehlman, West, & Pasahow, 1985).

EXPLANATORY STYLE AND COPING

Because they reframe stressors as coping tasks and have heightened perceptions of control and efficacy, optimists suffer fewer emotional consequences from setbacks and are more motivated to actively cope (e.g., Peterson, Bettes, & Seligman, 1985; Satterfield, 1995; Seligman, 1975, 1991; Weiner, 1974, 1985; Zullow & Seligman, 1990). Research suggests that coping abilities are improved when individuals frame stressors as challenges rather than as threats, perceive that they have control, and believe change is possible (e.g., Kobasa, 1979; Kushner, Riggs, Foa, & Miller, 1992; Lazarus & Folkman, 1984; Lazarus & Launier, 1978; McSherry & Holm, 1994). Perceptions of change/control foster lower post-stressor distress levels, minimize coping difficulties, and yield greater problem-focused coping (Folkman & Lazarus, 1980; Janoff-Bulman, 1979, 1992; Janoff-Bulman & Wortman, 1977; Kushner, Riggs, Foa, & Miller, 1992; Peterson, Schwartz & Seligman, 1981; Wortman, 1976).

Past research suggests that optimists use different, more effective coping strategies than pessimists. Using Lazarus's (1966) coping skills system, Scheier and Carver (1987) linked optimism with more problem-focused coping and with positive, adaptive distortions. Optimists also seek and receive more social support and develop an intense, task-specific focus (Coates & Winston, 1983; Coates, Wortman, & Abbey, 1979; Coyne & Gottlib, 1983; Scheier et al., 1986). Studies on academic transitions, coronary artery bypass surgery, coping with infertility, and cancer have further corroborated the optimism-resilience hypothesis (Aspinwall & Taylor, 1992; Carver et al., 1993; Litt, Tennen, Affleck, & Klock, 1992; Scheier et al., 1989; Stanton & Snider, 1993).

EXPLANATORY STYLE AND CONTENT ANALYSIS

The Attributional Style Questionnaire is the primary measure of explanatory style (Peterson et al., 1982). However, since obtaining questionnaire data is not always feasible, the content analysis of verbatim explanations or CAVE technique was developed (Peterson & Seligman, 1984; Schulman, Castellon, & Seligman, 1989). The CAVE technique relies on the extraction and rating of causal statements taken from verbatim spoken or written materials. Materials can include private letters, diaries, or speeches to study the individual and song lyrics, popular news magazines, newspapers, religious prayers or scriptures, mythologies, and folktales to study a culture as a whole. Given the adaptability of this technique, nearly any area of interest from any period of recorded history can be analyzed.

In brief, an unambiguous causal statement is extracted from the verbatim materials, then rated by blind, independent raters on the three explanatory style dimensions of internality, stability, and globality. Relevant explanatory style composite scores corresponding to levels of optimism and pessimism can then be derived. CAVE scores have proven reliable and both concurrently and constructively valid (r = -0.36 with the Beck Depression Inventory and r = .71 with the ASQ; Schulman et al., 1989).

INTEGRATIVE COMPLEXITY

Many current models of explanatory style are unidimensional—a subject falls somewhere on a single continuum between optimism and pessimism. However, it seems plausible that optimism or pessimism can be grounded in either rationality or illusions with varying consequences. Optimism may be helpful when faced with a surmountable challenge but hurtful when careful, conservative action or reflection is indicated (Baumeister, 1989; Seligman, 1991). By looking at the interaction between explanatory style and a measure of thought quality, one might be able to make more specific outcome and behavioral predictions.

Integrative complexity measures thought quality. It captures the breadth and depth of the search-inference (i.e., decision making) process around a circumscribed issue. There are two components of integrative complexity: 1) Differentiation, which refers to the search for alternatives, evaluative dimensions or values, and the survey of goals, and 2) Integration, which refers to the drawing of conceptual connections between differentiated dimensions or weighing pros and cons of differentiated alternatives. To assess integrative complexity, extractions are again taken from selected verbatim materials and rated on a 7-point scale by blind, independent raters. Scores of 1–3 indicate increasing levels of differentiation while scores of 4–7 indicate full differentiation plus increasing levels of integration (Baker-Brown, et al., 1992).

Most likely, because of integrative complexity's close ties to encodings, beliefs, goals and values, and competencies, measures of integrative complexity have proven useful in predicting an individual's behavior. Archival analyses of historical documents have shown integrative complexity to be useful in understanding military conflicts and outcomes, political roles and careers, civil unrest, political ideologies, resilience, and the impact of psychosocial stressors on cognitive processes (Raphael, 1982; Satterfield, 1995; Suedfeld, 1985, 1993; Suedfeld & Bluck, 1993; Suedfeld, Corteen, & McCormick, 1986; Suedfeld & Rank, 1976; Suedfeld & Tetlock, 1977; Suedfeld, Tetlock, & Streufert, 1992; Tetlock, 1983, 1985; Tetlock & Boettger, 1989; Wallace, Suedfeld & Thachuk, 1993). Stress and its consequent decision-making pressures are associated with reductions in integrative complexity, but increases in optimism and integrative complexity can make one more resilient (George, 1986; Hockey & Hamilton, 1983; Holsti, 1972; Kaltoff & Neimeyer, 1993; Linville, 1987; Morgan & Janoff-Bulman, 1994; Satterfield, 1995; Suedfeld, Tetlock, & Ramirez, 1977).

The interaction of integrative complexity with explanatory style offers four categories of cognitive subtypes—high complexity and low complexity optimism and high complexity and low complexity pessimism. It thus further differentiates already useful categories of explanatory style (i.e., optimism and pessimism) to enhance predictive power and better specify preventive or reactive interventions. The interaction term could provide the opportunity to separate the "depressive realists" from the depressives and the reckless optimists from simply hopeful individuals.

PESSIMISTIC RUMINATION

Rumination is broadly defined as the tendency to non-productively think about negative affects, situations, and attributions. Kuhl's (1981, 1984) critique of the learned helplessness reformulation argued that rumination about a "negative state orientation" and not just pessimism per se should be the better predictor of depression. In other words, the presence, frequency, and intensity of pessimistic attributions should all be considered. Empirical support for this hypothesis was found by Zullow (1984), who showed that depressive symptoms were best predicted by a pessimistic explanatory style in conjunction with high rumination. Other studies have offered further support for the relationship between rumination and depression (Hollon & Kendall, 1980; Kammer, 1983; Nolen-Hoeksema, Parker, & Larson, 1994). It then follows that an individual or culture high in rumination could more likely exhibit symptoms of learned helplessness and depression such as passivity, self-doubt, and negative cognitive distortions.

Using any sample of verbatim materials, content analysis scoring for rumination rates each sentence for the presence or absence of a rumination and derives a percent rumination score for each piece of verbatim materials. A rumination is scored for a focus on a bad event, an explanation for a bad event, or a negative emotion. High interrater reliabilities have been reported and the measure does not seem redundant with explanatory style (Zullow, 1995). To combine the measure of rumination with explanatory style, a final pessimistic rumination (PessRum) score is calculated using the sum of the standardized z-scores for rumination and explanatory style. The interaction of explanatory style and rumination yields four subtypes—ruminative and non-ruminative optimists and ruminative and non-ruminative pessimists.

MACRO-ANALYSIS: OPTIMISM AND CULTURE

Primarily due to the tremendous flexibility of the CAVE technique for deriving explanatory style, traditional optimism research has moved into the spheres of cultural psychology and cross-cultural work. Creative researchers have taken this unique opportunity to retrospectively tap into the levels of optimism for a given culture at any given time when verbatim materials might be available. Rather than look at an individual's verbatim utterances, one can look at materials indicative of a segment of society, such as myths, fairy tales, proverbs, song lyrics, newsmagazines, and prayer books, and derive levels of cultural optimism. These levels can then be used to predict any number of variables ranging from passage of political propositions to confidence in the economy. Comparisons of optimism between cultures have just begun and are faced with the traditional struggles of cross-cultural work, including issues of generalizability and conceptual validity (Oettingen, 1995).

The reliability and validity of the CAVE technique in assessing cultural levels of optimism was first demonstrated by Oettingen and Morawska in 1990. Religious written materials from late nineteenth-century Russian Jewish culture were selected with consultation from Russian Judaic scholars and CAVEd for explanatory style scores. As hypothesized, religious statements were found to be more optimistic than secular statements, suggesting a potential value/function of religious beliefs. This study was followed by a successful replication using materials from late nineteenth-century Orthodox Christian peasantry (Oettingen, 1995; Oettingen & Morawska, 1990). No specific predictions were made regarding mass behavior, but the research methodology was shown to be viable and held great promise for future studies.

Building on Oettingen's success, Harold Zullow (1991) used the explanatory style and rumination scores derived from North American culture to predict economic upswings and downturns. He CAVEd the lyrics to Top 40 pop songs and the captions of *Time* magazine covers from 1955–1989 in order to derive corresponding levels of cultural optimism. He expanded on the classic explanatory style model by adding a content analysis measure of rumination and combining the two measures to create a composite score of "pessimistic rumination." Zullow predicted that cultural shifts in optimism and rumination, especially shifts in pessimistic rumination, would be manifested in the verbatim materials and that these shifts could then be used to predict changes in consumer spending and confidence. Consumer spending and confidence would in turn contribute to later recessions or periods of high economic growth. Zullow's predictions were confirmed. The 2-year moving average of pessimistic rumination correlated significantly with the moving average of GNP growth in the subsequent two years ($r = -.63$), the occurrence of a recession in the following year ($r = .46$), the average of the index of consumer sentiment ($r = -.54$), and the change in consumers' personal consumption expenditures in the following year ($r = -.56$). Increases in pessimistic rumination predicted lower GNP, greater likelihood of a near future recession, and lowered consumer confidence and spending. By tapping into a "macro" level of optimism and rumination, the enigmatic behaviors of the masses and the economy became more clear.

Encouraged by growing research on cultural optimism, Oettingen and Seligman hoped to find two cultures they could compare, contrast, and better understand based on differences in cultural explanatory style. However, even if statistically significant differences in explanatory style and outcome variables were found, no meaningful conclusions could be made since the cultures would differ on multiple, uncontrollable dimensions. The ideal study would involve two cultures that differed on only one aspect. East and West Berlin, before the fall of the Berlin Wall, offered the perfect laboratory given their near identical cultural roots but vastly different political and economic structures. Oettingen and Seligman (1990) CAVEd East and West Berlin newspaper articles regarding the Sarajevo Winter Olympics. Given that East Berliners have less freedom and personal control in many areas of their lives, Oettingen and Seligman predicted they would find higher levels of pessimism in the East Berlin papers. Consistent with these predictions, the levels of pessimism in East Berlin were far higher than those of their Western counterparts despite East Germany's comparatively stellar performance in the Olympic Games. Given the higher levels of pessimism in the East, they also predicted that East Berliners would display more signs of depression. Through creative and perhaps risky direct observations of bar patrons in both East and West Berlin, their hypothesis was again confirmed. East Berliners displayed more depressive affect (Oettingen and Seligman, 1990; Zullow, Oettingen, Peterson, & Seligman, 1988).

MICRO-LEVEL: OPTIMISM, POLITICS, AND HISTORY

In other contexts, explanatory style has proven useful in predicting the behavior of individuals—students, medical patients, athletes, life insurance salesmen, and the like (Peterson, 1988; Peterson & Barrett,

1987; Peterson, Seligman, & Vaillant, 1988; Seligman, Nolen-Hoeksema, Thornton & Thornton, 1990; Seligman & Schulman, 1986). What if the individual under study was one of significant political or historical importance? By using the well-validated content analysis measures for explanatory style, integrative complexity, and rumination it would be possible to study leaders from afar in a way that would be both scientifically rigorous and interesting. It would only require reliable verbatim materials and a team of well-trained raters.

Within the realm of politics, content analysis derived explanatory style scores have been linked to electoral success, aggressive campaigning, resilience to stress, and military aggression and risk-taking (Satterfield, 1995, 1998; Satterfield & Seligman, 1994; Zullow, Oettingen, Peterson, & Seligman, 1988; Zullow & Seligman, 1990). I'll first review a series of electoral studies by Zullow and Seligman (1990) followed by predictions of behavior in the Persian Gulf War (Satterfield & Seligman, 1994) and psychohistorical analyses of the major world leaders during World War II (Satterfield, 1995, 1998).

OPTIMISM AND ELECTORAL SUCCESS

In the seminal Zullow and Seligman (1990) election studies, the nomination speeches for United States presidential candidates from 1900 to 1984 were analyzed for explanatory style and rumination. Zullow and Seligman predicted the optimistic, non-ruminative candidate would be more likely to win. In fact, they were able to correctly predict eighteen out of the twenty-two elections with the exceptions being the three re-elections of Franklin Roosevelt and Nixon's victory over Humphrey in 1968. Not only were they able to predict the winner, but the differences in pessimistic rumination (the combination score of rumination and explanatory style) between the candidates also predicted the margin of victory (Zullow & Seligman, 1990).

To answer challenges regarding third variables and directions of causality, further analyses were completed. Early spread in the polls might have caused the successful candidate to become more optimistic and less ruminative rather than the other way around. After controlling for initial margins, the correlation between the spread in pessimistic rumination and the spread in the popular vote increased to .89 ($p < .01$) and the correlation between pessimistic rumination and the change in support increased to .88 ($p < .01$). By controlling for the election year percentage increase in real per capita disposable income, Zullow and Seligman were able to rule out a thriving economy as a variable responsible for their election prediction results. Finally, they suggested and found partial support for two potential mechanisms. First, it appears that optimistic, non-depressed candidates are more well-liked by the electorate while ruminative candidates may have evoked avoidant responses (Coyne & Gotlib, 1983). Secondly, optimistic, non-ruminative candidates were more likely to be aggressive campaigners, making more campaign stops and raising more campaign funds (Zullow, 1995; Zullow & Seligman, 1990).

In response to critics of retrospective "predictions," Zullow (1988, 1995) set out to prospectively predict the 1988 presidential primaries, presidential elections, and Senate races. As anticipated, optimism and pessimistic rumination again predicted the presidential nominations and twenty-five of twenty-nine Senate races. For the presidential elections, Dukakis at first appeared more optimistic and less ruminative than Bush. As the race progressed, however, Dukakis became more ruminative. It was later discovered that the Dukakis camp had closely followed the earlier election studies and had rewritten early speeches to sound more optimistic and less ruminative. When Dukakis's true style emerged, the pessimistic rumination hypothesis was again confirmed. For perhaps the first time in the history of psychology, a major historical event was correctly predicted using sound scientific methods. Furthermore, combining a rumination measure with explanatory style seemed to be a significant improvement over using rumination or explanatory style scores alone.

The final set of studies were done by Satterfield and Seligman from 1990–1995. We looked at the role of explanatory style, pessimistic rumination, and integrative complexity in explaining something more significant than election results—predicting military aggression, risk taking, and resilience in some of the most significant events in world history. By content analyzing verbatim materials taken from world leaders, we demonstrated the viability of a new "scientific psychohistory," which relied on reliable and valid assessments of leaders' psychological states and predicted their subsequent actions and decisions as well as their ability to cope with significant personal and professional stressors.

OPTIMISM, AGGRESSION, AND RISK TAKING

The first study was born in late 1990 as Seligman and I, along with most of the country, anxiously watched the events around the Persian Gulf War begin to unfold. We wondered if we could use explanatory style to better understand the governmental policies and military actions advocated by both Saddam Hussein and George Bush. According to the learned helplessness theory, a world leader with an optimistic explanatory style would be more likely to take aggressive, bold, and risky actions than would that same leader in the same situation with a more pessimistic explanatory style. The pessimistic leader would be more indecisive and doubtful, overly concerned with policy costs and risks, less confident in the face of challenges, and less motivated to overcome the inertia of maintaining inadequate status quo policies. As a way to increase the number of analyzable events (and increase our statistical power), we also looked retrospectively at the 1980–1988 Iran-Iraq war and Operation "Just Cause," Bush's involvement in the search for and capture of Panama's General Noriega. We CAVEd verbatim materials taken prior to each military action. Each military action was rated on scales of aggression and risk (see Satterfield, 1998 or Satterfield & Seligman, 1994 for scale specifics).

Our hypothesis was partly supported for both Saddam Hussein and George Bush. Optimism prior to military action predicted subsequently higher levels of aggression and risk taking while greater pessimism predicted lower aggression and risk taking. Just prior to the invasion of Kuwait, Saddam was at his peak level of optimism. Prior to ordering the commencement of the air strikes and ground war, Bush was at his most optimistic point. And before Saddam's surrender and withdrawal, his optimism plummeted to its lowest level (Satterfield & Seligman, 1994). Although results were only correlational, all verbatim materials used in the content analysis were taken prior to the predicted actions, suggesting that the military actions did not cause the explanatory style shifts found in the verbatim materials.

Although we had statistically significant and potentially important findings, we were unable to do more than speculate about mechanisms—the roles of motivation and decision making. We suggested optimistic leaders were more likely to attend to benefits of an action, minimize costs, and overestimate chances of success while the inverse was true of pessimists. Optimists would be more motivated, act more quickly, and be less frozen with anxious or depressive ruminations.

The need to corroborate these speculations led to our second and more ambitious study. We wanted to replicate our findings with optimism and pessimism but add additional measures of decision making and rumination with a larger sample of leaders and a greater number of events. We chose to look at the pivotal players in the most destructive and violent conflict in human history—Churchill, Hitler, Roosevelt, and Stalin in World War II. A review of military histories and biographies yielded a list of primary military actions occurring within each subject's tenure as national leader. The final study sample consisted of fifty-one military and political actions dating from 1914–1945 and drawn from all four subjects. A full range of actions were included from full scale military operations (e.g., Operation Overlord) to the ultimate surrender (i.e., Hitler's suicide).

The fifty-one selected military actions were rated by two blind, independent raters on two 6-point scales quantifying the degree of aggression and risk taken by the leader. All historical information leading up to the decision and subsequent military action was taken into account to better determine risk and the level of aggression. A rating of 6 on the aggression/passivity scale reflected a highly aggressive act typified by rapid action and/or large scale military involvement. A rating of 1 indicated high passivity or inaction even in the face of a direct threat or reasonable cause. Raters were instructed to look for provocation, justification, amount of resources involved, time to action, hostility, inertia, presence of alternative plans or safeguards, etc. Interrater reliability was found to be good for both the aggression ($r = .86, p < .01$) and risk-taking ($r = .89, p < .01$) scales. Although the dimensions of risk and aggression clearly differ from one another theoretically, they were highly correlated ($r = .81$, $p < .01$) and subsequently combined in the final data analysis to create the variable AggRsk.

Public and private verbatim materials preceding the military actions were used to content analyze explanatory style, integrative complexity, and pessimistic rumination (Satterfield, 1998). We once again expected optimism to precede more risky and aggressive actions. With the addition of integrative complexity and pessimistic rumination we further refined our hypotheses to predict that low complexity, non-ruminative optimism would be the strongest predictor of aggression and risk-taking.

Multiple regression models were used to test the hypothesis that explanatory style, integrative complexity, rumination, and their interactions would predict subsequent aggressive and risky behaviors by world leaders. The most powerful and parsimonious model tested (as indicated by having the highest R-square with all variables still significant predictors) was AggRsk = constant + Subject1 + Subject2 + Subject3 + Explanatory Style + Integrative Complexity + Explanatory Style × Integrative Complexity (Overall *Adj R-square* = .397, $F[5,45] = 5.165$, $p < .05$, two-tailed for overall regression). After controlling for subject identity, optimism was associated with increases in AggRsk while pessimism predicted passivity and caution. Integrative complexity was also found to be a significant predictor of AggRsk with increases in integrative complexity predicting lower AggRsk. Rumination was not found to be a significant predictor of AggRsk in any regression model. The interaction (Explanatory Style × Integrative Complexity) was also found to be a useful predictor of AggRsk even after controlling for subject identity and main effects. Integratively non-complex optimists were most aggressive while integratively complex pessimists were most passive. No other two-way interactions were found to be statistically significant in any models.

As predicted, we found an inverse correlation between levels of pessimism and aggression and risk. As the leader became more pessimistic, he became less aggressive and risk-taking. The same relationship held true for integrative complexity. As leaders' thinking became more complex, as they searched for more alternatives and were better able to integrate information, their levels of aggression and risk-taking began to drop. Analyzing the interaction between explanatory style and integrative complexity enabled us to look at a high complexity optimism versus a low complexity optimism and a complex pessimism versus a non-complex pessimism. Again as predicted, the strongest relationship was between military aggression and risk taking and low complexity optimism.

Neither rumination scores nor combination scores for rumination and explanatory style significantly predicted aggression or risk taking. In other words, an overall increase in the frequency and intensity of negative state–oriented sentences did not seem to affect a leader's subsequent actions as measured by the aggression and risk scales. It is unclear why this measure was not useful. Rumination was thought to be important in aggression and risk because as a leader or decision maker non-productively ruminates on doubts and problems, he will be more likely to disengage from further action. He could be less motivated, less confident, and have a weaker sense of control (Carver, Blaney, & Scheier, 1979; Nolen-Hoeksema, 1991; Scheier & Carver, 1988; Zullow, 1984). However, the measure used in this study might simply be too vague to capture this process. Recall that any negative emotion, event, or explanation that did not directly involve coping was extractable. Hence much of Stalin's litany against the "perfidious fascists" or Hitler's passionately rousing pre-war speeches about German suffering at the hands of the communists and imperialists were rated as ruminations even though the content probably reflected rhetorical styles designed to consolidate and motivate public support. The validity of this particular content analysis measure clearly needs to be explored along with alternative scoring methods (e.g., rumination scores might have more utility if the ratio of negative state orientation to action orientation is used as the primary score rather than just negative state orientation scores).

Two primary hypotheses have been offered to explain the link between explanatory style and integrative complexity and aggression-risk—the intrapsychic cognitive model and impression management. In the intrapsychic model, shifts in a leader's cognitive-affective processes "leak" into his or her public pronouncements, reflecting the leader's explanatory style and abilities to search for alternatives and evidence, view different perspectives, and carefully integrate and weigh options.

Shifts in explanatory style and integrative complexity are thought to have causal significance perhaps through the mechanisms of motivation, decision making, and coping. With the impression management hypothesis, shifts in explanatory style and integrative complexity are merely reflections of a leader's conscious or subconscious attempts to sway public opinion toward a previously decided course of action. Disentangling these two hypotheses has proven especially difficult (Tetlock, 1985; Tetlock & Manstead, 1985).

In an attempt to test the impression management versus the intrapsychic cognitive model, we separated data taken from private verbatim materials (e.g., letters to wives, private memoirs) and public verbatim materials (e.g., prepared speeches, addresses). Unfortunately, the majority of data points were taken from public verbatim materials simply because of their greater availability. In total, only eight of the fifty-one time points had sufficient private verbatim materials to make reliable ratings of explanatory style, integrative complexity, and rumination. Statistical analyses were re-run for the reduced sample of forty-three public verbatim material events. All previously stated regression results were nearly identical to those found for the full sample. Although trends were similar, no analyses of the private sample yielded significant results, most likely because of the extreme lack of statistical power. Tetlock and Tyler (1996) more systematically compared integrative complexity scores from private and public verbatim materials for Churchill and found no differences in scores for public versus private verbatim utterances, suggesting that impression management was not a factor.

We are left with the intrapsychic cognitive model, which suggests a direct causal link between shifts in explanatory style and integrative complexity and aggression and risk perhaps via enhanced motivation and influenced decision making. In the present study, state optimism and low complexity optimism predicted aggression and risk taking. Ratings of aggression and risk reflected offensive action, rapid response initiation, action despite unfavorable odds, and high magnitude of response—all indicative of enhanced levels of motivation. In terms of decision making, the low integrative complexity leader would by definition be lower in both integration and differentiation. He or she would be attached to one option and fail to see other alternatives (low differentiation), and fail to acknowledge counter-evidence or to adequately assess the costs or limitations of his or her action (low integration). This "unflinching bearing" could feasibly motivate higher levels of aggression and risk taking. Alternatively, the integratively complex leader would carefully search for alternatives and weigh available evidence. If action were taken, it would certainly be more prudent and perhaps more passive. This does not mean that integratively complex leaders are unmotivated or are unable to act. Rather, integrative complexity could determine whether motivation would be manifested in impulsive action or in an energetic yet conscientious survey of available actions followed by the most prudent course.

OPTIMISM AND RESILIENCE

We assumed that a leader's ability to cope with the intense stress of leading a nation in a time of crisis would impact his or her actions and could help explain the course of historical events. Knowing their coping styles or abilities would be useful in predicting behavior but, more generally, would be helpful in understanding the psychological makeup of noteworthy individuals. This curiosity led to our next project, which analyzed each leader's ability to cope with significant personal and professional stressors and his cognitive-affective state preceding each stressor. To achieve this goal we again applied the innovative content analysis techniques for explanatory style, integrative complexity, and rumination to verbatim materials preceding significant personal and professional stressors. Another unique content analysis technique to derive a subject's level of functioning both before and after the stressor using biographical information was created to measure how much a subject was affected by an event or how well he coped (see Satterfield, 1995 for further details).

We hoped to further refine the links between explanatory style and resilience and coping by again adding integrative complexity and rumination. Although integrative complexity had not been directly linked to resilience, related concepts such as cognitive complexity and self-complexity have shown promise in predicting and understanding resilience. Several studies have found that, under high stress conditions, successful coping was best predicted by complex, positive self-representations (Hershberger, 1990; Kalthoff & Neimeyer, 1993; Linville, 1987; Morgan & Janoff-Bulman, 1994). In general, rumination about negative events has been shown to contraindicate successful coping and contribute to depression (Hollon & Kendall, 1980; Kammer, 1983; Kuhl, 1981, 1984; Nolen-Hoeksema, 1991; Nolen-Hoeksema, Parker, & Larson, 1994; Zullow, 1984). Rather than thinking about "action oriented" ways of coping with traumatic events, the ruminator becomes entangled with non-productive repetitions and detailed elaborations about the aversive event. We hypothesized that the complex thinking, non-ruminative optimist would be the most resilient.

Historical and biographical data sources were consulted to obtain a list of objectively significant psychosocial stressors for each subject in both the personal and public domains (e.g., marriage, health problems, electoral defeat). Stressors were selected if pre-dated verbatim materials and adequate historical accounts were available for analysis. Axis IV (A4) of the DSM-III-R, the Severity of Psychosocial Stressors Scale: Adults (American Psychiatric Association, 1987) was used by independent raters who were blind to the study's hypotheses to objectively measure the severity of each stressor. Axis V of the DSM-III-R (APA, 1987), the Global Assessment of Functioning Scale (GAF), was used to rate the subject's level of functioning both before and after the selected stressor. The subject's level of resilience was operationalized as the difference between GAF scores prior to and after the stressor (GAF pre-stressor - GAF post-stressor = resilience). In other words, larger drops in GAF after a stressor corresponded to less resilience. A small GAF drop meant high resilience. GAF scores were thought to be a useful measure of coping because of their attention to multiple expressions of distress (anxiety, depression, somatic complaints) and multiple contexts (occupational, social, interpersonal). Data for making GAF scores was obtained from biographies, family reports, memoirs, and medical records.

A multiple regression analysis was performed to test the predictive value of explanatory style, integrative complexity, rumination, and their interactions for resilience. The psychosocial severity rating (A4) was added to each model to partial out the effects of stressor severity. The most powerful and parsimonious model was Resilience = constant + Subject 1 + Subject 2 + Subject 3 + A4 + Integrative Complexity (Overall *Adj R-square* = .404, $F = 4.521$, $p < .05$ for overall regression). Not surprisingly, larger A4 scores predicted a significantly greater decline in functioning in every model tested. Explanatory style was not a significant predictor of resilience after controlling for stressor severity and was excluded from the final model. Integrative complexity was found to account for a significant portion of resilience variance with higher integrative complexity predicting greater resilience, even after controlling for subject identity and stressor severity. When Churchill was hit with significant stressors at two of his most integratively non-complex times—before his capture in the Boer War and before his dismissal from the Admiralty in World War I—he responded with great distress, causing his GAF scores to plummet more than thirty points. High integrative complexity prior to his near financial collapse and heart problems enabled him to cope exceptionally well, showing little change in GAF. Rumination did not meet minimal significance criteria in any regression model. Finally, none of the interactions (IntComp-ExStyle, ExStyle Rum, or IntComp-Rum) was found to be significant.

In summary, it appears that high integrative complexity predicts resilience to and successful coping with a wide variety of personal and professional stressors. Not only can these findings help us better understand these historically significant individuals and the course of world events, they may also be generalizable to average individuals who are faced with average stressors.

We were left with one primary hypothesis regarding a mechanism of action, the role of stressor and coping appraisal, which refers to the ability to correctly predict and prepare for the occurrence of a stressor as well as make an accurate estimation regarding available coping resources and abilities. In short, it appears that someone who is more optimistic and integratively complex would have a more hopeful (less negative) and motivated response to a stressor, a more differentiated and integrated appraisal of stressor likelihood and severity, and a more accurate assessment of coping resources and needs. For example, perhaps Churchill's complex, optimistic outlook when he accepted the position of prime minister in 1940 provided him with the strength and resilience to rally a nation and face Germany alone. Conversely, Churchill's low complexity before his post-Dardenelles dismissal from the Admiralty, contributed to the worst depression of his life. During this time he believed his career and all that he held important were gone.

Contrary to our hypothesis, explanatory style alone was not a useful predictor of resilience. It is possible that our operationalized measure of resilience was simply too non-specific to explanatory style. The GAF measure was chosen to capture resilience because it incorporates a wide range of functioning and coping indicators—anxiety, depression, social interaction, physical health. However, explanatory style has historically proven most useful in predicting depression and depressive symptomatology. Had we assessed level of depressive symptoms before and after each trauma, we might have uncovered a relationship between explanatory style and resilience to depression.

Despite past work linking depression and rumination, rumination did not significantly predict resilience in the present study. Again, perhaps a more specific measure of depressive symptoms would have shown results. However, recent evidence suggests a far more complicated relationship between rumination and resilience. In some instances, rumination about a stressor could enhance coping ability rather than amplify feelings of depression and hopelessness (Pennebaker, Colder & Sharp, 1990; Silver, Boon, & Stones, 1983). Perhaps rumination provides the necessary affective arousal to "work through" or restructure the meaning of a traumatic event. Recall, however, that in our sample pessimistic rumination was neither negatively nor positively related to coping or resilience.

CONCLUSIONS AND FUTURE DIRECTIONS

Content analysis methodologies have opened a broad range of new possibilities for the scientific study of optimism on both the cultural and the individual levels. By examining verbatim materials representative of a culture or group, we can now make predictions about the behavior of the masses or whole societies. The cultural methodologies developed by Oettingen, Zullow, and Seligman have only just scratched the surface of potential applications. By looking at the verbatim materials of politicians or historically significant figures, we can better understand the course of elections, political decisions, and propensities to advocate aggression and risk taking. With similar methods, we can predict how effectively an individual will cope with stress. With this knowledge, it is feasible to design interventions that promote individual resilience. Given these methodologies, it is also feasible to better study and understand how the optimism of mass messages (e.g., television, advertising, etc.) might influence the optimism of the individual and affect subsequent behavior.

The theoretical specificity and predictive power of explanatory style have likewise improved as theories and measurements of cognitive style and optimism have grown more sophisticated. By adding a content analysis measure of thought quality (i.e., integrative complexity) and a content analysis measure of rumination, optimism can now be classified into complex, non-complex, ruminative, and non-ruminative subtypes. Although much work remains to be done, the mechanisms through which these cognitive styles exert their influence (i.e., decision making, motivation, and coping) have become more clear.

Future research will most likely continue to broaden and deepen the scope of explanatory style within the contexts of culture, politics, and history. As we struggle to function and thrive in an increasingly dangerous, crowded, and depressed world, researchers have the opportunity to demonstrate the universality of optimism, the importance of hope, and how we might engender these attributes across vastly different cultures and peoples. This could mean critically looking at our past mistakes and current endeavors—educational systems, political systems, community units, and other contexts in which integrative complexity, explanatory style, or ruminative style are taught and shifted within the individual as well as the culture as a whole. Understanding those shifts would ultimately open the way for interventions designed to improve the well-being of the individual and society.

REFERENCES

Abramson, L.Y., Seligman, M.E.P., & Teasdale, J.D. (1978). Learned helplessness in humans: Critique and reformulation. *Journal of Abnormal Psychology, 87,* 49–74.

Ackerman, R., & DeRubeis, R.J. (1991). Is depressive realism real? *Clinical Psychology Review, 11,* 565–584.

Alloy, L.B., & Abramson, L.Y. (1979). Judgment of contingency in depressed and nondepressed students: Sadder but wiser? *Journal of Experimental Psychology, 108*(4), 441–485.

American Psychiatric Association. (1987). *Diagnostic and statistical manual of mental disorders* (3rd ed., revised). Washington, DC.

Aspinwall, L.G., & Taylor, S.E. (1992). Modeling cognitive adaptation: A longitudinal investigation of the impact of individual differences and coping on college adjustment and performance. *Journal of Personality and Social Psychology, 63,* 989–1003.

Baker-Brown, G., Ballard, E.J., Bluck, S., De Vries, B., Suedfeld, P., & Tetlock, P.E. (1992). The conceptual/integrative complexity scoring manual. In C.P. Smith (Ed.), *Motivation and personality: Handbook of thematic content analysis* (pp. 401–418). Cambridge: Cambridge University Press.

Bandura, A. (1977). *Social learning theory.* Englewood Cliffs, NJ: Prentice-Hall.

Baumeister, R.F. (1989). The optimal margin of illusion. *Journal of Social and Clinical Psychology, 8,* 176–189.

Buchanan, G.M., & Seligman, M.E.P. (1995). *Explanatory style.* Hillsdale, NJ: Lawrence Erlbaum.

Carver, C.S., Blaney, P.H., & Scheier, M.F. (1979). Reassertion and giving up: The interactive role of self-directed attention and outcome expectancy. *Journal of Personality and Social Psychology, 37,* 1859–1870.

Carver, C.S., Pozo, C., Harris, S.D., Noriega, V., Scheier, M.F., Robinson, D.S., Ketcham, A.S., Moffat, F.L., Jr., & Clark, K.C. (1993). How coping mediates the effect of optimism on distress: A study of women with early stage breast cancer. *Journal of Personality and Social Psychology, 65*(2), 375–390.

Coates, D., & Winston, T. (1983). Counteracting the deviance of depression: Peer support groups for victims. *Journal of Social Issues, 39*(2), 171–196.

Coates, D., Wortman, C.B., & Abbey, A. (1979). Reactions to victims. In I.H. Freize, D. Bar-Tal, and J.S. Carroll (Eds.), *New approaches to social problems: Applications of attribution theory*. San Francisco: Jossey-Bass.

Coyne, J.C., & Gotlib, I.H. (1983). The role of cognition in depression: A critical appraisal. *Psychological Bulletin, 94*, 472–505.

Folkman, S., & Lazarus, R.S. (1980). An analysis of coping in a middle-aged community sample. *Journal of Health and Social Behavior, 21*(3), 219–239.

Folkman, S., & Lazarus, R.S. (1985). If it changes it must be a process: Study of emotions and coping during three stages of a college examination. *Journal of Personality and Social Psychology, 48*(1), 150–170.

Folkman, S., Lazarus, R.S., Gruen, R., & DeLongis, A. (1986). Appraisal, coping, health status, and psychological symptoms. *Journal of Personality and Social Psychology, 50*, 572–579.

Garber, J. and Seligman, M.E.P. (Eds.) (1980). *Human helplessness: Theory and applications*. New York: Academic Press.

George, A. (1986). The impact of crisis-induced stress on decision-making. In Institute of Medicine (Ed.), *The medical implications of nuclear war*. Washington, DC: National Academy of Sciences Press.

Hershberger, P.J. (1990). Self-complexity and health promotion: Promising but premature. *Psychological Reports, 66*(3), 1207–1216.

Hockey, R., & Hamilton, P. (1983). The cognitive patterning of stress states. In R. Hockey (Ed.), *Stress and fatigue in human performance*. Chichester, England: Wiley.

Hollon, S.D., & Kendall, P.C. (1980). Cognitive self-statements in depression: Development of an automatic thoughts questionnaire. *Cognitive Therapy and Research, 4*(4), 383–395.

Holsti, O. (1972). *Crisis, escalation, and war*. Montreal: McGill-Queens University Press.

Janoff-Bulman, R. (1979). Characterological versus behavioral self-blame: Inquiries into depression and rape. *Journal of Personality and Social Psychology, 37*(10), 1798–1809.

Janoff-Bulman, R. (1992). *Shattered assumptions: Towards a new psychology of trauma.* New York: Free Press.

Janoff-Bulman, R., & Wortman, C.B. (1977). Attributions of blame and coping in the "Real World": Severe accident victims react to their lot. *Journal of Personality and Social Psychology, 35*(5), 351–363.

Kalthoff, R.A., & Neimeyer, R.A. (1993). Self-complexity and psychological distress: A test of the buffering model. *International Journal of Personal Construct Psychology, 6*(4), 327–349.

Kammer, D. (1983). Depression, attributional style, and failure generalization. *Cognitive Therapy and Research, 7*(5), 413–423.

Kobasa, S.C. (1979). Stressful life events, personality, and health: An inquiry into hardiness. *Journal of Personality and Social Psychology, 34,* 191–198.

Kuhl, J. (1981). Motivational and functional helplessness: The moderating effect of state versus action orientation. *Journal of Personality and Social Psychology, 40,* 155–170.

Kuhl, J. (1984). Volitional aspects of achievement motivation and learned helplessness: Toward a comprehensive theory of action control. In B.A. Maher (Ed.), *Progress in experimental personality research* (Vol. 13, pp. 99–171). New York: Academic Press.

Kushner, M.G., Riggs, D.S., Foa, E.B., & Miller, S.M. (1992). Perceived controllability and the development of posttraumatic stress disorder (PTSD) in crime victims. *Behavioral Research and Therapy, 31*(1), 105–110.

Lazarus, R.S. (1966). *Psychological stress and the coping process.* New York: McGraw-Hill.

Lazarus, R.S. (1993). Coping theory and research: Past, present, and future. *Psychosomatic Medicine, 55,* 234–247.

Lazarus, R.S., & Folkman, S. (1984). *Stress, appraisal, and coping.* New York: Springer.

Lazarus, R.S., & Launier, R. (1978). Stress-related transactions between the person and the environment. In L.A. Pervin and M. Lewis (Eds.), *Perspectives in interactional psychology.* New York: Plenum.

Lewinsohn, P., Mischel, W., Chaplin, W., & Barton, R. (1980). Social competence and depression: The role of illusory self-perceptions. *Journal of Abnormal Psychology, 89,* 203–212.

Linville, P.W. (1987). Self-complexity as a cognitive buffer against stress-related illness and depression. *Journal of Personality and Social Psychology, 52*(4), 663–676.

Litt, M.D., Tennen, H., Affleck, G., & Klock, S. (1992). Coping and cognitive factors in adaptation to *in vitro* fertilization. *Journal of Behavioral Medicine, 15,* 171–187.

Manchester, W. (1983). *The last lion: Visions of glory.* New York: Dell.

McSherry, W.C., & Holm, J.E. (1994). Sense of coherence: Its effects on psychological and physiological processes prior to and after a stressful situation. *Journal of Clinical Psychology, 50*(4), 476–487.

Morgan, H.J., & Janoff-Bulman, R. (1994). Positive and negative self-complexity: Patterns of adjustment following traumatic versus nontraumatic life experience. *Journal of Social and Clinical Psychology, 13*(1), 63–85.

Nolen-Hoeksema, S. (1991). Responses to depression and their effects on the duration of depressive episodes. *Journal of Abnormal Psychology, 100,* 569–582.

Nolen-Hoeksema, S., Parker, L.E., & Larson, J. (1994). Ruminative coping with depressed mood following loss. *Journal of Personality and Social Psychology, 67*(1), 92–104.

Oettingen, G. (1995). Explanatory style in the context of culture. In G. M. Buchanan & M.E.P. Seligman (Eds.), *Explanatory style* (pp. 209–224). Hillsdale, NJ: Lawrence Erlbaum.

Oettingen, G., & Morawska, E.T. (1990). Explanatory style in religious vs. secular domains in Russian Judaism vs. Orthodox Christianity. Unpublished manuscript, University of Pennsylvania.

Oettingen, G., & Seligman, M.E.P. (1990). Pessimism and behavioral signs of depression in East versus West Berlin. *European Journal of Social Psychology, 20,* 207–220.

Pennebaker, J.W., Colder, M., & Sharp, L.K. (1990). Accelerating the coping process. *Journal of Personality and Social Psychology, 58*(3), 528–537.

Peterson, C. (1988). Explanatory style as a risk factor for illness. *Cognitive Therapy and Research, 12,* 117–130.

Peterson, C., & Barrett, L.C. (1987). Explanatory style and academic performance among university freshmen. *Journal of Personality and Social Psychology, 53*(3), 603–607.

Peterson, C., Bettes, B., & Seligman, M.E.P. (1985). Depressive symptoms and unprompted causal attributions: Content analysis. *Behavioral Research and Therapy, 23,* 379–382.

Peterson, C., Maier, S.F., & Seligman, M.E.P. (1993). *Learned helplessness: A theory for the age of personal control.* New York: Oxford University Press.

Peterson, C., Seligman, M.E.P., & Vaillant, G. E. (1988). Pessimistic explanatory style as a risk factor for physical illness: A thirty-five year longitudinal study. *Journal of Personality and Social Psychology, 55,* 23–27.

Peterson, C., Semmel, A., von Baeyer, C., Abramson, L., Metalsky, G., & Seligman, M.E.P. (1982). The attributional style questionnaire. *Cognitive Therapy and Research, 6,* 287–299.

Peterson, C., Schwartz, S.M., & Seligman, M.E.P. (1981). Self blame and depressive symptoms. *Journal of Personality and Social Psychology, 41,* 253–259.

Raphael, T. (1982). Integrative complexity theory and forecasting international crises: Berlin 1946–1962. *Journal of Conflict Resolution, 26*(3), 423–450.

Ruehlman, L.S., West, S.G., & Pasahow, R.J. (1985). Depression and evaluative schemata. *Journal of Personality, 53,* 46–92.

Satterfield, J.M. (1995). Cognitive predictors of resilience: A content analysis of Churchill, Hitler, Stalin, and Roosevelt. Unpublished manuscript.

Satterfield, J.M. (1998). Cognitive-affective states predict military and political aggression and risk taking: A content analysis of Churchill, Hitler, Roosevelt, and Stalin. *Journal of Conflict Resolution, 42*(6), 667–690.

Satterfield, J.M., Monahan, J., & Seligman, M.E.P. (1997). Law school performance predicted by explanatory style. *Behavioral Sciences and the Law, 15,* 95–105.

Satterfield, J.M., & Seligman, M.E.P. (1994). Military aggression and risk predicted by explanatory style. *Psychological Science, 5*(2), 77–82.

Scheier, M.F., & Carver, C.S. (1987). Dispositional optimism and physical well-being: The influence of generalized expectancies on health. *Journal of Personality, 55*(2), 169–210.

Scheier, M.F., & Carver, C.S. (1988). A model of behavioral self-regulation: Translating intention into action. In L. Berkowitz (Ed.), *Advances in experimental social psychology,* (Vol. 21, pp. 303–346). New York: Academic Press.

Scheier, M.F., & Carver, C.S. (1992). Effects of optimism on psychological well-being: Theoretical overview and empirical update. Special Issue: Cognitive perspectives in health psychology. *Cognitive Therapy and Research, 16*(2), 201–228.

Scheier, M.F., Matthews, K.A., Owens, J.F., Magovern, G.J., Sr., Lefebvre, R.C., Abbott, R.A., & Carver, C.S. (1989). Dispositional optimism and recovery from coronary artery bypass surgery: The beneficial effects on physical well being. *Journal of Personality and Social Psychology, 57,* 1024–1040.

Scheier, M.F., Weintraub, J.K., & Carver, C.S. (1986). Coping with stress: Divergent strategies of optimists and pessimists. *Journal of Personality and Social Psychology, 48,* 1162–1172.

Schulman, P., Castellon, C., & Seligman, M.E.P. (1989). Assessing explanatory style: The content analysis of verbatim explanations and the attributional style questionnaire. *Behavior Research and Therapy, 27,* 505–512.

Seligman, M.E.P. (1975). *Helplessness: On depression, development, and death.* San Francisco: Freeman.

Seligman, M.E.P. (1991). *Learned optimism.* New York: Alfred A. Knopf.

Seligman, M.E.P., Nolen-Hoeksema, S., Thornton, N., & Thornton, K.M.

(1990). Explanatory style as a mechanism of disappointing athletic performance. *Psychological Science, 1,* 143–146.

Seligman, M.E.P., and Schulman, P. (1986). Explanatory style as a predictor of productivity and quitting among life insurance sales agents. *Journal of Personality and Social Psychology, 50,* 832–838.

Silver, R.L., Boon, C., & Stones, M. (1983). Searching for meaning in misfortune: Making sense of incest. *Journal of Social Issues, 39*(2), 83–103.

Stanton, A.L., & Snider, P.R. (1993). Coping with a breast cancer diagnosis: A prospective study. *Health Psychology, 12,* 16–23.

Suedfeld, P. (1985). APA Presidential addresses: The relation of integrative complexity to historical, professional, and personal factors. *Journal of Personality and Social Psychology, 49*(6), 1643–1651.

Suedfeld, P., & Bluck, S. (1993). Changes in integrative complexity accompanying significant life events: Historical evidence. *Journal of Personality and Social Psychology, 64*(1), 124–130.

Suedfeld, P., Corteen, R.S., & McCormick, C. (1986). The role of integrative complexity in military leadership: Robert E. Lee and his opponents. *Journal of Applied Social Psychology, 16,* 498–507.

Suedfeld, P., & Rank, A.D. (1976). Revolutionary leaders: Long term success as a function of changes in integrative complexity. *Journal of Personality and Social Psychology, 34,* 169–178.

Suedfeld, P., & Tetlock, P.E. (1977). Integrative complexity of communications in international crises. *Journal of Conflict Resolution, 21,* 168–178.

Suedfeld, P., Tetlock, P.E., & Ramirez, C. (1977). War, peace, and integrative complexity. *Journal of Conflict Resolution, 21,* 427–42.

Suedfeld, P., Tetlock, P.E., & Streufert, S. (1992). Conceptual/integrative complexity. In C.P. Smith (Ed.), *Motivation and personality: Handbook of thematic content analysis* (pp. 393–400). Cambridge: Cambridge University Press.

Sweeney, P.D., Anderson, K., & Bailey, S. (1986). Attributional style in depression: A meta-analytic review. *Journal of Personality and Social Psychology, 50,* 974–991.

Tennen, H., & Affleck, G. (1987). The costs and benefits of optimistic explanations and dispositional optimism. *Journal of Personality, 55*(2), 377–393.

Tennen, H., & Herzberger, S. (1985). Attributional style questionnaire. In D.J. Keyser, & R.C. Sweetland, (Eds.), *Test critiques* (Vol. 4, pp. 20–30). Kansas City: Test Corporation of America.

Tetlock, P.E. & Boettger, R. (1989). Cognitive and rhetorical styles of traditionalist and reformist Soviet politicians: A content analysis study. *Political Psychology, 10*(2), 209–232.

Tetlock, P.E. & Manstead, A.S.R. (1985). Impression management versus intrapsychic explanations in social psychology: A useful dichotomy? *Psychological Review, 92,* 59–77.

Vaillant, G.E. (1977). *Adaptation to life.* Boston: Little, Brown, and Company.

Vaillant, G.E. (1993). *The wisdom of the ego.* Cambridge, MA: Harvard University Press.

Wallace, M.D., Suedfeld, P., & Thachuk, K. (1993). Political rhetoric of leaders under stress in the Gulf Crisis. *Journal of Conflict Resolution, 37*(1), 94–107.

Weiner, B. (Ed.). (1974). *Achievement motivation and attribution theory.* Morristown, NJ: General Learning Press.

Weiner, B. (1985). An attributional theory of achievement motivation and emotion. *Psychological Review, 92*(4), 548–573.

Wortman, C.B. (1976). Causal attributions and personal control. In J.H. Harvey, W.J. Ickes, and R.F. Kidd (Eds.), *New directions in attributions research* (Vol. 1). Hillsdale, NJ: Lawrence Erlbaum.

Zullow, H.M. (1984). The interaction of rumination and explanatory style in depression. Unpublished master's thesis, University of Pennsylvania, Philadelphia.

Zullow, H.M. (1985). Manual for scoring negative state orientation. Unpublished manuscript, University of Pennsylvania, Philadelphia.

Zullow, H.M. (1991). Pessimistic rumination in popular songs and newsmagazines predicts economic recession via decreased consumer optimism and spending. *Journal of Economic Psychology, 12,* 501–526.

Zullow, H.M. (1995). Pessimistic rumination in American politics and society. In G.M. Buchanan & M.E.P. Seligman (Eds.), *Explanatory style* (pp. 187–208). Hillsdale, NJ: Lawrence Erlbaum.

Zullow, H.M., Oettingen, G., Peterson, C., & Seligman, M.E.P. (1988). Pessimistic explanatory style in the historical record. *American Psychologist, 43,* 673–682.

Zullow, H.M., & Seligman, M.E.P. (1990). Pessimistic rumination predicts defeat of presidential candidates, 1900 to 1984. *Psychological Inquiry, 1,* 52–61.

ACKNOWLEDGMENTS

The author would like to acknowledge the support of the John Templeton Foundation in the creation of this volume. Special acknowledgment goes to Martin E. P. Seligman for his personal and intellectual guidance in many of the studies presented in this chapter.

✦ CHAPTER 22 ✦

Comments: Optimism and the Laws of Life, History, and Culture

Christopher Peterson and Michael P. Bishop

JASON SATTERFIELD's work is interesting and important, but it had its beginning in science fiction, specifically in the fictional exploits of psychohistorian Hari Seldon, the hero of the *Foundation* trilogy (Asimov, 1983a, b, c). In a way, Satterfield has done Hari Seldon one step better. One of Seldon's cardinal principles was that social scientists could predict the behavior of collectivities but not the behavior of individuals. Because Satterfield has indeed predicted the behavior of individuals, the reality proves more intriguing than the science fiction.

When Peterson and Seligman (1984) first described the content analysis procedure used so profitably by Satterfield, it was referred to as Seldonics, after Hari Seldon. This label never caught on, which is just as well because it sounds like the science of antihistamines.

It should be emphasized, though, that the content analysis procedure had a beginning, and it was born of necessity. Peterson had gone to graduate school to be trained as an experimental social psychologist. Then he took his first job at a school that had only six hundred students enrolled and no introductory psychology subject pool. He was at a complete loss. How could he do research without "subjects"? He complained to one of his sociologist friends, who asked, "What's a subject?" Peterson explained that a subject is an 18-year-old college student who is required to participate in psychology studies.

The sociologist then asked Peterson what he wanted to study with these unavailable subjects, and he was told causal explanations, that is, how people offer accounts of events that befall them. Then the sociologist asked why Peterson needed a subject pool, given that most college students were better at excuses than explanations? When Peterson had no response, the sociologist went on to say, "The only thing you like to do is to read about sports, so go off and read the sports pages, and study whatever causal accounts you find there." And that is what Peterson did, and he content analyzed statements by basketball greats like George Gervin and Julius Erving (Peterson, 1980).

When Peterson brought this technique with him to Pennsylvania, Seligman and he started to apply it to therapy transcripts, and the results became more and more interesting. Satterfield's work has applied the technique—now dubbed the CAVE procedure (Content Analysis of Verbatim Explanations; Peterson, Schulman, Castellon, & Seligman, 1992)—to historical figures, which in turn has led Peterson and Bishop to study the causal attributions of famous generals who went head-to-head in battle with one another. Our guiding question was whether the more optimistic generals triumphed.

This work is ongoing, but let us describe some of the results concerning two of the most storied protagonists in military history: Ulysses S. Grant (1822–1885) and Robert E. Lee (1807–1870). The contrasts between these two Civil War foes are often told; they are stark and provocative. Grant was an uncouth and largely undistinguished individual, whereas Lee was cultured, brave, and respected even by his enemies. How could Grant have triumphed in the first example of modern warfare, a brutal war of attrition that gradually depleted Lee's resources until surrender at Appomattox was inevitable?

As it turns out, Grant was more optimistic. We demonstrated this difference by reading the personal memoirs, letters, and diaries of Grant (1894) and Lee (1896), locating bad events and associated causal attributions. Using the CAVE technique, we extracted six of these for each general and presented them in a random order to six blind and independent raters who scored them with 7-point scales along the dimensions of internality, stability, and globality. Examples are shown in table 23.1.

Table 23.1

Bad Events and Attributed Causes

Ulysses S. Grant

Event: The Wilmington expedition was a failure.

Cause: Delays and free talk of the object of the expedition enabled the enemy to move troops.

Event: The pontoon bridge which was to have been sent by rail to Franklin . . . had gone to Chattanooga.

Cause: Through a mistake of the wording of the order or otherwise.

Robert E. Lee

Event: The army was forced to retire from fighting.

Cause: The usual casualties of battles have diminished its ranks . . . [and] . . . its numbers have been greatly decreased by desertion and straggling.

Event: Many opportunities have been lost and hundreds of valuable lives uselessly sacrificed.

Cause: Because of a lack of strict discipline in the ranks.

Raters were told only that these statements were made by military leaders. Indeed, event-attribution units from Grant and Lee were embedded among those from several other generals we were studying. Our raters complained that more context would have been helpful to them as they completed their task, but their ratings nonetheless were reliable. We collapsed the ratings across raters, separately for internality, stability, and globality, and then we formed separate composite scores for Grant and Lee. Internality scores did not differ, but Grant's attributions were less stable than those of Lee and also less global.

We should not reduce the incredible complexity of the War between the States to the relative optimism and pessimism of the generals involved; however, these results still provide some food for thought.

Historians have frequently commented that Grant, if nothing else, was doggedly determined and patient, willing to suffer great losses in order to achieve greater gains. These descriptions are consistent with our characterization of Grant as optimistic and resilient. In contrast, historians have just as frequently commented on Lee's quiet dignity and demeanor in the wake of defeat; perhaps he accepted his losses too gracefully.

Let us close with mention of a few studies that we have done using content analysis that yielded absolutely nothing in terms of causal attributions, but importantly remind us that optimism and pessimism are not always rendered in terms of explanatory style. The CAVE technique is frequently used to analyze essays that people have written about bad occurrences in their lives. Causal explanations are identified and rated by judges as relatively optimistic versus pessimistic. These scores invariably relate to some other variable of interest.

There have been two collections of such essays that simply did not work out. One was a set of open-ended responses to questionnaires obtained by Jennifer Bryce, who was among the last Americans teaching at the American University of Beirut (Lebanon) right before all Americans had to leave. She had studied women living in the war zone. Her investigation was sponsored by UNICEF and was concerned with small children (Bryce, 1986). Perhaps surprisingly, all of these women were healthy and happy, and their children were healthy and happy as well. Such resilience in the midst of chaos seemed almost inexplicable. We wondered if these women employed optimistic explanatory styles that buffered them and their children against the events of war.

The women had provided their questionnaire responses in Arabic, which had then been translated into English. We read the translations, and we re-read them, and we re-read them yet again, and we could not find a single causal explanation for anything by anyone. Finally, we asked Bryce about a word that had not been translated—*Inshallah*—which showed up in virtually every sentence.

It means "God willing." Life is good, God willing. Life will be good, God willing. Here was a group of people who were optimistic, not because they circumscribed the attributed causes of bad events, but because they believed in God and in God's benevolence. This sort of optimism has nothing to do with explanatory style as we typically conceive it, but this belief is obviously a beneficial form of optimism. It should remind those of us in the explanatory style research tradition that there are different routes to optimism and the resilience that it can confer. The benefits of optimism may be a universal principle, but it is phrased differently depending on the jurisdiction.

The other set of responses in which we again could find no causal attributions came from the Federal Writers Project (Yetman, 1970). In the 1930s, when our country was in the Great Depression, not the DSM-4 major depression, but the economic depression, the federal government was trying to put unemployed people to work doing what they did best. The government officials had good ideas for what most unemployed people could do, but they did not know what to do with unemployed newspaper writers. What could journalists do if there were no newspaper to employ them? The answer was, of course, that they could talk to people and write about their conversations. So, the federal government sent dozens of journalists down south to interview two thousand African Americans who at that point were in their eighties or nineties or even older. All had lived as the last generation of slaves. What the journalists produced from their conversations with these individuals was a stunning set of first-person narratives about what it meant to live as a American slave. It is sobering reading even today.

Here were elderly people who were obviously healthy and had survived a way of life about which many of us today do not even want to think. Did they have an optimistic explanatory style? No, they had no explanatory style at all. Their descriptions of events were phrased not in terms of causes but rather in terms of—how else to say it?—the people who had owned them. Their accounts about their owners were detailed and articulate. Their descriptions were not benign, but they were rich, and we speculate that this richness was critical to their survival. They knew a great deal about what their situations did and did not afford.

If one is in a situation where one cannot exert literal control, at least one can exert what theorists call interpretive control (Rothbaum, Weisz, & Snyder, 1982). One makes sense of the situation and tries to understand whatever—people in this case—is in control. We can look at this sense-making as a form of optimism; certainly, its opposite entails giving up.

In sum, our content analysis technique makes it possible to study human beings across time, across place, and across cultures (Lee & Peterson, 1997). We think that is very exciting, and it seemed to start from Peterson's fondness for the sports pages. What is that old saying—the front pages of newspapers describe our tragedies, whereas the sports pages recount our triumphs? It seems fitting that Peterson's fascination with George Gervin and Julius Erving led in a small way to a method for studying what is best and most positive about the human condition.

REFERENCES

Asimov, I. (1983a). *Foundation.* New York: Ballantine.

Asimov, I. (1983b). *Foundation and empire.* New York: Ballantine.

Asimov, I. (1983c). *Second foundation.* New York: Ballantine.

Bryce, J.W. (1986). *Cries of children in Lebanon as voiced by their mothers.* Beirut: Express International.

Grant, U.S. (1894). *Personal memoirs.* New York: Charles L. Webster & Co.

Lee, F., & Peterson, C. (1997). Content analysis of archival data. *Journal of Consulting and Clinical Psychology, 65,* 959–969.

Lee, R.E. (1886). *Memoirs of Robert E. Lee, his military and personal history* (A.L. Lang, Ed.). London: Sampson, Law, Marston, Searle, & Rivington.

Peterson, C. (1980). Attribution in the sports pages: An archival investigation of the covariation hypothesis. *Social Psychology Quarterly, 43,* 136–140.

Peterson, C., Schulman, P., Castellon, C., & Seligman, M.E.P. (1992). CAVE: Content analysis of verbatim explanations. In C.P. Smith (Ed.), *Motivation and personality: Handbook of thematic content analysis* (pp. 383–392). New York: Cambridge University Press.

Peterson, C., & Seligman, M.E.P. (1984). Causal explanations as a risk factor for depression: Theory and evidence. *Psychological Review, 91,* 347–374.

Rothbaum, F., Weisz, J.R., & Snyder, S.S. (1982). Changing the world and changing the self: A two-process model of perceived control. *Journal of Personality and Social Psychology, 42,* 5–37.

Yetman, N.R. (1970). *Voices from slavery.* New York: Holt, Rinehart, & Winston.

✦ CHAPTER 23 ✦

The Contribution of Flow to Positive Psychology

Mihaly Csikszentmihalyi

IN CONTRAST to most other contributors to this volume, I can't claim the good fortune of having known Marty for a long time. We met for the first time only about three years ago. Of course, I had known his work as one of the beacons of good sense and excitement in psychology for a long time. As with many of the other contributors, in my own academic career I have also confronted with trepidation the rather narrow and pessimistic perspective of mainline psychology. Several times as a graduate student I had also entertained the notion of leaving the discipline for other fields, because the promise that psychology had offered was not being delivered. Instead of working out ways to improve the quality of life, the profession seemed bent on offering tired palliatives for maintaining the status quo.

I ceased to trust the status quo when I was only 10 years old, and I witnessed the dissolution of European culture during World War II. Moving with my parents from Hungary to Italy in an effort to avoid being caught in the front lines, I remember very clearly how struck I was by the realization that none of the adults around me knew what was happening, and the sense of amazement upon realizing that instead of having all the answers, adults had no idea as to what was going on. I also realized that most men and women who before the war had lots of money, and power, and education quickly deteriorated into helpless and hopeless individuals once they lost these external supports. And yet among all this debacle I noticed also that there were a few individuals who seemed to have been able to keep their heads and to function with optimism and hope. It is to these tragic experiences at the end of WWII that I trace my interest in understanding the strength that makes people able to keep their integrity when everything else is falling to pieces around them.

After many false starts, I turned to psychology to find out about human strengths. But during the late '50s and '60s there was very little knowledge available about what makes people able to lead happy lives in the face of adversity. Abraham Maslow and other humanistic psychologists were beginning to raise these issues, but their insights never developed into a systematic field of investigation.

Now thanks to Seligman and those who have been influenced by him this situation might change. It seems to me we have a lot to learn from the positive extreme of the distribution of mental states. Psychology has always looked at the pathological end of the distribution to understand the middle ground of normal behavior. We rarely look at the other end, where creativity and optimal functioning can illuminate the great middle regions of the bell curve.

In my own career, I decided to study people who appeared to like how they had chosen to live, who seemed to like what they were doing. People who were motivated by the very activities they did without much concern for rewards that they might get later on. I started interviewing musicians, chess players, rock climbers, artists, people who spent a lot of time and effort doing things for the sheer joy of it, and not for the usual rewards of everyday life, like a paycheck or a promotion. I thought that from such people I might be able to learn something useful about the positive end of the distribution of human experience.

This research started over thirty years ago, and at this point it has expanded quite widely. More than eight thousand interviews and a quarter of a million questionnaire responses have been collected by researchers around the world, from a great variety of different cultures and populations. (Csikszentmihalyi, 1975, 1997). One result that I didn't expect when I started these studies, but that soon became obvious, is that whenever people are doing something that they enjoy, something that they want to do, they keep doing it because of the experience they get from the activity. And despite the great variety of activities—

from chess to mountain climbing—the phenomenological state they report is very similar. The experience of enjoyment is described essentially in the same terms by mountaineers in Thai villages, by farmers in Somalia, by Navajo shepherds, and by industrial workers in Japan, Europe, and the United States. (Csikszentmihalyi & Csikszentmihalyi, 1988; Inghilleri, 1995). The results suggested that there is a universal mental state that cuts across cultural, gender, and age differences; it is a positive experiential state that our nervous system has been tuned in to appreciate, probably through evolutionary selection, and that we try to repeat whenever possible.

I have called this state the "flow" experience simply because people describe their thoughts and actions when they are in that context as spontaneous and effortless, even though what they are doing is often difficult and risky. But at the time it feels as natural as being carried by the flow of a river, a process which does not require effort or control. Let me briefly review the characteristics of this experience, the common conditions which seem to make it happen, and then consider how this relates to Sir John Templeton's *Laws of Life.*

First of all, the most universal trait of flow experiences is the sense of concentration, a complete immersion in what one is doing. Many people describe it as a merging of action and awareness—one does get so involved in the chess game, or the climb, or the music one plays, that action follows action seemingly without the conscious intervention of an agentic self. A corollary effect of this deep concentration is that we tend to forget the worries and concerns that take up our attention in ordinary life. All of one's mental resources are taken up by the task at hand. As one climber said, "It's as if your memory was cut off beyond thirty seconds in the past, and as if you can't imagine anything happening beyond five minutes in the future." This very narrow window of awareness is essential for maintaining the focus of concentration.

Another element of the phenomenology of flow is the sense of control. As Eckstein points out in this volume, control is an interesting phenomenon with a contradictory element in it. People in flow report a tremendous feeling of control, but actually this consists in not thinking about the possibility of losing control. Even though the possibility of failure or mistakes is always present, one is too busy to worry about it. Paradoxically, one is in control by giving up trying to be (Csikszentmihalyi & Larson, 1984).

A related feature is that in flow one forgets oneself. In our studies we find that in everyday life one of the worst contingencies occurs when a person is thinking about him- or herself. For reasons that are not entirely clear, when we think about ourselves the content of the thoughts is usually negative, in turn producing negative emotions (Csikszentmihalyi & Figurski, 1982). Our moods invariably deteriorate when we start worrying about our shortcomings, about what others think of us, whether we are dressed right, whether we are smart enough, or good-looking enough. These constant critical reflections on the ego disappear in a flow experience. We don't worry about how we look, about what others think about us. We are too focused on doing what needs to be done to worry about such things.

Another corollary of forgetting oneself is the feeling of transcendence that many people report as a result of experiencing flow. The climber feels at one with the rock, the wind, and the weather; the musicians feel that the sounds they produce link them with the "harmony of the spheres"; the surgeon becomes part of the choreography of the operating theatre; the dancer gets lost in the dance. After an episode of flow there is a sense that we have moved beyond our limitations, and have actually become a part of some great force, a system or process larger and more powerful than the individual selves we were before.

Another important element is the distortion of the sense of time. People in flow usually experience time passing much faster than usual. My brother who is now in his eighties has always been fascinated by minerals. Even now he often takes a complex crystal out of its display case early in the morning, and starts looking at it under a microscope. After a while, looking up, he notices that the weather must have turned stormy, because the room is quite dark. It takes him a few more moments to realize that actually the darkness is due to the fact that it is already evening, and he has spent the entire day exploring the intricacies of a chunk of rock the size of a walnut.

When all these elements are present, people feel that what they do is autotelic. That is, the goal of the activity is simply to do it, and no other reason for doing it needs to be there.

What are the conditions that make such experiences possible? One thing that people report is clarity of goals. When we are involved in an activity that produces flow, usually we know, moment by moment, what needs to be done. If you are playing a musical instrument, you know what the next note, the next chord is supposed to be. If you are playing tennis, you know that in a few seconds you will have to hit the ball, and you know where it is supposed to go. The actual long range goals—finishing the musical piece, winning the game—are not really why one does these things. The ultimate goals are simply an excuse for the activity, a point of closure. But the momentary goals are essential, because they keep the action flowing.

Another condition is the immediacy of feedback. To keep focused concentration, one needs to know how well one is doing moment by moment. If you are playing tennis, you see where the ball went after you hit it; if you are playing music, you hear the sounds you made. It's not important to be right every time, but it's essential to know whether one did right or not.

Finally, in activities that produce flow one feels that what can be done and what one can do are in balance. In other words, there is a one-to-one ratio between challenges and personal skills. In our studies we measure the average level of challenges a person reports during a typical week, and the average level of skills the person reports (Csikszentmihalyi & Le Fevre, 1989; Hektner, 1996; Moneta & Csikszentmihalyi, 1996). When a person is above his or her mean level of both challenges and skills, the optimal condition of flow is usually reported. When only challenges are above the mean, the person tends to feel anxious. When only skills are above the mean, the typical condition is relaxation. When both challenges and skills are reported to be below the weekly average, the person tends to be in apathy.

There are basically two ways one can get into flow: Either the activity is so structured as to induce the experience, or the person is able to induce the experience regardless of external conditions. In the first case sports, games, music, and rituals are activities that provide clear goals, immediate feedback, and the opportunity to balance skills and challenges. Every culture we know about has developed a great number of such activities that have one major purpose: To make flow possible.

The other way to experience flow is by gaining control over one's consciousness, so that one can transform almost everything one does into a semblance of a flow activity. Then one can set clear goals, read feedback, balance challenges and skills even when working at a routine job, or playing with one's children. It is especially in this aspect that flow resembles the disciplines that various religions, East and West, have developed over time in an effort to emancipate consciousness from the deterministic influences of genetic programming and of cultural conformity (Csikszentmihalyi, 1993; Massimini & Delle Fave, 1991).

There are stable individual differences in the ability to experience flow. For instance, in a longitudinal study of 240 teenagers, we find that the amount of time spent in flow (i.e., in high challenge, high skill situations) at age 12 correlates .53 with the amount spent at age 14 and .30 with the amount of flow at age 17 ($p < .0001$). Furthermore, the amount of time spent in flow at age 12 is correlated with the amount of hope students express at age 17 (but only for boys is the correlation significant), whereas the amounts of time spent in anxiety and apathy are very significantly correlated with lack of hope, and with physical pain—all these correlations being highly significant; $p < .001$ (Patton, 1998).

The flow experience has important implications with regard to religion. One of the things that colleagues from around the world have pointed out to me is that the elements of flow—concentration, forgetting the self, transcendence, clarity of goals—are very similar to elements of spiritual practice in many of the world's religions (Crook, 1980; Eno, 1990; Sun, 1987). For example Hinduism, Buddhism, Taoism, Christianity, and Islam have developed many techniques that seem in part designed to make life as a whole more like a unified flow experience, achieved primarily through the control of consciousness.

In looking through Sir John Templeton's book on the laws of life, I was struck by how many of them have to do with suggestions about how to transform life as a whole into what I have been calling a flow experience. For instance, 16% of the first one hundred laws—the largest category—have to do with selflessness and altruism. For instance, one of the laws, based on Matthew's Gospel, says: "As you give, so shall you receive." The primary constituent of these laws is giving up the need for controlling others, of adopting an autotelic attitude towards one's actions.

And yet, an equal number—15%—deals with the importance of controlling consciousness, which is also a central feature of the flow experience. For instance, one of the laws in this cluster reads: "Your life becomes what you think." Again this is an ancient notion, going back at least to Marcus Aurelius and the stoics. The insight that reality is constituted by our consciousness is also a central tenet of most Eastern spiritual disciplines.

The next largest category are the laws that deal with setting goals; for instance, "Failing to plan is planning to fail." There is an equal number of precepts about feedback—for instance, that wisdom is born of mistakes, that one learns by confronting error. Important as it is to set goals, it is equally important to evaluate one's actions in terms of their consequences.

The next largest category, including 5% of the "laws," has to do with seeking challenges. For example, "Every ending is a new beginning." These point to the fact that in life what one tries to accomplish is never completed. There is an ancient Chinese curse that is relevant here: "May you reach all your goals." If you think you have exhausted your goals, there is no point in living any further.

Finally, in looking at the laws of life, the next major category has to do with perseverance. Nothing very valuable can be accomplished without it. Here too the relationship to flow is intriguing: When in our studies we examined the relationship between the frequency of reported flow to an inventory measuring twenty separate personality dimensions, the trait that correlated highest with frequency of flow was "perseverance" (Moneta, 1998). Presumably this trait is necessary for developing new skills so as to confront ever increasing challenges.

In the Preface to the *Laws of Life*, Sir John writes that he hopes his book will help people in all parts of the world to make their lives not only happier, but also more useful. What I would like to stress is that contributing to happiness is perhaps the most useful result of his laws. And the greatest gift that the positive psychology heralded by Marty

Seligman could leave humankind is to help transform life into a cosmic game, giving everyone the keys to a feeling of total involvement and enjoyment.

REFERENCES

Crook, J.H. (1980). *The evolution of human consciousness.* New York: Oxford University Press.

Csikszentmihalyi, M. (1975). *Beyond boredom and anxiety.* San Francisco: Jossey-Bass.

Csikszentmihalyi, M. (1993). *The evolving self: A psychology for the third millennium.* New York: Harper Collins.

Csikszentmihalyi, M. (1997). *Finding flow.* New York: Basic Books.

Csikszentmihalyi, M., & Csikszentmihalyi, I. S. (Eds.). (1988). *Optimal experience: Psychological studies of flow in consciousness.* New York: Cambridge University Press.

Csikszentmihalyi, M., & Larson, R. (1984). *Being adolescent.* New York: Basic Books.

Csikszentmihalyi, M., & Figurski, T. (1982). The experience of self-awareness in everyday life. *Journal of Personality, 50*(1), 14–26.

Csikszentmihalyi, M., & Le Fevre, J. (1989). Optimal experience in work and leisure. *Journal of Personality and Social Psychology, 56*(5), 815–822.

Csikszentmihalyi, M., & Rathunde, K. (1992). The measurement of flow in everyday life: Toward a theory of emergent motivation. In J. E. Jacobs (Ed.), *Nebraska Symposium on Motivation* (pp. 57–97). Lincoln, NE: University of Nebraska Press.

Eno, R. (1990). *The Confucian creation of heaven.* New York: State University of New York Press.

Hektner, J. M. (1996). Exploring optimal personality development: A longitudinal study of adolescents. Unpublished doctoral dissertation, University of Chicago.

Inghilleri, P. (1995). *Esperienza soggettiva, personalita, evoluzione culturale.* Turin, Italy: UTET. (Translated as: *From subjective experience to cultural change.* New York, Cambridge University Press, 1999).

Massimini, F., & Delle Fave, A. (1991). Religion and cultural evolution. *Zygon, 16*(1), 27–48.

Moneta, G. B. (1998). Personality correlates of flow. Paper presented at The European Conference on Research on Adolescence, Budapest, June.

Moneta, G. B., & Csikszentmihalyi, M. (1996). The effect of perceived challenges and skills on the quality of subjective experience. *Journal of Personality, 64*(2), 275–310.

Patton, J. D. (1998). Exploring the relative outcomes of interpersonal and intrapersonal forces of order and entropy in adolescence: A longitudinal study. Unpublished doctoral dissertation, University of Chicago.

Sun, W. (1987). Flow and Yu: Comparison of Csikszentmihalyi's theory and Chuang-tzu's philosophy. In *Anthropological Association for the Study of Play,* Montreal, Quebec.

Section D. Discussion of Part III

✦

✦ CHAPTER 24 ✦

Pitfalls on the Road to a Positive Psychology of Hope

Barry Schwartz

THE PHENOMENON of learned helplessness may well be the most significant and most pervasively influential psychological discovery in the last thirty-five years. Learned helplessness is extremely important in its own right, but in addition, its impact has extended across a wide variety of different domains of psychological research. It has contributed to changing the way people think about basic learning processes. It has influenced the way people think about motivation. It has affected the way people think about child development. It has altered the way people think about education. It has affected the way people think about the relation between mind, brain, and behavior. It has influenced the way people think about personality. It has had a major impact on the way people think about attribution processes, the turf of social psychology. It has influenced the way people think about work. It has affected the way people think about aging. And of course, it has transformed the way people think about the causes and treatments of psychopathology, most especially, of depression.

And now it may have its biggest influence yet. For much of its history, psychology has been concerned with identifying human weakness and correcting or ameliorating it. Now, learned helplessness, in the guise of its complement, "learned optimism," may help to shape a positive psychology—a psychology that perhaps will someday illuminate what a human life at its best can be and show us how we can help people make their lives good lives.

Taken together, the contributions to the present volume provide an impressive blueprint for the beginnings of a positive psychology—a psychology of hope. As each of the specific research areas sketched in this volume continues to develop, psychology will be able to tell us more and more about how to nurture strong and resilient people. And yet, the contributions to this volume also provide hints about difficult questions that will have to be faced and addressed if a positive psychology is to evolve. I think it is important for people to be thinking about these questions while the psychology of hope is still in its infancy. Thus, in this general commentary on the prospects for a future "psychology of hope," I will enumerate the issues I think all contributors to that psychology should be addressing.

THE "DEPRESSION EPIDEMIC": IS PSYCHOLOGY PART OF THE SOLUTION OR PART OF THE PROBLEM?

Learned helplessness has taught us about the importance of control and autonomy to mental health. In particular, helplessness has taught us that a lack of control, coupled with a certain characteristic style of causal explanation, creates candidates for clinical depression. Given that having control over important things in one's life is important to preventing clinical depression, we can ask ourselves what we might expect the incidence of depression to be like in modern American society.

Most of us now live in a world in which we experience control to a degree that people living in other times and places would think quite unimaginable. Extraordinary material wealth enables us to consume an astonishing quantity and variety of goods. And the magical mechanism of the market allows us an almost limitless array of choices: milk with or without lactose and with whatever percentage of fat one wants; jeans of every conceivable cut; restaurants serving foods from all over the world; cars of almost an infinite variety of shapes, sizes, colors, and prices. On and on it goes: if you want something, no matter how odd it is, chances are there is someone, somewhere, ready to sell it to you.

With regard to higher education, curricular requirements have almost vanished, and to the extent they still exist, they can be satisfied in so many different ways that they might as well not be there.

With regard to entertainment and culture, the range of what is available is staggering. Cultural invention has enormously expanded the variety of options, and advances in media technology have made most of these options accessible, in one way or another, to almost everybody.

With regard to careers, there is an enormous degree of mobility, both in career-type and in geographical location. People are not constrained to do the work their parents did, in the place in which their parents did it. Nor are people constrained to have only a single occupation for their entire working lives. And for the most part, success and advancement in work are based on talent and achievement. So almost anything is possible.

With regard to personal life, religious, ethnic, racial, class, geographic, and even gender barriers to mate selection are rapidly disappearing. Moreover, one is free to choose whether to have children or not, whether to have them early or late, whether to bear them or adopt them, whether to have them as part of a traditional marriage and family or as part of any of a host of non-traditional family arrangements. And it is remarkably easy to get out of marriages that have turned sour, and having done that, to arrange child custody in ways that suit the involved parties.

In sum, I think it is only a slight exaggeration to say that for the first time in human history, large numbers of people can live exactly the kind of lives they want, unconstrained by material, economic, or cultural limitations. Based on this fact, coupled with the helplessness theory of depression, one might expect clinical depression in the United States to be going the way of polio. With so many opportunities for control available, why would anyone become depressed?

Instead, what we find is an explosive *growth* of depression (e.g., Klerman, et al., 1985; Robins, et al., 1984). Some estimates are that depression is ten times as likely to afflict someone now than at the turn of the century. This result demands explanation and two explanations come readily to mind. The first is that the helplessness theory of depression is wrong; that there is no relation between control and depression. The second is that despite appearances to the contrary, people don't really *have* more control over their lives than they once did.

I think both of these explanations are mistaken. I'm quite convinced by the literature that there is a strong relation between lack of control and depression. And I find it hard to imagine the possibility that people had more control in pre-technological, culturally rigid times than they do now. So in my view, we have a puzzle. It is this puzzle that led to the question at the heading of this section: Is psychology part of the solution or is it part of the problem?

The correct answer to this question, I believe, is yes. That psychology is part of the solution is obvious; our understanding of depression allows us to help alleviate human misery far more effectively than ever before. Thus, I will dwell on the respects in which psychology is part of the problem. Here, I think three distinct forces are at work:

1. *Increases in experienced control over the years have been accompanied, stride-for-stride, by increases in expectations about control.* The more we are allowed to be the masters of our fates in one domain of life after another, the more we expect to be. Education is expected to be stimulating *and* useful. Work is supposed to be exciting, socially valuable, *and* remunerative. Spouses are supposed to be sexually, emotionally, and intellectually stimulating and also loyal and comforting. Friends are supposed to be fun to be with *and* devoted. Children are supposed to be beautiful, smart, affectionate, obedient, *and* independent. And everything we buy is supposed to be the best of its kind; with all the choice available, people should never have to settle for things that are just "good enough." In short, life is supposed to be perfect. Psychology has, I believe, contributed to these unrealistic expectations via its cultivation of a kind of cult of psychotherapy intended not to relieve suffering but to engender "self-actualization"—satisfaction in all things. And a future "positive psychology" may subvert itself by feeding into these expectations.

2. *American culture has become more individualistic than it ever was before.* What this means, I think, is that not only do people expect perfection in all things, but they expect to produce this perfection themselves. When they (inevitably) fail, I believe that the culture of individualism biases them toward making causal attributions that focus on internal rather than external causal factors. That is, I believe that the culture has established a kind of officially acceptable style of causal explanation, and

it is one that focuses on the individual. As Seligman's research has led the way in demonstrating (e.g., Peterson & Seligman, 1984), this kind of causal attribution is just the kind to promote depression when people are faced with failure. And if my first point is correct, despite their increased control, people will be faced inevitably with many occasions that, by their own lights, count as failure. Psychology has contributed significantly to this excessive focus on the individual with its emphasis on personal growth and autonomy, and on "looking out for number one."

3. *Finally, the emphasis on the individual to which psychology has contributed may well be undermining what may be a crucial vaccine against depression: deep commitment and belonging to social groups and institutions—families, civic institutions, and faith communities*, as several contributors to this volume (e.g., Fincham, Garber, Myers, Miller, Nolen-Hoeksema) have suggested. There is an inherent tension between doing one's own thing, or being one's own person, and meaningful involvement in social groups. Doing the latter right requires submerging "one's own thing." So the more people focus on themselves—with respect both to goals and to the means of achieving those goals—the more their connections to others will be weakened. Political scientist Robert Putnam has recently attracted a great deal of attention to this deterioration of social connection in modern America (e.g., 1993, 1995, 1996). And in this connection it is relevant to note a study by Egeland and Hostetter (1983), which showed an incidence of depression among the Amish of Lancaster County, Pennsylvania, that was about half the national rate while other forms of psychopathology were much closer to national averages. The Amish, of course, are an extremely cohesive, tightly knit, traditional community.

It goes without saying that psychology is not solely, or even principally, responsible for these trends. It is clearly reasonable for people to place increasing reliance on themselves as the various social and public institutions they once could count on for support (for a social as well as an economic "safety net") stop serving that function. And we all know for the last twenty years or so it has been official government policy, at all levels, to allow that safety net to fray. Nevertheless, psychology has done plenty to exacerbate these trends and nothing to ameliorate them. A future psychology of hope must grapple with these issues. An effort to cultivate optimism of the wrong kind—optimism that does not take the three points I just raised into account, may well make the problem worse rather than better.

COGNITION AND HOPE: HAPPIER OR WISER?

Much of the focus in the helplessness theory of depression is on cognition. From this perspective, depression largely *is* a cognitive disorder. People think about success and failure, and about their role in it, in a way that is harmful. If we can change the way people explain their successes and failures to themselves, we can break up or (as Chapter 11, the Shatté, Gillham, & Reivich contribution to this volume, suggests) prevent depression. And to shift the emphasis from negative to positive, if depression represents the wrong way to think about success and failure, then getting people to think about success and failure in the right way should engender optimism and hope.

Armed with the view that depression results from disordered cognition, people who want to treat or prevent it would develop techniques designed to order cognition. But what do the words "disordered" and "ordered" mean? At first blush, one would assume that "disordered" means distorted—that the task faced by clinicians and educators is to get people to see the world accurately.

Alas, this assumption is wrong; things are not this way. In 1979, Alloy and Abramson published a landmark study that showed that under some significant circumstances, depressed people judge their ability to control the world more accurately than do non-depressed people. This phenomenon has come to be known as "depressive realism," or as "optimistic bias." I had always been troubled by this finding, not because I doubted its validity, but because it raised for me a very serious ethical dilemma: Should we be aspiring to develop techniques that get people to see things as they are, or should we be aspiring to get people to see things in a way that is good for them? Are we after truth or happiness in the people with whom we work?

In a context in which this ethical dilemma arises in connection with treating depression—with efforts to alleviate significant pain and suffering—it seems to me to be only a minor nag in the back of one's mind. People come to therapy in real misery, and by teaching them habits of optimistic (if inaccurate) thinking, one can alleviate that misery. Therapeutic drugs have side effects, but we learn to live with them because the therapeutic effects far outweigh the side effects. So too, perhaps, with non-drug therapies. We should be able to live with optimistic bias as a side effect of cognitive treatments of depression because their therapeutic effects are so beneficial.

Unfortunately, this minor nag grows much larger when we shift the context from negative to positive—from alleviating suffering in the depressed to inculcating optimism and hope in everyone. Now it seems we are talking about putting these "drugs," with their "side effects" into the water supply. Now, the temptation will be all around us even in dealing with perfectly healthy people to induce them to color or distort their cognitions just a little bit because such distortion is "good" for them.

We see in the Shatté, Gillham, and Reivich discussion of the Penn Optimism Project (POP) that what we might call the "advance guard" of a positive psychology is concerned with engendering accuracy rather than foolish optimism in middle-school children. But if it should turn out that illusions of control or optimistic bias work just as well, or even better, than accuracy, how long will it be before the insistence on maintaining the accuracy of cognition slides away because there is a very effective distortion that protects kids against depression?

And the opportunities to nurture such distortions are legion. Here are a few examples:

1. Carol Dweck (see Dweck & Leggett, 1988) has shown that children can be divided into those with a helpless orientation and those with a mastery orientation, that these orientations in turn stem from "entity" (intelligence is a fixed entity that can not be increased through one's individual efforts) or "incremental" (people can get smarter) theories of intelligence, and that children with a mastery orientation (and an incremental theory of intelligence) do better when faced with school challenges than those with a helpless orientation. Suppose that as empirical

research proceeds on the vexed question of the nature of intelligence it turns out that intelligence actually *is* a fixed entity (this is the claim of Herrnstein & Murray, 1994, and while I do not believe it is correct [see Schwartz, 1997], it certainly *could* be). What role are we supposed to play in creating a positive psychology of hope when the facts as we know them are not positive?

2. Related to the work reported by Satterfield in this volume, Zullow and Seligman (1990; see also Zullow, Oettingen, Peterson, & Seligman, 1988) have shown that politicians whose speeches tend to be optimistic are more likely to win elections than politicians whose speeches are pessimistic. When I first read this work, it sent chills down my spine. It made me think of a quote from a very popular disc jockey who said, when asked to explain his popularity, "The secret of success in this business is sincerity; if you can fake that, you've got it made." To say that we currently have a credibility problem with political leaders is an understatement. But if it were widely known that the way to impress the electorate is to sound optimistic, then we could count on the credibility problem getting a good deal worse, as politicians, no matter what they actually thought, gave speeches that were full of optimism.

3. Suppose it were to turn out that women who accepted some responsibility for being sexually assaulted ("I flirted," or "I was out walking alone late at night") showed a better prognosis for recovery from the psychological consequences of the assault than women who did not accept responsibility, a perfectly plausible possibility since to accept responsibility is to acknowledge a degree of personal control that might prevent a similar assault in the future. Does a practitioner of the "psychology of hope" attempt to get such assault victims to assume responsibility whatever the truth of the matter might be?

4. Suppose that, as some of the contributions to this volume indicate (Nolen-Hoeksema, Myers, Miller), religious faith and commitment reduce dramatically the risk of depression. Does a practitioner of the positive psychology of hope encourage people to embrace a faith for instrumental, rather than metaphysical and spiritual reasons? What does such an "instrumental" view of faith do to faith in the long run?

5. Suppose it were to turn out, as I deeply suspect, that the only real predictor of the behavior of financial markets is people's expectations

about those markets, that such economic variables as inflation rates, interest rates, unemployment rates, trade balances, and the like all pale in importance when compared to people's optimism or pessimism about the economic future. As a psychology of hope develops, what role is psychology to play as it watches members of the financial community use that psychology to drive up market values and drum up commissions—until the bubble bursts? A dose of "realism" in this context might harm people both psychologically and financially.

Each of these examples points out a possible tension between truth and happiness that a future positive psychology will face. I don't want to be taken here to suggest that people working in this area are not mindful of this dilemma. What I do want to suggest is that while the dilemma is not especially significant when one is working to alleviate suffering, it will loom very large indeed when the focus shifts from repairing the negative to nurturing the positive. It would be good for the field to think this dilemma through before it grows in significance.

CHANGING COGNITION OR CHANGING THE WORLD

Another thing that is troubling to me about the helplessness/optimism-derived focus on changing cognition to promote a positive psychology is that it can foster a tendency to ignore or minimize attention to what people are actually experiencing in the world. It suggests that we can fix the world by fixing the way people think about it. What is troubling to me about this is that often people are miserable for very good reasons. And if we were able actually to develop a positive psychology of hope, then perhaps we would know how to make people happy without very good reasons. I would rather see us finding a way to make people happy for good reasons, but that would suggest an emphasis on things other than developing the most effective way to engender optimistic cognitive styles in people. That would suggest an emphasis on finding ways to change the world rather than changing the way people think about it. Since it is almost certainly easier to change the way people think about the world than it is to change the world, my concern here is that over time, a successful positive psychology will develop techniques that induce people to tolerate intolerable living conditions.

The contributions to this volume that struck me as especially relevant in this connection are Csikszentmihalyi's discussion of "flow" as it relates to human activities, and Fincham's discussion of marriage and the family. These papers address the two central features of human life—work and love. I certainly aspire to a world in which the majority of people can experience "flow"—a kind of timelessness that comes from intrinsic satisfaction—in their work lives. I think that there are two distinct ways in which this might be achieved. The first, and harder, way is to restructure the nature of work so that most people's jobs contain the characteristics that Csikszentmihalyi has identified as critical to flow. Deadeningly repetitive, unchallenging, and oversupervised jobs are not the sort of things to produce flow. The second, easier way is to change the way people think about their work, without changing the nature of the work itself. I fear that a successful positive psychology of hope will give us the tools to make people satisfied with work lives that should not satisfy them.

In connection with the family, and with marriage in particular, I have a similar kind of concern. Sociologist Arlie Hochschild has written an important book on the modern, two-career couple, *The Second Shift* (1989). The book includes a series of detailed case studies of harried, overworked, two-career couples. A significant source of tension in these marriages is what Hochschild calls "the economy of gratitude." The problem of the economy of gratitude is not the sharing of household responsibilities between wife and husband, but rather each one's interpretation of what he or she is doing. So, for example, the husband takes out the garbage four times a week instead of two, and thinks that for this he deserves some sort of distinguished service medal, and wonders why his wife isn't full of praise, affection, and gratitude for his sacrifices. Meanwhile, the wife is wondering why *all* her husband can see his way clear to do is take out the garbage, as if all household chores are her responsibility and whatever he does is a favor. So each partner is contributing to the household, and each partner thinks he or she is doing a lot, while the other thinks he or she is not doing nearly enough. The conflict, Hochschild argues, has more to do with mismatched perceptions or interpretations of actions than with the actions themselves.

This kind of marital conflict would seem to be just the sort of thing for which modification of cognition is made to order. But Hochschild also observes that "each marriage bears the footprints of economic and cultural trends which originate far outside marriage" (p. 11). Among the economic trends she has in mind are the decrease in real wages that has made it almost impossible for a single full-time wage to support a family, coupled with an attendant rise in the need for child-care services and flexible work schedules without nearly enough initiative, in either the public or the private sector, to meet this need. So by using a positive psychology to change the way people think about their marriages, we may paper over the need to change the actual detailed workings of these marriages.

My concern about changing cognitions rather than changing the world can be summarized as follows: when the world needs changing, we should change the world and not how people think about it.

LIBERAL INDIVIDUALISM AS THE MAIN OBSTACLE TO A POSITIVE PSYCHOLOGY

I want to conclude this commentary by indicating what I think may be the main obstacle ahead to developing a positive psychology of hope. In the short run, a positive psychology that follows the trail blazed by "learned optimism" can make a real contribution to human welfare. Teaching people adaptive ways to think about their efficacy in the world will almost certainly reduce the incidence of debilitating depression. Teaching people that they *do* control their destinies in important respects will almost certainly increase the energy with which they face life's challenges, and that in turn will almost certainly increase the chances that they can get the world to do for them what they want it to do. And this would be no small achievement.

The problem, I think, is that a richly developed positive psychology has to do more than teach people *how* to do things—it has to do more than teach people effective techniques for getting what they want out of life. It must also tell them something about *what* they should be trying to get. That is, it must be informed by a vision of what a good human life contains. Thus a positive psychology will have to be willing to tell people that, say, a good, meaningful, productive human life includes commitment to education, commitment to family and to other social groups, commitment to excellence in one's activities, commitment to virtues such as honesty, loyalty, courage, and justice in one's dealings with others, and so on.

The official "ideology" of modern America poses an enormous barrier to this kind of contentful positive psychology. The ideology of America is the ideology of liberalism—let people decide for themselves what is good. Modern liberal culture is extremely reluctant to tell people what to do. And social science has internalized that credo: don't be "judgmental"; help people get what they want, but don't tell them what they should be wanting. Some modern social theorists, like philosopher Alasdair MacIntyre (1981), have even argued that the nonjudgmental character of the culture has become so pervasive that we no longer have the cultural resources with which to speak intelligibly about "the good life," even if we want to. MacIntyre argues that the language of "virtue" must be supported by social practices that embody that language in order for virtue terms really to mean anything, and that modern society lacks those practices. The result is that even when people are willing to talk about virtues and "the good life," they spend most of their time talking past one another.

It is one thing to encounter people in extreme psychological pain and to tell them, gently, how to change the content of their lives so as to relieve that pain. Few people will object to psychologists who "impose" their values in this way to relieve suffering. But a positive psychology is a whole other story. A positive psychology will be indiscriminate in imposing its values; it will be putting its values in the community water supply, like fluoride. Is psychology prepared to be a science that promotes certain values instead of one that encourages "self-actualization"? And if it is, will modern, liberal society stand for it?

Notice how the very notion that psychology might articulate a vision of the good life contradicts the emphasis on freedom, autonomy, and choice that are so much a part of modern aspiration, and not coincidentally, so much a part of learned optimism, as we currently understand it.

To summarize this final concern of mine about a future positive psychology: Once, clinical psychologists had "patients." Over the years, as the discipline grew concerned that "patient" implied illness, which in turn implied a conception of "health," a conception of the goal of therapy that the field did not really have, "patients" became "clients." Doctors have patients. The patients come in sick, and the doctors make them well. Restoring and maintaining physical health and alleviating suffering is the goal of medicine. Lawyers, in contrast, have clients. Lawyers don't have goals for clients the way doctors have goals for patients. Rather, lawyers are there to help the client achieve his or her own goal. Clients define their goals in a way that patients do not. So in moving from "patients" to "clients," psychology moved from having the practitioner define the goal to having the recipient define the goal. What will we call the recipients of our services if and when a positive psychology comes to fruition? I don't think that either "patients" or "clients" does justice to the grand vision that informs these beginnings of a positive psychology. The right term, I think, is "students." Are we prepared to argue that it is future generations of psychologists of hope who should be society's teachers? I think that unless we are prepared to say yes to this question, and to develop arguments about the content of a good human life, the potential achievements of a future positive psychology will always be limited. And I also believe that the time to be thinking and talking about this very big and difficult issue is now, at the beginning, and not later, in the face of angry critics trying to put us in our place.

REFERENCES

Alloy, L.B., & Abramson, L.Y. (1979). Judgment of contingency in depressed and non-depressed students: Sadder but wiser. *Journal of Experimental Psychology: General, 108,* 441–485.

Dweck, C.S., & Leggett, E.L. (1988). A social-cognitive approach to motivation and personality. *Psychological Review, 95,* 256–273.

Egeland, J.A., & Hostetter, A.M. (1983). Amish study, 1: Affective disorders among the Amish, 1976–1980. *American Journal of Psychiatry, 140,* 56–61.

Herrnstein, R.J., & Murray, C. (1994). *The bell curve.* New York: Free Press.

Hochschild, A. (1989). *The second shift.* New York: Viking.

Klerman, G.L, Lavori, P.W., Rice, J., Reich, T., Endicott, J., Andreasen, N.C., Keller, M.B., & Hirschfeld, R.M.A. (1985). Birth cohort trends in rates of major depressive disorder among relatives of patients with affective disorder. *Archives of General Psychiatry, 42,* 689–693.

MacIntyre, A. (1981). *After virtue.* Notre Dame, IN: Notre Dame Press.

Peterson, C., & Seligman, M.E.P. (1984). Causal explanation as a risk factor in depression: Theory and evidence. *Psychological Review, 91,* 347–374.

Putnam, R.D. (1993). The prosperous community. *The American Prospect, 13,* 34–40.

Putnam, R.D. (1995). Bowling alone: America's declining social capital. *Journal of Democracy, 6,* 65–78.

Putnam, R.D. (1996). The strange disappearance of civic America. *The American Prospect, 24,* 34–48.

Robins, L.N., Helzer, J.E., Weissman, M.M., Orvaschel, H., Gruenberg, E., Burke, J.D., & Regier, D.A. (1984). Lifetime prevalence of specific psychiatric disorders in three sites. *Archives of General Psychiatry, 41,* 949–958.

Schwartz, B. (1997). Psychology, "idea technology," and ideology. *Psychological Science, 8,* 21–27.

Zullow, H.M., Oettingen, G. Peterson, C., & Seligman, M.E.P. (1988). Pessimistic explanatory style in the historical record: CAVE-ing LBJ, presidential candidates, and East versus West Berlin. *American Psychologist, 43,* 673–682.

Zullow, H.M., & Seligman, M.E.P. (1990). Pessimistic rumination predicts defeat of presidential candidates: 1900–1984. *Psychological Inquiry, 1,* 23–37.

Part IV

✦

Seligman Address

✦ CHAPTER 25 ✦

Positive Psychology

Martin E. P. Seligman

I AM FIRST going to discuss the notions of negative psychology and negative social science and contrast them to the notions of positive psychology and positive social science. Then I will ask the question, "Why has social science in my lifetime been negative and remedial?" I will then turn to a specific problem, which I think the notion of positive social science and positive psychology addresses: the remarkable epidemic of depression occurring among young people in the United States today. The epidemic is a paradox in a nation that should be grateful for the blessings that have fallen on it and that it is has created. But instead our young people are imbued with depression and pessimism and sadness. What could cause a situation like this? What could cause a nation—prosperous, at peace, with virtually no starvation, with the hands on the nuclear clock farther from midnight than ever before—to suffer such a wave of pessimism and depression in its young people? I am going to suggest that there are three causes. First, the balance between the I and the We is badly askew now. Second, we have become a nation of immediacy, a nation concerned with hedonics, a nation concerned with self-esteem. This has backfired and the self-esteem movement has helped to create youth with the lowest self-esteem in memory. Third, there is an ideology that has come to pervade America, an ideology of victimology, in which psychology and the social sciences are not only observers, but central participants.

Finally I am going to ask what can we do to remedy this malaise. I will share my vision of a positive social science, the vision of a science that measures and nurtures the best qualities of human life. This is the science that embodies what Sir John Templeton advocates in the *Worldwide Laws of Life.*

POSITIVE SOCIAL SCIENCE

How has it happened that the social sciences have come to view the human virtues—courage, altruism, honesty, faith, duty, responsibility, good cheer, perseverance—as derivative, as illusions, and as defensive, while the human weaknesses—greed, anxiety, lust, selfishness, fear, anger, depression—are viewed as authentic? Why aren't human strengths and human weaknesses symmetrical in their authenticity? Myers points out that the literature in psychology for the last 30 years has 46,000 papers about depression and only 400 papers about joy (Myers, see Chapter 18). How did a science of the negative become enthroned? Psychology, the science I know best, has, since World War II, looked at and documented the negative effects of isolation, trauma, abuse, physical illness, war, poverty, discrimination, early parental death, and divorce voluminously. Somehow it has managed to ignore the very common observation that these undesirable events often produce extraordinary growth, strength, and creativity. Social scientists look at authoritarianism, at religion, at faith, at childhood discipline and document the negative consequences of these human undertakings. How is it that social science has managed to overlook the enormous positive consequences of these human endeavors?

Another way of putting the problem is to ask how social science became a science of the "isms" of racism, of sexism, of age-ism. How have we come to attribute so much of what has gone wrong in this nation to these "isms"? Finally, how is it that the social science of today has a world view that excludes responsibility, decision-making, and free will, while viewing human beings as puppets of their race, class, and gender, as well as of "stimuli" in their environments?

Here is one possible explanation: when a culture faces military threat, poverty, social upheaval, a shortage of goods, it is very natural that the science and art and humanities that it underwrites will be concerned with damage and with defense. What it will do by way of intervention is an attempt to undo damage and defend against further damage.

Modern psychology has been preoccupied with the negative side of life. It has understood human functioning in a disease model. Its main mode of intervention has been the repair of damage. And theoretically, it has been until recently a victimology. Learning theory construed human beings as passive, as "responding" (if you think about the word "responding" it is really quite extraordinary) to external goads called "stimuli." Psychoanalysis saw people as consumed by unresolved conflicts from childhood, dictated by childhood trauma. Biological psychology saw people as acting from tissue needs, drives, and instincts. Social psychology saw people as helpless victims of oppressive cultural and economic forces. All high cultures are not like ours in this way. Athens of the fifth century B.C., Victorian England, and Florence of the fifteenth century, are interesting counterexamples. Athenian prosperity gave birth to philosophy and democracy. Victorian England, enriched by the bounty of empire, enshrined honor, duty, and valor. Fifteenth-century Florence's successful wool and banking industries made it the richest city/state on the peninsula. The Florentine leaders decided not to use their surplus to become the most powerful military force in Europe. Rather they decided to use their surplus to create beauty.

I want to suggest to you that the United States today stands in a similar world-historical moment. The United States can choose to continue its preoccupation with defense and with undoing damage and with being a victimology. But also it can choose to build a different kind of monument. I am not going to propose to you that we try to create an aesthetic monument. Rather I propose that we create a humane scientific monument: positive psychology. My vision of psychology and social science in the twenty-first century is that it will move from being muckraking and remedial to becoming a positive force for understanding and nurturing the highest qualities of personal life and civic life. I propose that psychology in the twenty-first century will become a science of human strength and of personal fulfillment. I propose that social science will become a science of civic virtue.

Negative psychology and negative social science have had their victories. There are fourteen mental illnesses now, which because of negative psychology are understandable and treatable both biologically and psychologically. And our concern with "isms"—racism, age-ism, sexism—has indeed helped to undo some of the injustices of the past. But in its preoccupation with the negative, social science now finds itself in almost total darkness about the qualities that most make life worth living. The qualities that make life most fulfilling, most enjoyable, and most productive on the individual side are not the objects of science. On the civic side the conditions that promote civility, progress, and stability within a society are not the objects of science. We do not have a science of personal strength, or of social responsibility, or of human virtue now, but I believe it is within our grasp.

Such a science is possible. This volume is a testimony to that. The major psychological theories, furthermore, have undergone a change. They are not all victimologies any longer. The investigation of strength and responsibility and resilience has underpinnings now. Dominant theories no longer view the individual as passive, but rather see human beings as decision makers with choices, with preferences, with responsibility, with free will, with the possibility of becoming masterful, efficacious, or in malignant circumstances, of becoming helpless. And best of all, negative social science and negative psychology developed methods that can be applied to the study of personal strength and to the study of civic virtue. The first method was ingenious and reliable measurement: measuring subjective negative states like depression, fear, anomie, aggression, and measuring the neurochemistry of hopelessness and helplessness (Maier & Watkins, see Chapter 2). The second method was the understanding of causality: experimentation to isolate the causes of untoward states and causal modeling to unravel the causal skein by observation and statistics. The third method was intervention and testing the effectiveness of intervention: social science pioneered ways of undoing negative states and verifying the active ingredients.

Psychology can use the same three methodological advances to measure, to understand the causal structure, and to build the personal strengths and civic virtues. Positive psychology does not have to be constructed from the ground up. It merely involves a change of focus from repairing what is worst in life to creating what is best.

THE EPIDEMIC OF DEPRESSION

I want to turn to the epidemic of depression. This epidemic is an astonishing paradox. The nation is at peace, the standard of living is enormously high, nuclear war is less of a threat, the age of the dictator may have come to an end. There are fewer soldiers dying on the battlefield today than at any time since the Boer War more than one hundred years ago. A lower percentage of children are dying of starvation in the world than in any time in human history. And yet in spite of this, by our measurements we have an unprecedented epidemic of depression, of pessimism, and of low self-esteem among our young people.

Starting about twenty years ago, the National Institute of Mental Health, concerned with the allocation of therapeutic resources, decided to measure how common each of the mental illnesses were. To do this, interviewers went door to door to more than ten thousand representative Americans and interviewed them in depth about their experience of psychological difficulties. The lifetime prevalence of depression across the century became known. Researchers expected that the lifetime prevalence of depression would look just like the lifetime prevalence of broken hips: that is the older people get, the more chances they have had to break a hip, and therefore lifetime prevalence should go up with age. Astonishingly, it was just the reverse. For example, for females born around the time of World War I, the lifetime prevalence of depression was about 1%. In other words, about 1% of your grandmothers experienced depression. For females born around World War II, the lifetime prevalence was about 3.5% even though they had less time to get depressed than the World War I cohort. For females born around the Korean War, the lifetime prevalence was about 7%. For females born during the Vietnam era, it seemed to be about 10% (Klerman et al., 1985; Robins et al., 1984).

The latest findings indicate that by the time our children graduate from high school in the United States today, their chances of having a major depressive episode are between 12% and 15% (Garrison et al., 1992; Lewinsohn, Rohde, Seeley, & Fischer, 1993). This is conservatively a ten-fold increase in the risk for depression in our children over this century (Reich et al., 1987).

How could there be an epidemic of depression in a nation like ours with the opportunities that our young people have before them? When I talk about depression, I am not just talking about mental suffering. Depression as you can see from this volume is linked to productivity, to the capacity for happiness, and to physical health. So the epidemic does not merely augur that we are going to have a bunch of whiners twenty years from now, but it also augurs that the very economic wellbeing of the nation will be threatened if the epidemic continues. This is an epidemic of considerable political and economic concern as well as a mental health concern.

Let me first say what the epidemic is not. First, it is not about bad events. By every statistic that we have, life is objectively better for our young people. All of our national statistics are going north, except for those regarding mental health, which are going south. Depression is not in lock step with the quality of external events. Compare the rates of depression in African Americans and Hispanics to the rates for white middle-class Americans. Blacks and Hispanics have between 60% and 80% of the depression of white middle-class people, but blacks and Hispanics have more bad events (Kessler et al., 1995). Depression is a marvelously psychological phenomenon: John Milton told us that a person can make a heaven of hell or a hell of heaven.

The epidemic is not an ecological phenomenon. It is not caused by the air we breathe or the water we drink, and the best control group to study this epidemic lives thirty miles down the road from my house: the Old Order Amish. If you compare the rate of mental illness in the Amish to that of the people in Philadelphia, you find the Amish have the same rate of manic depression—which I believe is a physical illness. But they have one-tenth the rate of unipolar depression (Egeland & Hostetter, 1983). Since the Amish breathe our air and drink our water and they actually provide a lot of our food, the epidemic is not ecological. The epidemic is not biological. Our chromosomes, our genes, and our hormones have not changed enough in this century to produce a ten to one increase in depression.

THREE POSSIBLE CAUSES OF THE EPIDEMIC OF DEPRESSION

I am now going to speculate on what I take to be the three possible causes of the epidemic. Much of depression is a disorder of individual thwarting. It is what happens when you can't get the things that you most cherish and most want—and you believe that is going to last. That's what hopelessness is. Depression is a disorder of the I-We Balance.

America has always been an individualist nation. This is one of the country's great strengths. But now I think we live in the most rampantly individualistic time of all. There are delicious freedoms that come with that, but young Americans believe more than we did, and we in turn believe more than our parents' generation did, that "I am the only thing in the world, that my successes and my failures are of monumental importance." That's what I mean by the "big I." At the same time the "we" has gotten smaller.

Why didn't our grandparents become depressed at the same rate we do when they were thwarted? What buffered them against depression when the people they loved rejected them and they didn't get the jobs they wanted? They had large consolations: They had their relationship to God. They had belief in a nation, patriotism. They had belief in a community, and they had large extended families. This was the spiritual furniture that our parents and grandparents sat in when they failed. This spiritual furniture—belief in God, community, nation, and abiding family—has become threadbare in our lifetime.

So the first factor causing the epidemic, I speculate, is that the "I" has gotten very big and the consolations of the spirit have become small, smaller. So the I-we balance is out of kilter.

THE SELF-ESTEEM MOVEMENT

I have five children. They range in age from 7 to 31. So I've had the unusual privilege of reading children's books aloud at night for the last 29 years. The children's books have changed. Twenty-five years ago, as it was during the Great Depression, the emblematic children's book was *The Little Engine that Could*. It is about doing well in the world. Children's books now are about feeling good, about having high self-esteem, about having confidence. I am not against self-esteem and I am not against confidence and I am not against feeling good. I believe that notions like self-esteem are meters that read out the state of the system. The meter reads low when you're doing badly with the people you love, when you're doing badly at school, and when you're doing badly at work. In general, when you're doing well with the people you love, at school, and at work the meter reads high. The meter is not perfectly accurate.

We now have a movement that originated in California in the 1960s, which tells us to jiggle the meter. It says that our primary duties as educators, as parents, and as therapists is to bolster self-esteem. From my point of view, this is a movement that tells us to rig the meter without changing the underlying motor. This movement cares nothing about the difference between unwarranted and warranted self-esteem. Warranted self-esteem has to do with learning and exercising the skills of getting along with other people, the skills of work, and the skills at school and sports. Unwarranted self esteem gets our kids to recite mantras like "I am special." This is the movement. But this movement has teeth. This is the movement that ended IQ testing in the schools, lest kids who score low on IQ tests feel bad. It is the movement that ended tracking in schools, lest kids on lower tracks feel bad. It is the movement that made competition a dirty word among young people. It is a movement that has led to less hard work. It is a movement that has paradoxically tried to create children with high self-esteem, but, that I believe has created children with footless and enormously fragile self-esteem.

THE THREE GOOD USES OF FEELING BAD

Why is the teaching of unwarranted self-esteem actually damaging rather than just vacuous? The self-esteem movement tells us that our first duty as educators, as parents, as therapists, when our charges feel sad or anxious or angry, is to intervene and relieve that state. It systematically deprives our charges of the three good uses of feeling bad. The first good use of feeling bad is that evolution has been tremendously interested in the dysphorias. Each of the dysphorias has a message about the world. When you feel anxious, the message is that there is danger around. When you feel sad, the message is that there is loss around. And when you feel angry, the message is "look out for trespass." Now these are imperfect messages. But it is these and not the immune system that are our first line of defense against nasty things happening in the world. To the extent we have a movement that tells us to get rid of the dysphorias, we remove our children from the real message.

The second good use of feeling bad has to do with persistence. Engage in an exercise for a moment. Pretend we have met at a bar, and you want to tell me about the thing in life you have done, either in love or in work, of which you are most proud. I am not going to try to describe what specific thing you have in mind, but there is a great deal of commonality to the form of what most of us choose. It is the following: there was either some person or some achievement that you wanted very much, you worked hard to get it and you failed, and you regrouped, and you worked hard again and you failed, and you regrouped and finally you got it. A central ingredient is to be able to feel the dysphoria and then to overcome it—to learn that you can overcome sadness, frustration, anxiety, and anger by your own actions. So a movement that tells us to intervene right away when our kids are sad or anxious, afraid or angry deprives them of persistence.

Finally, encroaching on Csikszentmihalyi's territory a bit, happiness itself is impeded by the self-esteem movement. Flow is the most measurable part of happiness. Flow occurs when time stops for you, when you feel completely at home and you want to be no place else. The conditions that produce flow occur when the highest of your abilities just matches the highest of challenges that you face. Now you don't have to think for very long about the match between ability and challenge to come up with the conclusion that if you haven't learned to tolerate and overcome sadness, anxiety, and anger, you can't have flow. So paradoxically, in attempting to create a happy generation of children, the self-esteem movement has created a generation of children for whom it is very hard to be happy.

VICTIMOLOGY

This nation, which used to be a nation of individual responsibility, has somehow become a nation of victimologists. You had to be blind and made of stone in September 1997 not to feel the genuine outpouring of grief across the world about Princess Diana's untimely death. The grief was not matched by John F. Kennedy's death, or by Marilyn Monroe's. More people, it is estimated, watched that funeral than any event in human history. Diana made every political mistake and yet was enormously loved and popular. Any student of political science had better pay at least as much attention to the reaction to Princess Diana as they will to Monica Lewinsky. Why was Diana so popular? Diana, I believe, was the princess of victims. In being the princess of victims and evoking that mourning, she told us that heroism has changed in our world. Diana was bulimic, anorectic, suicidal, she called herself a victim, she blamed her troubles on everyone else but herself. She was oppressed by the royal family, she was seen by the world not as the mother of the heirs to the throne but as a victim of Prince Charles's infidelity and indifference. It used to be that our heroes were people who did extraordinarily courageous and unusually positive things. Diana was not unusually courageous or unusually civic minded. But we could identify with her in a world in which we prize victimology. She was our princess, and we deserve her.

Victimology has a very fine providence, a great lineage—but it has gone much too far. In 1887 in Chicago, the Haymarket Square riot took place. Seven policemen were killed by rioting immigrants protesting the conditions of their work. In that era, bad action, and mental illness itself, was usually explained by bad character. You were a bad person, and bad action showed a moral deficit. A group of liberal Protestant theologians got together and argued that the immigrants were not bad people. The killings resulted from deprivation, ignorance, and poverty, not bad character. These theologians suggested founding a science, a "social science" whose mission would be to explain events like this, not as bad character, but as bad environment (Kuklick, 1985). This is a tradition in which psychology and sociology, anthropology, to this day, squarely stand. We are part of the problem.

After Haymarket Square, victimology underlies two other quite positive ventures. Before the 1930s if you were an alcoholic the label you applied to yourself was "evil," "sinner," and "bad" character. What Alcoholics Anonymous did was to supply a new attribution, "you've got a disease." It made you the victim of a disease. In so doing, it replaced a very malignant attribution, self-indulgent and evil, with the possibility of change. Diseases can be cured.

Then, best of all in 1953, the civil rights movement used victimology in a noble way. African Americans in the United States were, by every statistic, doing badly. White people whispered "stupid, lazy, and immoral," but in 1953 the Supreme Court said "unequal opportunity and discrimination." Failure in blacks was now explained as a result of discrimination. That opened a door and changed the attributions both externally and among young black people from "stupid, lazy, and immoral" to "I've been a victim."

But now this ideology has gone overboard. It has become completely routine to blame your troubles on being a victim. One of my students fell asleep in class and said to me, "I am sorry, Dr. Seligman, I have attention deficit disorder." The Menendez brothers were almost excused from a heinous premeditated murder of their parents on the grounds of alleged childhood sexual abuse. I could go on and on.

Now let me contrast the benefits of victimology with its costs. The first benefit is that you side with the underdog, and this is something that American social scientists have always wanted to do. Second, when you can blame something outside yourself—a disease, the establishment, or your race or your sex—for your failures, you feel better. Your self-esteem goes up, at least it goes up temporarily. Third, being a victim changes the usual wages of failure from contempt and pity to compassion and support. You now have groups of peers who love you and support you. And most important, it is sometimes correct that you are a victim.

The first cost of victimology is its temporary nature. It enables people to feel good in the short term. It is about feeling good now as opposed to finding out what the real causes are and correcting them in the long term. The second cost of victimology is that sometimes it is wrong. Sometimes the problem is you, the things you've done, the bad decisions you've made, and even the bad character you might have. Third, the notion of victimology erodes responsibility. Fourth, it deforms the nature of heroism, as exemplified by the astonishing contrast in the amount of mourning after the death of Diana versus Mother Teresa.

The most important cost of all is that victimology induces learned helplessness. Young people who believe that they are victims, that important events are uncontrollable, may exhibit the passivity and sadness of learned helplessness (Seligman, 1975).

WHAT WE CAN DO

That is my diagnosis of the epidemic of depression: the I-We balance is out of whack, we are teaching unwarranted self-esteem to our young people, and a flabby victimology is replacing rugged individualism as America's central ideology.

I want to close with what we can do. The vision of a profession that works on individual responsibility, on mastery, on optimism and hope coincides with the vision of Sir John Templeton and the Templeton Foundation. I do not think there is too much the science of psychology can do to correct the I-We balance. But there is a great deal that religion and spiritual reawakening can do about the I-We balance. One example: I was at a White House conference on daycare in 1997. The Clintons told us that they were going to advocate a budget to increase the quality of daycare. Stricter licensing qualifications and higher salaries would be the aim. While this would be very good for some of our children, I have a different view of what most needs attending to. It is not increasing the budget, but getting parents to spend more time with their children and less time on self-centered activities. The more time parents log with their children, the better off the children are. Many people perceive a tension between making daycare more attractive and parents' spending time with their children. This is not the tension to focus on: working mothers are here to stay, and many children will inevitably be in daycare. But in the last 100 years, adult leisure time has increased on average from 10 hours to 40 hours of per week (Demuth, 1997). The

Boomer generation has grown up and they are now the parents. They are using this leisure time, not to be with their children, but in isolated, self-indulgent activities: watching football on Sunday, working out, and going to the hairdresser. I believe that we need to change the I-We balance of the Boomer parents. We need moral suasion, a campaign of the Smokey the Bear variety, encouraging parents to use their leisure time to do things with their children.

What can we do about the self-esteem movement? I think we can end it. Psychology and education, more than any other disciplines, have been responsible for the myth that self-esteem is causal.

What we want to teach is not unwarranted self-esteem but warranted self-esteem. We can do that with the research that shows that having the skills to do well at school, to do well at work and on the playing field, and learning the skills to do well with other people produces warranted optimism.

Finally, we must engage the ideology of victimology that pervades social science and more alarmingly the body politic. The work set forth in this book has changed psychological theories from centering on the passive individual responding to stimuli to active individuals with responsibility, decision, choice, and mastery. This is the main virtue of the great work that my colleagues have done.

This work suggests a new vision of the future of social science. The social science of this century will become a science, not only engaged in correcting what is worst in the human condition, but a science of our best possibilities. Work on prevention gives us a window on this future. Effective prevention of mental illness will not, I believe, come from the disease model. It will not come about by changing the chemical balance of the brain. It will not come about by repairing psychological damage already done. Rather effective prevention will come from measuring and building human strengths. I want to suggest to you in closing that there is a set of human strengths that are the great buffers against mental illness: optimism, hope, courage, interpersonal skill, loving-kindness, work ethic, responsibility, faith, future-mindedness, honesty, and perseverance just to name a few. I want to suggest to you that the positive psychology, the positive social science that I envision for the twenty-first century, will therefore have the useful side effect of the prevention of

much of mental illness. But more importantly it will have the direct effect of creating a scientific understanding and a profession concerned with the practice of civic virtue and the pursuit of the best things in life.

REFERENCES

Demuth, C. (1997). The new wealth of nations. *Commentary, 104,* 23–28.

Egeland, J., and Hostetter, A. (1983). Amish study 1: Affective disorders among the Amish, 1976–80. *American Journal of Psychiatry, 140,* 56–61.

Garrison, C., Addy, C., Jackson, K., et al. (1992). Major depressive disorder and dysthymia in young adolescents. *American Journal of Epidemiology, 135,* 792–802.

Kessler, R.C., Sonnega, A., Bromet, E., Hughes, M., & Nelson, C.B. (1995). Posttraumatic stress disorder in the national comorbidity survey. *Archives of General Psychiatry, 52,* 1048–1060.

Klerman, G., Lavori, P., Rice, J., Reich, T., Endicott, J., Andreasen, N., Keller, M., & Hirschfeld, R. (1985). Birth cohort trends in rates of major depressive disorder among relatives of patients with affective disorder. *Archives of General Psychiatry, 42,* 689–93.

Kuklick, B. (1985) *Churchmen and philosophers: From Jonathan Edwards to John Dewey.* New Haven: Yale University Press.

Lewinsohn, P., Rohde, P., Seeley, J. & Fischer, S. (1993). Age-cohort changes in the lifetime occurrence of depression and other mental disorders. *Journal of Abnormal Psychology, 102,* 110–120.

Reich, T., Van Eerdewegh, P., Rice, J., Mullaney, J., Klerman, G., & Endicott, J. (1987). The family transmission of primary depressive disorder. *Journal of Psychiatric Research, 21,* 613–624.

Robins, L., Helzer, J., Weissman, M., Orvaschel, H., Gruenberg, E., Burke, J., & Regier, D. (1984). Lifetime prevalence of specific psychiatric disorders in three sites. *Archives of General Psychiatry, 41,* 949–958.

Seligman, M. (1975). *Helplessness.* San Francisco: Freeman.

ACKNOWLEDGMENTS

This work was supported by grants MH19604 and MH52270 from the National Institute of Mental Health.

Contributors

Lyn Y. Abramson, Ph.D.
Professor of Psychology & Associate Chair and Director of Graduate Studies, University of Wisconsin-Madison, Madison, Wisconsin

Lauren B. Alloy, Ph.D.
Professor of Psychology, Temple University, Philadelphia, Pennsylvania

Lisa G. Aspinwall, Ph.D.
Associate Professor of Psychology at the University of Maryland, College Park, Maryland

Michael P. Bishop
Graduate Student, School of Public Health, University of Michigan, Ann Arbor, Michigan.
Interested in health behavior and health education.

Janay Boswell
Graduate Research Assistant, Department of Educational Psychology, University of Texas, Austin, Texas

Susanne M. Brunhart, B.S.
Designs and conducts public outreach on recycling and waste reduction for Montgomery County, Maryland

Alexandra M. Chiara, M.A.
Graduate Student in Clinical Psychology, Temple University, Philadelphia, Pennsylvania

Caroline M. Clements, Ph.D.
Assistant Professor of Psychology, University of North Carolina-Wilmington, Wilmington, North Carolina.

Mihaly Csikszentmihalyi, Ph.D.
Professor of Psychology and Director, Quality of Life Research Center, Claremont Graduate University, Claremont, California

Robert J. DeRubeis, Ph.D.
Professor and Director of the Clinical Psychology Training Program, University of Pennsylvania, Philadelphia, Pennsylvania

Robert C. Drugan, Ph.D.
Associate Professor of Psychology, University of New Hampshire, Durham, New Hampshire

Yechiel Eckstein, Rabbi
Founder and President of the International Fellowship of Christians and Jews. He has degrees from Yeshiva and Columbia Universities and is the author of a number of books.

Frank D. Fincham, Ph.D.
Professor of Psychology, University of Wales, Cardiff, Wales

Judy Garber, Ph.D.
Professor of Psychology and Human Development, Vanderbilt University, Nashville, Tennessee

Jane E. Gillham, Ph.D.
Research Associate in Psychology, University of Pennsylvania and Visiting Assistant Professor, Swarthmore College, Swarthmore, Pennsylvania

Benjamin L. Hankin
Graduate Student, University of Wisconsin-Madison, Madison, Wisconsin

Michael E. Hogan, Ph.D.
Senior Database Administrator, University of Wisconsin-Madison, Madison, Wisconsin

Thomas E. Joiner, Jr., Ph.D.
Professor and Director, University Psychology Clinic, Florida State University, Tallahassee, Florida

Steven F. Maier, Ph.D.
Department of Psychology, University of Colorado, Boulder, Colorado. Interest in the neurobiology of motivation and emotion as well as in neural-immune interactions.

Lisa Miller, Ph.D.
Assistant Professor of Psychology and Education at Teachers College, Columbia University and Assistant Professor of Psychology, Deparment of Psychiatry, Columbia University, New York, New York

David G. Myers, Ph.D.
John Dirk Werkman Professor of Psychology at Hope College, Holland, Michigan

Susan Nolen-Hoeksema, Ph.D.
Professor of Psychology, University of Michigan, Ann Arbor, Michigan

Christopher Peterson, Ph.D.
Arthur F. Thirnall Professor, Department of Psychology, University of Michigan. Interested in explanatory style and health.

Stanley Rachman Ph.D.
Emeritus Professor of Psychology, University of British Columbia, Vancouver. Fellow, Royal Society of Canada

Karen Reivich, Ph.D.
Member of the research faculty at the University of Pennsylvania and Vice-President of Research and Development for Adaptiv Learning Systems

Jason M. Satterfield, Ph.D.
Assistant Professor and the Director of Behavioral Medicine at the University of California, San Francisco, California

Barry Schwartz, Ph.D.
Dorwin Cartwright Professor of Social Theory and Social Action at Swarthmore College, Swarthmore, Pennsylvania

Martin E. P. Seligman, Ph.D.
Fox Leadership Professor of Psychology, University of Pennsylvania, Philadelphia, Pennsylvania. In 1998 he was President of the American Psychological Association.

Andrew J. Shatté, Ph.D.
Member of the research and teaching faculty at the University of Pennsylvania and Vice-President of Research and Development for Adaptiv Learning Systems

C. R. Snyder, Ph.D.
Professor and Director of the Clinical Psychology Program, University of Kansas, Lawrence, Kansas. He also is Editor of the *Journal of Social and Clinical Psychology*.

Kevin D. Stark, Ph.D.
Professor and Director of the Doctoral Program in School Psychology at the University of Texas, Austin, Texas

Linda R. Watkins, Ph.D.
Department of Psychology, University of Colorado, Boulder, Colorado. Interest in the neurology of pain as well as in neural-immune interactions.

Wayne G. Whitehouse, Ph.D.
Adjunct Associate Professor of Psychology, Temple University, Philadelphia, Pennsylvania

Everett L. Worthington, Jr., Ph.D.
Professor and Chair of Psychology, Virginia Commonwealth University, Richmond, Virginia

Lin Zhu, M.A.
Graduate student in Clinical Psychology, Temple University, Philadelphia, Pennsylvania

Index

H

I

L

P